Charles J. Kokaska
California State University—Long Beach

Donn E. Brolin
University of Missouri-Columbia

Career Education for Handicapped Individuals
Second Edition

Charles E. Merrill Publishing Company
A Bell & Howell Company
Columbus Toronto London Sydney

Published by
Charles E. Merrill Publishing Company
A Bell & Howell Company
Columbus, Ohio 43216

This book was set in Quorum
Production Coordinator: Christina Anagnost
Text Design: Cynthia Brunk
Cover Design: Cathy Watterson
Cover Photo: Roman Spalek

Photo Credits: Pages 1, 75, 88, 108, 128, 225, 263: © Randall D. Williams.
Reproduced by permission of The Licking County Board of Mental
Retardation. Pages 67, 384: Linda Ordway. Pages 121, 374: Strix Pix. Page
221: Roman Spalek. Page 247: © Harvey R. Phillips/Phillips. Page 26:
Courtesy of the President's Committee on Employment of the Handicapped.

Library of Congress Card Catalog Number: 84-61331
International Standard Book Number: 0-675-20282-5
1   2   3   4   5   6   7   8   9—
90   89   88   87   86   85
Printed in the United States of America

Dedicated to our colleagues and students
who transform career plans
for handicapped people
into reality

Preface

Career Education for Handicapped Individuals was written for parents, teachers, counselors, administrators, rehabilitation workers, psychologists, business and industrial leaders, and all other persons who are concerned about the career development of handicapped individuals. This book can be used by university educators to teach regular and special education, vocational education, guidance and counseling, psychology, and rehabilitation classes or by anyone who prepares their students for working with handicapped individuals. Curriculum planners, inservice trainers, state department administrators, community agency personnel, and educational consultants can also use this book to design and implement effective career education programs.

This book presents career education as a whole life process for all handicapped individuals regardless of how they are categorized or labeled. We see career education as a sequence of planned learning activities that prepare individuals to participate in various occupational, avocational, family, civic, and retirement roles. We examine all career development needs and provide a mix of daily living, personal-social, and occupational activities for elementary students through adults.

We define career education as the systematic coordination of all school, family, and community activities that can be used to actualize each person's potential. We present an eclectic approach to the concept, structure, and teaching of career development in educational settings. The Life-Centered Career Education model includes 22 competencies for different settings (home, school, and community) and four stages of development (awareness, exploration, preparation, placement, and follow-up).

Career Education for Handicapped Individuals provides a structure for career education that can be infused into the curriculum and adapted to fulfill the unique needs of handicapped learners. This book furnishes strategies and resources for teaching career skills and suggests ways to involve both family and community. This material results from our years of experience in career education with teachers, counselors, administrators, and researchers.

We have learned that far too many handicapped citizens continue to have problems participating as contributing members of society. The ability to conduct their daily affairs and to earn a decent wage are two major problems affecting over half of our handicapped adults. If these individuals are to achieve their rightful place in society, schools must help handicapped individuals develop the skills they will need to actualize their potentials and lead productive lives. Infusing career education into the schools can make this goal a reality.

Career Education for Handicapped Individuals differs from the first edition in several ways. This book is divided into three sections: Introduction, Application, and Implementation. Each of the 13 chapters features the "Point of View" of a person who has contributed to career education for handicapped individuals. Two new chapters on career and vocational assessment and career education for adult learners have been added to this edition.

In addition, we have included more activity tips, sample lesson plans, program descriptions, and photographs to illustrate the application of the Life-Centered Career Education competencies. Career quotations provide another dimension to the chapter discussions. The book is accompanied by an *Instructor's Manual* that includes numerous suggestions for instructional activities, discussions, essays, and test items for each chapter.

We greatly appreciate the several people who contributed their materials and ideas to make this text valuable to our readers. We thank the following field reviewers for their suggestions on improving this second edition: Lon S. Kriner, Ernest L. Pancsofar, and Patricia Cegelka. We recognize the contributions of many school district personnel, university and state department leaders, and representatives from the Office of Special Education and Rehabilitative Services who have supported and assisted us in our efforts. We especially appreciate the work of Christina Anagnost for improving the quality of our prose and our administrative editor, Vicki Knight, whose patience rivals that of Job.

C.J.K.
D.E.B.

Contents

**PART III
IMPLEMENTATION**

13

Issues and Future Directions   371

I
Introduction

Part one presents basic background information about the development and current status of educational services for handicapped individuals and explores the concept, need, and organization of career education. This information forms the foundation for the Life-Centered Career Education (LCCE) approach that is presented in subsequent chapters of the book.

Chapter 1 describes some major historical events that have influenced this country's provisions for individuals with handicaps. Various instructional settings are identified and a definition of mainstreaming is presented. The chapter discusses the major forces that have molded positive educational change: parent organizations, litigation, and legislation. The Individualized Education Program (IEP) and its components and implications for career development are presented. The chapter concludes with a discussion on how technological change can expand the range of career possibilities for handicapped people.

Chapter 2 outlines the historical development of career education in relationship to handicapped individuals. The problem of finding a universally accepted definition of career education is presented. Life-Centered Career Education (LCCE) is also presented as an approach that defines career education within a broad context. The concepts, infusion techniques, and design models for this competency-based curriculum are discussed. The curriculum model focuses on 22 career development competencies and 102 subcompetencies, which are classified under three curriculum areas: daily living skills, personal-social skills, and occupational skills. School, family, and community relationships, and four stages of career development are also discussed in relation to their contributions to the competencies. The chapter concludes with suggestions for implementing Life-Centered Career Education.

The Education of Handicapped Individuals 1

There is no universal definition of handicap or disability. In many cases, public and voluntary organizations create their own definitions so that they may achieve specific goals. However, in reality, many factors determine whether these individuals become differentiated from the able-bodied. Generally, a distinction is made between the terms *disability* and *handicap*. Disability may or may not be considered a handicap. If a disabled individual is perceived as being unable to resume normal activities, he is described as being handicapped. Factors such as body impairment, functional limitations, mental ability, emotional level, communication, environment, self-care, age, education, and social skills are major determinants of the extent to which an individual may be considered handicapped.

The Office of Information and Resources for the Handicapped, established by the Department of Education, is responsible for examining programs and needs for handicapped people throughout the country. It defines a handicapped individual as follows:

A handicapped individual is one who has a physical or mental impairment or condition that places him at a disadvantage in a major life activity such as ambulation, communication, self-care, socialization, vocational training, employment, transportation, or adapting to housing. The physical or mental impairment of condition must be static, of long duration, or slowly progressive.

This definition excludes handicaps of short duration and minimally limiting conditions, yet it is broad enough to accommodate narrower definitions.

The Rehabilitation Act of 1973 contains another definition used by rehabilitation personnel throughout the country. "Severe handicaps" are defined by the following:

> A disability that requires multiple services over an extended period of time and results from amputation, blindness, cancer, cerebral palsy, cystic fibrosis, deafness, heart disease, hemiplegia, mental retardation, mental illness, multiple sclerosis, muscular dystrophy, neurological disorders (including stroke and epilepsy), paraplegia, quadriplegia and other spinal cord conditions, renal failure, respiratory or pulmonary dysfunction, and any other disability specified by the Secretary in regulations he shall prescribe.

This definition is similar to the one presented in the regulations of the Education for All Handicapped Children Act of 1975 (PL 94–142), which describes handicapped children as "mentally retarded, hard of hearing, deaf, speech impaired, visually handicapped, seriously emotionally disturbed, orthopedically impaired, other health impaired, or as having specific learning disabilities, who because of those impairments need special education and related services."

The definitions presented thus far seem to agree that handicapped people deviate from the average in mental, physical, or social characteristics to the extent that they require special education or rehabilitation services in order to develop to their maximum level of potential.

A significant proportion of the American population is handicapped in some way. However it is difficult to ascertain exactly how prevalent these conditions are since the figures obtained by prevalence studies are dependent upon which definitions and survey methods are used. Results from various studies have been diverse and therefore can only be used as estimates. Gearheart (1980) even proposed that it would be best to project a *range* of prevalence for each major category based on a composite of estimates from the federal government, professional organizations, and advocacy groups. In table 1.1, Halloran (1978) presents the estimated incidence of various types of disabilities in the school-age population. The best possible estimate reveals that 10 million children and 30 million adults are handicapped and that they comprise the largest and possibly least understood minority groups in this country (Gliedman & Roth, 1980).

These individuals need special assistance in preparing for and securing employment, in earning wages that will permit them to maintain a decent level of living for their families, and in gaining acceptance as worthwhile, contributing members of our society. Over the past two decades this country's provisions for handicapped individuals have changed markedly. Various forms of media and legislation have focused on numerous aspects of the handicapped individual's life. These aspects include the etiology of the condi-

TABLE 1.1
Incidence level of various types of handicaps.

Handicapping Condition	Incidence (percentage of school-age population)
Speech impaired	3.5
Mentally retarded	2.3
Learning disabled	3.0
Emotionally disturbed	2.0
Orthopedically impaired	0.5
Deaf	0.075
Hard of hearing	0.5
Visually handicapped	0.1
Other health impaired	0.06
Total	12.035

Source: Halloran, W. E. Handicapped persons: Who are they? *American Vocational Journal*, 1978, *53*(1), 30–31.

tion; the family's struggle to cope with the situation; infant and child development; methods of instruction; organization of educational programs; peer relationships; vocational training and placement; and success in the adult years.

Education is one element of the entire picture, although it can be an important ingredient in the success of an individual's life. Major changes in the educational structure include increased allocations of monies to support special programs; integration of handicapped students into regular education classrooms; and applications of technology in the development of instructional media to assist teachers and students.

This book deals with several major concerns that have emerged from these changes in the educational system. First, career education has sparked new interest in the scope and content of the schools' efforts to prepare individuals for their adult roles and responsibilities. Second, the integration of handicapped students, sometimes referred to as *mainstreaming*, also places certain demands on personnel within the school program. For some, these demands are not new. For others, the combination of mainstreaming and career education may require a dual adjustment in curriculum design and teaching techniques.

"Handicapped people are members of a minority group that inspires not only sympathy, but fear, guilt, terror and superstition. It's the one minority group you or I could join at a moment's notice."

Bethell (1979)

This chapter provides a historical overview of the education and training of handicapped individuals and includes discussions of the various instructional settings, the emergence of the mainstreaming concept, and the major forces that have influenced society's provisions for handicapped students.

HISTORICAL DEVELOPMENT

The history of handicapped individuals is as old as the human race, but their education is a relatively recent achievement. Blind Egyptian harpists and singers are depicted on the walls of tombs that date back to approximately 1400 B.C. Individuals with various disabilities have been recorded in other civilizations, such as on the pottery of the Incas or Oriental ink drawings. Their hardships are told in the stories of the Greek poets, of whom the most notable, Homer, was blind.

Historical records indicate that the experiences of handicapped individuals were harsh during a period when humans had to strive daily for mere physical survival. The deformed, disabled, and slow-witted were at a constant disadvantage. They were viewed as a burden to the community and denied any claim to worth and status. The Spartans, who recognized the expedience of the "survival of the fittest," simply threw defective infants off a cliff or abandoned them in the surrounding countryside. This freed the community of another mouth to feed. Those who weren't destroyed in the Spartan custom had little to look forward to in other Greek city states and the European cultures that followed for the next eighteen hundred years. This situation was partly influenced by such prominent philosophers as Plato, who in describing the ideal society, envisioned no place for an individual with handicaps. He recommended in the *Republic* (1941) that

> . . . the offspring of the inferior, or of the better when they chance to be deformed, will be put away in some mysterious, unknown place, as they should be. (Book V)

Those societies that followed the Greeks only expanded the basic "survival doctrine." Occasionally, handicapped individuals were protected or were able to achieve status in royal courts. In the Middle Ages religious orders established various types of homes and asylums. This practice stemmed from the Christian belief that humans' divine qualities should be manifested in acts of sacrifice and kindness toward the suffering and afflicted. However, for every individual who may have been assisted, for example, by St. Vincent de Paul and the Sisters of Charity, hundreds were viewed as physical manifestations of the evil powers at work in the world, and were tortured, burned, or punished. For every individual who entertained in the courts as a jester or buffoon or had access to the royal family in the role of an escort to the king or tutor of his children, there were thousands who maintained themselves as beggars. It is no wonder that classical art and literature often portrayed handicapped individuals as thieves, scoundrels, or as refuse of the social system. The vast majority met with little favor or advantage among the councils of the rich, knowledgeable, and powerful.

POINT OF VIEW

Are all students who are enrolled in special education programs "carved by nature" to be "truly" handicapped? Or are they regarded as "handicapped" only because they fall below a statistical cutting point on one dimension of aptitude or performance?

The answer is some of both. Some categories of students are basically taxonomic, as in clear cases of genetically determined disorders such as Down's syndrome. However, we are still using arbitrary cutting scores to categorize many individuals.

If we adapted to individual differences in our mainstreamed classes, those cutting scores could be moved and there would be less need for classifying students as handicapped. Recent public policies, including those expressed in PL 94–142, clearly call for educators to work on making mainstream education more powerful and thus more inclusive.

Maynard C. Reynolds is a professor in the Department of Educational Psychology at the University of Minnesota-Minneapolis (formerly President of The Council for Exceptional Children).

European Antecedents

The beginnings of education and hope for handicapped individuals can be traced to a cluster of French philosophers, scientists, and physicians who advocated an enlightened view of human beings. Jacob Rodriques Pereire was the first of these leaders. In 1749 at the Academy of Science in Paris, he presented his method of teaching deaf mutes to speak and read. His accomplishments received so much attention that King Louis XV requested Pereire and his pupil to appear at court (Kanner, 1964). Pereire's work has been identified by some scholars as being the beginning of special education as a distinct discipline.

If there are classics in the history of the education of handicapped individuals, then one of the first is the efforts of Jean-Marc-Gaspard Itard with Victor, as documented in *The Wild Boy of Aveyron* (1962). Few texts in special education are without a reference to Itard. Itard's hopes as a humanitarian and rigor as a scientist set an example for the field that has endured for generations. In 1799, Victor, a boy of 10 or 11 years old, was captured by hunters in the forest of Aveyron located in the southern part of France. He was literally placed on exhibit to the public and curious scientists, who were investigating whether Victor could be a representative sample of Rousseau's "noble savage." The boy was far from noble as he trotted and grunted like the beasts of the forest, ate most anything placed before him after sniffing it, rocked back and forth in his cage, and did not seem to feel heat and cold.

Pinel, a leading physician of the period and Itard's mentor, put an apparent end to the speculations about the boy's hidden human intelligence by declaring that Victor was an incurable idiot. Itard had a different opinion, which did not please his mentor, and he ventured upon a 5-year experiment to educate the boy. His goals were to ease Victor through the transition between the solitary life he led in the forest and the social world; awaken his nervous sensibilities through intense stimulation and emotion; extend his range of ideas by increasing his social contacts; lead him to the use of speech through imitation but based on necessity; and use instruction to stimulate mental operations associated with physical needs.

Itard did not achieve his goals, and Victor never became a "normal" individual. But, Itard did achieve significance by attempting techniques with what could be described as the most unlikely candidates for success. In reviewing the significance of Itard's work, a physician (Richard Masland), a psychologist (Seymour Sarason), and a social scientist (Thomas Gladwin) termed the efforts and accomplishments *phenomenal.*

> Over the long period of training one could see the development of various ego functions, the capacity to delay responsiveness—in short, one saw the development of a surprisingly complex personality. (Masland, Sarason, & Gladwin, 1958, p. 325)

Itard's efforts characterized a growing interest in the nineteenth century with the *possibility* that the deaf could communicate, that the blind could be mobile, and that the mentally retarded could learn. Other individuals such as Thomas Hopkins Gallaudet, Samuel Gridley Howe, and Edouard Sequin continued to expand the means by which handicapped individuals could realize those possibilities.

The American Scene

The expansion of education for handicapped individuals in the United States during the nineteenth century was due to the singular efforts of such men as Gallaudet, Howe, and Sequin. Although the first residential setting, the American Asylum for the Deaf and Dumb, was established in Hartford, Connecticut in 1818, it took almost half of a century before the first day-school classes were initiated in Boston, Massachusetts, as illustrated in table 1.2. By 1922 the United States Office of Education had conducted a survey of enrollments in programs for handicapped students in 191 cities with a population of 100,000 or more. These programs reported that most of their 26,163 students were enrolled in classes for the mentally retarded.

The education of handicapped individuals expanded slowly between the two world wars. School districts increased course offerings in all areas of exceptionality but were hindered by the drain on personnel and finances created by the wars and the Great Depression. Nevertheless, two significant events took place during this period that later influenced development of new programs and assistance.

In 1922 Elizabeth Farrell and the students enrolled in her course at Columbia University founded what was to become the dominant professional organization in special education, The Council for Exceptional Children (Aiello, 1976). The Council has continued to function as an advocate for the rights of

TABLE 1.2

Commonly reported dates for the establishment of the first day classes for handicapped students.[a]

Deaf	Boston, Massachusetts	1869
Retarded	Providence, Rhode Island	1896
Crippled	Chicago, Illinois	1899
Blind	Chicago, Illinois	1900
Lowered Vitality	Providence, Rhode Island	1908
Partially Seeing	Roxbury, Massachusetts	1913

[a]United States Office of Education. *The unfinished revolution: Education for the handicapped,* 1976 Annual Report, National Advisory Committee on the Handicapped. Washington, D.C.: Government Printing Office, 1976, p. 11, Table 2.

handicapped individuals and works in conjunction with parent groups as a strong lobbying organization.

The 1930 White House Conference on Child Health and Protection was the first to recognize that special education contributed to the education and well-being of children. The conference resulted in the creation of a department of special education in the Office of Education. This one-person department grew into the Office of Special Education and Rehabilitative Services; its projected budget is now in the billions of dollars.

Public apathy toward individuals with handicaps diminished as handicapped World War II veterans returned to their families and friends who remembered them as healthy and able. Faced with the contradictions between traditional stereotypes and reality, the nation finally had to confront the question of whether capable handicapped individuals would be provided with the training and opportunity to achieve the freedoms they fought for. The organization of the President's Committee on Employment of the Handicapped in 1947 was a beginning in this direction and helped start what was to become the most dramatic period of expansion and activity in the history of the education of handicapped individuals.[1]

The remainder of this chapter will focus on several components that were a vital part in the expansion. Each component has its own story and contributes to the development of the field. We have divided these components into specialized instruction, mainstreaming, parent organizations, litigation, legislation, and medical and technological advances.

SPECIALIZED INSTRUCTION

The varied characteristics and instructional needs of handicapped students, combined with the evolution of programs within school districts, has led to a variety of instructional settings. But one of the dominant concepts that has emerged in the field of special education in the United States is the application of the "least restrictive alternative" to the education of handicapped students. It is based, in part, on the efforts and experiences of European educators and humanists to normalize the education, work, and social environments in which handicapped individuals must function. The concept requires that a range of instructional alternatives become available to accommodate the specific learning characteristics and requirements of the student. Reynolds (1962) has arranged the various administrative approaches on a continuum of services, ranging from the most segregated to the most integrated:

---

[1]Harold Russell, chairperson of the President's Committee on Employment of the Handicapped, won an Academy Award for his authentic role as an injured veteran in the 1946 movie, *The Best Years of Our Lives.*

- hospital and treatment centers
- residential schools
- special day schools
- full- and part-time special classes
- resource rooms
- regular classrooms with consultation from specialists
- regular classrooms

Deno (1970), Dunn (1973), and Reynolds and Birch (1982) expanded the "cascade model of services" in order to shift the emphasis from administrative settings to specialized forms of instruction. Specialized instruction would alter the classroom to fit the multiple needs and abilities of the individual.

The ultimate goal is to place the disabled individual in as normal an educational setting as possible. This goal is reflected in specific references to free, appropriate public education and individualized education programs contained in The Education for All Handicapped Children Act (PL 94-142). To achieve this goal, a coordinated effort is required between the specialists, who previously taught in limited settings, and regular classroom teachers, who may need help on how to tailor instruction to specific learning styles.

MAINSTREAMING

In April 1976 the delegate assembly at the 54th Annual International Convention of The Council for Exceptional Children adopted the following definition of mainstreaming as a statement of policy.

> Mainstreaming is a belief which involves an educational placement procedure and process for exceptional children, based on the conviction that each such child should be educated in the least restrictive environment in which his educational and related needs can be satisfactorily provided. This concept recognizes that exceptional children have a wide range of special education needs, varying greatly in intensity and duration; that there is a recognized continuum of education settings which may, at a given time, be appropriate for an individual child's needs; that to the maximum extent appropriate, exceptional children should be educated with non-exceptional children; and that special classes, separate schooling or other removal of an exceptional child from education with non-exceptional children should occur only when the intensity of the child's special education and related needs is such that they cannot be satisfied in an environment including non-exceptional children, even with the provision of supplementary aids and services.
>
> (The Council for Exceptional Children, 1976)

The delegate assembly had to take this action because both professional and popular publications were using the term *mainstreaming* without reaching consensus on a definition. Everyone, it seemed, had their own view of the term. Some parents of handicapped students visualized wholesale elimination of the special schools and facilities that they established through state legislatures and local school boards. Regular classroom teachers envisioned that a wave of students with special needs would converge on their classrooms and require additional time and skills. Special educators were torn between meeting the needs of all handicapped individuals while insuring that the student would receive the best possible instruction. These problems and solutions generated much attention in the print. For example, in preparing one of the most comprehensive bibliographies on mainstreaming, Clarkson (1982) collected approximately *3000* entries including literature written on areas of instruction for eight categories of exceptionality.

It is hoped that the definition given by The Council for Exceptional Children will eliminate much of the confusion and will focus attention on three critical points. First, the concept of the *least restrictive environment* should be used to determine the appropriate educational setting. Second, an *appropriate educational setting* meets the unique needs of the exceptional student and includes integration of these individuals with nonexceptional students as much as possible. Third, a *continuum of settings* is acceptable in order to meet the varied needs and abilities of the student.

There are some problems in implementing mainstreaming. An evaluation report by Rice (1976) on a series of meetings that included 11 state directors of special education lists four major obstacles as identified by those administrators:

- attitudes of regular classroom teachers toward handicapped students;
- attitudes and willingness of general administrators toward means of integrating handicapped students;
- lack of fiscal resources;
- insufficient number of specialists on the staff.

Of course, these major obstacles overlap. Regular classroom teachers may be reluctant to accept mainstreaming when they are acutely aware that they lack prior experience or assistance from specialists to bolster daily activities. Administrators may want to integrate handicapped students on a gradual scale if the faculty needs extensive inservice training in order to attend to some serious concerns. These concerns may have to do with

- attitudes of regular students toward handicapped individuals;
- modifications in the physical environment to accomodate handicapped students;

- appropriate curriculum materials, evaluation instruments, and teaching techniques;
- use of resource personnel; and
- coordination of several programs that interface with the regular curriculum.

Discussions on the pros and cons of mainstreaming are academic. Mainstreaming, integration, least restrictive environment—whatever the term—will occur because the major forces at work within the American social and political setting will move society toward those goals. It is only a matter of whether we are to achieve first-class citizenship for handicapped individuals as effectively and quickly as possible. The following section examines those major forces that affect positive changes on behalf of handicapped individuals.

"Motivation is much more important than disability."

Roberts (1982)

MAJOR FORCES AFFECTING POSITIVE EDUCATIONAL CHANGE

The explosion of services and public attention on behalf of handicapped individuals has not been a matter of chance. Distinct forces in American society will continue to foster change and increase the possibilities that handicapped individuals will fulfill their maximum potential. We have divided these forces into three headings for the sake of discussion. In reality, the forces of parent organizations, litigation, and legislation interact with one another and build upon the success that each has fostered within the society.

Parent Organization

It is appropriate to begin a discussion of major forces with a review of the numerous organizations that have been founded by the parents of handicapped individuals. Such organizations date back to the founding of the National Society for Crippled Children in 1921. But the biggest surge of progress was made in 1949–50 when the National Association for Retarded Children (now the Association for Retarded Citizens) and the United Cerebral Palsy Association were organized within a few months of one another. Membership in such organizations is open to parents, students, and professionals and numbers in the hundreds of thousands.

These organizations were created by parents as a response to public inaction manifested by the absence of school programs, treatment centers, or even skilled personnel who were interested in working with handicapped children. A well-known example of the parents' plight can be found in the story of the beginnings of the New York State Cerebral Palsy Association. A parent advertised daily in several local newspapers that those individuals who were interested in receiving help should call or write to her (Killilea, 1960). There are numerous examples of parents seeking each other out in order to receive and provide solace and find answers to basic questions about their children's condition and future. Today these organizations also function as viable representatives of handicapped individuals in affecting political and social action.

The organizations had initial problems in working with professionals. Parents were forced into combined action because very little was being provided by agencies in which the doctor, teacher, and psychologist were employed. At first, bitter memories and feelings forced parents to rely upon themselves for counsel and direction; but in time, they learned to use the

Parent groups have been a major force in improving education for persons with handicaps.

professional's skill as the organization continued to expand its role and influ ence. At the current stage of development, numerous parent groups have professionals as consultants and members of their board of directors, although the parents still control the overall intent and direction of policy.

Their strongest drive and accomplishments have been to promote legislation from the local level through the statehouses and Congress. Several organizations have active legislation committees that monitor the progress of bills, organize attempts to lobby on behalf of favorable legislation, produce witnesses during committee hearings, and function as a source of information to its members, legislatures, and representatives of the media. These efforts have been rewarded. Repeated laws that support the rights of handicapped individuals have been passed at all levels of government.

Parent groups have also served other purposes. For example, they have

1. organized educational facilities and services when public schools or agencies were unavailable;
2. promoted public awareness and support for programs and efforts to assist handicapped individuals;
3. supported parents through counseling, guardianship plans, respite care programs, and medical services;
4. promoted research into causes, treatments, education, and other aspects of the individual's life;
5. sponsored training for teachers, teacher aides, community leaders, doctors, and other individuals who may be involved in the care, education, and treatment of handicapped individuals;
6. built permanent structures for sheltered workshops, day schools, and diagnostic centers; and
7. developed programs to prepare the handicapped for such necessary functions as daily care, mobility, recreation, leisure, and raising a family.

Finally, parent groups have established themselves as advocates by representing handicapped individuals as plaintiffs in litigation involving public agencies. One of the most prominent suits, *Pennsylvania Association for Retarded Children* v. *Commonwealth of Pennsylvania*, will be reviewed later in the chapter. The case and decision have been termed *landmark*, and it is appropriate that one of the parent organizations was so intimately involved in a decision that affirmed the constitutional right of every child to an education.

What are the future directions and roles for the parent organizations? Cain (1976) identifies several in his review of the historical position of parent groups. First, more instances of coordinated activity will occur across organizations that have previously been working in isolation. This cooperation is evident in the areas of vocational training and placement. The Department of Labor has awarded several contracts to the Epilepsy Foundation of America and the Association for Retarded Citizens so they may develop and expand their training and placement services (*National Spokesman*, 1983; Association for Retarded Citizens, n. d.). Second, parent groups will continue to focus on the total life of the individual. The emphasis on the customary "poster child" will change as the organizations and the consumers they serve move toward the problems of adulthood. Organizations that have been founded by adults with disabilities will probably influence parent organizations through mutual action in the areas of transportation, adult education, and employment. Third, as the public sector becomes more responsible for providing services, parent groups will become more concerned with initiating and monitoring services. For example, the contracts made by the Department of Labor illustrate that parent groups are capable of initiating projects when school systems fail to meet the needs of handicapped students. These services will eventually become absorbed by the education sector. The role of monitor is already evident in several cases brought before the bar in which parent organizations challenged school districts and other public agencies to meet a standard of due process procedures that determine the appropriate education or training program for the handicapped individual. As more laws establish these procedures, parent groups will be able to work on improving the *quality* of service instead of having to fight for the right of handicapped individuals to that service.

Litigation

As important as the doctor, teacher, or psychologist may be in the history of special education, the lawyer and judge are not to be forgotten. Since 1960 legal suits and judicial decisions have had a direct effect upon the education, training, care, and protection of handicapped individuals.

The Supreme Court decision in *Brown* v. *Board of Education of Topeka, Kansas* (1954) set a major precedent in litigations involving the right of every citizen to an education. The court ruled that state laws could not permit segregation of students on racial grounds and that the doctrine of "separate but equal" educational facilities was unconstitutional. The court stated:

> In these days it is doubtful that any child may reasonably be expected to succeed in life if he is denied the opportunity for an education. Such an opportunity, where the state has undertaken to provide it, is a right which must be made available to all on equal terms.

Although racial discrimination was the prominent concern in the *Brown* case, the Supreme Court's ruling helped to establish arguments used in labor cases involving handicapped individuals who had been denied equal education because of the unfounded belief that they would not be able to profit from it and contribute to society.

Hobson v. Hansen (1968) was one of the first litigations that included special education within the broader context of segregation and labeling of children. Judge Skelley Wright ruled that the five part track system used in grouping students was unconstitutional since it deprived students who were black or from lower socioeconomic families of an opportunity to experience equal educational service. The school system was unable to demonstrate that the system allowed students to advance within and across the tracks or that instruction at the lower levels was meeting the needs of the students. The Hobson case established additional precedent for future right-to-education suits in the following ways:

1. It established that school districts had to provide evidence that programs were yielding adequate results. It was not enough for school districts to intend to design adequate programs for students.
2. It indicated that placement of students into appropriate programs had to be substantiated by adequate procedures and supporting evidence. The courts would not accept procedures that violated the constitutional rights of the child or tests that were inappropriate for the intended educational objectives.
3. It forced the field of special education to examine its unwilling partnership in de facto segregation and the practice of placing students into categories of disability.

A third major decision was reached in Pennsylvania Association for Retarded Children v. Commonwealth of Pennsylvania (1971). On behalf of the parents of 13 retarded children, the association filed a class action suit in the United States District Court against the state of Pennsylvania for failing to provide publicly supported education for all retarded students. The class action suit was a strategic move by the plaintiff's lawyer, Thomas Gilhool, since the court decision would affect all children with mental retardation in the state. His second strategic move was to base the case on the right of every American child to an education. Using expert witnesses before a panel of three judges, Gilhool elicited testimony establishing that mentally retarded individuals could profit from an education and contribute to society. After two days of hearings, the parties reached an agreement.

The court ordered the state to provide the necessary education and rejected the argument that a lack of funds, personnel, and facilities were legitimate reasons for substandard education. The court maintained that if, in fact, the state did not have the resources to educate all the children, then handicapped children must take a share of the burden with other children but that they should not have to bear the entire load of the state's financial difficulties. As a postscript to the decision, which further substantiated the plaintiff's contention that there was a general absence of programs, a survey of all eligible children who were mentally retarded and not enrolled in school was conducted by the state of Pennsylvania. The survey indicated that 14,267 children had been denied access to the public schools (Gilhool, 1973).[2]

The *Pennsylvania* case signaled the beginning of a succession of suits in other states for the following reasons:

1. It established that every normal and handicapped child had a right to an educational program appropriate to his ability.
2. It established the precedent that every state has the obligation to provide the personnel and resources to meet the instructional needs of the child.
3. It itemized a due process procedure whereby parents and students would be able to approve or challenge the school system's action on a change of educational status to the extent that the final decision would be settled in the courts, if necessary.
4. It established the necessity of fulfilling an individual's present rights (i.e., those that must be immediately exercised and safeguarded).

The *Pennsylvania* case was a major breakthrough in behalf of the handicapped individual's right to receive an appropriate education. A previous case, *Diana* v. *State Board of Education of California* (1970), and a related decision in *Mills* v. *Board of Education of the District of Columbia* (1972) helped this cause. The *Diana* decision led to modifications in state codes related to the testing, assessment, and assignment of individuals from minority groups to classes for handicapped students. The *Mills* decision extended the results of the *Pennsylvania* case by affirming that *all* handicapped individuals had the right to a public education. These cases also established a judicial foundation for organizations working on behalf of handicapped individuals by encouraging state legislatures to enact further laws. If those laws were not forthcoming, the same groups had the option of turning to the courts. Both of these alternatives required time, effort, and money. Furthermore, states were inconsistent in supporting legislation for various groups of handicapped individuals. What was needed? Simply, a form of legislation that would apply to all states and all forms of disability, with a funding basis to support the necessary education. That form of legislation was in its early

---

[2]Lippman and Goldberg (1973) provide an extensive review of the background, development, and impact of the case, including a copy of the final court order.

stages of development when the *Pennsylvania* case became prominent in the field of special education.

Legislation

The growing urgency of appropriate education for handicapped individuals can be documented by the increased number of laws that were passed in the states. According to the Constitution, each state should assume the responsibility of establishing school law, districts, procedures, and, in some instances, financial support. In effect, there are 50 state plans and definitions of state and local partnership in the conduct and funding of education for all children, youths, and adults. Thus, states differ in the extent of their support of education for handicapped individuals, as well as medical facilities, research, and employment possibilities.

In 1961 President John F. Kennedy appointed a panel to prepare a "national plan to combat mental retardation." He recognized that the office of the president could be used to develop approaches to a problem that existed in every state when no one state had the means to the solution. The panel's *Report* (The President's Panel on Mental Retardation, 1963) established long-term goals in the following areas:

- research and scientific manpower
- prevention
- clinical and social services
- education, vocational rehabilitation, and training
- residential care
- the law
- public awareness
- planning and coordination of services

The Panel's findings and recommendations were applicable to other areas of disability and, more importantly, were placed into law by Congress. These laws have generated more equal-opportunity legislation guaranteeing the rights of handicapped individuals to use public facilities, receive an education, or obtain employment. The following discussion focuses on significant legislation of the 1970s.

MAJOR EDUCATIONAL LEGISLATION

The Education for all Handicapped Children Act, PL 94–142 (1975)

The Education for All Handicapped Children Act (PL 94–142) has already been hailed as a Bill of Rights by numerous organizations and sponsors who labored for several years in its drafting and passage. It established the federal government's commitment to a full and free appropriate public education for all handicapped children. The term *children* is used in the act, although it includes funds for individuals between the ages of 3 to 21.

> It is the purpose of this Act to assure that all handicapped children have available to them, within the time periods specified . . . a free appropriate public education which emphasizes special education and related services designed to meet their unique needs, to assure that the rights of handicapped children and their parents or guardians are protected, to assist States and localities, to provide for the education of all handicapped children, and to assess and assure the effectiveness of efforts to educate handicapped children.
>
> (Section 601 (c) of the Act)

Many of the initial regulations may possibly be modified over time, although each attempt will meet serious resistance on the part of parents, advocates, and handicapped citizens. For example, Terrel H. Bell, Secretary of Education during Ronald Reagan's administration, proposed the first major changes in the law; however citizens and members of Congress raised such a "storm of protest" that the modifications were withdrawn (*Los Angeles Times*, 1982). The episode has made participants more wary of attempts by administrations to weaken the act.

Funding

The federal government has provided the public school with funds based on a percentage of the excess cost involved in educating handicapped individuals. This percentage equals the National Average Per Pupil Expenditure (NAAPE) in public elementary and secondary schools multiplied by the number of handicapped students who are between the ages of 3 and 21 and who are being served by the local educational agency (LEA). In 1984, the amount of funding reached 40% so that the appropriations for the fiscal year amounted to approximately $998 million.

Due Process Procedures

In the year of the nation's bicentennial anniversary, a historian made the observation that one of the most important aspects of the celebration was the development of 200 years of law. A key ingredient in this system of law is the concept of *due process*.

> Due process is a course of legal proceedings in accordance with established rules and principles for enforcing and protecting individual rights.

Section 615 of the act is directed toward the rights of handicapped individuals and their parents and, although not immediately evident, it contains safeguards for those who work in systems of public instruction.

An example of the safeguards is contained in Section 615 (e) 3. It specifies that a child will remain in the public school while the procedures of identification, evaluation, and determination of educational program, including all impartial hearings and appeals, have run their complete course. The procedures prevent instances in which children are held outside the public school program while their fate is being decided. This outside status had the effect of denying them an education.

In reviewing PL 94-142, previous legislation, and court orders, there are several basic elements of due process procedures in programs for handicapped individuals. Basic elements of due procedures are listed in figure 1.1; however when school systems apply due process procedures to the student population, these elements overlap with one another. In reviewing the elements listed in figure 1.1, educators can begin to anticipate the amount of communication that is required in the whole process of identification, assessment, program planning, instruction, and evaluation. A great deal of accountability is required, especially if parents press the education agency into

---

- The child is represented by a parent surrogate when the parent or guardian are not known, the parents are unavailable, or the child is the ward of the state.
- The parents have the opportunity to participate in the evaluation and determination of the child's program.
- The parents receive written and oral notification in their native language before the child's status in the educational program becomes the subject of evaluation, hearings, or reviews.
- The educational agency establishes a specific period of time for the completion of each procedure.
- The parents receive written results of identified procedures and have the opportunity to respond to all notifications.
- Impartial hearings are conducted if parents disagree with decisions. In conjunction with hearings, parents can examine all relevant records, obtain independent educational evaluation, be represented by counsel, produce and examine witnesses, present evidence, receive records of hearings, and obtain written findings of fact and decision.
- Parents may appeal decisions to an appropriate civil court.
- The burden of proof for recommended action is upon the educational agency.
- The educational agency conducts a periodic review of procedures.

FIGURE 1.1
Basic elements of due process procedures.

a hearing or court case. Yet, professionals should not suppose that hearings will flourish like the spring grass. Many hearings are a result of the lack of communication between parent and educator and can be avoided if the educational agency develops adequate due process procedures for the whole identification-instruction cycle.

Individualized Education Program

The act specifically requires LEAs to establish a written individualized program (IEP) for each handicapped student who is receiving or is expected to receive special education. The law mandates that each state and local educational agency shall insure policies and procedures for developing, implementing, reviewing, maintaining, and evaluating the IEP regardless of what institution or agency provides special education for the student. The IEP should be developed, reviewed, and revised at the beginning of each school year. Although the program will contain references to services and goals to be obtained by the student, parents, and teachers, it should not be interpreted as a binding contract for the school system or agency. State and local educational agencies are responsible for establishing appropriate services so that the individual will achieve specified goals, but the agencies have not violated federal regulations if an individual falls short of the projected objectives.

The formulation of the individualized education program will be the responsibility of the LEA. Each meeting for the purpose of writing, reviewing, or revising the IEP shall include the following participants:

- one or both of the student's parents
- the student, when appropriate
- other individuals, at the discretion of the parent or agency

The list in figure 1.2, derived from various state standards and federal regulations, describes several components of an individualized instruction program.

Although there are limitations in the number of services that can be required from a school district, many of the basic components in the IEP process have been upheld in the Supreme Court case of *Hendrick Hudson School District* v. *Rowley, No. 80–1002.* The IEP is a complex document outlining the present and projected status of the student. It has generated so much interest that numerous articles and materials have been published specifically relating to the effective design and execution of the IEP. Turnbull, Strickland, and Brantley's (1982) publication is one of the most complete guides on the topic.

The IEP also provides numerous opportunities for professional personnel to improve educational measures in career development.

- A statement of the student's present levels of educational performance, including academic achievement, social adaptation, prevocational and vocational skills, psychomotor skills, and self-help skills.
- A statement of annual goals describing the educational performance to be achieved by the end of the school year, according to the IEP. These goals would correspond to the areas of performance as identified in the above component and could include other domains.
- A statement of short-term instructional objectives, which are measurable, intermediate steps between the present level of educational performance and the annual goals.
- A statement of specific educational services needed by the student includes all specific education and related services that are required to meet the unique needs of the student, including the type of physical education program in which he will participate, any special instructional media and materials that are needed, and the career education program in which the student may participate.
- The date when the above services will begin and end.
- A description of the extent to which the student will participate in regular education programs.
- A justification for the type of educational placement that the student will experience.
- A list of the individuals who are responsible for the implementation of the IEP.
- Objective criteria, evaluation procedures, and schedules for determining, on an annual basis, at least whether the short-term instructional objectives have been achieved.

FIGURE 1.2
Components of an individualized education program.

- It can be a focal point for a parent-teacher cooperation in meeting mutually defined objectives. These objectives will be the primary responsibility of the teacher and other professionals involved in educational services. However, the parents' assistance and areas of cooperation should be identified in order to continue basic themes and activities that were first introduced in the educational setting. The parents' role and efforts will be discussed separately in chapter 6.
- It requires that the teacher specify long-term goals and short-term instructional steps required to obtain the goals. The IEP functions as a broad scale marker of the direction in teaching content and skills and can be used as a tool in the management of resources. These resources can be interpreted as services (vocational training in cooperation with a community facililty), personnel

(therapists, instructors from other disciplines), and materials (System FORE individualized instruction, System 80 individualized instruction via teaching machine methods.)

■ It provides other personnel with an overview of the student's educational program and career objectives. This total view would be valuable for curriculum coordinators, counselors, therapists, aides, substitute teachers, and cooperating instructors from such disciplines as physical education, home economics, and vocational education. The overview also defines the responsibilities of cooperating professionals who design curriculums that are aimed at intermediate objectives.

■ It contributes to the continuity of educational efforts as the student progresses through the system or moves from one system to another. Each step in the development of the plan and its subsequent evaluation and revision adds an increased amount of information about the student's abilities and difficulties. Hopefully this composite will decrease the amount of time and effort that instructors must expend in establishing baseline measures of competence. As a fundamental reference, the plan is extremely helpful for students who must change systems because of personal circumstances or because other services that meet their particular needs have become available.

■ It identifies the "who, what, when, and how" of educational services and evaluation. "Who" refers to the learner and professionals involved in the instructional process. "What" refers to the forms of instruction, assistance, or review that will be conducted within a given period of time. "When" refers to the period of time covered in the plan or the specific period during which the student will receive designated services. "How" refers to the measures and means by which program planners will determine student achievement. Although these four questions have been simplified in this discussion, they are extremely important in meeting the multiple needs of the handicapped student.

■ It is another means through which the instructor can specify and obtain career development objectives. The sections dealing with statements of educational performance, objectives, and services should contain references to the student's progress in career development.

The Education Amendments of 1976 (PL 94–482)

The Education Amendments of 1976 (PL 94–482) contain several provisions within a Vocational Education Section that affect training programs for handicapped individuals. These provisions built upon prior legislation, such as the Vocational Education Act of 1963 and the Vocational Education Amendments of 1968 (PL 90-576). The 1968 amendments required that states spend at least 10% of the basic federal and state grant-in-aid funds on vocational programs that would meet the unique training needs of handicapped students. This provision is continued in the 1976 amendments with the stipulation that half of the 10% set-aside money is provided by state and local funds. This prevents the practice of substituting federal monies for state funds in vocational education programs for handicapped students and should increase the total amount of fiscal support available for future efforts.

The law is also consistent with the following provisions contained in the Education for All Handicapped Children Act (PL 94-142).

1. States are directed to use set-aside funds to help handicapped individuals participate in regular vocational education to the maximum extent possible.

2. States are directed to provide written assurance that the use of funds will be consistent with the state plans submitted under PL 94-142. The references to state plans and provisions under PL 94-142 means that the safeguards contained in that legislation would be extended to handicapped individuals who obtain services through the vocational education section.

"Karl has just ended an employment interview with the personnel manager of a large firm. Both are in agreement that Karl is well qualified for the position as a typographer. As Karl leaves the room, the personnel manager remarks: 'But you're limping!' Karl replies: 'Yes Sir, you are right but only when I walk.'"

Elmfeldt, Wise, Bergsten, & Olsson (1983)

The Rehabilitation Act Amendments of 1973 (PL 93-112)

Section 503

Section 503 of the Rehabilitation Act Amendments of 1973 (PL 93-112) is intended to regulate the hiring, training, advancement, and retention of qualified handicapped workers by employers under contract with the federal government for more than $2,500. It requires employers to initiate "affirmative action" for all employment openings, including executive level. Affirmative action can also cover such employment practices as upgrading, transfer, demotion, layoff, and termination. A government contractor holding a contract of $50,000 or more or having at least 50 employees is required to develop and maintain an affirmative action program. This program can be integrated with others but must be reviewed annually. Any changes in the program must be made available to employees and applicants for jobs.

The affirmative action program makes employers responsible for the following:

1. Employers will initiate outreach practices reflecting the affirmative action plan. These practices could include adequate use of employment and placement services, active recruitment through the public media, cooperative ventures with organizations that

Pat Long, Handicapped American of the Year, receives the President's Trophy.

represent handicapped individuals, and company efforts to expand all employees' understanding of and cooperation with affirmative action.

2. Employers will accommodate the job and work environment to the physical and mental limitations of the qualified handicapped worker. Such accommodations may include the elimination of architectural barriers, modifications in the work setting or machine, and changes in the work process.

3. Employers will train the worker in routines that are within individual's general capabilities. Training may encourage handicapped workers to enter the labor force whereas previously they were denied the opportunity of competing for jobs they were capable of handling.

4. Employers will refrain from discrimination against handicapped workers who are qualified to advance to other levels of employment. This is particularly important in eliminating situations in which handicapped individuals were locked into a certain work role and corresponding economic returns.

5. Employers will refrain from attempting to fulfill affirmative action obligations through the process of subcontracting with sheltered workshops for handicapped individuals. Sheltered workshops are to be considered as another source of manpower for the employer and not as a means of meeting obligations without changing employment policies.

The handicapped applicant should recognize limitations to the affirmative action program. First, the handicapped worker must be "qualified" (i.e., capable of performing a particular job with a reasonable accommodation to his limitations). Second, the applicant must declare that he is handicapped in order to be covered by affirmative action policies. Even with these limitations, employers and handicapped workers may work together to increase the skills and productivity of the labor force.

Section 504

Section 504 of the Rehabilitation Act has been described as the most comprehensive civil rights protection extended to handicapped individuals in America. It affects fundamental modifications in the actions and attitudes of individuals in organizations that receive funds from the federal government. Such recipients include all levels of the education community (elementary, secondary, adult, and university systems), hospitals, and social service agencies. Section 504 states that

> No otherwise qualified handicapped individual . . . shall, soley by reason of his handicap, be excluded from the participation in, be denied the benefits of, or be subjected to discrimination under any program or activity receiving Federal financial assistance.
>
> Section 504
> The Rehabilitation Act Amendments of 1973

Two important features of Section 504, program accessibility and elimination of discrimination, are highlighted in the following discussion.

Program Accessibility. A fundamental principle is that programs must be accessible to handicapped individuals. Modifications in class schedules, use of mechanical devices, and changes in degree requirements or changes in the way that such requirements can be met enable individuals to participate in the program. Accessibility is also defined to include the institution's responsibility for integrating the handicapped person as much as possible with normal citizens.

Program accessibility has been used in subsequent court cases. For example, in the case of *Jones* v. *Illinois Department of Rehabilitation Services and the Illinois Institute of Technology,* the Seventh Circuit Court of Appeals in Chicago found that state vocational rehabilitation services were responsible for providing interpreters to deaf clients who were enrolled in college. However, if the student is not an eligible client, then the federally funded college, which is also subject to Section 504, must pay for the interpreter's services.

Elimination of Discrimination. Program personnel must abolish materials and practices that discriminate against handicapped individuals. These practices may include admission procedures, testing, and interviews related to health, welfare, or social service benefits. The procedures are especially crucial in hiring practices, and if employers can make the accommodations prescribed in Section 503, they may not refuse to hire handicapped individuals. Employers are also directed to eliminate mandatory pre-employment physical examinations that can be used to discriminate against a handicapped person.

Any person who has a complaint about discriminatory practices in a program funded by the Federal government should file a letter with the Director, Office for Civil Rights, Department of Health and Human Services, Washington, D.C. 20201.

Although the Rehabilitation Act was passed by Congress in 1973, it took until April 28, 1977 before the final regulations were signed by Joseph A. Califano, Jr. who was then the Secretary of the Department of Health,

Education, and Welfare (HEW). His action focused attention on the long delay in implementing the law, and various groups of handicapped citizens and groups representing their interests rallied in protest. Repeated attempts to decrease the extent to which government agencies enforce regulations has only caused handicapped citizens and their advocates to become more wary of the way that laws become implemented (*ACCD Action*, 1982; *Capitol Observer*, 1983; *Programs for the Handicapped*, 1983c).

TECHNOLOGICAL ADVANCES

Medical and technological improvements have made significant changes in the daily lives of handicapped individuals. The use of corrective surgery for physical and sensory damage has assisted individuals in maintaining acceptable levels of performance in the classroom, community, and place of employment. Developments in the field of medicine has led to greater success in preventing or decreasing damage caused by illness or injury and have added to the amount of time and effort the individual can devote to learning. Refinements in the technology of metals and synthetics used to make prosthetic devices and other mechanical aides have allowed many handicapped individuals greater mobility within the environment. Finally, advancements in the field of microcomputers have provided individuals with the tools for more effective communication, education, training, mobility, and employment. However changes in technology will also contribute to an *increase* in the number of people who will become handicapped because of industrial injuries, automobile accidents, and prolonged life spans.

Developments in research, products, and information have expanded the scope and applications of technology and have improved the lives of handicapped people and the work of professionals in the fields of special education, vocational education, rehabilitation, and health services. Participants in a series of workshops held at the Library of Congress (*Programs for the Handicapped*, 1980) discussed new developments in information resources such as the print media and telecommunications, educational machinery that can be used to evaluate and teach handicapped students, mechanical and electronic aids that can be used to help rehabilitate handicapped individuals, devices that help to restore, facilitate, and augment communication of handicapped individuals, and accessibility and usability of environmental facilities.

Advances in the microcomputer link these categories together. Various devices such as the Optacon, which converts printed images into tactual representations, and the Kurzweill reading machine, which translates printed material into English speech, are examples of inventions that were made possible by computer science. The use of computer technology will continue in such areas as communication aids, robotic aids, wheelchair control systems, and functional electrical stimulation to assist movement and ameliorate pain (Fenderson, 1983).

The average reader or television fanatic is hard pressed to avoid the increasing attention to computers, computer literacy, and technology. The economic recession of 1982–83 and subsequent unemployment demonstrated that the structure of previously vital smokestack industries was changing. Those industries laid off workers and replaced them with computers, robots, and technicians.

We are in the second stage of technological innovation which Naisbitt (1982) describes as a transition from the industrial to information society. This same technological innovation is necessary if handicapped persons are to achieve self-sufficiency and independence. The key question is how handicapped people can benefit from and participate in a society and economy that is changing toward a greater emphasis on high technology.

This is not an easy question to answer, since throughout history handicapped individuals have not participated in the mainstream of society. During the Renaissance and the Industrial Revolution, they were denied the opportunity of making contributions to society. They were even late arrivals to the Civil Rights Movement and have still not received their share of programs in the public schools. For example, when PL 94-142 was passed in 1975, Congress stated that 1 million of the estimated 8 million handicapped children in the United States were *excluded entirely* from the public schools and 3 million were not receiving appropriate educational services. In testimony before the Senate Committee on Labor and Human Resources, Razeghi (1983) indicated that the percentage of handicapped students in vocational education was 1.7% in 1974–75 and increased to 2.5% in 1978–79. Although the number of students almost doubled during that time, the percentage gain was small compared to the estimated percentage of handicapped students in the total school population which range from as little as 8% to as much as 12%. These previously excluded or minimally prepared students are tomorrow's potentially unemployed or welfare cases.

"Today we are seeing only the tip of the technological iceberg. Getting to the solid mass needs and deserves a nationwide program which every agency concerned with the handicapped—both public and private—can support with research, information and other resources. We have long talked about humanizing technology. The chance is here to do so by using technology to open up opportunities for disabled persons to live independently."

Cunerd (1980)

Guide Posts in the Technological Society

Our emphasis on long-term career development is based on years of experience and research revealing that if they are given the opportunity, handicapped individuals can develop their potentials and can make significant contributions to society. The following approaches may serve as markers along a path that will be shaped by major trends in society.

- Technological and medical advances that, on one hand, may cause injury may also be used to enrich the life of the handicapped person. This is vital if professionals, parents, and disabled persons are to approach technological changes with a positive view rather than a resistive one. Resistance will only produce yet another barrier to long-term success, and we definitely do not need any more barriers.

- Handicapped people are accomplishing more in society and, most certainly, in the work world. For years information on limitations and inadequacies have filled introductory textbooks on the education or psychology of handicapped people. It is no wonder that a person like Helen Keller was regarded by the popular media as a "super hero." She was exceptional, but there was also an absence of background against which she could be contrasted. This "information gap" about millions of other handicapped people is another form of exclusion and we still experience these omissions. For example, you could probably count on one hand the number of handicapped people you have *seen* in commercials on television.

The following examples document the success of handicapped people in the work world. Since we cannot keep up with their expanding accomplishments, the list is not all inclusive.

- Merchant and Coriell (1981) and Owens, Redden, and Brown (1978) compiled directories of handicapped scientists and educators. The two directories include approximately 1300 entries. Kenney (1981 & 1982) surveyed these entries and published two articles on the characteristics of disabled scholars. She concluded that scholarship should be a part of the full range of career options and would contribute to the disabled person's pursuit of happiness.

- The Association for Retarded Citizen's On-the-Job Training Project placed approximately 25,000 mentally retarded individuals in competitive jobs from 1969 to 1979. Most of these workers were

31

retained by employers who were willing to provide training (Association for Retarded Citizens, 1980).

■ Most issues of such publications as *Disabled USA, NTID Focus, Rehabilitation Gazette, Accent on Living,* and *Mainstream* contain accounts of disabled individuals who have achieved success in an array of careers.

■ The Epilepsy Foundation of America's Training and Placement Service Project (TAPS) has trained or found jobs for over 4,800 participants in 13 cities. A list of over 200 types of jobs is available in an issue of *National Spokesman* (1982).

■ The National Center on Employment of the Deaf in Rochester, New York, part of the National Technical Institute for the Deaf, advocates career opportunities by providing services to employers. The center maintains a clearinghouse of employment information and a career matching system that compares employers' needs with resumes from qualified deaf persons across the nation (Foote, 1982).

■ Handicapped people have participated in the "high tech/high touch" change from an industrial- to an information-based society (Naisbitt, 1982). Some of the earlier references to disabled people as participants in data processing and computer occupations occur several years prior to Naisbitt's projections of megatrends in the society (Hallenbeck, 1973; Jamison, 1976; Knorr & Hammond, 1975; Nichols, 1970; Smith, 1973).

The professional community has finally recognized the potential of the microcomputer. National conferences and an increasing number of publications have focused on the applications of microcomputers in special education and vocational rehabilitation (Apple Computer Inc., n. d.; Nave, Browning, & Carter, 1983; Taber, 1983). However, the emphasis in the professional realm has been largely on the microcomputer as a teaching device. Information about the development of the handicapped person's career in computer technology is mostly found in project reports.

■ Disabled Programmers Inc. (DPI), Campbell, California, is a nonprofit, tax-exempt institute and development center that specifically trains, places, or employs disabled persons in the computer programming field (Puorro, 1983). In 1980, International Business Machines (IBM) provided the first large contract that was later followed by successive training programs for disabled persons funded under a California law. The majority of trainees were new to the computer field and subsequently placed in private industry. DPI's letterhead contains the motto "Ready with a helping mind."

Electronic Industries Foundation (EIF) is a private, nonprofit ganization that was created by the Electronic Industries Association to perform a variety of research and public education functions. EIF also administers a Projects with Industry program which includes training of disabled workers for positions in the electronics industry. During 1982, EIF placed more than 500 workers by matching the disabled applicant's capabilities with job openings (Pati, Adkins, & Morrison, 1981; *Programs for the Handicapped,* 1983).

- International Business Machines Corporation (IBM) initiated computer programmer training for severely physically disabled persons in 1972 and has continued to expand the program. By 1982, IBM in cooperation with vocational rehabilitation agencies, training facilities, and the business sector trained 895 persons in 22 active projects. Between 1974 and 1981, placement of computer programmers from these projects ranged from 86% to 100% per year (IBM, 1983).

We have not cited every training program or example that has enabled handicapped people to contribute to our technological society. However, we do know that there are not *enough* programs, projects, and examples to meet the long-term needs of handicapped people. We advocate opportunities. Handicapped people are capable, but they need education and training in order to contribute.

CONCLUSION

Some of the highlights in the history of the education of handicapped individuals include distinct landmarks, significant persons, and concerted efforts by groups of people. These actions are not over but truly have just begun. Professionals, advocates, and handicapped individuals, who have defended and lobbied for legislation, have just opened up the realm of possibilities. Career education is a vital ingredient to the possibilities for handicapped people. It can provide its participants with the preparation and experiences that are necessary for personal growth in a complex and changing society.

Life-Centered Career Education 2

In a scathing report, the National Commission on Excellence in Education pronounced that a "tide of mediocrity" was devastating public education. After 18 months of study, the Commission revealed that for the first time in the history of the country, the educational skills of the newer generation would not surpass that of their parents. Among a host of reforms, they recommended that education focus on "the new basics" by including more English, math, science, social studies, foreign languages, and computer science in programs for all students. Speaking at a national conference on career education, a top executive for one major American industry (Miller, 1983) reported that this country has fallen behind in the use of technology despite the fact that the majority of new and existing jobs will become more technically oriented. He indicated that the one constant that exists when looking at job prospects for the 1980s and 1990s is *change* and that what students learn in school today will no longer be adequate to carry them through a lifetime of work.

The need to change our educational practices has been the subject of considerable discussion and debate for many years. Although there is unanimous agreement that change is needed, the major question is *how should education change*? Career education is one good vehicle for meeting the National Commission's recommendations. When properly integrated into the educational system, career education can help teachers make the basics more relevant to the world of work and each student's career interests and potentials. Active involvement of parents and community resources are two vital ingredients in this process. Although not a magic elixir, career education can be a valuable instructional strategy in helping students acquire up-to-date information and skills that they will need in today's fast-moving society

35

(Jesser, 1984). Career education does not replace basic skills education; instead it focuses on the roles, settings, and events that will comprise the future work life of the learner.

In this chapter we will briefly review the career education movement (particularly in relation to handicapped individuals) and describe Life-Centered Career Education (LCCE), an approach that has gained considerable attention throughout the country. Subsequent chapters will detail various aspects of the LCCE approach.

HISTORY

Career education was proclaimed as a major educational reform in 1971 when the U.S. Commissioner of Education, Sidney P. Marland, Jr., introduced the concept to a group of secondary school principals at a national educational convention in Houston, Texas. Marland and his associates believed that the high dropout rate in American schools was partly caused by the failure of the education system to provide students with knowledge that would be relevant to their future goals and potentials. Many educators voiced more practical and meaningful approaches to education. Thus, career education was born.

During the decade of the 1970s and into the 1980s, career education progressed rapidly in most states. When Dr. Marland returned to Houston in 1976 to keynote the first National Commissioner's Conference on Career Education, he reported that "probably never in our educational history has there been such enormous movement toward a central concept of reform over such a brief span of time" (Neil, 1977). At the Helen Keller Centennial Conference, Hoyt (1980) noted that the career education concept has survived for a full decade—three times as long as the typical educational reform movement.

Some of the major historical events having direct implications for handicapped individuals have been the following:

- *In 1972 the federal special education agency (then the Bureau of Education for the Handicapped) endorsed career education.* The Bureau's director, Edwin Martin, declared career education a top priority and made funds available for a large number of curriculum and materials development projects, in-service and pre-service training, and research studies.
- *In 1973 a National Topical Conference on Career Education for Exceptional Children and Youth was held.* This important conference, cosponsored by the Council for Exceptional Children (CEC) and the American Vocational Asssociation (AVA), launched the concept of multidisciplinary career education, which received endorsement from professional teacher associations. The conference

POINT OF VIEW

The issues raised by the National Commission on Excellence describe a sociological phenomenon and should not serve as an indictment against the educational process. The facts were before us a decade ago, but only now are we able and willing to accept the report and the challenges it presents for those of us who are concerned about the future of mankind and the young people who will lead us. Career education may be one of the best vehicles for meeting the National Commission's recommendations.

Career education has survived for a decade—three times as long as the typical educational reform movement—because it is not a gimmick or experimental program. Instead it serves as a conceptual scalpel that cuts through all the superficial short-term cures our creative minds can conjure in the scheme of professional education and lays bare the fundamental obligation of education to offer a systematic, competency-based, sequentially built curriculum. Career education also emphasizes the skills of students and the attitudes of families, communities, and schools that will help handicapped individuals grow as people and mature as members of society. In doing so, career education gives its graduates confidence in applying knowledge and skills to the real world and provides them with a sense of comfort in knowing that their skills have been clinically developed, measured, and explored. Instead of having to face the world with limited academic knowledge, students who have been through a career education program are able to use their educational experience to cope with the demands of adult life.

Leonard Hall is the executive director of the American Association of University Affiliated Programs for the Deveopmentally Disabled in Washington, D.C. (formerly assistant Commissioner of Special Education and Special Services which is a branch of the Missouri Department of Elementary and Secondary Education).

37

brought together legislators, lawyers, advocates, business and industry leaders, and an array of educators from various disciplines who presented service-delivery models, methods, and materials for providing career education.

- *In 1974 a U.S. Office of Career Education was officially established within the Office of Education.* Kenneth B. Hoyt was appointed the director of the U.S. Office of Career Education and established leadership for career education within the federal bureaucracy. The office wrote and disseminated important position papers and monographs, sponsored workshops and mini-conferences with significant individuals and organizations, funded special projects, and promoted legislative and programmatic developments.

- *In 1975 the Bureau of Education for the Handicapped (BEH) sponsored a conference for nationally recognized leaders on "Research Needs Related to Career Education for the Handicapped."* After several days of intensive group interactions and problem solving, members of the conference established priorities that set BEH funding patterns. In St. Louis later that year, a small band of concerned educators organized a committee to establish a new division within the CEC that would focus on and promote implementation of career education. The new division was entitled the Division on Career Development (DCD). A similar group formed within the AVA became known as the National Association of Vocational Education Special Needs Personnel (NAVESNP).

- *In 1976 the Division on Career Development (DCD) was provisionally approved as the 12th division of the Council for Exceptional Children by an overwhelming vote of its Board of Governors.* The division elected its officers and became a significant branch of CEC. Two other important events that occurred during this year were the first *National Commissioner's Conference on Career Education* and the passage of the *Vocational Education Amendments.* The Commissioner's Conference drew over 8000 enthusiastic participants who exchanged ideas about providing career education to all age groups. The Vocational Amendments required that 10% of federal funds be allocated for handicapped students as outlined in PL 94–142.

- *In 1977 the Career Education Implementation Incentive Act (PL 95–207) helped states infuse career education into school curricula so that it became part of ongoing local instruction, and was not just considered vocational education.* Congress declared: "A major purpose of education is to prepare every individual for a career suitable to that individual's preference. . . career education should be an integral part of the Nation's education process which serves as preparation for work" (including students with handicaps).

- *In 1978 the Council for Exceptional Children issued a position paper supporting career education.* Career education was described as the "totality of experiences through which one learns to live a meaningful, satisfying work life. . . provides the opportunity for children to learn, in the least restrictive environment possible, the academic, daily living, personal-social and occupational knowledges and specific vocational skills necessary for attaining their highest levels of economic, personal, and social fulfillment. The individual can obtain this fulfillment through work (both paid or unpaid) and in a variety of other social roles and personal life styles . . . . student, citizen, volunteer, family member, and participant in meaningful leisure time activities."

- *In 1979 Special Institutes and the National Topical Conference on Career Education for Exceptional Individuals were held in conjunction with one another.* This conference, sponsored by the CEC, and the institutes brought together a wide variety of professional workers who demonstrated that career education could be infused and implemented into a variety of settings by numerous methods. Approximately 1000 people weathered the blizzard of 1979 in St. Louis and expressed enthusiasm for continuing the conferences on a more frequent basis.

- *In 1980 the Division on Career Development started to form state DCD units.* The division's membership became the fastest growing in CEC and states began to organize at the grass roots level. As of 1984, 25 DCD state units had been approved by the national organization.

- *In 1981 the DCD conducted an International Conference on Career Development for Handicapped Individuals.* Despite severe nationwide financial constraints, the conference was highly successful and set into motion the planning of a similar conference that was held 2 years later. In addition, several states started organizing and conducting conferences at the state and local levels.

- *In 1982 the Career Education Incentive Act was repealed on October 1, and the Office of Career Education began the process of phasing out.* The Career Education Incentive Act was never intended to be renewed; instead it was designed to provide federal incentive funds so that state and local districts could initiate career education and make it part of their educational effort. The Omnibus Budget Reconciliation Act of 1981 moved career education into the block grant program with the hope that most state departments of education and local school districts would make career education a priority and appropriate even more funds. Thus, the block grant approach could be a significant boon to the future of career education.

■ *In 1983 two important career education national conferences were held.* The Second National Conference on Career Education was held June 13–16 in Louisville, Kentucky. Kenneth Hoyt, on leave from the federal government to serve as Distinguished Visiting Scholar at Embry-Riddle Aeronautical University, spearheaded its development. In polling career education proponents across the country, Hoyt found an overwhelming positive response to having such a conference. The other important conference was sponsored by the CEC's Division on Career Development (DCD) in cooperation with NAVESNP and the Special Needs Division of the American Vocational Association. It was held October 20–22 in Chicago. Both of these conferences demonstrated that interest

Sandra Squires, past president of DCD, presents an award to Kenneth Hoyt for his leadership in the career education movement. Fred Weintraub, assistant director of CEC, looks on.

and enthusiasm for career education was not waning but progressively growing (Brolin, 1983, 4–6).

Many other significant activities have had direct implications on the education of students and adults with handicaps. First, several career education curriculum models can be used successfully with special education students. These are the School-Based Model (Clark, 1979), Experience-Based Model (Larson, 1981), Career Development Model (Egelston-Dodd & DeCaro, 1982), and Life-Centered, Competency-Based Model (Brolin, 1978; 1983). The reader is encouraged to review the models, curriculum, and in-service techniques discussed in these publications and other sources. Second, a substantial body of career education literature has become available in the form of journals, textbooks, monographs, curriculum guides, and teacher and student materials. Third, over 20 states have career education legislation, and most have career education coordinators and resource centers. The career education approach is still endorsed by the Council of Chief State School Officers and many other influential groups (Hoyt, 1982b). In his 1982 study surveying state career education coordinators and several hundred practitioners, Hoyt discovered that in most states career education was at least holding its own and in many others it generated more interest and involvement than ever before. Fourth, a number of schools that have implemented career education models could serve as demonstration sites for exemplary practices (Brolin, 1983).

Readers interested in an in-depth description of the historical aspects of career education are encouraged to read an excellent article by Kenneth Hoyt in the Fall 1982 issue of the *Journal of Career Education.*

TOWARD DEFINING CAREER EDUCATION

Career education was launched without a commonly accepted definition. Months before Commissioner Marland introduced the term in 1971, his staff had labored over an appropriate term in response to a White House directive to increase the federal government's involvement with vocational education. Marland saw this as an opportunity to promote reform by embracing vocational education and the occupational aspects of human development for all of education (Herr, 1976). Since that time, career education has become a priority in American education, and numerous attempts have been made to conceptualize and define the term on the federal, state, and local levels.

One of the major problems career education has experienced is the widespread tendency of professional workers to conceptualize the words *career* and *occupation* synonymously. Donald E. Super (1976), a recognized pioneer and leader in career development theory, wrote a monograph on career education for the U.S. Office of Education that placed career education into an appropriate perspective. He wrote:

> Career education must take into account the many theaters in which careers take place, the numerous roles which can constitute a career, and the non-occupational roles which acquire prominence in society as that of occupation diminishes. Educators need to think of aptitudes, interests, and values as traits which may be utilized, find outlets, and seek satisfaction in available occupations, avocational activities, in civic activities, and in family activities. We need to ask ourselves which roles seem likely to provide the best outlets for each student and in what combination . . . (and) to ascribing honor and importance to appropriate non-occupational roles as they begin to take on more significance in a leisure-oriented society (p. 42).

In presenting a "Career Development Glossary for Career Education," Super defines *career* as

> The sequence of major positions occupied by a person throughout his preoccupational, occupational, and postoccupational life: includes *work-related roles* such as those of student, employee, and pensioner, together with complementary avocational, familial, and civic roles. Careers exist only as people pursue them; they are person-centered (p.20).

Thus, a career is multifaceted and consists of occupational, social, leisure, and interpersonal roles—*occupations are only a part of one's career.*

One's *career* consists of many roles—occupational, avocational, family, and civic.

Hoyt (1975) originally defined career education as "the totality of experience through which one learns about and prepares to engage in work as part of her or his way of living" (p. 4). In this context, *career* is defined as the totality of work that a person engages in during his or her lifetime; *education* is the totality of experiences through which one learns. Thus, career education is conceptualized as considerably less than all of life or one's reason for living. The emphasis is on paid or unpaid *work*, which is defined as "conscious effort, other than that involved in activities whose primary purpose is either coping or relaxation, aimed at producing benefits for oneself and/or for oneself and others" (Hoyt, 1975, p. 3). Later, Hoyt took a broader view of career education than before. In "A Primer for Career Education," Hoyt (1977a) redefined career education in a work context, by emphasizing that teachers and learners should consider it to be only one of several basic educational goals. In another publication, Hoyt (1977b) emphasized that in career education, the word *work* included productive use of leisure time and the unpaid activities of the volunteer, homemaker, and student. Thus unlike many of the people who tried to conceptualize career education, Hoyt clarified his position on work by using a broad definition.

The definition of career education should include the many roles and positions occupied by a handicapped individual during his or her lifetime. This distinguishes career education from vocational education and emphasizes the important knowledge, skills, and attitudes students and other individuals need for various life roles and settings. Paid employment will become a large part of handicapped individuals' careers if they can receive the necessary occupational guidance and preparation that will permit them to earn a decent wage. For many other handicapped individuals, paid employment will not necessarily comprise a major part of their careers. Although their vocational functioning is limited, these individuals may have successful careers and productive lives by learning how to function meaningfully in avocational, family, and civic activities. If the focus of career education is based on each individual's unique set of abilities, needs, interests, and ultimate potentials, career education can work for everyone (Brolin & D'Alonzo, 1979).

Career education does not de-emphasize the fundamentals. Rather, it brings meaning to the curriculum by making individuals more aware of themselves, their potentials, and their educational needs.

The Authors

In this book we have conceptualized career education as a purposeful sequence of planned educational activities that assist individuals in their career development. This eclectic approach requires professionals to seek substantial contributions from families, community agencies, business and industry, and other community organizations.

> Career education is the process of systematically coordinating all school, family, and community components together to facilitate each individual's potential for economic, social, and personal fulfillment and participation in productive work activities that benefit the individual or others.

Career education is a life-centered approach focusing on the individual as a productive worker in many different jobs. Individuals perform both paid and unpaid work at home, in the community, and on a job. Productive work includes that of a homemaker and family member, citizen and volunteer, student, retiree, employee, and participant in meaningful avocational pursuits. Thus the challenge of career education is to provide learners with opportunities that will help them function adequately in these various life roles.

THE LIFE-CENTERED CAREER EDUCATION (LCCE)

Life-Centered Career Education (LCCE) is a competency-based approach to providing handicapped individuals with educational services. It has developed as a result of many years of work involving several hundred educators, special and career education experts, professional workers from various agencies and organizations, parents, and others (Brolin & Thomas, 1971, 1972; Brolin, 1973; and Brolin, Malever & Matyas, 1976). These individuals helped identify the competencies that are critical to the successful community adjustment of handicapped students after they have left the school system. These competencies were then broken down into subcompetencies and organized into a curriculum guide that was eventually published by The Council for Exceptional Children (CEC) as *Life Centered Career Education: A Competency-Based Approach* (1978, 1983). A companion publication, *Trainer's Guide to Life-Centered Career Education* (1978), is also available to help school personnel conduct in-service or staff development activities.

The LCCE Curriculum has been implemented in many schools, residential facilities, and sheltered and rehabilitation workshops across the country. A second edition of the curriculum guide was released in 1983 because of high demand from the field. Descriptions of some representative programs are presented in chapter 9.

The LCCE Curriculum Model

American education focuses on the question "What must the individual know?" Students are taught reading, spelling, mathematics, and other skills that facilitate knowledge about history, chemistry, and economics. When the important skills needed for community functioning are ignored, students are unable to fulfill fundamental educational needs. Instead, educators might ask, "What skills must the individual know to become a more effective person?" *Process education* addresses this question by focusing on "the development of cognitive, affective, perceptual, motor, and social interactive skills" (Bailey, 1976, pp. 40–41).

The LCCE Curriculum, a competency-based model for grades K–12, helps the students acquire 22 major competencies that can be broken down into three major curriculum areas: (1) daily living; (2) personal-social; and (3) occupational skills. These competencies represent what research, practitioner experience, and expert opinion have deemed essential for successful career development. Table 2.1 presents the three curriculum areas, 22 competencies, and 102 subcompetencies that comprise the LCCE curriculum.

The LCCE Model interfaces the 22 competencies with two other important dimensions of career education: (1) school, family, and community experiences; and (2) four stages of career development—awareness; exploration; preparation; and placement, follow-up, and continuing education. Figure 2.1 presents a three dimensional model illustrating the interaction of

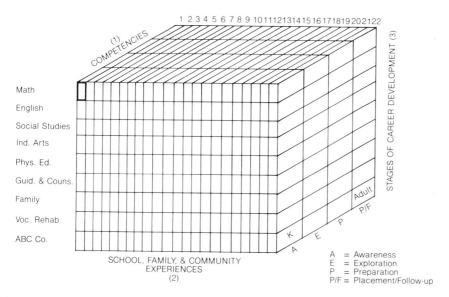

FIGURE 2.1

Competency-based model for infusing career education into the curriculum.

these components in the LCCE approach. Although the model is not intended to be factorially or mathematically pure, it demonstrates that one or more resources, available in the school, family, or community, can be used to teach any of the competencies at each career development stage. For example, competency 1 (Managing Family Finances) could be taught in a math class at the elementary, junior high, and senior high level. Before the competency is taught, the elementary teacher should provide the student with a sufficient *awareness* of the importance of this skill, including how people acquire the skill, what kinds of things are involved in learning the skill, and what people can do with this skill (e.g., family responsibilities, job possibilities). With this background, the student becomes more aware of the importance of this competency in the real world and therefore becomes more receptive to learning the necessary skills. The student begins by learning how to identify money and make correct change. As upper-level elementary school students learn basic skills, they should be provided with *exploration* experiences in and out of the school so they can observe how other people make wise expenditures, obtain and use bank credit facilities, and so on. During late junior high and early senior high, students should crystalize their skills in this competency area *(preparation)* with further complementary community and family experiences. Finally during the preparation stage, students have the opportunity to independently display their skill for this competency. Students may use this competency for family living and may have the interest to get a job that requires this skill.

TABLE 2.1
Career education curriculum competencies.

Daily Living Skills

1 Managing family finances
1.1 Identify money and make correct change
1.2 Make wise expenditures
1.3 Obtain and use bank and credit facilities
1.4 Keep basic financial records
1.5 Calculate and pay taxes

2 Selecting, managing, and maintaining a home
2.1 Select adequate housing
2.2 Maintain a home
2.3 Use basic appliances and tools
2.4 Maintain home exterior

3 Caring for personal needs
3.1 Dress appropriately
3.2 Exhibit proper grooming and hygiene
3.3 Demonstrate knowledge of physical fitness, nutrition and weight control
3.4 Demonstrate knowledge of common illness prevention and treatment

4 Raising children—family living
4.1 Prepare for adjustment to marriage
4.2 Prepare for raising children (physical care)
4.3 Prepare for raising children (psychological care)
4.4 Practice family safety in the home

5 Buying and preparing food
5.1 Demonstrate appropriate eating skills
5.2 Plan balanced meals
5.3 Purchase food
5.4 Prepare meals
5.5 Clean food preparation areas
5.6 Store food

6 Buying and caring for clothing
6.1 Wash clothing
6.2 Iron and store clothing
6.3 Perform simple mending
6.4 Purchase clothing

13 Maintaining good interpersonal skills
13.1 Know how to listen and respond
13.2 Know how to make and maintain friendships
13.3 Establish appropriate heterosexual relationships
13.4 Know how to establish close relationships

14 Achieving independence
14.1 Understand impact of behaviors upon others
14.2 Understand self-organization
14.3 Develop goal-seeking behavior
14.4 Strive toward self-actualization

15 Achieving problem-solving skills
15.1 Differentiate bipolar concepts
15.2 Understand the need for goals
15.3 Look at alternatives
15.4 Anticipate consequences
15.5 Know where to find good advice

16 Communicating adequately with others
16.1 Recognize emergency situations
16.2 Read at level needed for future goals
16.3 Write at the level needed for future goals
16.4 Speak adequately for understanding
16.5 Understand the subtleties of communication

Occupational Skills

17 Knowing and exploring occupational possibilities
17.1 Identify the personal values met through work
17.2 Identify the societal values met through work
17.3 Identify the remunerative aspects of work
17.4 Understand classification of jobs into different occupational systems
17.5 Identify occupational opportunities available locally
17.6 Identify sources of occupational information

18 Selecting and planning occupational choices
18.1 Identify major occupational needs
18.2 Identify major occupational interests
18.3 Identify occupational aptitudes
18.4 Identify requirements of appropriate and available jobs
18.5 Make realistic occupational choices

7 Engaging in civic activities
7.1 Generally understand local laws and government
7.2 Generally understand the federal government
7.3 Understand citizenship rights and responsibilities
7.4 Understand registration and voting procedures
7.5 Understand Selective Service procedures
7.6 Understand civil rights and responsibilities when questioned by the law

8 Utilizing recreation and leisure
8.1 Participate actively in group activities
8.2 Know activities and available community resources
8.3 Understand recreational values
8.4 Use recreational facilities in the community
8.5 Plan and choose activities wisely
8.6 Plan vacations

9 Getting around the community (mobility)
9.1 Demonstrate knowledge of traffic rules and safety practices
9.2 Demonstrate knowledge and use various means of transportation
9.3 Drive a car

Personal-Social Skills

10 Achieving self-awareness
10.1 Attain a sense of body
10.2 Identify interests and abilities
10.3 Identify emotions
10.4 Identify needs
10.5 Understand the physical self

11 Acquiring self-confidence
11.1 Express feeling of worth
11.2 Tell how others see him
11.3 Accept praise
11.4 Accept criticism
11.5 Develop confidence in self

12 Achieving socially responsible behavior
12.1 Know character traits needed for acceptance
12.2 Know proper behavior in public places
12.3 Develop respect for the rights and properties of others
12.4 Recognize authority and follow instructions
12.5 Recognize personal roles

19 Exhibiting appropriate work habits and behaviors
19.1 Follow directions
19.2 Work with others
19.3 Work at a satisfactory rate
19.4 Accept supervision
19.5 Recognize the importance of attendance and punctuality
19.6 Meet demands for quality work
19.7 Demonstrate occupational safety

20 Exhibiting sufficient physical-manual skills
20.1 Demonstrate satisfactory balance and coordination
20.2 Demonstrate satisfactory manual dexterity
20.3 Demonstrate satisfactory stamina and endurance
20.4 Demonstrate satisfactory sensory discrimination

21 Obtaining a specific occupational skill (Subcompetencies will depend on the student's occupational choice.)

22 Seeking, securing, and maintaining employment
22.1 Search for a job
22.2 Apply for a job
22.3 Interview for a job
22.4 Adjust to competitive standards
22.5 Maintain post-school occupational adjustment

This curriculum model can form the basis for infusing career education experiences or concepts and materials into the educational program for handicapped students, whether it is in the school, family, or community. It requires a holistic career education plan involving various disciplines and levels of education to assure that each student acquires all competencies that he is capable of mastering. Procedures for developing this kind of plan will be presented in chapter 8.

The Competencies

All 22 competencies and their 102 subcompetencies have been subjected to rigorous review by hundreds of school personnel who have agreed that the competencies reflect major outcomes required for successful community living and working. The LCCE model has been described as an *adult adjustment approach* because it focuses on skills and competencies needed for a successful career (Clark & White, 1980). The following discussion briefly describes the three curriculum areas and the 22 competencies.

Daily Living Skills

The competencies under the daily living skills category include the following: (1) managing family finances; (2) selecting, managing, and maintaining a home; (3) caring for personal needs; (4) raising children and family living; (5) buying and preparing food; (6) buying and caring for clothing; (7) engaging in civic activities; (8) utilizing recreation and leisure; and (9) getting around the community. These competencies are directly related to the avocational, family, and civic roles that were mentioned earlier in this chapter. But the attainment of daily living skills can lead to many occupational possibilities. Handicapped students must learn these competencies in order to survive in today's fast-moving society. Educators do not emphasize daily living skills enough because they assume that these competencies will be learned incidentally in the home and elsewhere. For handicapped students, this typically doesn't happen. The school must make a deliberate effort to provide this instruction since it is not usually provided in the home and other community settings.

Daily living skills and interests lead to job possibilities such as clerk, stockperson, nursing aide, child-care worker, grocer, cook, maintenance worker, forklift operator, food service worker, housekeeper, press cleaner, laundry worker, furniture upholster, photographic finisher, and barber.

Personal-Social Skills

The competencies under the personal-social skills category include the following: (10) achieving self-awareness; (11) acquiring self-confidence; (12) achieving socially responsive behavior; (13) maintaining good interpersonal relationships; (14) achieving independence; (15) achieving problem solving skills; and (16) communicating adequately with others. Lack of the personal-social skills contributes to the major downfall of all individuals, including handicapped individuals, in work and other settings—no matter how competent the individual may be in other skills. Curricular emphasis on these competencies is critical.

> Personal-social skills are critical for successful performance on most jobs. Skills in this area include getting along with others, taking criticism, accepting supervision, making vocational decisions, knowing proper behavior, respecting the rights of others, following directions, and being honest and loyal.

Occupational Skills

The competencies in occupational skills category include the following: (17) knowing and exploring occupational possibilities; (18) selecting and planning occupational choices; (19) exhibiting appropriate work habits and behaviors; (20) exhibiting physical and manual skills; (21) obtaining a specific occupational skill; and (22) seeking, securing, and maintaining employment. Occupational skills are most often associated with *career education*. They deserve major curricular emphasis; however since the occupational skills are subsumed under daily living and personal-social skills, the three curriculum areas are inextricably linked. The first two occupational competencies, awareness of occupational possibilities and making appropriate occupational choices, should be taught within a broad context: educators should not pressure the student into making a premature occupational choice. Knowing and exploring occupational possibilities, exhibiting appropriate work habits and behaviors, and developing physical and manual skills should be tackled almost immediately after the student enters school. The senior high school is the appropriate time for emphasizing the remaining three competencies.

> Occupational skills development begins in the elementary school and depends on substantial career awareness and career exploration activities, experiences, instruction, and assessment.

49

In presenting our competency-based approach, we do not intend to de-emphasize the importance of basic academic instruction. Students should still be taught reading, mathematics, social studies, science, but a specific purpose should underlie the traditional practice of bringing an individual to a certain grade level at the end of a year or teaching the student to master some kind of physical activity. In this instance the specific purpose is the development of 22 important life-sustaining competencies, and every teacher at every grade level has a stake in each student's career development.

SCHOOL, FAMILY, AND COMMUNITY RELATIONSHIPS

A competency-based curriculum involves changes in the roles of teacher and counselor and requires more involvement from family and community agencies, including the business and industrial sector. Students should also be allowed to express their opinions and must be given the opportunity to influence the direction of the curriculum.

School Personnel

All members of the school community should share responsibility for providing career education and competency development for handicapped students. Unfortunately, little is done to assure that this responsibility is applied systematically. Many educators wish to hold on to the traditional mode of imparting knowledge. They concentrate on grade level content and manipulate the classroom environment for that purpose (Moore & Gybers, 1972). Career education responsibilities must be clearly delineated and assumed by various personnel. Many regular classroom teachers have opposed mainstreaming because they feel that handicapped students will be pushed on them. These teachers must be shown that they have important roles in teaching knowledge, information, and *skills* that will result in a successful career for the student in later years. Special considerations for teachers and in-service personnel assuming such a role must be provided by the school administration.

Regular class teachers are important in helping students develop feelings of self-worth and competence by providing situations where each student can learn and be accepted by other class members. Almost every regular class teacher can help the student develop at least one competency. Home economics and industrial arts teachers are particularly significant in helping students acquire daily living and occupational skills, while counselors are integral helpers in the personal-social and occupational guidance areas. Table 2.2 (Brolin, 1978) presents examples of the types of school personnel who could assist the student *in learning various competencies* at the junior and senior high school levels.

50

TABLE 2.2
Possible competency instructional responsibilities*.

Competency	Junior High	Senior High
Daily living skills		
1. Managing family finances	Business, math	Home economics, math
2. Selecting, managing, and maintaining a home	Home economics, vocational education	Home economics
3. Caring for personal needs	Home economics, health	Home economics
4. Raising children—family living	Home economics	Home economics
5. Buying and preparing food	Home economics	Home economics
6. Buying and caring for clothing	Home economics	Home economics
7. Engaging in civic activities	Social studies, music	Social studies, music
8. Utilizing recreation and leisure	Physical education, art, music, counselors	Physical education, art, music
9. Getting around the community (mobility)	Home economics	Driver's education
Personal-Social Skills		
10. Achieving self-awareness	Music, physical education, counselors	Art, music, counselors
11. Acquiring self-confidence	Art, music, physical education, home economics, counselors	Physical education, counselors, social studies, art, vocational education, music
12. Achieving socially responsible behavior	Physical education, counselors, music	Social studies, music
13. Maintaining good interpersonal skills	Counselors	Music, counselors
14. Achieving independence	Counselors	Counselors
15. Achieving problem-solving skills	Math, counselors	Science, counselors
16. Communicating adequately with others	Language arts, music, speech, physical education	Language arts, speech, music, art
Occupational Skills		
17. Knowing and exploring occupational possibilities	Vocational education, home economics,	Counselors
18. Selecting and planning occupational choices	Business, vocational education, counselors	Counselors
19. Exhibiting appropriate work habits and behaviors	Vocational education, math, home economics, art	Home economics, vocational education, music
20. Exhibiting sufficient physical-manual skills	Vocational education, physical education	Vocational education, physical education, art
21. Obtaining a specific occupational skill	Vocational education, home economics	Vocational education, home economics
22. Seeking, securing, and maintaining employment	Counselors	Counselors

Note: *Regular educators only. Special education teachers and others should assume these responsibilities as needed.

51

Special education teachers assume a different role within this competency-based career education curriculum. The special educator becomes more of a consultant or advisor to other school personnel, parents, and community agencies and industries by coordinating services and integrating the contributions that the school, community, and family can make in meeting each student's career development needs. They will become increasingly important as resource personnel to the regular classroom teachers who will need in-service assistance, methods and materials consultation, modification and materials development assistance, and relevant information on the students' basic academic skills, values, and attitudes. Special classroom instruction will still be needed for many students who cannot be appropriately educated in regular classes. The special educator should monitor each student's progress and should also direct the energies of the school staff to ensure that the student acquires these competencies.

Family

The handicapped individual's family is extremely important in his or her career development. The family can provide meaningful assistance to school efforts by providing the handicapped person with hands-on experiences, positive reinforcement for achievements, a secure psychological environment, community experiences and involvements, participation in family decision making, specific job tasks around the house, an atmosphere that encourages the development of independence, work habits and values, family projects, meaningful leisure and recreational pursuits, and other career development opportunities. The family must work closely with the school personnel to coordinate their efforts sequentially and consistently, assist in the development of community resources, assist as a volunteer or aide in school settings and functions, and serve on advisory and action committees related to career education. Families of handicapped students can help schools in public relations, fundraising, resource development, and other efforts needed to enhance school operations. Chapter 6 is devoted to "Family Contributions," where more information relevant to these ideas is discussed.

Community Involvement

A wide array of agencies and organizations can assist school personnel and families in helping the student acquire the 22 career education competencies. Agencies, organizations, and civic clubs such as YMCA, YWCA, Red Cross, League of Women Voters, Jaycees, Kiwanis, Rotary, Chamber of Commerce, Planned Parenthood, Parks and Recreation, Public Health, 4-H, Boy Scouts, churches, libraries, Girl Scouts, and Campfire Inc. are all resources that can be used to help students acquire daily living skills and career education experiences. Groups that may help students to acquire personal-social skills include many of the preceding organizations as well as state employ-ment services and mental health, counseling, and university organizations. Occupational skills can be developed by using a wide variety of agencies and organizations including vocational rehabilitation and state employment ser-vices, Community Action Programs, Veterans Administration, rehabilitation workshops, and the Governor's Committee on Employment of the Handi-capped. Business, industry, and labor also offer a wealth of assistance: banks, grocery stores, department stores, factories, insurance companies, repair shops, gas stations, loan companies, and many other businesses can be used effectively in planning daily living and occupational learning activi-ties.

The interaction and interface of these three curriculum areas to ca-reer development cannot be overemphasized. It will take considerable time and effort to develop these relationships into an effective, meaningful oper-ating mechanism. But once achieved, the benefits will be obvious and the ca-reer education of handicapped students will be more fully realized.

STAGES OF CAREER DEVELOPMENT

Career education consists of several different stages or phases. As illustrat-ed in figure 2.2 (see page 54), our model includes four stages of develop-ment: career *awareness*, career *exploration*, career *preparation*, and career *placement*, *follow-up* and *continuing education*. Since severely disabled stu-dents need more time to develop the skills required for successful career functioning, these stages will begin earlier and last longer.

Career Awareness

During the elementary years, career awareness should be emphasized. When learning daily living skills, students must become aware of how to manage and use money appropriately, how to manage and maintain a home, how to take care of personal needs properly, how to assume responsibility for rais-ing children and living as a family, how to purchase and prepare food, and how to select and care for clothing. In addition students will learn how to as-sume civic responsibilities and roles, how to fulfill interests and needs by be-coming aware of recreation and leisure activities, and how to achieve greater mobility in the community.

Personal-social skills will help students develop a sense of self-worth and confidence as well as help them become more aware of their feelings, values, and potentials. In addition, students will develop communication skills such as reading, writing, and speaking. They will become more aware of socially desirable behavior and learn how to interact appropriately with

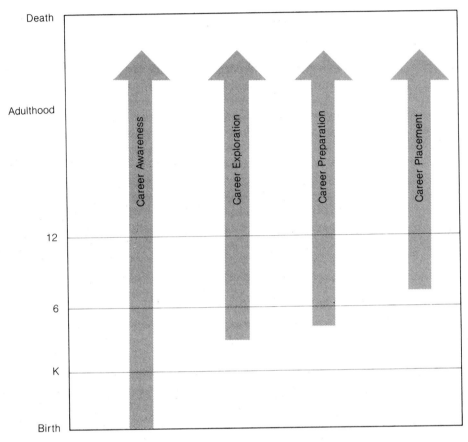

FIGURE 2.2
Stages of career development.

others, and as students gain confidence, they will develop independent relationships. Finally personal-social skills will enhance students' awareness of how to approach and solve problems and will teach them to think independently.

As they acquire occupational skills, students will begin to develop positive attitudes about work. They will begin seeing themselves as potential workers and will begin to explore different types of jobs and their requirements. As they become more aware of work habits and behaviors needed for success in work, they will develop a work personality based an a unique set of needs and physical and manual skills.

Attitude, information, and self-understanding are three main elements of career awareness. Attitudes are the foundation on which the career education structure is built. Young children must learn that people make many conscious efforts at producing some benefit for themselves and others, including working. They can learn that people work for many reasons: economic, psychological, and societal. They need to understand that work can provide a major source of personal identification and satisfaction. Information helps the student learn the variety of ways people earn a living and how they use their time in avocational, leisure, and other life pursuits. Self-understanding enhances the development of students' careers by making them more aware of their relationship to the world and by helping them identify their eventual adult roles (Kolstoe, 1976).

Career awareness is not that difficult to infuse into the elementary curriculum. To a limited extent, most teachers are already taking the time to talk about various careers such as police officer, fire fighter, mail carrier, doctor, nurse, and homemaker. But the career education concept requires that this be done in a purposeful manner so that students become aware of career aspects in relation to themselves. Like any other form of education, career education must be designed sequentially so that whatever happens at each grade level is built upon and leads toward competency attainment.

Career Exploration

Career exploration begins at the elementary level, but it should receive greater emphasis during the junior high school years. During this phase, students begin a more careful self-examination of their unique abilities and needs in relation to the world of work, avocational interests, leisure and recreational pursuits, and all other roles related to career development. It is important for school personnel to design curriculum and instructional experiences so self-exploration can occur. This process should include the use of a variety of techniques, experiences, and settings relevant to each individual. The incorporation of community resources is crucial during this stage of career development.

Daily living skills instruction should encourage students to explore various methods of managing family finances, selecting and managing a home, caring for various personal needs, childrearing and family living methods, buying and preparing nutritious food, buying and caring for clothing, engaging in civic activities, pursuing recreation and leisure activities, and trying various modes of community transportation. These explorations can be personalized to each individual student's emerging set of attitudes, values, and needs by using various courses, field experiences, clubs and organizations, home activities, and community involvements such as part-time jobs, hobbies, reading, and conversation.

Personal-social skills exploration should help students begin to seriously question who they are and assist them in leaving the child status they assumed during the elementary years. Guidance and counseling help students identify unique abilities, needs, and interests as they relate to career development. Individual and group counseling activities such as role playing, modeling, values clarification, and other inter- and intrapersonal activities should be available to help students gain better understanding of themselves and others.

Occupational skills preparation helps students to examine carefully several occupational clusters and engage in a variety of hands-on experiences, both in and out of school. To fully understand characteristics of various occupational possibilities, students need to observe and analyze them firsthand, try them out in simulated situations, and talk to employers about various aspects of jobs and work. To select and begin planning *tentative* occupational choices, they will need assistance from guidance personnel so they can receive a thorough assessment of their vocational aptitudes, interests, and needs. At this time, occupational choices can be only generally related to any specific area, since the student's interest and needs will change during the high school years. Students should be encouraged to try various work samples, simulated job tasks, and community jobs, and should develop work habits and behaviors, physical and manual skills, and other competencies needed in the work place. Prevocational classes such as industrial arts and home economics will be beneficial during the junior high school years.

Career exploration is the link between career awareness and career preparation. During this stage, young students begin to think seriously about their particular set of aptitudes, interests, and needs and how these can be directed toward meaningful and successful adult roles. Sequential exploration activities and experiences should be planned so that by the time students are ready for high school, a more highly individualized educational plan can be designed, and a more relevant career preparation program can be offered.

Career Preparation

Career preparation is not solely confined to one period of schooling. Like other stages of career development, it begins in the early grades and continues throughout life. But for most individuals, particularly for those who do not go on to post-secondary training, the high school years are critical for reaching the necessary level of competence in the three curriculum areas that comprise the 22 life career development competencies.

Educators should monitor and promote a curriculum that will help the student master the nine competencies involved in daily living skills. Home economics, math, business, health, driver's education, social studies, and physical education will help students attain these nine competencies.

If development of personal-social skills has been satisfactory at the elementary and junior high levels, students are ready to learn and practice those personal-social skills needed for community living and working. The professional should identify any specific difficulties that students may have in learning these seven competencies and design procedures for their remediation. This may be accomplished by consulting with classroom teachers on procedures for remediating the difficulty, by altering classroom instruction to fit the needs of students, or by using individual and group counseling. Counseling, role playing, modeling, values clarification, and other techniques are effective with most students. Professionals should perceive each student as an independent and nearly adult-functioning individual who is to be listened to and respected. Their job is to help students identify specific interests and aptitudes and help them find an effective life style.

Development of occupational skills can be more specifically directed toward the student's tentative career choices. Students should be able to select from a variety of vocational courses and community job experiences that fit the aptitudes, interests, and abilities comprising their work personality. If the student has acquired work habits and behaviors, physical and manual skills, and work values and attitudes during the elementary and junior high years, he or she can begin to select an appropriate occupational area and develop specific occupational skills. However this may be counterproductive if the student is forced into making a premature career decision. Some handicapped students may choose to enter college or other post-secondary programs. In the process of learning a specific occupational skill, students also acquire a much more positive self-concept, gain confidence in their ability to learn a specific skill, and master other personal-social skills. Guidance and special education workers are responsible for teaching students how to seek, secure, and maintain employment. This competency should be emphasized throughout the high school program.

Since experience will be a major part of handicapped student's career preparation, they should be encouraged to use community resources. Intensive vocational assessment is also necessary to help students test the realism of their career choices and training needs. Finally many handicapped students may need more than the traditional amount of time to prepare for a successful career and should be given additional time in either the high school or post-secondary setting.

Career Placement, Follow-Up, and Continuing Education

Career placement can occur during the secondary or post-secondary years depending on the student's readiness for this stage of career development. The work-study program gives students the opportunity to be placed in an actual job as if they were being employed as regular workers. This may be either on a full- or part-time basis and may last longer than one semester, depending on each student's ability level and needs.

Although career placement is usually associated with job placement, students should also be given the opportunity to assume avocational, family, recreation, civic, and other nonpaying adult work roles so they can assess their abilities and needs in these areas, as well as in paid employment. School personnel should work closely with the family. For example, the student should be given specific household responsibilities, which include managing family finances, managing a home, caring for personal needs, living as a member of a family unit, buying and preparing food, buying and caring for clothing, becoming involved in civic activities, engaging in self-planned recreation and leisure-time activities, getting around the community, and developing and maintaining satisfactory social relationships. Although the school and family have probably worked on these competencies together before this stage, students should now practice these skills without assistance from the family.

Career placement pulls all previous stages together. During the career placement stage, educators will identify whether the student still needs to refine any of the competency skills. It is the most realistic stage of the career education program and may extend intermittently over several years for many of the students. Therefore, community resources are crucial to the student's life career development and success and should be included in this final stage. Like other people, most handicapped persons will have important lifelong learning needs. Provisions must be made to account for these needs. Therefore, follow-up and supportive services are an important aspect of career placement.

The four stages of career development interface with the competency-based, career education-oriented curriculum designed to prepare handicapped individuals for adult adjustment. If conducted accordingly, all handicapped individuals will be given full opportunity to learn the competencies they need to successfully assimilate into our complex society.

FEATURES OF THE LCCE APPROACH

The LCCE and other career education approaches differ from vocational education in many respects. Vocational education focuses on training people in a variety of technical and subprofessional job skills. Career education, on the other hand, is a broader concept that focuses on preparing the person for a satisfying and productive work life at all developmental stages.

One way to distinguish career education and LCCE from vocational education, life skills education, and other subject matter curriculums is to describe its unique contribution to the educational system (Brolin, 1983):

- *Career education interfaces education with work.* Work is a primary need for the vast majority of adults. An individual who engages in productive work activity, paid or unpaid, gains status as an adult. Productive work is performed on the job, in the community, or at home and includes leisure-time and recreational pursuits. Adults spend much of their productive work time on their job; others may work at home or on volunteer projects that benefit their community. Thus, students should be prepared to engage in the various roles and settings where meaningful, productive work activity occurs. The school curriculum provides students with the opportunity to learn many of the cognitive, affective, and psychomotor skills that they will need to perform various work roles.

- *Career education is a K–12 effort that involves all possible school personnel.* Individuals begin developing their personalities in early childhood. Work attitudes, values, interests, motivation, needs, habits, and behaviors develop early and are very susceptible to the influence of parents, teachers, peers, and experiences. Teachers are very important in helping students clarify work values and potentials. Career maturity depends on the type and level of experiences provided.

- *Career education is an infusion concept.* Career education concepts, materials, and experiences can be integrated into traditional subject matter. For example when teaching mathematics concepts, the teacher should use practical examples of how to relate mathematics to productive work activities in the home, community, job, and avocational situations. The use of gaming, role playing, simulated businesses, occupational notebooks, job analysis assignments, and many other stimulating activities can be used to enhance learning.

- *Career education does not replace traditional education or subject matter.* Career education requires that traditional education reassess why and how various subject matter are taught. Career education may already be involved in much of what is being taught in the classroom. Generally, however, the effort is too limited and unfocused. Educators can be taught how to expand their career education effort without discarding most of what they have done in the past.

- *Career education conceptualizes career development as a process that occurs in stages.* The *career awareness stage* occurs during the elementary school years. It is a time when students need instruction and experiences that will help them become more aware of themselves. They will explore various work settings and job requirements and think about how they might fit into the work world someday. During the junior high school years, the *career exploration stage* not only provides students with further career awareness opportunities but also gives them the opportunity to explore areas of interest and aptitude. During this period, students start to determine the direction of their future roles as citizens, family members, employees, and participants in productive avocational activities. The high school period, or the *career preparation stage*, focuses on career planning, prepares students for the world of work after high school, and provides them with further training. The curriculum should include these three stages of career development so students can develop the work personality and level of career maturity that are necessary in the last stage, *career placement, follow-up, and continuing education.*

■ *Career education requires a substantial experiential component.* Many special education students learn best if hands-on experience is a major focus of their instructional program. If students are busily engaged in activities that are relevant to their future lives, their motivation will increase, and behavior problems will diminish. A basic principle is that the school must meet the needs of students; students should not have to fit into the exact needs and structure of the school and its personnel.

■ *Career education focuses on the development of life skills, affective skills, and general employability skills.* Life skills are important for productive work activity in the home and community. However, they are also directly related to job functioning. Individuals must be able to dress and groom themselves properly, have good table manners, make decisions about money, and use transportation to get to work. Interest and aptitude in certain life skill areas (e.g., cooking, cleaning, mending clothes, taking care of children, participating in athletics) provide valuable indices of possible job interests, training, and employment areas. Affective skills are important for successful acceptance by others in the home, community, and job site. General employability skills such as work motivation, dependability, promptness, consideration of others, perseverance, and handling criticism are skills that all educators can help students acquire.

■ *Career education requires the school to work more closely with the family and community resources.* The majority of what one learns occurs outside of school. Career education promotes a partnership with parents and community resources who help to extend what students learn about the world of work beyond the confines of the school environment. As parents and the community become more aware and appreciative of the school's program and objectives, they will become more supportive of and cooperative with the school.

An individual's career is more than one's occupation. It includes all the productive work activities that individuals engage in during a day and throughout life. In this manner, career education encompasses the whole person, not just one part. Career education should be a pervasive part of a student's education. Vocational educators can expand their role by providing more career awareness and exploration experiences related to a variety of occupations, home, and community experiences. General educators should not view vocational teachers and counselors as the only people who can provide career education. They too can offer many important career education activities. If all educators have a common goal, namely preparation of students for productive work activity as adults, students will be able to achieve greater success.

The LCCE Curriculum approach requires school personnel to focus on the students' career development needs by initiating competency-based instruction in the early elementary years and continuing to pursue the program until the student leaves school. Some competencies, or some of their subcompetencies, must be taught during the elementary years, whereas others are included during the junior high and senior high years. The LCCE Curriculum does not specify when this instruction should begin. Rather, since school personnel are more familiar with their students, resources, and administrative posture, they should decide when the program should be implemented. (Brolin, 1982).

The approach taken in the LCCE Curriculum is to infuse the competencies into the students' programs, not to use the competencies as specific lessons, courses, or minicourses. The sample lesson plan illustrated in table 2.3 can be used as an example of how the subcompetency "Identify Money and Make Correct Change" could be implemented in a math class at the primary level.

Another example of infusing competency instruction can be illustrated at the junior high level. The sample lesson plan in table 2.4 can be used to implement the subcompetency "Exhibit Proper Grooming and Hygiene" in a regular home economics and special education room.

The sample lesson plans demonstrate that instructional activities can be used in familiarizing students with vocational, avocational, home, and community or volunteer career roles. As pointed out by Lamkin (1980), career education

> brings meaningfulness to the learning and practice of basic academic skills by demonstrating to students and teachers alike the multitude of ways in which these skills are applied in work and daily living. A career education emphasis brings observable, experimental relevance to social studies, health, and science curricula, assisting students in perceiving the relationship between educational subject matter and the larger world outside the classroom (p. 71).

61

TABLE 2.3
Sample lesson plan.

INSTRUCTIONAL UNIT

Curriculum Area: Daily living skills	**Competency:** Managing family finances	**Subcompetency:** Identify money and make change
Career Education: Awareness	**Grade Level:** Primary	**Subject:** Math

Lesson Plan

Career Role	Instructional Objectives	Activities and Strategies	Resources and Materials
Vocational	Identify coins and make change in activities related to job experience	Use play money and have students set up a lemonade stand in the room; give each student an opportunity to be the owner	Toy cash register, play money, stand, lemonade, and cups
Avocational	Identify coins and make change in leisure activities	Show a movie and set up a snack bar for the students to purchase snack items	Snack bar, food items, and money drawer
Work in home	Identify coins and make change in the home	Instruct parents to assist child in counting money in the home (i.e. piggy bank, father's change)	Home, parents, and change
Community/Volunteer Work	Identify coins and make change as a volunteer in a community setting	Involve students in collecting and counting money for United Way	United Way

TABLE 2.4
Sample lesson plan.

INSTRUCTIONAL UNIT

Curriculum Area: Daily living skills	**Competency:** Caring for personal needs	**Subcompetency:** Exhibit proper grooming and hygiene
Career Education: Exploration	**Grade Level:** Junior high	**Subject:** Home economics and junior high special education classes

Lesson Plan

Career Role	Instructional Objectives	Activities and Strategies	Resources and Materials
Vocational	Demonstrate proper grooming and hygiene for job situation	Invite employers to discuss the importance of personal grooming in obtaining and maintaining a job	Employers from the community
Avocational	Exhibit understanding of certain grooming needs in the area of leisure and recreation	Discuss how grooming and hygiene needs change as activities change	Physical education teacher
Work in home	Exhibit independent grooming and hygiene skills	Discuss *proper bathing* techniques and show students how to keep a chart of grooming skills	Filmstrips, booklets, and free samples of products
Community/Volunteer Work	Recognize that good grooming and hygiene skills should be maintained at all times	Discuss the importance of first impressions	

The LCCE Competency-Based approach does not advocate elimination of current courses or change in the structure of education. Instead, it recommends that educators change the focus of instructional content to serve career needs of students and that family and community resources be used to a greater extent in helping students gain experience. Each instructor must decide how competencies can be taught and how career education concepts can be infused into existing course offerings. Although basic academic skills should be emphasized at the elementary and junior high levels, more attention to career awareness and exploration activities is also highly recommended.

The LCCE approach lends itself well to mainstreaming. With current emphasis on the least restrictive environment in education, many regular class teachers are being asked to provide instruction to handicapped individuals. Educators and counselors should familarize themselves with the competency needs of exceptional students and should learn how to help handicapped individuals acquire competency skills. The competencies lend themselves to an Individualized Education Program (IEP) format such as the one presented in appendix A. In addition, the LCCE Curriculum offers a Competency Rating Scale (CRS) (chapter 9) which provides a cumulative record of student progress in each competency area. Interested readers can secure the CRS Manual from *Life-Centered Career Education: A Competency-Based Approach*, published by the Council for Exceptional Children.

CONCLUSION

The career education movement continues to be a significant force in American education despite the expiration of the Career Education Incentive Act on October 1, 1982. Unlike most Federal laws, the Career Education Incentive Act never made career education a mandate but rather, provided Federal funds as an incentive for the voluntary participation of the Department of Education in each state. Forty-seven SEAs, the District of Columbia, Puerto Rico, and the territories decided to participate (Hoyt, 1982a). Thus besides legislation, funding, and a Federal Office of Career Education which expired at the end of the legislation, state and local agencies responded with definitions, guides, policy statements, and curriculum modifications. Many national and state workshops and conferences were conducted.

Hoyt (1982b) grouped the major accomplishments of the first decade of the career education movement in relation to three major goals:

1. Career education attempted to provide students with 10 career-related skills. Evidence strongly indicates that career education succeeded in improving students' abilities to (1) understand the private enterprise system; (2) explore themselves and identify educational and occupational opportunities; and (3) overcome

bias and stereotyping as deterrents to full freedom of career choice. Promising but not yet conclusive evidence suggests that career education can help students to (4) improve basic academic skills; (5) develop and use personally meaningful work values; (6) develop career decision-making skills; and (7) seek, find, obtain, and hold jobs. Evidence does not indicate that career education can provide skills that enable students to (8) practice good work habits; (9) make productive use of leisure time; and (10) humanize the work place.

2. Career education attempted to strengthen the relationship between the school and community so that students could apply what they learn in the classroom to the work world. Evidence strongly indicates that the school and community are successfully coordinating their efforts.

3. Career education attempted to infuse careers into the K–12 curriculum. Evidence very strongly indicates that this can occur and, when it does, it receives very wide support from diverse segments of the community.

The Life-Centered Career Education competency-based approach focuses on the life career development needs of handicapped individuals. The Life-Centered Career Education (LCCE) Curriculum has gained considerable acceptance and adoption across the country. Subsequent chapters of this book will reveal its widespread use in many different settings and levels.

The career education approach encompasses all kinds, types, and levels of education and prepares individuals for all phases of productive work activity. It is a personalized approach that provides individuals with a balance of content and experiential learning. Career Education is also a *total person* approach that views occupations as one part of the individual's career and attempts to prepare the student with vocational, avocational, civic (volunteer work), and family work skills. Finally career education views unpaid work as an activity that not only benefits society but also endows the individual with a sense of dignity and purpose.

II
Application

Part two presents information in regard to teaching handicapped students and adults in a career education context. First, this section presents objectives and activities that professionals can use in teaching the 22 competencies and 102 subcompetencies. Second, part two describes ways that the family and business and industry can support and enrich teaching efforts.

Chapter 3 is devoted to the daily living skills competencies. These competencies are important in helping students develop community living skills and vocational possibilities. The chapter provides many suggestions on teaching the nine daily living skills and the 42 subcompetencies and includes activity tips and sample lesson plans. It is recommended that school personnel identify areas of the curriculum that already contain lessons relative to the competencies. Chapter 3 includes a curriculum check sheet that teachers can use to facilitate review of texts, programmed materials, or learning aides, and that corresponds with the competencies, curriculum areas, and methods of instruction.

Chapter 4 discusses the personal-social skills. The seven competencies in this area help students develop satisfactory interpersonal relationships, both at work and in the family and community. Suggestions for teaching the 33 personal-social skills are presented, and several strategies—bibliotherapy, classroom discussions and meetings, individualized learning centers, role playing and sociodrama, self-concept scales, and values clarification—are discussed. Particular attention is given to the development of the individual's self-concept and additional activity tips and sample lesson plans are included in the chapter.

Chapter 5 focuses on the occupational skills. The six competencies comprising this area can be divided into two groups: Three competencies relate to occupational guidance, and the remaining three are involved in occupational preparation. The 27 subcompetencies that relate to five competencies are discussed in relation to suggestions for their provision in and out of the classroom. The sixth, obtaining a specific occupational skill, is discussed relative to why students should acquire this competency before employment. The occupational guidance techniques include counseling, job-task analysis, simulations of business and industry, career seminars, field trips and speakers, and career information centers and systems. Occupational preparation techniques include work tasks and projects, simulations of business and industry, on- and off-campus training, skills development systems, and behavioral task analysis.

Chapter 6 examines the contributions that the family can make to the student's career development. Principal attention is given to suggestions for working with parents. Parent power is discussed in light of the several court cases that led to expanded provisions for the education of handicapped students. The influences that parents have upon the student regarding career roles and other matters concerned with the realities of the modern world are stressed throughout the chapter. Efforts at training parents in career education are reviewed as well as the family involvement in the competencies that were presented in chapters 3 through 5.

Chapter 7 discusses what business and industry can contribute to programs for handicapped individuals, how educators can involve business and industry in career development programs, and what procedures professionals can follow in approaching prospective employers. Business and industry personnel can identify trends in the economy, provide job leads, become advocates for handicapped people, provide program consultation, offer work experiences, sponsor conferences and workshops, and provide resources for classroom use. The chapter also includes suggestions for involving members of business and industry through advisory committees, workshops, and publications. Continuous contact with this sector of society is important to maintaining a successful career education program.

The Daily Living Skills 3

Daily living skills are necessary for successful, independent living and working in modern society. Acquisition of these skills can lead to vocational possibilities for students, depending on their particular abilities, interests, and needs. Skills should be systematically included in daily classroom lessons rather than taught haphazardly or overlooked entirely. Teachers may need to consider the individual's particular learning characteristics before they plan objectives and methods and evaluate the student's progress. These efforts will help teachers and learners to notice improvements in such daily functions as maintaining personal appearance, managing finances, and mobility in the community. The following lists the nine daily living competencies that are important to the career development of handicapped individuals.

---

1 Managing Family Finances
2 Selecting, Managing, and Maintaining a Home
3 Caring for Personal Needs
4 Raising Children—Family Living
5 Buying and Preparing Food
6 Buying and Caring for Clothes
7 Engaging in Civic Activities
8 Utilizing Recreation and Leisure Time
9 Getting Around the Community

This chapter does not contain all possible objectives and activities that teachers can use from the time the student enters school at primary grades through adult education. However teachers should modify these objectives and activities to fit the needs of individual learners. This modification is especially important when teachers help students acquire daily living skills. Fortunately, the professional literature contains numerous articles and research studies about the daily living skills. For further information, you should review issues of such journals as *Mental Retardation*, *Education and Training of the Mentally Retarded*, *Behavior Therapy*, and *The Journal of the Association for the Severely Handicapped*. In addition, Wehman (1983) and

the Division on Career Development's Committee on Severely Handicapped compiled a resource list of community, domestic, vocational, and avocational skill areas. Information is available from Paul Wehman, Rehabilitation Research and Training Center, School of Education, Virginia Commonwealth University, Richmond, VA 23284.

We have provided a series of goals toward which the daily lesson plans and individual education programs for most handicapped individuals can be directed. Each competency is divided into subcompetencies that con-

POINT OF VIEW

Career education is not a separate course of study, but is rather a body of concepts that should be integrated into the school curriculum (elementary through high school, and beyond). Career education experiences become increasingly more important as the severity of the handicapping conditions increases.

Teachers can use the classroom as a learning facility that can help students learn daily living skills. For instance, in teaching employability skills, the teacher becomes the employer and the child's occupation becomes student. Grades and, in some instances, token money may become the wages. A classroom store can be set up where students can purchase school supplies with token money they have earned from working in the classroom. The idea of incorporating a money system leads the way to setting up a classroom banking system, savings accounts, and loans. In this way, the students will be learning not only the expected curriculum, but also survival skills such as budgeting money.

There is hardly a subject within the school curriculum that does not have some relationship to daily living skills. Math (e.g. time, money, measurement), English (e.g. reading), language arts (e.g. writing skills), and social studies (e.g. map skills) include teaching career concepts. Teachers do not have to change the curriculum. However they should work toward helping their students become happy, self-adjusted individuals who are achieving to their fullest capacity.

The importance of parent involvement cannot be stressed too much. Parents are an important resource who can supply help in the classroom (as teacher aides or career speakers), on field trips, as well as projects at home. This valuable resource costs no more than a little time and can be the backbone of any program.

Carol Ellington teaches learning disabled and mentally handicapped students in Hillsborough County, Tampa, Florida.

tain narrative discussions and suggestions relative to objectives and teaching activities. Teachers should fashion additional objectives and activities to meet the specific abilities and learning difficulties of their students.

We have also presented several *activity tips* and *sample lesson plans* to facilitate infusion of the competencies into the curriculum. The *activity tip* is only one example that can be modified to meet the student's progress through the stages of career awareness, exploration, preparation, and placement. Each *sample lesson plan* has been prepared by professionals who applied our competencies and suggestions to the instructional situation. The discussions of the competencies, suggestions for activities, and sample lessons should enable the teacher and counselor to integrate career concepts and materials into the daily curriculum. The chapter concludes with a discussion of techniques for teaching daily living skills to handicapped learners.

COMPETENCIES

1   Managing Family Finances

The ability to regulate finances is a crucial determiner of adult success for average as well as handicapped citizens. Therefore teachers should include numerous activities that prepare students for their roles as spenders, savers, and managers.

1.1   Identifying Money and Making Correct Change

The beginning skill for this subcompetency is the successful identification of several forms of currency. Students with visual disability may accomplish this skill by becoming familiar with the size of metal coins and by folding paper money of various denominations at different corners. Arithmetic exercises or "play stores" can be used to teach primary grade students how to count and manipulate coins and bills.

Numerous teaching aides and commercial workbooks are available to help teachers initiate activities that would require students to make correct change and use money in various situations. Parents can provide students with money to buy lunch or spend on field trips. Other objectives related to this subcompetency should include demonstrating ability to make change and identifying uses of money in society.

1.2   Making Wise Expenditures

The ability to select goods and services is valuable in a society that experiences inflation, economic stagnation, and prosperity. This subcompetency focuses upon the student as a consumer who can use tags and labels to evaluate merchandise, who considers the advantages and disadvantages of discount stores, and who develops strategies for buying during bargain sales. These skills will be especially helpful to those handicapped workers with low incomes. Teachers can acquire commercial materials that include specific exercises in consumer education. However in general, the instructor should conduct classroom activities that require students to compare products sold at different stores or markets, itemize their family's purchases during a given period of time, or construct a shopping list and record prices of items at a given store. These assignments can begin at the primary level, and experience has taught us that students use these skills repeatedly through the adult years. These practices also sharpen the student's ability to make decisions regarding which products and services to use. A final consideration for all consumers is an awareness of common advertising gimmicks and traps. Local consumer protection agencies and groups can provide the class with materials and demonstrations that will further supplement this

Learning to identify money and make correct change is an example of an LCCE subcompetency that can be infused into the regular curriculum.

75

part of the curriculum. Other objectives should include distinguishing essential items from luxuries and identifying sources of consumer information.

ACTIVITY TIP

Students can keep a record and calculate their parents' expenditures for a week or their own expenses for a longer period of time. The student should place budget headings on the left hand side of a ruled sheet of paper. The days of the week or months of the year are placed at the top of the page. Dollar amounts are entered for the following budget headings: rent, utilities, food, transportation, clothing, medical expenses, insurance, taxes, entertainment, savings, others. Advanced students can calculate the percentage of expenditures per budget heading.

1.3 Obtaining and Using Bank and Credit Facilities

This complex subcompetency includes the use of a checking and savings account, credit or charge account, and obtaining a loan. Many students will not engage in the latter step until their adult years, but initial familiarity with banks, pass books, checks, deposits, and the like can begin in the elementary grades. Teachers can establish classroom banks and accounts in conjunction with exercises on the use of money. Shopping trips, as discussed in subcompetency 1.2, can be financed by checking, savings, or charge accounts maintained through the classroom deposits. All of these exercises depend upon an actual acquaintance with the community's financial establishments. Although teachers have an opportunity to visit banks, savings and loan facilities, and credit unions, the family has access to these establishments over a longer period of time. Teachers should encourage parents to explain how to use these facilities when they take their children with them to make deposits or withdrawals. Teachers can supplement these activities by asking representatives from these establishments to show the class how to use these services. Other objectives should include identifying benefits in saving money and identifying information required to open a charge account or obtain a loan.

1.4 Keeping Basic Financial Records

Successful adults can maintain a minimum number of records. But, they must be able to identify those receipts, bank statements, or contracts that should be preserved in order to plan a budget, meet bills, and file tax returns. The goal of these activities is to help the student develop a personal system of record-keeping and filing. Children are introduced to logical systems when they develop hobbies that involve organizing events or materials, such as collecting stamps, pictures, or bubble gum cards. Several commercial publishers provide instructional materials explaining banking procedures and how to maintain records and calculate taxes. The crucial concern for the teacher is whether the student *has practiced* and *uses* a record-keeping system. Once students incorporate a system into their daily activities, they have acquired the necessary skills for the development of this subcompetency. Other objectives should include constructing a personal budget for a given length of time and identifying community agencies that help individuals develop an adequate record system.

1.5 Calculating and Paying Taxes

The students will not need these skills in authentic situations until they have earned incomes subject to local, state, and federal taxes. However, the instructor should prepare the student by conducting classroom activities examining the several kinds of taxes (sales, luxury, gas) that affect the student's earnings and savings. These activities can help students identify which items are taxed, how much tax they should pay, and how taxes are collected and used. Secondary school programs should include exercises that will familiarize students with income tax forms, procedures for filing returns, and agencies that provide tax assistance. Other objectives should include demonstrating ability to complete a tax form.

Magic Valley (Idaho) Rehabilitation Services (1978) developed a daily living skills curriculum that includes several lessons on income taxes. The curriculum is intended for handicapped adults who live in group and sheltered homes and also contains lessons in other competency areas such as money, cooking, housekeeping, clothing, self-care, and shopping.

2 Selecting, Managing, and Maintaining a Home

A major portion of the average person's salary is spent on housing. In certain parts of the country, the monthly rent for apartment or house may exceed the costs for food. Housing costs that exceed the average worker's salary place increased stress on her ability to maintain independence. The young handicapped person may have to reside with the family for a longer period of time or seek peers who will share costs. These situations require the individuals to be alert for ways in which they can minimize expenses for maintaining a home.

2.1 Selecting Adequate Housing

Awareness of a family's needs for living space and facilities begins in the primary grades. Students can draw their homes or apartments, collect pictures of various rooms, and identify family functions in each part of the dwelling. This general inquiry leads to expanded knowledge of various types of housing available in the community. The teacher should stress the advantages and disadvantages of each dwelling. This would include discussions about space, costs, utilities, and location. Students in the intermediate grades can gather information by interviewing realty agents, family members, and newspaper advertisers. Secondary students should continue with specific exercises related to renting a home or apartment, deposits, leases, tenent rights and responsibilities, and community agencies that can assist the individual with more complicated decisions involving the purchase of property. Another objective should be identifying important considerations in renting an apartment or buying a house.

2.2 Maintaining a Home

Maintaining a home includes basic skills such as sweeping, dusting, cleaning, and washing household fixtures, furniture, and utensils. The physical skills required in using brooms, mops, and vacuum cleaners can be acquired through practice in the classroom. But a far better learning situation exists in the student's home. Teachers should coordinate their activities with those of the parents so that handicapped individuals will become familiar with household routines and instruments and practice maintaining a clean and attractive home. Another objective should be demonstrating a housekeeping routine or system.

ACTIVITY TIP

Students and parents cooperate in constructing a large diagram of their house or apartment. Symbols that represent various tools required to maintain and clean the dwelling and that the student can use successfully should be entered at the bottom of the diagram. Students can create their own symbols for such functions as sweeping and dusting. A chart can be added indicating the functions and the days of the week. The chart can help parents and teachers keep track of the student's progress. Both the diagram and chart can be expanded to fit the student's abilities.

SAMPLE LESSON PLAN 3.1

Author: Lynn S. Miller

Level: Elementary Situation: Multi-handicapped day class

Period: Language arts Time Span: One week

Objective: Competency 2.3: Students will identify and demonstrate the use of basic appliances and tools found in the home.

Activity Title: *Field Trip to an Appliance Store*

Goal of Activity: Students will participate in a field trip to a local appliance store and will identify a variety of home appliances and tools.

Activity: Students will take a field trip to an appliance store in the community. While touring the store, each student will compile a list of as many appliances and tools as possible. Students may need assistance from the teacher to develop a list. The students should ask a store employee for any catalogs or advertising material concerning home appliances and tools that are available. Students should also collect a business card that they can put into their field trip file.

Activity Title: *My Home Appliances and Tools Notebook*

Goal of Activity: Students will compile a booklet picturing basic home appliances and tools.

Activity: Students will look for pictures of a variety of home appliances and tools found in magazines, newspapers, catalogs, and brochures that they have received from an appliance store. After pasting their pictures onto a piece of construction paper, students will label each tool and appliance. These pages will be placed in a booklet form and titled *My Home Appliance and Tools Notebook*. The students will also discuss the function of each appliance and tool.

Activity Title: *Are You Using Your Appliances and Tools Correctly?*

Goal of Activity: Students will become familiar with safety procedures involved in using various home appliances and tools.

Activity: The teacher will bring several home appliances and tools to the classroom and will discuss and demonstrate procedures for using these materials safely. While showing students how to use each device, the teacher should explain what the appliance or tool is used for. Before each student has the opportunity to operate the appliance or tool, the student should be aware of the safety procedures involved in operating the device. A photograph will be taken as the student demonstration is taking place. Students will construct a bulletin board using these photos. They will label each appliance and tool and make a list of safety procedures that will accompany each photo.

Evaluation: After discussing their field trip to the appliance store, students will illustrate and write a sentence or a short story about their experience. Students will also share *My Home Appliance and Tools Notebook* with their parents and should list the appliances and tools found in their homes. Finally students will discuss the function and safety procedures of a variety of home appliances and tools.

Related Subcompetencies: 4.4 Practice family safety in the home
  12.2 Know proper behavior in public places
  16.4 Speak adequately for understanding

2.3 Using Basic Appliances and Tools

Appliances can be used to clean or repair the home. The latter includes such tools as a hammer, saw, screwdriver, or wrench. The teacher's goal is to develop student competencies with appliances and tools that would be used in the home to maintain cleanliness and insure that doors, windows, and locks are in working order. This means that students would be able to make basic home repairs and improvements such as replacing screens or light bulbs, tightening screws or bolts, and painting doors or walls. The special education teacher should plan these activities with the assistance of home economics and industrial arts teachers. Other objectives should include identifying financial benefits of home repairs and improvements and using safety procedures in working with tools and appliances.

2.4 Maintaining the Home Exterior

Although the majority of young adults will live in apartments, they should understand and practice skills that contribute to the preservation of the exterior of the dwelling. These skills include mowing, raking, trimming, watering, painting, and removing ice or snow. Students should be aware of safety procedures and should know how to use various tools such as rakes, shovels, and lawn mowers. Again, home economics and industrial arts teachers should be asked to help the teacher plan these activities. Other objectives should include identifying appropriate tools for each procedure and identifying community sources of tools and advice for maintaining exterior conditions.

"Career education at the elementary level consists primarily of an evolvement of social skills necessary in job, family, and societal adjustment; an understanding of oneself; a development of basic communication and computation skills; an introduction to the general idea of the world of work; and an exploration of a variety of meaningful careers."

Gillet (1980)

---

3 Caring for Personal Needs

Adequate hygiene, physical condition, and health care are of special importance to those handicapped individuals who are susceptible to injury, illness, or irritation associated with their impairment. Relatives will probably try to help these individuals learn how to take care of personal needs, but the teacher's objectivity can help to balance the emotional involvement of relatives who identify with the handicapped individual.

3.1   Dressing Appropriately

Social standards concerning acceptable attire for both men and women have become less rigorous. The broad range of acceptable attire presents a new burden to teachers who must instruct students on the types of clothing that are appropriate for different weather conditions, social settings, and work situations. Elementary school students could construct bulletin boards containing displays that illustrate the major forms of dress. When planning activities related to this skill, teachers should focus on the relationship between health and appropriate attire. Teachers can also use role-playing techniques to help adolescents become more aware of the social ramifications involved in dressing to meet the occasion. Students can use the feedback provided by role-playing experiences to evaluate the appropriateness of their attire. Another objective should include demonstrating competence in selecting appropriate leisure and work attire.

3.2   Exhibiting Proper Grooming and Hygiene

Students should demonstrate ability to brush their teeth, wash their hands and face, use handkerchiefs, towels and napkins, and maintain a clean appearance. Teachers from intermediate grades through adult education should continue to help students develop these abilities and expand their awareness of personal hygiene and grooming habits that are appropriate for males and females. This is one of the most vital subcompetencies since acceptance of an individual by peers, adults, and employers is usually based on personal appearance. Another objective should include demonstrating the use of appropriate health and grooming aids.

ACTIVITY TIP

Each student constructs a "grooming card" that she can carry in a wallet or purse. The grooming card is similar to an identification card but contains specific reminders of grooming appropriate to the student's concern (i.e. hair style, make-up, and clean glasses). Teachers, counselors, and parents periodically check the "grooming card" for proper identification!

3.3   Demonstrating Knowledge of Physical Fitness, Nutrition, and Weight Control

Development of the Special Olympics was motivated by the fact that mentally retarded individuals had received little or no instruction in physical education or recreation in public schools and institutions. The Special Olympics help to dramatize that all individuals possess physical competence. Proper care and development of the body is vital for handicapped people so that

81

they may be able to meet the physical demands of everyday life. The child should demonstrate knowledge of major body parts and perform exercises or activities that benefit development. As students develop fundamental knowledge of basic food groups, nutrition, and weight control, teachers should enlist cooperation of physical education, recreation, and home economics professionals. Students can maintain their own health charts by recording maturation, eating habits, or games and exercises. Other objectives include performing activities that maintain appropriate physical fitness and demonstrating eating practices that contribute to proper nutrition.

3.4 Demonstrating Knowledge of Common Illness Prevention and Treatment

Demonstrating knowledge of illness prevention and treatment methods is one of the most complex subcompetencies. This area includes information about illnesses and basic symptoms, hazards to health that occur in the home, basic first-aid techniques, and obtaining assistance for various medical problems. The lessons on illness will be significant to handicapped individuals who must guard against dangers in the environment that can complicate the primary disability—for example, respiratory infections for the physically disabled, or an inflamed eyelid for the deaf. Students in the primary grades should begin learning basic health measures that will prevent illnesses or injury. The students' experiences will provide ample subject matter, and the instructor should provide numerous practice sessions requiring students to contact emergency facilities in the event of illness or injury. The range of subject matter increases as instruction includes first aid, safety considerations, health facilities, and professionals. Local public health facilities or agents can provide demonstrations and audiovisual aides to assist instruction in these competencies.

SAMPLE LESSON PLAN 3.2

Author: Lynda Glascoe

Level: Junior high school   Situation: Handicapped students in a resource specialist program

Period: Four (home activity included)   Time Span: One week

Objective: Competency 3.4: The student will differentiate between healthful and unhealthful products advertised in magazines and on television. These activities should be used after basic instruction on nutrition and chemical abuse.

Activity Title: *Do Magazines Advertise Healthful Products?*

Goal of Activity: Students rate products advertised in magazines according to their appropriateness to good health.

Activity: The teacher leads a discussion on how advertising affects eating habits and how this could influence health. Provide different types of magazines (women's, teens', and sports). The student cuts out advertisements of products that can be eaten or are related to health (e.g. food, drinks, medicine, and cigarettes). The student glues each advertisement on a separate piece of paper and answers the following questions about each product (this can be done in questionnaire form or written in a paragraph).

1. Is this product good for you?

   Yes   No   Don't know
2. Do you like it?

   Yes   No   Dont't know
3. Would you use it?

   Yes, a lot
   Yes, sometimes
   Yes, but only when an adult says it's okay
   No

Activity Title: *Does Television Advertise Healthful Products?*

Goal of Activity: Students rate the appropriateness of products advertised on television to good health.

Activity: Students will watch television during *normal* viewing hours and will record the time and the program they watched. Since this activity will probably be conducted almost entirely at home (unless a television is available for classroom use), parent involvement is important. Teachers should contact the parents to explain the objectives of this activity and encourage their assistance. After students have listed all commercials that advertise products to eat or drink (including medicines), students will answer the questions given in the previous activity. These activities will be included in a folder with the previous cutouts.

Evaluation: Students will list five healthful and five unhealthful products that are frequently advertised in magazines or on television. Given five advertisements, the student will state reasons why the product is healthful or unhealthful.

Related Competencies: 3.4   Demonstrate knowledge of common illness prevention and treatment
                            15.3   Look at alternatives
                            15.4   Anticipate consequence

4   Raising Children—Family Living

Raising a family begins with the individual's experiences as a family member. Teachers should help students observe childrearing practices of their families, relatives, or neighbors. Many of the skills required in mastering the subcompetencies will be based on the observational and reporting skills of students. Students' observations can help teachers prepare lessons on successful child-parent interactions. Experience is the best teacher, but when room for experimentation is limited, observation of others' experiences also avoids needless trial and error. Teachers in secondary and adult programs can also provide students with ample opportunity to ask questions about raising children and can provide them with enough sources of information so that students may obtain in-depth answers.

4.1 Preparing for Adjustment to Marriage

The focus of the teacher's lessons should be on the personal adjustments that each partner must make during marriage. Students can certainly observe the "give and take" in decision-making processes that occur in their families. They may also have some experience adjusting to brothers and sisters, playmates, club members, or peers. Of course, these situations hedge around the actual experiences accompanying marriage. Nevertheless these experiences test students' abilities to plan cooperatively with others, express their opinions, and develop other basic skills that contribute to a successful marriage. The teacher may discuss various aspects of marriage that require careful decision making. Mutual concern and respect, shared responsibilities in the home, earning a living, managing the household, visiting relatives, and planning a family are just a few issues for discussion. They certainly provide enough subject material for the hundreds of hours of television that these same students may view throughout their childhood and adolescent years! Other objectives should include identifying personal adjustments in life style necessary in marriage, listing reasons for family planning, and identifying sources of assistance in family planning and marriage problems.

4.2 Prepare for Raising Children (Physical Care)

Children have various needs at successive developmental stages. Infant care and feeding, innoculation for diseases, appropriate diet, clothing, exercise, and protection are important throughout all stages of development. The intensity of these needs may vary depending upon all particular characteristics of the individual. Students can use their own life experiences with each topic area to develop appropriate methods of working with their future children. This is one way the teacher can emphasize childrearing procedures when, in actuality, the main topic of consideration is projected to some time in the future. Other objectives should include demonstrating proper care of a child and demonstrating basic protection measures for a child.

ACTIVITY TIP_____

> Each student is given an egg and a shoe box. The egg represents a new baby and the shoe box is a bed or home. The student is to provide and care for the "child." The student must plan a schedule which includes bathing, feeding, changing, etc. Classroom discussions can include the difficulties and fun aspects of the assignment.

4.3 Prepare for Raising Children (Psychological Care)

In preparing the student to meet the psychological responsibilities of marriage and childrearing, the teacher must develop the student's awareness of some basic emotional needs. Discussions of love, support, and acceptance probe the structure of the student's sense of self and identify the conceptions and attitudes that are basic to the individual's behavior. These encounters may include identification of the student's needs as a child or at various stages of development, reflections on behaviors that meet these needs, and the parent's role in providing for this aspect of the child. In understanding their emotional needs as children, students can approach the problem of building a psychological environment that fosters personal growth. Other objectives should include identifying potential family problems, and identifying community agencies that provide assistance with family problems.

ACTIVITY TIP_____

> The teacher or counselor arranges the class into a "family circle." All students are members of the same family. Each session focuses on an incident or problem that confronts a family (i.e., planning a vacation or sending a child to summer camp). Teachers should select problem areas that have particular importance to the class. The students can question the professional for more details but must present alternative solutions to the problem. Various activities can evolve from the session, such as drawing, writing, and other creative endeavors that reflect individual and group solutions.

4.4 Practicing Family Safety Procedures in the Home

This subcompetency is founded on the active measures that a child, adolescent, or adult may take to protect the family against potential danger. It includes the identification of emergency situations that can occur in the home (fire, damage by storm) or with members of the family (injury, accident). Each emergency situation involves an appropriate action that should be taken by members of the family. This would include first-aid procedures and contact with rescue, fire, or safety units. Another objective should be identifying the appropriate safety procedures in a hazardous situation.

5 Buying and Preparing Food

This competency relates to the purchase, preparation, and consumption of food. It also involves an area of life that functions as a reward; thus food is used frequently as a reinforcer for student performance in the classroom. The role of food as both a necessary substance for life and reward for behavior places an additional responsibility on teachers who must develop student abilities in distinguishing between the two. The following subcompetencies are by no means the last word in planning, purchasing, and preparing food, so teachers should expand this area to meet the particular needs and abilities of their students.

5.1 Demonstrating Appropriate Eating Skills

Society has developed standards of behavior pertaining to eating in the company of other individuals, whether it be in family or public situations. These standards of etiquette are bent only slightly for handicapped individuals. Individuals who are blind must eat peas with the same skill as their sighted companions who can watch peas rolling around on the dinner plate. An inability to conform to these standards even with some slight modification to accommodate the disability places handicapped individuals in situations that elicit disapproval and rejection by other members of society. Therefore, the student should be made aware of these standards and should demonstrate the abililty to use necessary eating utensils and the accessories that are available to people with physical limitations. These skills should be taught in the primary grades, reinforced in the home, and practiced in specifically designed field trips in the community. Another objective should be demonstrating abilities in restaurant or other public eating places.

5.2 Planning Balanced Meals

It is quite a step from eating properly to planning appropriate foods for breakfast, lunch, and dinner. Planning does not need to include actual preparation of a meal. Even if students are unable or do not choose to prepare foods, they should know the nutritional value and relationships between food, health, and growth so that they can choose meals that provide the greatest benefits. Many individuals eat "junk foods" that are high in sugar content but low in protein. This is the type of situation that the individual with handicaps must avoid. Second, adequate meals are important for those individuals who receive supplementary ingredients to their diets, such as calcium for bone development, medications of various sorts, and injections.

These supplements balance and interact with other nutrients. If a student is careless about her diet, her mental and physical performance will be lowered and her health endangered. Teachers should note that this subcompetency is also related to the one on physical fitness, nutrition, and weight (3.3). Other objectives should include developing a list of foods that are beneficial to health and planning meals within a specified budget.

5.3 Purchasing Food

Purchasing food is related to the subcompetency on making wise expenditures (1.2) and provides ample opportunity for teachers to train students in the use of measuring units of food and calculating costs. Unfortunately, students are often immersed in a world of advertisements for foods. Buying "goodies" can become the subject matter for daily assignments in purchasing meals at the school cafeteria, calculating the cost of a "bag lunch," or projecting future expenses for after-school snacks. In later years, with the recommended assistance of home economics instructors or representatives from community consumer organizations, students should be exposed to lessons that will help them recognize differences in the quality of foods, various types and cuts of meat and fish, and the advantages of sales and specials. Other objectives should include identifying community sources of information about food prices and constructing a shopping list within a budget.

ACTIVITY TIP

The teacher provides the class with a list of basic food items. Students price each item at their local store or supermarket. These prices form the basis for activities in which students are required to compare prices of food items, compute costs for a given number of items, and select items based on fixed amount of money. The complexity of the activity can be adjusted to the ability of the individual student.

5.4 Preparing Meals

To prepare an entire meal the student will need to know how to use utensils, follow directions, identify various forms of measures, clean, cut, and prepare food, and use devices for cooking and baking. Every school curriculum should train the handicapped individual in the skills involved in managing the preparation of a meal, either by direct manipulation or instruction. Teachers can certainly include parents in the instruction of buying and preparing food. Hughes (1981) provided a letter to the parents that outlined two weeks of home assignments, activities, and instructional hints that

Learning to plan and prepare nutritious meals is an essential daily living skill.

moved the student from the planning to the final preparation of meals. Other objectives should include preparing a meal according to directions and demonstrating kitchen safety measures.

5.5 Cleaning Food Preparation Areas

Teachers should stress that the cleaning process is just as important as preparation of foods. After all, food disappears, but dirty dishes remain for the next meal. This subcompetency includes skills involved in the use of various cleaning measures and materials, disposal and removal of waste products, and storage of utensils. Cleaning up is also an appropriate area for lessons emphasizing safety factors and measures involved in the entire preparation and clean-up process.

5.6 Storing Food

Proper food storage is useful in the overall management of financial resources and family health. This process requires that students learn how to store food and identify when food is spoiled. Teachers can use numerous instructional aides available from consumer organizations or companies that manufacture storage devices. Another objective should be demonstrating techniques for storing food.

6 Buying and Caring for Clothes

The old expression that "clothes make the man" has undergone some alterations, but it still signifies a cultural standard that serves as a powerful tool in the classroom. Whether it be blue jeans or formal dress, sport shoes or high heels, students from elementary through adult education classes will be interested in fashions, styles, and the latest "in thing" because clothes are related to identity and social acceptance. Proper choice or modification of clothing can improve the handicapped individual's appearance and minimize any physical deficiencies she may have.

6.1 Washing Clothing

The principal objective in this subcompetency is to teach students how to care for clothing. This skill will enhance the student's appearance and use of financial resources. Primary grade students can become familiar with the effects of various laundry detergents and water temperatures by washing dust cloths, handkerchiefs, and towels. When students begin to wash their clothes, they will need instruction about the various laundry products and operating washers and dryers. These steps require cooperation from parents who, in all practicality, are in a better position to evaluate these skills.

Teachers may be especially interested in an extensive discussion by Cuvo, Jacobi, and Sipko (1981) based on a 37-step task analysis for using a clothes washer. Although the study was based on mentally retarded students, the task analysis is applicable to other handicapped people.

6.2 Ironing and Storing Clothing

Home economics teachers can help students acquire skills involved in preparing and ironing various types of clothing. Teachers should provide instruction about the why, when, how, and where of storing seasonal clothing. Once again, every attempt should be made to coordinate classroom and home instruction.

6.3 Performing Simple Mending ˙

Skills for this subcompetency include matching thread color and learning the mechanics of preliminary planning and basting, simple hand sewing, machine sewing, and appropriate stitches for different types of tears.

ACTIVITY TIP

Each student should have access to a "repair kit" either at school or home. The classroom or home economics teacher should assign specific repairs to be completed at home, or the student may bring items from home to repair sessions at school. Teachers and parents can monitor materials for the kit, its location, and use according to the abilities and attitude of the student.

6.4 Purchasing Clothing

Some students will have experience or influence over the purchase of clothing and food products before they have learned other basics of consumer buying (i.e. shelter, health, transportation, and leisure). The observant teacher will recall the numerous children who accompany their mothers on shopping ventures in the supermarket and clothing stores. These same teachers may face a bitter battle in attempting to counteract students' impulse buying habits. If successful, the teacher will have impressed the student with such considerations as how to select appropriate clothing for different occasions, balance clothing needs with available funds, identify well made versus poorly made garments, and coordinate purchases relative to the student's needs and finances. Other objectives should include recording one's measurements, identifying clothing for a basic wardrobe, and planning a wardrobe based on a specific budget.

"When I go out and talk to leaders in business and industry, I do not talk about weakness and sickness. There are plenty of people in our society who are ready to portray the disabled as sick, weak, helpless, or unable. I talk about the strengths."

Roberts (1979)

---

7 Engaging in Civic Activities

Over the past decade the participation of handicapped people in civic activities has steadily increased. This participation has been encouraged by the success of other groups of individuals who have demonstrated and lobbied for legislation to insure equality in housing, education, and employment. Once significant laws have been passed at the local, state, and federal levels, handicapped citizens must be prepared to continue their roles as advocates in order to translate legislation and regulations into daily social practice.

7.1 Understanding Local Laws and Government

The teacher should help each student understand fundamental reasons for the existence of laws, government, and the various roles and duties of government officials. Instead of emphasizing the consequences of violating a law, the teacher should explain how officials and citizens within the community affect changes in the law and how already existing laws benefit handicapped individuals. Another objective should be identifying the duties of various civic officials.

7.2 Understanding the Federal Government

The teacher may approach the larger federal structure from the same vantage point as in the previous subcompetency. Local and federal structures contain three major administrative, legislative, and judicial areas, as well as a set of statutes, regulations, and agencies. The student should be aware of the instances in which federal law takes precedence over local and state laws. Another objective should be identifying appropriate elements of the Constitution and Declaration of Independence.

7.3 Understanding Citizenship Rights and Responsibilities

Citizenship rights and responsibilities is a major element in the entire competency. Subcompetency 7.1 involves identification of laws that were enacted to assist handicapped citizens. But, each right contains a responsibility of citizenship, and students should be aware of obligations that include obeying laws, voting, paying taxes, and being informed on problems and issues within the society. Another objective should be identifying community services available to handicapped individuals.

ACTIVITY TIP

Students collect an "Advocacy Notebook" of pictures, articles, and information pertaining to the rights of handicapped individuals. The material should reflect the expanding role of handicapped individuals in civic and social functions. It can be gathered from newspapers, magazines, or brochures collected on field trips or distributed by classroom speakers. Teachers should enlist the cooperation of handicapped individuals who have been active in community affairs.

7.4 Understanding Registration and Voting Procedures

The reasons for voting should be emphasized throughout the elementary years. Many secondary students who have the opportunity to register and vote will enroll in training programs. This situation provides teachers with a chance to use practical lesson plans based on student experiences with the process of registering and voting. Another objective should be identifying the dates, issues, and offices to be decided in coming elections.

7.5 Understanding Selective Service Procedures

Students should register for selective service classification at age 18. In some instances, the military may be a possible occupational choice. For example, former students in classes for the mentally retarded have served in the military. Another objective should be identifying information required for registration with the selective service.

7.6 Understanding Civil Rights and Responsibilities When Questioned by the Law

This subcompetency includes knowledge of the individuals' rights when being questioned by officers of the law, and sources of legal assistance that can be used to help individuals answer the questions. Teachers cannot help students develop this combination of skills very easily. Students should role play situations in which they are confronted by officers. Law enforcement officials or members of legal aid associations may also give classroom presentations that concern violations and citizen responses during interrogation.

8 Utilizing Recreation and Leisure

Steady decrease in the number of hours in the average work week has resulted in an increase in the amount of time, energy, and attention that workers can devote to recreation and leisure. Handicapped individuals should be able to share in these experiences. Various professional and parent organizations have placed new emphasis upon physical education, leisure, recreation, and art. Expanded programs, special events, and conferences will contribute to the development of physical abilities, as well as public acceptance of the handicapped individual's participation in society. The activities involved in this competency prepare individuals for yet another area of integration and, therefore, must be considered a distinct and valuable part of the overall curriculum. Furthermore, the career cluster of hospitality and recreation occupations also provide opportunities for employment if the individual demonstrates particular interest and skill in these competencies.

8.1 Participating Actively in Group Activities

Adequate participation in group activities depends, in part, upon the individual's physical fitness (refer to subcompetency 3.3) and ability to interact with other members of the group (refer to subcompetency 1.3). Therefore the teacher should design or adapt games and group activities that contribute to both goals. The student's physical characteristics are a consideration, but we have enough examples from blind skiers to basketball players in wheel-chairs to know that physical constraints do not always prevent an individual from engaging in particular activities. Horst, Wehman, Hill, and Bailey (1981), for example, describe three case studies of severely mentally and physically handicapped youth who learned how to throw a frisbee, bowl electronically, and operate a cassette tape recorder. Each case study includes a task analysis of the skill. For example, the task analysis used in operating a cassette recorder includes the following steps:

1. Sit or stand in front of cassette deck.
2. To turn it on, reach toward the cassette.
3. Extend index finger toward buttons.
4. Place finger on appropriate button.
5. Push "play" button down.
6. Listen to music.
7. To turn it off, reach toward the cassette.
8. Extend index finger toward buttons.
9. Place finger on appropriate button.
10. Push "stop" button down.

Other objectives should include identifying group activities available in the community, demonstrating competence in a selected activity, and demonstrating proper care of equipment used in an activity.

8.2 Knowing Activities and Available Community Resources

Teachers can begin to teach elementary school students about functions, events, and facilities that are available in community agencies, schools, or churches. The next step includes cooperative efforts between teachers, parents, and recreation leaders to encourage and include handicapped individuals as participants, as well as observers. Based on this encouragement, students can develop an awareness of the range of recreational activities in which they can participate, as well as the resources and facilities that are accessible to them in the community.

8.3 Understanding Recreational Values

Understanding recreational values is closely linked to development of self-awareness (refer to subcompetency 1.4). It includes students' understanding of the role of recreation in the overall development of life and can function as a balance to everyday pressures that the individual may confront in striving toward independence. But students can only internalize this understanding by using leisure time effectively and by becoming involved in activities, clubs, or hobbies. This requires coordinated effort between parent, teacher, and recreational personnel.

93

ACTIVITY TIP

Teachers, recreation and physical education personnel, parents, and students should contribute to the construction of a "leisure grid ". The grid lists the skills required of students as (1) participants, (2) observers, and (3) employees in each leisure area. Each sport, activity, or hobby provides students with opportunities to record their observations about recreation and employment possibililties. The grid can be supplemented by pictures, newspaper or magazine articles, and student essays.

8.4 Using Recreational Facilities in the Community

Learning how to use recreational facilities and equipment is the primary objective of this subcompetency. This skill may be demonstrated to teachers, parents, or recreational personnel but should be observed on a firsthand basis and not simply reported by the student. A secondary objective is related to the student's competency in mobility and traveling in the community (refer to competency 9).

8.5 Planning and Choosing Activities Wisely

Many of the previous subcompetencies related to the utilization of recreation and leisure require actual "field" experiences. These experiences enable the student to plan leisure activities. Planning should include factors such as cost, location, travel, physical requirements, use of equipment, and number of participants. The planning and decision making will incorporate the students' experience with prior activities and test their self-awareness (refer to competency 10).

8.6 Planning Vacations

Adults initiate vacations, but children can be included in some of the planning. Children can wrestle with such major questions as, "When should the family take a vacation? Where should we go? Why should we go there? What will we do when we get there? How much will it cost? Do we have enough money for a vacation?" Throughout the questioning process, teachers and parents should present several considerations so children can understand that the final plan is really composed of several decisions involving family needs and resources. Another objective should be identifying available sources of information that assist in planning.

9 Getting Around the Community (Mobility)

In a society that encourages mobility and places importance on such things as cars, campers, ski trips, and coast-to-coast air flights, it is no wonder that teenagers and adults value their ability to move at will. This ability is even more important for those who struggle to commute between home and places of employment, recreation, or health services. Diligent training can prepare individuals who have visual, physical, and mental handicaps to move freely within the community. These individuals should receive training on how to use guide dogs or canes, drive cars, wheelchairs, or carts, and use other forms of transportation. The following subcompetencies are based on the assumption that individuals are able to move within the community with or without the assistance of devices such as artificial limbs, mechanical devices, or sonic sensory aides.

9.1 Demonstrating Knowledge of Traffic Rules and Safety Practices

The basics of traffic rules, signs, symbols, and sounds should be taught in the elementary grades. Their importance is based on safety for all members of the community. Teachers should use posters, field trips, and numerous audiovisual aids to emphasize the responsibilities of both pedestrians and motorists.

9.2 Demonstrating Knowledge and Using Various Means of Transportation

Students should be acquainted with specific forms of transportation that are available within the community. Teachers should construct lessons that emphasize advantages and disadvantages, costs, schedules, availability, and convenience of various forms of transportation. The lessons should include information on how students can use aids such as tickets or tokens, route maps, and illustrations provided by various carriers. A second important area of instruction would include the student's ability to interpret maps and locate addresses within the community. Finally students use appropriate forms of transportation to reach school, work, or recreational destinations.

ACTIVITY TIP

The treasure hunt game can be used to test the students' mobility skills. Parents, friends, and other teachers can assist on "hunts" that expand from the classroom or home, to the neighborhood, and to the larger community. The hunt should emphasize all aids that students may use to reach their final destinations and should help them understand the roles of various community workers who can provide assistance.

9.3 Driving a Car

One of the major goals of most high school students is to sit behind the wheel of a car. Teachers can use this to help students develop several other subcompetencies, as well as academic skills. The teacher should work with other instructors to coordinate driver's education lessons. This is especially important if driver educators are responsible for instruction in the driver's manual, state examination and "behind-the-wheel" training. Classroom teachers could also be of assistance in teaching aspects of the manual. Costa and Welch (1981) developed a "simulated traffic scene" that uses visual and kinesthetic senses to develop the students' awareness of rules and improve their driving skills. Teachers can construct layouts of highways and streets (from posterboard or plywood) that contain numerous traffic signals and signs. Other objectives should include identifying appropriate procedures for a driver after being involved in an auto accident and demonstrating ability to make minor repairs on a vehicle.

TEACHING THE DAILY LIVING SKILLS

All of the prior competencies should be mastered by the handicapped individual in the adult years. The great challenge of teaching daily living skills is to translate educational goals into manageable components of instruction for individual students, given the circumstances that teachers encounter during the average day. It is important to consider the teacher's circumstances as well as the unique learning styles of the several students who comprise the class or therapeutic case load for that day. Increased emphasis upon the integration, normalization, or "mainstreaming" of handicapped individuals with regular students places greater demands upon the abilities of teachers, counselors, and coordinators to handle the complexities of meeting all students' needs.

The art of teaching has always required a certain amount of management. After all, the instructor must decide on the progression of lessons that will accomplish an objective, materials that will be used at specific points in the progression, and alternatives that will meet the intended goals once she and the learner encounter barriers. This section focuses on the management of the teacher's efforts in planning programs because of two reasons:

1. The Individualized Education Program plan has emerged as a focal point for conceptualizing the direction that educators and parents should take in providing handicapped students with appropriate instruction and services. Among other things, the plan is a tool used in managing diverse sources, and all the participants should be well versed in its strengths and limitations.

2. The numerous demands upon the average educator's time and ability will require her to use every means available to provide students with experiences in the competency areas.

The remainder of this chapter will suggest steps for the identification, co-ordination, specification, and integration of these competencies so that the school, home, and community become integral sources of these experiences.

The Individualized Education Program (IEP)

The competencies discussed in this chapter, as well as those in the chapters on personal-social and occupational skills, are a foundation for the long-term instructional goals for many handicapped individuals. The severity of disability will often determine the appropriateness of the competency objectives. Most likely, the actual competency statements contained in chapters 3 through 5 could appear as goal statements in the plan for students in secondary and adult education programs. For example, subcompetency 9.3, driving a car, is an appropriate goal in the secondary curriculum area of driver education. This may be specified as an appropriate goal in the planning sessions between the educational agency representative, parents, teacher, and students. Physical and intellectual ability can be used to develop training devices and programs that will enable the student to obtain the goal. However these factors may be considered less of a barrier than in previous years because driving a car is an adult skill necessary for mobility and chances at employment.

Once subcompetency 9.3 is designated as a final goal, then the several major steps contained in a driver education curriculum can function as short-term objectives. Participants do not need to record every lesson plan on the IEP if a standard curriculum text or manual is used in the course. Progress through the lessons in the text can provide a basis for evaluation.

Driving a car is one of the easiest daily living skills to use as an example because it meets IEP requirements and involves subcompetency skills. Although formalized training does not begin until the secondary level, primary grade students have had exposure to several stages of career development within the broader context of getting around the community. For example, the student's *awareness* of traffic rules, safety, and means of transportation in the community should be nurtured in the elementary grades. Field trips, various means of transportation to and from school, and family-directed outings can provide individuals with *exploration* experiences. The actual driver education curriculum is the strongest example of the *preparation* stage, although mobility training also includes the use of other mechanical aides, canes, or guide dogs for certain handicapped individuals. The final stage of *placement and follow-up* incorporates the skills and techniques acquired through instruction and can be applied to the individual's daily living and work situations. The follow-up component can be neglected by school personnel; yet it is very important to handicapped individuals who encounter difficulties in adjusting to new environments and routines, or who need periodic evaluation of their skills and means of getting around the community.

This progression of stages alerts teachers and parents to the fact that students may acquire parts of subcompetency skills from the primary to adult education grades. For example, the primary level student may not drive a car, but cars, racers, hot rods, and the "cult of wheels" are important and available in the student's experiences at successive stages of physical, social, and psychological development. A second important consideration is that it reminds teachers and parents to include provisions for nurturing the subcompetencies in their planning and activities. These small provisions will probably not be identified in the IEP. The plan will be geared toward such curriculum skill areas as arithmetic, language arts, and reading. Teachers tend to focus on the established progression of skill components that exist in the dominant curriculum areas. Over time, these skills begin to build upon one another so that students can use them to achieve competence in other areas. For example, driving a car requires, among other things, gross and fine motor coordination, perceptual abilities, and reading skills.

Teachers at all levels (primary through adult education) should review the competencies discussed in *chapters 3 through 5* because of their prior training and present emphasis upon mastery of the academic skills. These skills will continue to be dominant parts of the student's program at the elementary levels. The tragedy of the situation is that secondary and adult education instructors *must* concern themselves with competencies for daily living, social-personal relations, and occupational pursuits. These competencies are integral to the handicapped individual's success as an adult. Thus, teachers of adolescent and adult handicapped individuals must often de-emphasize instruction in the academic skills so that they can meet demands in the areas of personal-social and vocational skills. This is a difficult assignment if particular competencies require prerequisite ability with reading, communication, or computation.

As a statement of instructional objectives, the IEP and the life-centered career competencies can complement one another. First, the competencies combine several academic skills and therefore, function as long-term objectives in various curriculum areas. Why should a student be able to read at a certain level or complete calculations? These abilities enable her to obtain a driver's license, manage personal finances, and repair home equipment, all of which are listed as daily living skills. Second, the individualized education program can be used by various personnel and parents to check whether the student is acquiring both academic and competency skills. Has the student used various forms of public transportation that are available in the community? Does she need more instruction in personal hygiene?

The competencies and IEP function as checks against one another. They can be interlaced in such a manner as to add direction to programming, provide objectives for evaluation, and major steps for instruction. The teacher can use identification, coordination, specification, and integration of curriculum areas to insure that each handicapped student receives appropriate instruction at various levels in the development of each competency.

Identification

The instructor should identify areas of the curriculum that already contain lessons relative to the competencies. The ideal teacher should develop specific lessons for each subcompetency so they can meet the multiple learning characteristics of the student. Such a task would take years to accomplish, and many teachers become discouraged by the very idea of writing that many lessons or learning modules. This is one reason why publishers are experiencing such demand and success with packaged curriculums or programs for handicapped learners.

The daily living skills form the theme material for texts and programmed learning packages in mathematics, reading, language arts, and the like. Curriculum texts do not directly include the competencies as we define them, but nevertheless, they contain activities such as shopping, civic participation, and vocations as a motivating element within the stories. Teachers should review these texts and programs so that they can use several curriculum areas to enhance the competencies and decrease the amount of material that they have to prepare.

Figure 3.1 contains an example of a curriculum check sheet that the teacher can construct to facilitate a review of texts, programmed materials, or learning aides. Major competency areas are identified by number in the left margin, with specific references to the subcompetencies that are topics within the curriculum materials. The teacher may also emphasize certain competencies during a particular academic year, depending upon the student's stage of physical, social, psychological, or vocational development. The page references listed below the curriculum areas indicate where competencies can be located within the materials. The two remaining columns, *Other Materials* and *Resources*, refer to personnel, activities, or devices that are suggested by the teachers' guides which accompany curriculum texts or are used in conjunction with the lessons.

The teacher should modify the curriculum check sheet to correspond with the competencies, curriculum areas, and method of instruction she has chosen. For example, she may use group activities to identify major forms of money (competency 1) with individual lessons to follow. However this is *not* a lesson plan; it is a form that encourages teachers to review curriculum areas methodically and identify competencies that students will encounter during the school year.

"1 Handicapped + 1 Job = 1 Unhandicapped"

President's Committee on Employment of the Handicapped (n.d.)

Intermediate   Daily
—————————————   —————————————
Class or Student   Period

DAILY LIVING SKILLS

Curriculum / Competency	Arithmetic	Gross Motor	Language Arts	Reading	Other Materials	Resources
1. Identifying money	p. 15–18					Filmstrip
wise expenditure	p. 101–110					
2. Using basic tools		Industrial Arts			Hobby magazines	Parent: Mr. Brown demonstrates use of saws
3. Demonstrating physical fitness		Physical Education			Sports magazines and newspaper	Swimming coach and film of the Olympics
4. Family safety				p. 53–57		Film on control of fires in the home

FIGURE 3.1
Curriculum check sheet.

Coordination

The instructor should identify competencies that will be taught by other professionals and cooperate with them to meet common objectives. Daily living skills appear in so many curriculum areas that instructors in home economics, driver's education, industrial arts, vocational education, physical education, and other professionals share the teacher's interest in helping students develop certain competencies. In addition, the family may provide the handicapped individual with opportunities to practice daily living skills.

It would be logical and rewarding to learn as much as possible from the skills and commitments of other professionals and parents. The classroom teacher (or counselor, curriculum coordinator, supervisor) may need to coordinate these resources, but this is a better alternative than attempting to prepare each student for every competency. The teacher may also need to coordinate the skills of professionals and parents to meet the needs of students. Other professionals may have already used certain competencies as a part of their curriculum. Parents may provide experiences in the home and

100

community that facilitate classroom instruction. The instructor should be aware of the efforts and direction provided by these resources. An additional column could be added to the curriculum check sheet that describes the efforts of other professionals and parents.

On occasion, the instructor may suggest that lessons or activities be added to the curriculum in, for example, home economics or vocational education. Expansion of competency units corresponds with the idea that career development is the responsibility of every instructor. The instructor can improve the quality and availability of education by enlisting the efforts and interest of professionals in all disciplines. It has only been in recent years that an increased number of professionals from skill areas such as home economics, physical education, industrial arts, and vocational education have expanded their programs to accommodate the handicapped student. This increased attention is welcomed by handicapped individuals, their parents, and advocates, but it requires a corresponding refinement of the teacher's ability to coordinate programs and professionals.

Specification

The instructor should include statements concerning the student's career development on the IEP. As mentioned previously, the IEP gives professionals the opportunity to specify present levels of performance in career development, projected objectives, and educational services required to meet those aims. These statements can also include reference to the personnel who are deemed essential to the student's success.

It is recommended that the participants in the formulation of the IEP involve as many professionals as possible. This involvement provides the student with greater access to individuals who have the skills to teach particular subcompetencies. Instructors from industrial arts, for example, could function as the primary source of information and activities in subcompetency 2.3, using basic appliances and tools, while those from home economics could offer assistance in several major competency areas, such as competency 5, buying and preparing food, and competency 6, buying and caring for clothes. But, the professional's participation and role should be clearly defined so that the instructor and program coordinator are aware of the expected objectives that can be reached. Professionals from the area of physical education or recreation may either provide direct instruction to the student or advise the classroom teacher as to the appropriate activities that can be conducted during the period in the school day designated for "physical development." In the first situation, the instructor functions as the primary source of direction for the student; in the second instance, she is a support person to the classroom teacher. This distinction may not be included in the actual student plan, but it must be clearly understood among the participating professionals.

101

Integration

One of the obstacles to the introduction of career education into the average student's school experience is that it does not have the progressive characteristics of standard curriculums in areas such as reading, writing, and arithmetic. Advocates of career development have attempted to build a sequential chain of career themes and objectives that range from career awareness to career placement and follow-up. Several states have published guides for educators describing appropriate objectives for career lessons that can be conducted at various stages of the student's experience. The objectives most often conform to a design that allows teachers and counselors to integrate lessons in career development at grade levels and during parts of the school day. During these periods, instructors can initiate activities that are specifically related to the competencies. Thus, if a competency is not covered in other curriculum areas or by other professionals, the classroom teacher must develop lesson plans that provide the student with experiences in the competency areas.

Lesson plans for any instructional area range from the simplest to the most complex design. Some teachers merely record the title of an activity on a sheet of paper and consider that a "lesson plan." More than likely, this kind of planning will not place the teacher in high regard with those parents and advocates who demand evaluations of the intermediate objectives that are listed in the individual education program plan. The basic plan should include the lesson's objectives, activities, and forms of evaluation. The several sample lesson plans that appear in this text contain core elements of the competency unit and should provide several ideas for instruction.

Several school districts have applied our competencies and instructional suggestion to their curricula (see Chapter 10). For example, the Irvine Unified School District (1982) in California received funding for their project "Applied Career Tasks." The project provided resource specialists with lessons that focus on ten learning and communication competencies for physically handicapped students in grades four through eight.

The tasks include 41 lessons with themes and activities that could be implemented in a formal procedure or indirectly added to the regular class curriculum by the resource specialist (Huff, 1983). Each lesson includes 12 sections. Due to limitations of space, we have abbreviated the example, but the reader should be able to understand the scope of the lesson plan.

Title: *Good Looks Here and Now*
Domain: Daily living skills
Goal: Student's skill in caring for personal needs
Objective: Student will demonstrate knowledge about grooming.

Academic Objective: Conclusions or generalizations

Overview: Student describes techniques for cleansing body and caring for hair, hands, nails, and teeth.

Materials: Includes guides and teaching aides

Time: 40 minutes

Procedure: Includes steps and activities for each item in overview

Follow-Up: Includes suggestions for review activities

Ways to Demonstrate Skills in the Classroom: Includes additional activities

CONCLUSION

The daily living skills should be the easiest group of competencies to integrate and teach in the normal span of a school year. This is partly because they are already evident in the curriculums from primary through adult education. However, the instructor has a wealth of knowledge about and personal experiences with daily living skills that may surpass the offerings of a textbook or filmstrip. It is hoped that this chapter contains an adequate number of suggestions and examples that encourage teachers, counselors, or parents to form daily requirements for successful living into objectives and themes. These endeavors, whether they are based on the instructor's experience or classroom materials, will supply the handicapped individuals with the tools to shape successful lives.

The Personal-Social Skills 4

The **personal-social skills** curriculum area involves those abilities that are necessary for personal achievement and satisfactory interpersonal relationships. The daily living skills form the structure of the individual's abilities, while the personal-social skills are the muscle and blood that propel him toward fulfillment. This sense of achievement and fulfillment determines the quality of life. In other words, the handicapped individual's potential for successful, independent living cannot be judged merely on the basis of academic grades or competency scales. The individual's ideas about his present status, potentials, and interactions with other people should also be considered. These thoughts often determine how other skills will be used and toward what goals.

The seven personal-social competencies we have identified as important to the career development of handicapped individuals are listed as follows:

10 Achieving self-awareness
11 Acquiring self-confidence
12 Developing socially responsible behavior
13 Maintaining adequate interpersonal skills
14 Achieving independence
15 Achieving problem-solving skills
16 Communicating adequately with others

These competencies are integral to the individual's role in the home, community, work setting, and avocational activities.

Concepts of self, others, and their interactions include the elements of risk and trust in classroom activities. Risk is one element in the process of problem solving, while trust is essential to self-respect. Risk can be defined by such social factors as self-esteem, popularity with peers, and even teacher approval. The student who explains a personal problem to the teacher or in a group setting is taking a risk. Teachers cannot expect students to gamble with social status based upon traditional methods. The students must be assured through word and deed that their risks do have rewards. If this is successful, the risk-reward interaction contributes to the trust that students must build in themselves and other dependable individuals.

These two elements, risk and trust, are interwoven throughout the 34 subcompetencies of the personal-social skills curriculum area. Teachers may identify other factors and objectives that contribute to the student's self-awareness and his relationships with others. Activity tips and sample lesson plans are presented throughout the chapter as teaching examples. The chapter concludes with a discussion of techniques for teaching personal-social skills.

COMPETENCIES

10   Achieving Self-Awareness

Handicapped individuals are part of the new sense of freedom in America. They have been the subjects of an increased number of television documentaries, magazine articles, and newspaper reports. Legislation guarantees that handicapped individuals have equal rights to transportation, education, housing, and employment. Handicapped individuals are entering the "mainstream" of society, but there is another shell aside from the structure and restrictions that society imposes upon these individuals. It consists of the individual's body, abilities, limitations, and needs. The achievement of self-awareness has as much to do with becoming a contributing and productive member of society.

10.1   Attaining a Sense of Body

Exploration of the body helps infants differentiate themselves from the surrounding environment. This discovery does not end with childhood. Every maturational change requires a modification in the individual's concept of the body. This process includes a changing image of the self. This body image is visualized as positive when the individual recognizes limitations but still regards the physical shell as an instrument that can be developed and controlled to achieve objectives. A positive body image contributes to the individual's sense of ability and worth. Teachers, parents, and therapists can help the individual develop a positive body image by providing adequate information relative to the parts of the body, their functions, and the person's unique physical characteristics. The information should be accurate and presented within an atmosphere of support. This support helps the person confront the implication of the information and initiate appropriate personal adjustments objectives. Each stage of development requires different kinds

POINT OF VIEW

It is no accident that the seven personal-social competencies appear in the middle of the 22 competencies. Acquisition of these skills is essential to the fulfillment of handi-

capped individuals; moreover, once these individuals have command over personal-social skills, it is easier for them to learn and incorporate the daily living and occupational competencies into their lives.

The growth of self-esteem is woven into the personal-social competencies. Self-understanding (i.e. abilities, interests, needs, wants) and learning to interact constructively, appropriately, and responsibly lead to heightened positive attitudes about the individual's self-worth.

We must provide an environment in which self-esteem can be nurtured with the systematic infusion of the personal-social skills into a structured, continuous program. Isolated lessons and career education "classes" are fragmented efforts that yield fragmented results. This chapter provides educators with a focal point for weaving the competencies into a program that will raise the esteem of handicapped individuals.

Paul Joseph Perencevic teaches individuals with learning handicaps and behavior disorders in Los Angeles, California.

and amounts of information. Children at 7 will not ask the same questions as adolescents or adults at 40 years of age. Their needs vary and, more importantly, the answers must match the unique physical characteristics of the individual.

10.2 Identifying Interests and Abilities

Individuals with handicaps discover their abilities through their interests. How can a child cry or attempt to accomplish anything if his interest cannot be aroused? Aren't childhood hobbies a means of building confidence through interest? If handicapped individuals are to achieve independence through competent behavior, then they must have numerous experiences with those things they like to do, can do, and would attempt to do if given adequate support. With support, trial and error can help the individual build an awareness of physical and spiritual capabilities. This is especially important for the "able-bodied" person who, through accident, injury, or operation, has passed into the category of "disabled." In this situation, the rehabilitative process would involve supportive efforts that would help the individual

Interests help students develop abilities that are essential to career development.

identify interests that correspond to his altered abilities. Teachers should plan activities that require students to identify interests, list personal abilities, and plan strategies to implement selected goals (refer to subcompetency 15.2). Another objective should be identifying the interests of others and ranking them according to their interests.

ACTIVITY TIP

> The want ads of the local newspaper can provide a rich resource of ideas that can help students identify personal needs. People advertise so they can gain employment, sell home furniture, or join a car pool. Students can cut, paste, and place ads in various categories of interest.

10.3 Identifying Emotions

Teachers can begin classroom activities that deal with emotions by creating a nonjudgmental climate in which the student (whether child or adult) feels free to talk about feelings. Primary grade students should identify such emotions as happiness, sadness, and anger and should have had exposure to these emotions long before entering school. Older children should begin to work with the problem of recognizing the various ways in which emotions can be expressed. Students should be involved in role-playing situations or should report observations that emphasize various indices of emotions, for example, body language, facial expressions, and tone of voice (refer to subcompetency 16.5). A second major objective should be for teachers to develop the student's ability to distinguish the consequences of the emotion for others, but particularly, for self. For example, an expression of anger by an employer may have different consequences than a similar demonstration by an employee. The employer is allowed to let off steam, but the employee may lose his job. Finally, teachers should identify means through which students can release emotions in a constructive manner. An appropriate expression of emotion is unique to each individual. Teachers and parents should exert a great deal of time and effort in establishing a foundation of trust that will encourage the individual to explore feelings and find adequate ways of expressing them. Another objective should be identifying ways in which emotions affect behavior.

ACTIVITY TIP

> *The Emotions Bulletin Board* is a sure hit. Students can photograph each other in "typical" expressions, cut photos from newspapers and magazines, superimpose one photo on another, and add their own zany captions and quotes.

10.4 Identifying Needs

The skills involved in identifying needs enter into the physical, psychological, and social domains. There are some minimal needs for physical existence, but it is much harder to describe basic requirements in the social and psychological realms. How do we measure quantities of security, self-worth, esteem, and love? One way to determine the answer to that question is for students to identify their needs, talk about them, draw them, collect examples of them, and examine the ways in which other persons attempt to meet their needs. Varied classroom activities concerning the necessities of life will lead students to a realization about those things that they regard as essential to their lives. Another objective should be identifying several personal values.

10.5 Understanding the Physical Self

Understanding the physical self contains objectives that are specific to the sexual role of the individual. The activities should enable students to develop an awareness of the similarities and differences in the anatomy and functioning of the male and female. This subject material has received increased attention among researchers, parents, consumer groups, and publishing firms primarily because of the long absence of discussion on the sexual role of individuals who are mentally retarded or physically disabled. Teachers should be aware that if they encourage classroom or small group discussion and questions, they must be prepared to provide information. Another objective should be identifying sources of information relative to one's future sexual role.

"If you think you are handicapped, you might as well stay indoors; if you think you are a person, come out and tell the world."

Loomis (1980)

---

11 Acquiring Self-confidence

Handicapped individuals have been confronted for centuries with stories, fairy tales, works of art, and popular expressions depicting them as incapable. In some instances, they were not even regarded as human beings but as the embodiment of evil spirits. These ideas and stereotypes linger to this day, and most individuals with disabilities have had experience with abuse or pity by peers or elders. Despite these opinions and attitudes, the individual must build a concept of himself as a capable human being so that he can reach personal objectives and attain dreams.

11.1 Expressing Feelings of Worth

An individual begins to feel worthy when he experiences expressions of value from parents, teachers, and friends. These declarations of worth may be difficult for the nonhandicapped person to formulate. In our society, an individual's perceived worth is based upon comparison to other people. Comparitive statements are common in a culture that rewards individuals who demonstrate the drive to excel. The problem is that "doing better" is often determined in comparison to someone else. Individuals with handicaps can find themselves at a serious disadvantage if their abilities are always placed in some type of "better than the other person" derby. If the individual loses the race, he might perceive himself as being inferior to others which, in turn, may cause him to lose his sense of self-worth. The parent's and teacher's ability to work with the assets an individual has at his disposal is the key to this potential dilemma. They must move away from "you versus them" situations to "I can do" experiences. By emphasizing the "I can," the parent and teacher opinions change, with a corresponding influence on the attitudes and values of the handicapped individual. "I can" is a positive statement of value and worth in this society. How many times have we heard stories about individuals who were told they would never walk, run, or dance only to accomplish that very thing and more? The emergence and success of such events as the Special Olympics and Wheelchair Games illustrate that handicapped individuals have a strong desire to demonstrate their worth through physical accomplishments regardless of how long it may take them to run a certain distance. Of course physical ability is a variable, but so are the attitudes of an individual toward that ability. Teachers and parents should provide opportunities in which students express how they feel about themselves in relationship to their accomplishments, successes, and failures. What experiences cause students to feel good, worthy, or pleased with their accomplishments? What experiences frustrate them? These expressions provide professionals with an opportunity to plan subsequent activities that will increase the quality and quantity of success experiences. Another objective should be identifying ways in which other people affect an individual's feelings of worth.

11.2 Telling How Others See Him

Students should be able to describe the overt expressions and subtle hints that are made by other people (refer to subcompetency 16.5). Since most people are more sensitive to communications relative to themselves, they are more apt to interject their own interpretations onto the behavior of another person. The handicapped individual encounters a particularly puzzling situation when he wonders whether a person is reacting to his personality or to the particular disability. If someone does not invite him to another party, was it because he did not conduct himself properly, or was it due to his artificial limb? He may never get the answer, and repeated instances of these nebulous situations damage the individual's self-confidence. What others think of us influences our attitudes toward the self. These attitudes are used as a basis for further judgments. Parents and teachers cannot control the attitudes of other people—in some cases, their own attitudes may be enough of a challenge. But they can instruct the handicapped student to observe another person's overt and subtle responses that reflect either positive or negative attitudes. Many of the lessons on communication (refer to competency 16) should include such reactions that convey attitudes of pity, disgust, condescension, and the like. The lessons should, however, emphasize positive reactions that reflect the handicapped individual's self-respect. He must guard against reactions that would be interpreted by other members of society as justification for their folly. Another objective should be constructing personal views of others toward him.

ACTIVITY TIP

An effective exercise requires all students to say positive things about an individual. The class may be seated in a circle or at their desks, but the student under discussion should be facing the class. Each student has 15–20 seconds during which time other students say such things as: "He helped our team win the game. He came to school on time every day of the week. He knew the right answer to the weekly quiz." This activity helps build class unity, as well as individual confidence.

11.3 Accepting Praise

The handicapped individual needs legitimate experiences in which others confirm and show respect for his behavior. Legitimate experiences include those daily activities in home, school, or other environments that *involve* the student as a contributing member. The individual may receive respect and validation for this contribution from family, peers, teachers, or others. The student should not only receive recognition for his accomplishments but should also be supported for behaviors that will eventually result in accomplishment. Otherwise, the student is only rewarded for one achievement, and this may be disproportionate to his total effort at home, in school, or on a team. It is easier to know how to accept praise when he has experienced various forms of reward. Other objectives should include listing effects of praise on the self and others and demonstrating ability to offer praise to others.

11.4 Accepting Criticism

Criticism can have a positive effect when it refers to astute judgments relative to standards; however it is more often taken in the negative vein of fault finding. Unfortunately, criticism often causes individuals to feel less than adequate about themselves. This is one reason why students in secondary or college classes hate to receive a critical analysis of their assignments.

Fearing a potentially harsh review, they produce less than they can. In a sense, they are already protecting themselves from devaluation. Is it any wonder, then, that when teachers begin to criticize, students become disinterested? Teachers have the arduous task of first convincing students to be open to criticism, and second, helping them recognize situations in which critical statements are of little value in changing or improving on a mistake. The teacher can accomplish these goals by providing as much respect for the student while his work is being analyzed. Respect with criticism builds self-confidence. An attitude of respect says to the student: "You are someone." The critical element conveys the message: "You are someone who can improve on this mistake." The improvement reinforces the previous steps in the process. Another objective should be identifying positive and negative effects of criticism on self and others.

ACTIVITY TIP

The teacher leads the class in a role-playing activity in which the classroom is the "work setting," half of the class are "employees," and the other half of the class are "employers." For one day, the "employers" will make note of characteristics such as promptness, response to instructions, attitude, proper attire, and quality of work. The "employers" will share their reviews at the end of the day only to become "employees" on the next day.

11.5 Developing Confidence in Self

Students should be aware of their innate dignity. At times, they may have to assert their rights in order to protect that dignity. These actions are founded upon a trust in their ability to accomplish objectives. Trust begins with the first completed task in infancy and is subsequently nurtured by the individual's efforts to accomplish more difficult objectives. More often than imagined, the act of attempting a task strengthens the individual's trust in himself. Once an individual has developed faith in himself, he can begin to form objectives and seek the means, appropriate to his ability, of accomplishing his goals. For example, the movie *A Matter of Inconvenience* (Stanfield House, 1974) is based on individuals who, without sight or a leg, attempt to ski. The war veterans without a limb use one ski and two poles fashioned with small runners at the ends. The three skis function as supports to balance the transfer of weight at each turn. The females who are blind are followed by experienced skiers who provide instructions on turning, plowing, and breaking. These individuals experience skiing and enjoy themselves. Their accomplishments are judged by them and not in comparison to Olympic competitors. The experience is of value because it accomplishes an objective through a means that is appropriate to the individual. We are sure that these individuals' self-confidence is extended and that they will attempt other tasks because their trust in their abilities has been reinforced. They are, in a sense, developing faith in themselves. Another objective should be evaluating the self in a variety of activities.

12 Achieving Socially Responsible Behavior

Society is held together by laws and understandings relative to the conduct of individuals toward each other. These laws have been gradually increased to extend protection to handicapped people. But acceptance of the individual depends more upon his ability to demonstrate responsible behavior in various kinds of social situations.

12.1 Knowing Character Traits Needed for Acceptance

Students should be familiar with those personality factors which generally allow them to participate in a group situation that results in a positive attitude of others toward the individuals. What are some of these positive traits? Cooperation, cheerfulness, and dependability would form a solid foundation and are also considered necessary in employment situations. There are other traits, but the individual must discover them for himself. This is where experience and observation of others are important factors in helping the individual to change. The ability to look at oneself with a critical eye is not reserved for those with advanced degrees. It comes from practice, with encouragement, at home and in the classroom. Teachers can help students build their observational skills by assigning projects in which students interview or consider someone of their choice and list outstanding characteristics. Once the characteristics are defined, teachers can translate them into behaviors students should attempt. Together, students and teachers should work on a plan of practicing and reporting the behaviors. For students who experience problems in performing acceptable behaviors, the teacher may structure a system in which there is a conscious effort to modify the behavior toward prearranged objectives. Another objective should be identifying character traits that inhibit acceptance.

12.2 Knowing Proper Behavior in Public Places

The student should be able to identify behaviors that are appropriate and expected of him in such places as restaurants, transportation facilities, churches, recreational settings, and public meetings. The student acquires this behavior by imitating other members of the family or peer group. If it is necessary for the teacher to modify these behaviors, the student, teacher, and family should agree on common objectives. There are common denominators to acceptable behavior across all public places. Teachers should examine these similarities in classroom role-playing encounters, where the student reports on experiences with family or friends, field trips, or critical

---

SAMPLE LESSON PLAN 4.1

Author: Paul Perencevic

Level: High school

Situation: Self-contained class composed of students with behavior disorders

Time Span: Over one
semester

Objective: The student will be able to demonstrate proper behavior in public places and learn to follow instructions.

Activity: This is a field trip activity in which members of the class visit a local mall. Teachers should identify target behaviors for the class as well as for individual students. They should give students instructions for following certain procedures, selecting items, standing in line, and responding to questions or comments by sales personnel.

Examples: (1) Students are told to stand in line with the selected items and wait their turns at the cash register; (2) students are provided with written instructions on how to purchase certain items. They follow the instructions from entrance to exit of the mall.

Evaluation: Teachers or aides should observe the target behaviors that they identified prior to the activity. The teacher can make immediate evaluations and should reinforce acceptable behavior while the students are in a community setting.

Related Activities: Prior practice of the expected behaviors can be accomplished through role-playing exercises in the classroom.

---

reviews of televised events. Like a seasoned athlete before the "big game," the student needs practice that should be supervised by teachers or parents. Another objective should be identifying reasons for appropriate behavior in public places.

12.3   Developing Respect for the Rights and Properties of Others

Developing respect for the rights and properties of others involves one of the fundamental concerns upon which the country was founded. It is a continuous subject of interest in television, radio, and newspaper reports and, therefore, offers ample opportunity for teachers and parents to pinpoint the reasons for respecting the rights of others and their possessions. Parents are the initial vital link in this competency. They are the ones that have to teach children to differentiate between what belongs to them from what belongs to someone else. Teachers will reinforce these basic lessons as instances of ownership that will, no doubt, occur in the classroom. Respecting the rights of others becomes more complicated as individuals grow older and begin to exert their own opinions and power in taking command of possessions. This fact will require teachers to initiate lessons and draw upon the student's experiences that emphasize the relationships of laws, ownership, and the protection of the community.

ACTIVITY TIP

Who Owns This? focuses on situations and decisions related to ownership of property. School situations, newspaper articles, and student experiences provide the teacher with material for discussions and students' essays. The teacher constructs the situation and possible questions to consider. For example, a boy brings a pair of goggles to a swimming pool. He lays them on a deck chair and goes for a drink. He returns to put them on, and another swimmer says that the goggles are his. There is one pair of goggles and two swimmers. What should the boys do?

12.4 Recognizing Authority and Following Instructions

Just about everything a student does in the school setting is preceded by directions. The routine and even monotony of the school situation makes it difficult for the teacher to impress upon the student that things are different in the employment world. If the student doesn't pay attention or forgets an instruction, he may have to do the assignment again, visit the principal, or lose points. The results become commonplace if they are experienced enough times. But if this occurs in an employment situation, the student must face the consequences (i.e., "You're fired!). An equally difficult task is for the teacher to determine whether a student has the ability to accomplish an objective or if he lacks the skills to follow directions. Teachers often infer that a student is unable to follow instructions because the assignment has not been completed. For example, a student is instructed to clean a room in the home economics model house. He is to dust, sweep, and operate a vacuum cleaner. If he did not receive prior instructions on how to use a vacuum cleaner, he may be unable to fulfill the assignment. One possible teacher response is "Didn't you hear what I said?" This is one reason why students must be encouraged to ask questions or identify those things they do not know how to do before attempting a task. Employers have often said that an employee who is mentally retarded is easier to work with because he will tell the employer about those things he doesn't understand. Another person may try to fake his way through the job.

12.5 Recognizing Personal Roles

Several roles are identified across competency areas. Some of these roles would be employee, citizen, parent, relative, and friend. Students should be able to describe and demonstrate responsible behavior to individuals identified with a specific role (employer, parent, child), as well as groups (union, passengers, clubs). This competence requires students to be actively involved in each role so they can realize its full meaning. For example, a student may be a member of a family by birth, but not in actual practice. Parents should involve their children in as many family activities and decisions as possible, especially if the handicapped individual has chosen a future role as parent and spouse. Teachers should place students in situations that provide them with an understanding of the expectations of others for a particular role. For example, community personnel such as police officers, fire fighters, and employers should discuss their expectations of student behaviors and responsibilities in the role of citizen and employee. Another objective should be identifying all possible future roles.

13 Maintaining Good Interpersonal Skills

This competency explores the skills needed to establish and maintain successful forms of interpersonal relationships. It does not include all skills or offer a "cookbook" approach to an area that has received enough attention in books, magazines, and newspapers to fill a lifetime. It is a skill that interacts with the individual's feelings of confidence and independence and is a key to successful career functioning. Practice is the most crucial element of these competencies for teachers, parents, and students. Handicapped students need the opportunity to role play expected behaviors and responses for such everyday events as listening to another person, asking questions, providing information, telling a story, and expressing emotion.

13.1 Knowing How to Listen and Respond

Communication depends upon the correct interchange of ideas or objects between people. Computers can be programmed to exchange information, but people depend upon the meaning and implications of the message. They accomplish this by attending to the source of the message, as well as other nonverbal clues that may accompany it (refer to competency 16). The teacher should develop several abilities so students can complete this competency. Students should be able to attend to the message by using all available senses, develop adequate means of response, such as speaking, signing, or typing, determine the appropriate meaning of the message (verbal or nonverbal), and determine the correct manner of response. Another objective should be identifying effective interpersonal skills.

13.2 Knowing How to Make and Maintain Friendships

"Dear Abby" columns in newspapers and magazines are filled with the laments of people without friends. "What is a friend? What do students want in a friendship? What can they offer as a friend to someone else? How can they meet people who may become friends? What happens when a friend leaves? Do friends change as one becomes older?" These are just a few of the topic questions that can be used in individual and group activities throughout the year. Students can identify what they want in a friendship, various ways of meeting people and sharing interests, and responsibilities involved in being a friend. Teachers should help students form personal solutions to problems, because in the final analysis, the formula for "how to make friends and keep them" is unique to each person. Another objective should be identifying activities that can be shared with friends.

ACTIVITY TIP

The teacher should use a coming event in students' lives to help them practice interpersonal skills. For example, a class member has been invited to a party given by a relative. All students can rehearse appropriate questions and responses by taking on the various roles of participants at the party. These rehearsals are applicable from elementary school through the adult years and can be applied to a variety of social situations.

13.3 Establishing Appropriate Heterosexual Relationships

Students should understand the process of dating, various customs relative to the relationship of individuals in the dating situation, and the responsibilities that are included with each role. Parents and teachers face many difficult questions when they counsel young people. "When do I start dating? Should I date this type of person? How do I act on a date? Where do I go on a date?" Those few questions provide enough fuel for years of classroom discussions, heart-to-heart talks, and personal growth. Other objectives should include identifying activities in the community that are appropriate for dating relationships and identifying ways to demonstrate that one is pleased on a date.

13.4 Knowing How to Establish Close Relationships

The skills for developing close relationships can be nurtured by the family. Children learn about personal reactions and respect by observing their parents and by interacting with brothers, sisters, or relatives. Before the primary grades, students may have already developed relationships of varying intensities with family members, neighbors, playmates, and therapists. The teacher can begin with exercises that help students identify the different types of relationships that already exist or can be observed in the family and community. Students should formulate answers to such questions as "What are the characteristics of a close relationship? In what manner do people respond to one another in a close relationship? What is its function?" By trying to find answers to questions like these, students will develop an awareness of those individual needs that leads to the development of close relationships. The final objective would be for each student to maintain a close relationship based on characteristics that are important to him. Another objective should be identifying persons with whom the student could talk about personal matters.

"Teachers of exceptional individuals must extend their thinking about career education far beyond the world of paid employment to the total lifestyle of the persons being served."

Hoyt (1979)

---

14   Achieving Independence

There is no magic in the term *independence,* and yet it looms as an ever present goal in the lives of most handicapped individuals. Writers have debated whether an individual can ever be *truly* independent. Our lives involve a mixture of relationships from dependence, through independence, to an interdependence. Writers, who already have a measure of freedom, can debate concepts; but handicapped individuals, who have been only recently acknowledged as first-class citizens, would just like to experience the feeling. Independent persons can assume responsibility for their jobs and other daily affairs in a competent manner.

14.1   Understanding the Impact of Behaviors on Others

The goal of personal independence involves the student's awareness of those behaviors that promote acceptance or rejection within society. This anticipation influences interaction within a family, social, or employment setting. Teachers and parents want students to understand and to foresee the effect that their conduct will have on other individuals. Teachers at the primary level can begin with simple exercises in which students identify the way one person's behavior produces another's response. This is not a difficult task since the basic "cat and mouse" cartoons on television and in the comics depict these cause and effect relationships. The attraction of these stories is contained in the viewer's anticipation. Children know what is going to happen, and it does. The teacher can apply this principle to lessons in the classroom. Given a specific behavior, what will be the response? Of course, the subtleties of behavior and communication become more complicated at

119

successive levels of development, but understanding consequences should receive emphasis throughout the educational process (refer to subcompetencies 15.4 and 16.5). Another objective should be identifying several aspects of behavior (i.e., appearance, manner, speech) and their effect on others.

14.2 Understanding Self-Organization

Numerous proverbs and sayings in our culture convey the idea that larger goals are accomplished by taking one step at a time. Self-organization is the process of arranging these steps into a pattern. The importance of self-organization is found in the fact that a task, like getting dressed in the morning, has to be repeated daily and is subject to a pattern of behavior that facilitates its accomplishment. Among other things, children's puzzles convey the idea that there is an organization—a pattern—involved in solving the problem. After a child learns to piece the puzzle together, he may use the same steps to complete the task again—because the method was efficient or just because he enjoys solving the problem in that particular way. Once students have developed the fundamental ability of creating and replicating patterns of behavior to solve problems, teachers can present an overview of a problem and ask the students to choose the best course of action. In other words, students learn to make current decisions. Completing mazes and the yearly income tax forms are examples of such a whole-part-whole approach. Most of the students will have had experience with organizing behavior. However, such things as commuting, dating, and shopping are subjects for further review, analysis, and organization. Another objective should be demonstrating ability to organize daily activities.

ACTIVITY TIP

Teachers and parents can cooperate effectively on the familiar *Things to Do* lists that students make for weekly projects or tasks. The lists provide the student with an opportunity to identify goals and can serve as reminders of resources for accomplishing the objectives. They can also be used as sources for classroom discussions related to daily events and accomplishments. Some students may organize such a list for each subject in the curriculum.

14.3 Developing Goal-Seeking Behavior

Behavior leading to the accomplishment of a goal is one of the most powerful ingredients to the success of the handicapped individual. Indeed, the successful individual who obtains a goal despite an inconvenience is often used as a role model for others who have handicaps. In order to replicate those successes, students should be able to identify goals and execute the appropriate behavior that will help them reach defined objectives. Teachers should discriminate between short- and long-term, realistic and unrealistic goals.

Students should practice the organization of goals, outline behaviors they will need to reach those goals, practice the behaviors, and evaluate the results. Other objectives should include identifying potential barriers to goals and identifying resources that can help a person to achieve his goal.

ACTIVITY TIP

Goal of the Week activity sheets require students to identify successive steps to accomplish objectives. The objective should include activities that are outside of the classroom such as fixing a bike, shopping for clothes, or attending a school event. The reports provide a weekly record of *accomplishments* that reinforce goal-seeking behaviors.

Achievement of goals helps students to develop the confidence necessary to actualize their potentials and meet the challenges of adult life.

14.4 Striving toward Self-Actualization

Self-actualization is the point at which an individual is producing as near to his potential as possible, is aware of these accomplishments, and feels a sense of fulfillment in them. The emphasis is upon current talents and abilities and the individual's feeling that he is "doing the best he can." This competency may remind parents, counselors, teachers, and therapists of the part self-actualization plays in their own lives. Teachers can create an atmosphere that is conducive to self-actualization by emphasizing students' positive qualities and by teaching them that what they can do is more important than what they cannot do. Self-actualization is not a final end-all goal but a realization that comes through many incidents that cause individuals to achieve and feel satisfaction. During the first 20 years of life, children and adolescents become aware of physical changes in their bodies and become too concerned about whether they measure up to standards. The psychological aspects will be realized in later years, but their beginnings are established during those days when children have so little time for them. It is the responsibility of parents and professionals to plant those seeds of discovery. Other objectives should include identifying elements necessary for a satisfactory day and identifying important characteristics of personal growth.

15 Achieving Problem-Solving Skills

The process of problem solving is intrinsic to education. Reading, writing, and calculating and other basic skills prepare students to make appropriate decisions. Problem solving is usually identified with the previous curriculum areas and the sciences. But, several facets of methodology can be applied to the broad area of personal-social skills to help students examine and improve their relationships with other individuals.

15.1 Differentiating Bipolar Concepts

Bipolar concepts include such examples as good and evil, positive and negative, pro and con. These terms are often used in reference to issues and relationships. However more often than not, problems and relationships do not fall into such a neat dichotomy. There may be several solutions to a problem or positions on an issue. The favored solutions are of greatest advantage to the individual and his set of values. Students should demonstrate ability to identify the extreme positions within a problem area, search for many solutions, and place each alternative on a progression. In using a methodology that includes this ordering of possible solutions, alternatives, or approaches, the student is able to identify several ingredients that are intrinsic to the problem. Another objective should be examining various positions relative to a group's interpretation of ideas, feelings, and behaviors.

15.2 Understanding the Need for Goals

Parents and teachers should deal with the question, "What are the purposes of goals?" Students should identify ways in which goals affect their lives and relationships with the people around them. Teachers should conduct activities requiring students to set model goals that can be attained within a short span of time so that students can record behaviors and results. Students can set goals that concern personal behavior, appearance, academic accomplishment, and group participation (refer to subcompetency 10.2). Attainment of goals is most meaningful when students are the foremost advocate in their formulation. In other words, goals established by teacher or parent may be noteworthy or even achieved by the student. However, if this competency is to contribute to the student's move toward independence and responsibility, then he must be in the dominant position of advocate and main participant, while teacher and parent assume the role of facilitator. Another objective should be listing outcomes of attaining goals.

15.3 Looking at Alternatives

At first glance, a problem may appear to have only one or two possible solutions. The student obviously limits the range of alternatives if he accepts the visible solutions. Exercises related to differentiation of bipolar concepts expose him to the possibility that other solutions or positions can be used to solve problems, and that he must search for alternatives. The deep attraction of fictional mysteries, whether they include Sherlock Holmes or Nancy Drew, is that the characters refuse to accept answers that are easily available and seek other solutions to the puzzle. This principle should be applied to human relationships. Students should demonstrate ability to seek information and examine alternatives involved in individual and group relationships.

15.4 Anticipating Consequences

Anticipating the consequences of a decision is the most difficult component to examine in the problem-solving process and the most neglected component of the process. How can students examine what is only anticipated? At this point, observation and inquiry will be of greatest assistance to the student. Although the individual student may have had little, if any, experience with potential consequences of a course of action, he may ask other individuals how they handled a similar problem and what the consequences were. Everyday decisions are experienced by all of us, and their consequences can be used as guides for those who are first examining similar problems and alternatives (refer to subcompetency 10.3).

15.5   Knowing Where to Find Good Advice

Throughout the discussions on subcompetencies, teachers and parents were reminded that students should identify the resources in their communities that can provide assistance in personal and family decision making. These resources should be experts in their given subject area, have experience in advising members of the community, and should be able to subdivide the decision-making process for their given subject area into sequential parts.

16   Communicating Adequately with Others

Without adequate communication, the handicapped individual is isolated. No person, handicapped or not, is an island. The individual who cannot convey his thoughts and feelings to others will have difficulty reaching fulfillment. In the final analysis, educators should focus upon helping students develop communication skills. With these skills, students can gain protection, companionship, and understanding.

16.1   Recognizing Emergency Situations

Darley and Latané (1968) developed *The Decision Tree* to describe people's reactions in emergency situations. In order for a person to assist another who is in need, the bystander must (1) recognize that something is happening; (2) interpret the occurrence as an emergency; (3) assume some personal responsibility in relationship to the situation or person; and (4) intervene. If any of these steps is not completed, then the needed assistance will not be provided. This progression gives teachers a structure for planning training activities. Students must first be able to attend to instances within the environment that either are direct signs of an emergency (fire, earthquake) or could be interpreted as a danger signal (screeching car brakes followed by a loud "thud," or an individual collapsing in a restaurant). Assuming that the student does take a personal responsibility for action (which is a test of his values), he should be able to provide the appropriate form of communication with participants ("Can I help you?" or "What do you need?") and emergency personnel ("I wish to report an accident;" or "I observed the following things."). These skills can be practiced in conjunction with subcompetencies 3.4 and 4.4. Another objective should be preparing a list of emergency information to be carried by the student.

16.2   Reading at Level Needed for Future Goals

The primary objective of this subcompetency is for the individual to develop independence by learning how to read. Depending upon the handicap, students may need to use visual or tactile cues to achieve this skill. Reading ability should include interpretation of symbols within the environments that are important for safety, health, and mobility. A second important consideration is that the symbols and meanings to be mastered facilitate the individual's overall achievement and development of self-confidence. Some students' goals and abilities will include reading Gibbon's *Decline and Fall of the Roman Empire.* For others, reading the shopping specials in the newspaper or braille directions for repairing a car will provide a sense of accomplishment. A teacher should seek every opportunity to use reading material that includes career themes or skills. This will require the teacher to use discretion as to whether a student should read books about history or car repairs. These decisions will be enhanced if the teacher coordinates his efforts with the opinions of the parents. Another objective should be demonstrating ability to use sources of information (i.e., newspapers, magazines, library).

16.3 Writing at Level Needed for Future Goals

This subcompetency emphasizes the production of written or printed symbols that individuals can use to communicate with others. The term *printed symbols* includes the use of typewriter, stylus, or other machine and computer assisted production of words and symbols that convey information. Once again, the level of accomplishment should be commensurate with the abilities and ambitions of the individual. From a career or vocational orientation, students should receive training in abilities to complete informal notes, letters, job applications, and a variety of forms they will encounter in applying for credit, completing a lease form, or opening a checking account (refer to competency 1).

ACTIVITY TIP

A mock *Employment Bureau* should be established in each classroom or school. It could be another learning center in the elementary classroom or part of the career center at the high school and community college level. Students would have the opportunity to practice several skills required in applying for a job. The bureau would maintain job descriptions, employment applications, audio and video cassette recordings or printed transcripts of interviews, and programmed material that provide information related to employment.

16.4 Speaking Adequately for Understanding

In a society that places value upon verbal skills (singing, acting, political oratory, salesmanship), the individual who has speech disabilities or problems speaking fluently is at a disadvantage. Van Riper (1978) identifies the succession of penalties, frustration, anxiety, guilt, and hostility that individuals with speech problems experience in their everyday dealings with other members of society. Even the competent person has occasional "dark days" when

he mispronounces the boss' name, flounders among sentences in an interview, or is tongue-tied when meeting a prospective date. Teachers, parents,
counselors, and therapists have a formidable task in preparing students to
demonstrate proficiency in basic language skills, skill in regulating the loud-
ness of voice according to the social setting, ability to participate in conversation, and verbal expression of emotion, information, and inquiry.

SAMPLE LESSON PLAN 4.2

Author: Christine Hughes

Period: Second   Situation: Handicapped students in a resource
Time Span: Six weeks   room or special day class setting

Activity Title: *Using the Telephone*

Objective: Competency 16.4: Students will be able to communicate adequately
with others and will use the telephone as a means of obtaining information.

Goal of Activity: Students will role play and practice various telephone skills using a classroom telephone learning center.

Activity: Upon written request, local telephone companies are usually willing to
provide used, gutted telephones that are no longer in use. Obtain a set of phones
and organize a telephone learning center in your classroom in which students can
practice various telephone skills. On separate pieces of posterboard, creatively
describe and illustrate situations for students to role play and practice. Include
the following sample student responses or invent your own.

Situation 1   Call a friend to talk for a while.

What to Say: "How did your day go today?"
              "What did you do last weekend?"
              "What do you plan to do this weekend?"

Situation 2   Call a friend to make plans to go somewhere.

What to Say: "Where would you like to go this weekend?"
              "I would like to go to _____."
              "I agree. We should go to _____."

Situation 3   Place an emergency phone call to the police department, fire
              department or family doctor.

What to Say: "I want to report a prowler at _____ ." (Give address)
              "I want to report an accident at the corner of _____
              and _____."
              "I want to report a fire at _____." (Give address)

Situation 4   Call a business establishment to determine job openings.

What to Say: "Does your company have any job openings at this time?"
              "What positions are available?"
              "What is the application procedure?"
              "Could I schedule an interview at this time?"

Situation 5   Practice taking messages.
What to Say: "May I ask who is calling, please?"
               "May I take a message?"
               "What is your phone number?"

Situation 6   Call to schedule an appointment with your doctor, dentist, etc.
What to say: "My name is _____ , and I'd like to make an appoint-
               ment with Dr. _____ on _____ for
               _____ ."

Evaluation: Let students choose partners and act out the situation of the week. Students will take turns being the caller and receiver of the call. Inform parents of your classroom activities. Encourage them to allow students to make these types of calls at home.

Activity Title: *Dialing for Information*

Objective: Competency 16.4:   The student will be able to communicate adequately with others and will use the telephone as a means of obtaining information.

Goal of Activity: Under teacher supervision, students will use school telephones to obtain simple information.

Activity: Let students use school telephones under your supervision to make simple phone calls. Listed below are some suggested calls to make.

1. Call to order a pizza for the class.
2. Call to find out bus routes and schedules for a class field trip.
3. Call to find out the business hours of a field trip destination.
4. Call to find out the business hours of a local bank or store.
5. Call to find out the cost of bowling for a class field trip.
6. Call to find out the admission price to the local zoo, museum, or amusement park.
7. Call to find out what movie is playing and the admission price at a local theatre.

Help students write a script to use while calling. Allow them to practice several times before making the call. This could be done individually or as a group. Have the student making the call look the phone number up in the telephone directory. If the number is unlisted, have the student call directory assistance. Provide students with a checklist of skills to keep in mind while making the call. This checklist could include such items as speaks clearly, speaks with expression, requests correct information, and accurately records information received.

Evaluation: Allow a different student to place calls for you or the class whenever necessary. Use the checklist as a means of evaluation. Inform parents of your classroom activities. Encourage them to allow students to make these types of calls.

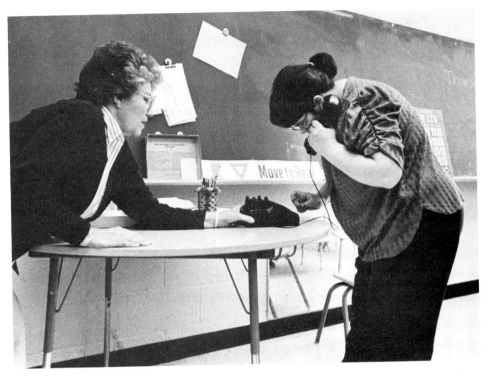

Students need to develop skills in using the telephone so they can report emergencies, fulfill social needs, and obtain information about jobs.

16.5 Understanding the Subtleties of Communication

Teachers should explore the area of "what is meant" in communication in contrast to "what is said, signed, or written." In other words, we live in a world of intention. Students should realize that sometimes people disguise their messages to protect themselves. They may say or imply things so they cannot be held accountable. School children soon learn that they can only be held accountable for what they say. They realize that communication can occur through many channels and can operate at both the overt and covert levels. Commercials can be, perhaps, the biggest and most accessible source of lessons. Numerous advertisements on radio and television and printed matter use nonverbal components—the subtleties—on communication to convey messages other than what is stated or pictured. Students should be able to distinguish between the verbal and nonverbal messages so that they can improve their communication skills. They should be aware of those instances in which they are producing dual messages (i.e., one level of acknowledged symbols and another one of intended meaning). Another objective should be practicing verbal and nonverbal forms of communication that are congruent with an individual's feelings.

TEACHING THE PERSONAL-SOCIAL SKILLS

In the beginning of this chapter, we made the statement that before professionals can add another dimension to classroom instruction, they must consider the ideas an individual has about his present status, potentials, and interactions with other people. These numerous personal ideas provide teachers and counselors with reflections of the student's self-concept. As so often happens with terms derived from the field of psychology or sociology, the words *self-concept* and *self-image* often appear in newspaper responses to the lovelorn, as well as in textbooks for teachers and counselors and have been absorbed into the mainstream of popular expression. This may be because the personalized picture that a person may have of the self, with all the attributes and deficiencies, appeals to the average individual, as well as to artists and scientists.

Each subcompetency is one part of a spectrum that describes the self-concept. It is appropriate to emphasize the self-concept at this stage of the text, since classroom activities in the personal-social skills include more than a strict adherence to academic performance. Teacher-student efforts in the areas of self-awareness, self-confidence, responsible behavior, interpersonal skills, independence, problem solving, and communication depend upon an accurate understanding of the student's opinions of his abilities and subsequent efforts to meet his level of expectation.

West (1977) reviews 27 strategies that teachers can use with educable mentally retarded students. Aside from the use of media and consultant support, 22 of the strategies require that teachers initiate and supervise these activities. The strategies include the following:

brainstorming	review of material	simulation
consensus forming	hands-on activities	games
role playing	oral reports	learning packages
discussion	peer tutoring	interviews
demonstration	practice sessions	projects
explanation	lecture	contract teaching
questions and answers	panel	learning centers
recitation		

Although West's list of strategies were obtained from classes for the educable mentally retarded, each strategy may be used with all students. Many may be familiar to the reader, while others may be of less importance depending on teacher's style or characteristics of the classroom situation. We are primarily concerned with strategies that encourage students to learn about themselves, their self-concepts, and ways they can change with each new piece of information. Several other strategies that have been developed in recent years include bibliotherapy, classroom discussions and meetings, individualized learning centers, sociodrama, self-concept scales, and values clarification.

Teachers and counselors can use these strategies to change the student's behavior and self-concept. All of the strategies can be used at each one of the four stages of career development (i.e. awareness, exploration, preparation, and placement and follow-up). The use of any one strategy will depend upon the teacher or counselor's objectives for a particular individual or group of students. These objectives should reflect an evaluation of the behaviors and abilities of the individual or group. The essential consideration is that the instructor uses an approach through which the competencies are infused into the daily curriculum. The approach also offers a means by which the teacher or counselor can judge whether particular competencies in the personal-social domain have been confronted and hopefully, mastered by the student. A discussion of the self-concept will be followed by reviews of several strategies.

" We've got to get the disabled to improve their perceptions of themselves. We need to have them say, 'Hey, what the hell am I ashamed for? Other people's limitations are the problem.' "

Siller (1977)

The Self-Concept

Self-concept occupies a central position in the development of personality. Carl Rogers, a leading proponent of client-centered counseling, provided the definition that we will use in this discussion. He spoke of the self-concept as

> an organized configuration of perceptions of the self which are admissible to awareness. It is composed of such elements as the perceptions of one's characteristics and abilities; the value qualities which are perceived as associated with experiences and objects; and goals and ideals which are perceived as having positive or negative valence.
>
> (Rogers, 1951, pp. 136–37)

The self-concept is generally regarded as the totality of the way a person perceives himself. This multifaceted image includes our abilities and characteristics, as well as the positive and negative evaluations that are placed on each person. The image changes with the individual's experiences; in other words, self-concept is *learned*, and new learnings change the composite image that the individual maintains from one moment of time to the next. Some psychologists and counselors refer to self-concept and self-esteem as both the image and the process of change. The individual reflects his experiences against his self-concept; in turn, his self-concept influences what he will learn from his experiences. Therefore the formation of a self-concept is a process in which the individual is constantly changing his awareness of himself and the way he perceives the world.

A second important element in this process is that the self-concept is influenced by *significant others*, such as parents, teachers, or those who foster change. For example, numerous inductees to the Professional Football Hall of Fame in Canton, Ohio deliver acceptance speeches in which they attribute their successes to specific individuals who coached them at the high school, college, or professional levels. In some instances, the athletes doubted whether they would have succeeded as professional football players, let alone achieved such a prominent distinction, without the teaching and encouragement of their mentors.

A third recurring element in definitions and discussions of the self-concept is related to the way people perceive themselves and their environments. Physical reception and transmission of sensations to the brain are basic components of perception. Individuals with an impediment in one of the senses will experience difficulties gaining accurate information about the environment. Bateman (1967) developed a model of human data processing to illustrate the effects that blindness has upon expression. She likened the various human functions to those of a computer. An individual's expression (output) is a product of the sensory input, prior knowledge (storage), and procedures for processing sensory information (program). Blindness limits the amount of input into the system, while individuals with hearing impediments may miss the rules for processing information that are contained in the learning of language. Also, individuals with severe emotional problems (paranoia, hallucinations, and the like) might have difficulty with input processes.

Perception also refers to the psychological interpretations that people place upon events or the behaviors of others. For example, an individual perceives that his host is ignoring him at the party or that people do not want to stand next to him in line for the theater. These interpretations constitute the basis for the ideas people develop about the self. Psychologists have postulated that changes in perception will affect behavior. Simply stated, our behavior is based on perception. If a person perceives differently, then he will behave differently.

How an individual feels about himself is a final element in discussions about the self-concept. Self-concept is especially crucial in relationship to how an individual feels about his physical characteristics. When people are asked how they are feeling at a particular moment, they may respond "O.K." "Great." "Awful." "I have Excedrin Headache Number 82." "Happy." "Can't complain." Although these responses may reflect the person's feelings at that moment, they cannot accurately describe the self-concept. Self-concept includes numerous component values that are placed on specific forms of demonstrated ability, aptitude, and disability. Thus, an individual may perceive himself as being an adequate tennis player, terrible when it comes to completing income tax forms, quick to form an opinion, and a dependable neighbor. These values, or the ways in which an individual regards himself, are influenced by the appraisals of significant others; in turn, the individual's subsequent behaviors affect the opinions of the appraisers. With time, the values given to the several components can change as the individual encounters new experiences and other appraisals. This is known in the average American lexicon as "Taking stock," or "Changing priorities." These new or modified values constitute the foundation for what the individual expects to accomplish (aspirations) and tries to achieve (endeavors).

An individual's opinion of his ability and his subsequent efforts to obtain goals are crucial to career education. In chapter 2, we mentioned that career education also involves the attempts made by members of the school, family, community, and business and industry to help students perceive that they may successfully take on many useful roles in society. These efforts attempt to expand the student's perception by placing a positive value on productive roles in society. The student's behaviors often depend upon the preconceived notions of ability and requirements for success. Thus, personal-social skills include the elements that form a basis for a concept of self.

Special educators have been interested in the implications of self-concept discussions for the personal development of handicapped individuals since the early beginning of the theory. With the availability of support monies and changes in social policy, research on the self-concept of individuals with various types of disabilities expanded during the 1960s. The term appears in research on all areas of exceptionality. Educators are particularly concerned about how physically disabled students develop a self-concept. Alterations in appearance, mobility, or physical abilities set in a culture that emphasizes the mistaken notion of "body whole, body beautiful" generate stereotypes about "inherent inferiority." Several writers have analyzed the social dynamics and suggested classroom activities and necessary behaviors that physically disabled people could initiate to enhance their self-concept (Foster, Szoke, Kapisovsky, & Kriger, 1977; Wright, 1960 & 1974).

"Some children who are physically disabled may yet reach young adulthood without the self-awareness, skills, and self-esteem that contribute to personal adjustment. Thus there is the need to provide opportunities for these youngsters to acquire the interpersonal skills, the coping orientation, the independent living skills and, above all, the acceptance of self that leads to self-actualization."

Palmer (1980)

Several reviewers (Bartel & Guskin, 1973; Cruickshank & Paul, 1980; Lawrence & Winschell, 1973) have identified major complications that should be resolved before researchers and practitioners can soundly state that their instruments and methods do, in fact, improve the individual's self-concept and corresponding behavior. These can be summarized as challenges in (1) defining the several components of the self-concept, (2) identifying the progressive stages in the development of the self-concept, and (3) improving the validity and standardization of the instruments that are used to measure the self-concept or its components.

Aside from these problems that are directly related to the formulation of self-concept theories and instruments to indicate the individual's status vis-à-vis the projected developmental stage, researchers also encounter difficulties when they apply their methods to specific categories of disability. If you consider the amount of variation existing among individuals with, for example, behavior disorders or physical disability, then you must be cautious in generalizing research findings. This is also complicated when there are differences of opinion concerning the definition of a disability and its characteristics. For example, the category of "learning disability" is a fledgling in the field of special education. Several attempts have been made at the national level to develop a definition that reflects current understanding of individuals with this impairment. But, given the relative newness of the category (or as some would have it, the label), combined with previously identified limitations in the measurement of the self-concept, people should have reservations while reading a research report on, for example, the effects of mainstreaming on the self-concept of children with learning disabilities.

Despite these difficulties and limitations, we feel that teachers and counselors should be encouraged to probe the personal-social skill areas that fall within the larger framework of the self-concept. This statement is based largely upon our observations of the status of handicapped individuals within society and their experiences in attempting to shape an image of themselves that includes positive values. Educators must be concerned with the development of the individual's self-concept for the following reasons:

1. In some instances, the individual's disability interferes with an accurate perception of the environment including people's reactions to him. For example, in using subcompetency 16.5, understanding the subtleties of communication, educators should train students to be aware of clues relative to others' reactions to them. But since a great many of these clues involve visual cues, individuals with visual disability will have difficulty receiving accurate information. There are very few ways in which the visually limited individual can change the behavior patterns of others. Such things as winks, physical gestures, or the raising of

133

an eyebrow have been learned and perfected over a long period of time and are used to convey additional information about the meaning or emphasis of another form of communication. Educators must train the individual to rely on other channels of communication to clarify the information and thereby provide a foundation for accurate perceptions.

2. In some instances, the individual's disability hinders his interaction with the environment and may limit the range of his experiences. Experiences provide information about the environment and an individual's ability to maintain himself within it. Physical development and recreation programs that are designed to meet special needs give handicapped individuals an opportunity to test themselves. These tests, whether swimming, camping, or racing, allow individuals to gain new insights about their physical and psychological selves. New possibilities for success are available, and the aura of limitation that constantly surrounds individuals with disabililty is diminished. These changes will be reflected in modified self-concepts.

3. In some instances, evaluations that are made by significant others will affect the individual's perception of his aptitude. Their opinions of the individual's "special" aspect and its unique effects can supersede the actual limitation. Individuals with disabilities have often been more limited by these reactions and concepts than by the physical limitation. Those of us in special education can recount numerous stories of students who regarded themselves as less than adequate, based solely upon the opinions of others. For example, have you ever heard the following statements?

> My parents will always treat me like a baby until the day I die.
> They've called me names so often that it doesn't bother me. I just don't talk to anyone, that's all. They're not missing much, and neither am I.
> Most of the time, I wish I was someone else.
> After a while, it just isn't worth trying. The teacher will always find something wrong with my work.

4. In some instances, the individual's identity develops as a result of his "inadequate" status. These "inadequacies" are first projected by significant others. Parents, relatives, and teachers link the individual's identity to the disability through such references as my "blind child" or "retarded student." At one stage of development, the use of such terms is passively accepted. The terms may even impart some forms of attention and distinguish the in-

dividual from other children. But at some stage of development, the same individual begins to realize that certain references or labels bear negative connotations and only decrease his perceived value. This realization marks the break in the path. One road leads to increased independence and an identity generated from accomplishments, while the other leads to a status built on labels and stereotypes. We suspect that some of the emphasis of individuals with special needs upon their role or identity as "people first" may be due, in part, to labels that always marked the disability prior to any other human characteristics.

5. In some instances, the individual will resort to evasive means in order to avoid devaluation and buttress a self-concept that has been under assault. Our society is characterized as one of accomplishment. We value success whether measured in gold medals at the Olympics, orbiting satellites, or gross national product. If an individual is unable to accomplish what amounts to the phantom of success, he is in jeopardy. As a society, we are now beginning to realize that the individual has value and his value does not decrease because he is unable to succeed. But because we are in the early stages of realizing the relationships between success, value, identity, and self-concept, numerous individuals with disabilities have had to resort to masking their shortcomings and evading detection.

Two researchers, Goffman (1963), a sociologist, and Edgerton (1967), an anthropologist, have documented the attempts of ex-mental patients, drug addicts, prostitutes, mentally retarded individuals, and others with "spoiled identities" to become assimilated into a society that maintains standards for normal behavior and appearance. Goffman devotes most of his book to the means by which those who bear a stigma attempt to avoid detection. Edgerton provides extensive histories of individuals who were released from institutions for the mentally retarded, but exhibited behaviors that project competence to the observer. These various "covering" techniques protect the self-concept but, in fact, only form *The Cloak of Competence* (Edgerton, 1967).

It is no wonder that individuals with special needs experience a whole range of contradictory feeling about themselves when they analyze their role as depicted in such popular media as magazines, newspaper comics, television, and movies. You can no doubt recall the classic examples of evil in such fairy tales as *Jack and the Beanstalk* (the giant ogre), *Peter Pan* (Captain Hook), or *Rumpelstiltskin*. Comedians have often used the popular stereotypes and expectations that are associated with a certain disability as the focal point of their jokes. For example, Mel Brooks has been associated with several comedy routines and movies. We need not elaborate on them as that would constitute its own chapter, but one routine in his movie *Young Frankenstein* illustrates his use of a stereotype to "play on" the audience. Dr. Frankenstein, Jr. (played by Gene Wilder) returns to his father's home town and is met at the railroad station by Egor, Jr. (played by Marty Feldman). After an exchange of lines relative to the pronunciation of their names, Dr. Frankenstein notices that Egor has a hunchback. He is seized with pity and, touching Egor's back, states that he is a surgeon and can help Egor with his hump. Egor looks puzzled and responds, "What hump?" The public usually laughs at that point, but we wonder whether they realize that they bear the brunt of the joke? Or does the individual who is sitting in the audience with a noticeable physical difference bear the brunt of the joke in the final analysis?

Bibliotherapy

You are probably familiar with examples of disabilities that are central to such classic literature as Victor Hugo's *The Hunchback of Notre Dame* and William Shakespeare's *Richard III*. The characters Quasimodo and Richard III encounter various difficulties, but they are not sterling examples of an individual's ability to cope with stress in his environment. There are other works of literature that do present the handicapped individual in a favorable light.

Bibliotherapy is one means of helping individuals with disabilities to understand their difficulties by exposing them to works of literature in which characters with limitations confront and, in most instances, succeed in life's challenges. The key element to the process, aside from the physical act of "reading" the book, occurs when the individual identifies with the character or circumstances, transfers insights from the literature, and applies them to his own situation. Teachers and counselors can use bibliotherapy to develop an informational background of the personal-social subcompetencies. For example, characters will often reflect upon their need for certain skills, difficulties they encountered in solving problems related to interactions with "normal" people, or the attitudes of others toward disabilities. Students can be asked to relate their experiences to similar events in the book. The student indicates whether he has gained insight into the circumstances that confront the character and, more importantly, notes those pieces of wisdom that can be transferred to his own repertoire of behavior.

Bibliotherapy has received expanded interest among teachers, counselors, and therapists who are attempting to broaden the individual's perspective of his situation and potential problem-solving behaviors that increase the student's self-confidence. This interest has been aided by the fact that a greater number of literary works by individuals with a disability and their parents have found their way into print. Bibliographies, interviews, and selections of literature appropriate for various ages and disabilities can be found in publications by Baum (1982), Bower (1980), Cohen (1977), King (1975), Landau, Epstein, and Stone (1978), and Orlansky and Heward (1981).

Professionals should also write to The National Easter Seal Society for Crippled Children and Adults, 2023 W. Ogden Ave., Chicago, Illinois, 60612, for a bibliography of books about handicapped persons that is organized according to areas of disability. This organization has been reviewing such books in its publication *Rehabilitation Literature* so that professionals may research specific works in order to gain more information prior to recommending it to students or their parents. Readers who are interested in expanded discussions of the method should refer to the works of Moody (1971) and Riggs (1971). Other sources include *Notes from a Different Drummer* (Baskin & Harris, 1977), which contains an annotated guide to juvenile fiction portraying handicapped individuals and *Don't Call Me Handicapped* (Vocational Biographies, 1980) which can be used as career or vocational instructional materials.

Classroom Discussions—Meetings

Classroom discussions or meetings is one of the most popular means by which teachers and counselors lead students in exchanges on the subcompetencies that are covered in chapters 3 through 5. Most professionals have participated in discussions during their training experiences and, no doubt, attempt to conduct similar activities with students in small or large groups. However, few have seriously dissected the functions and anatomy of a discussion as thoroughly as Glasser (1969). He devotes three chapters in his book *Schools Without Failure* to "classroom meetings" and their importance for relevant education.

Glasser projects the teacher or counselor as one who leads the class in a nonjudgmental discussion about the important concerns of the students. His suggestions and concepts are applicable particularly to teacher-student activities in the area of personal-social skills. Students are sensitive to the opinions and judgments of teachers and peers in such competency areas as achieving independence, acquiring self-confidence, and communicating with others.

The professional's attitude toward meetings determines whether discussion methods can function successfully in the school curriculum. If they are viewed as part of the daily routine, students and professionals begin to acquire an open and honest attitude toward topics that, under other circumstances, would warrant guarded and evasive behaviors. The professional cannot afford to lead small or large groups into such sensitive topics (and student concerns) as accepting criticism, understanding behaviors, and expressing feelings without establishing an atmosphere of trust. At the same time, the professional should not avoid such topics, because they constitute the building blocks of a positive self-concept.

137

The classroom meetings have particular benefits for those students with handicaps who are being integrated into the regular classroom. Some meetings may provide students with the opportunity to explore questions about feelings and attitudes toward individuals who are different. The student with disabilities may not be the best spokesperson for *all* people who share his inconveniences, but he can describe his experiences in the neighborhood and the school. It is hoped that the open and honest atmosphere that encouraged students to exchange views will also help them to accept individuals who differ from the group.

Individualized Learning Centers

Classroom learning or work centers have become increasingly popular as a means of facilitating independent learning. The center is a designated area in which the student works at a specific task at his own rate of speed. Elementary school teachers use this type of programming to direct students into various activities or buttress previous group instructional sessions. It was not until the introduction of Hewett's (1968) engineered classroom that the concept was expanded into what might be considered a model for special education.

Hewett's program was originally designed for students who were classified as educationally handicapped or behavior disordered. The program was modified subsequently to meet the needs of individuals with various types of disabilities. The work center concept lends itself particularly to situations in which the teacher must design a minimum amount of knowledge or skill that all members of the class should master but is faced with the problem of teaching students who learn at different rates. In other words, students must have the opportunity to cover the same amount of material at their own speed without imposing their limitations upon other members of the class. The main requirements of the work center are the following:

1. Activities should be conducted with a minimum of direct supervision.
2. Instructions and materials should be available at each center to meet the needs and abilities of the student.
3. Students should be introduced to the themes in each center as a normal part of their classroom routine.
4. Reinforcement of some form should be available to encourage the student's continued success and effort.
5. The work center should be considered part of the curriculum so that the teacher provides assistance and records observations of student behaviors.

The learning center can be contained within one room or dispersed throughout the school and may include such activities as visual perception, auditory discrimination, listening skills, fine motor skills, communication skills, and arts and crafts (Kokaska & Kokaska, 1971). The resource room is an increasingly popular method of mainstreaming handicapped students into the regular curriculum. Learning centers can be designed to serve as specific curriculum study modules within the larger resource room.

Most of the activities mentioned so far are associated with physical and academic development. However, Noar (1974) describes "The Center for Learning about Me," which helps students practice skills that foster positive attitudes and feelings about the self. The center contains personal grooming materials, as well as a wash basin and mirror. Noar also suggests that teachers use a camera so that students may have their pictures taken at periodic intervals. Students relate to positive images projected on pictures of themselves and, thus, build better self-images.

Individualized learning centers can concentrate on themes relative to the personal-social skills. For example, a Communications Center may contain a tape recorder on which a student may practice using the telephone to obtain an interview or introduce himself to a member of the opposite sex. Each student can play, erase, and record over his personal tape or cassette until he has produced the appropriate level of skill to meet criteria.

A second center may be assigned to personal reflections about self. Students may use the center to record their ideas about daily accomplishments, new goals, or the way others perceive their behavior. These reflections may be written in a log, diary, or notebook, or contained on the personal tape or cassette. In all instances, teachers and counselors must be mindful of the privacy required by students in disclosing ideas about themselves. This type of center will certainly test the amount of trust that has been established between professional and student, as well as student and peers.

Another center may be assigned to listening or viewing video recordings, slide-tape material, or other illustrations appropriate to personal-social skills. Commercial materials are available covering the wide range of behaviors appropriate to dating, controlling one's emotions, problem solving, developing objectives, communicating with friends and employers. At times, teachers and counselors may have more material available than they can use in classroom or small group sessions. This type of center would enable students to explore topics of interest at their rate of learning, which may generate more pertinent questions about abilities and areas of improvement. Letting students create their own learning centers can also be a positive experience.

"Once in a while, I still get out and fool around with the kids. A lot of them come up to me and say, 'You Pete Gray? How'd you ever play in the majors with one arm?' I just look at 'em and say, 'You know, son, there's a lot of guys with two good arms that don't make it.'"

Gray (1982)

139

Role Playing—Sociodrama

Role playing and sociodrama consist of several techniques that include spontaneous responses by participants within a given situation. The early origins of the techniques can be traced to therapists who encouraged their clients to "act out" frustrations, fears, or antagonisms. More recently, educators have found that role playing is a valuable technique that can be used in regular classrooms. This is due to the realization that each one of us is expected to assume a wide range of roles during the adult years with very little direct preparation in the classroom. Each role is assigned a set of expected behaviors. For example, employers expect certain behaviors from employees, and pedestrians from motorists. But what about the reverse expectations of the employees and motorists?

The manner in which children, adolescents, and adults learn role expectations and appropriate behaviors is often left to chance. Teachers and counselors recognize that most people, and particularly those individuals with handicaps who have had limited opportunity to engage in social interaction, need experiences in which they can "practice" certain roles. This practice is generally referred to as making believe, but the topics that are confronted in a role-playing situation are more significant than those associated with the usual "Let's pretend" themes. One may recall his experiences at the first formal dance of his life or junior prom. Everyone stood around looking for clues as to the appropriate things to do and say. Some prior role playing in a classroom may have made the experience less awkward. For example, Veatch (1980) described the development of a three part videotape series with captions designed to teach job interview skills to deaf applicants. The series includes acceptable and inappropriate behaviors from the preinterview preparation to the closing moments between the employer and applicant. Students then have the opportunity to rehearse the successful behaviors that are demonstrated in the model tapes.

Role playing provides the student with an opportunity to experiment with his feelings and explore behavior for a given situation while he is in a protective environment. Role playing allows the student to express feelings that may not be acceptable outside the classroom, to make mistakes, and to be different. After all, most of us know that actors are only filling a part and don't really believe their lines! The key to the encounter between members in the play is the spontaneity of the participants. Although the students assume the role of different characters, the teacher and counselor hope that the students will bring their true feelings, attitudes, and responses for the role to the forefront. If the responses are guarded, then the professional has no real basis upon which to judge whether the sessions have successfully demonstrated expected behavior for the role. The student ideally displays his behavior, receives constructive suggestions, and undergoes the necessary changes. Of course, the final test is whether the student initiates practice behaviors during actual encounters.

Several authors have suggested a series of steps by which professionals should prepare students for role playing or sociodrama. We have organized them into the following sequence.

1. *Identify the problem.* The problem may have already been identified by the student (i.e., "What do I wear to a prom?") or may occur in the normal sequence of the curriculum (i.e., "Goals for this school year"). Teachers and counselors could use some of the 102 subcompetencies as problem topics. The important aspect of this initial step is to define the problem so that each student understands its significance for his life.

2. *Warm-up.* This step is necessary in breaching the identification of the problem and the subsequent involvement in role playing. The warm-up prepares the student by getting him interested in solving the problem. "Should he read a book? Will an authority give him the answer? Can the class help him find the answer?" The warm-up helps the class realize that the group may be the best source of information that students can use in confronting the problem. The question of "What does one say at the junior prom?" may best be answered by the group in a role-playing situation.

3. *Specify the situation and various roles.* Simply stated, everyone should know his part and what is happening. At first, the teacher and counselor may have to organize the participants. With time and practice, students can adequately project situations and role behaviors, especially concerning those problems that are particular to their age group and circumstances.

4. *The play.* Response and timing are critical to the play. Students must carry the conversations and responses, but teachers and counselors have to judge whether the play is successful, when to bring it to a conclusion, or whether the participants should be encouraged further. There are no "hard and fast" rules regarding these decisions. Students can sense when they are not on the right track, but both students and professionals need practice at the process of role playing before it can be a vibrant part of the curriculum.

5. *Discussion.* The play should generate additional questions: "What happened? Why? What would you do differently? Is there another way of reacting in that situation?" These questions and others are intended to amplify alternative behaviors that could apply to all members of the group. Alternative decisions should

141

be discussed and, in turn, could provide the topics for other role plays.

6. *Replay.* The same situation could be recast and played again. New participants create new possibilities that students could review and discuss. Eventually, the situation will lose its luster. Teachers and counselors should be sure to end the play before that point so that students maintain a favorable attitude toward the entire process. If they wish, they can initiate the role play at some future date.

Readers who are interested in further discussion of the use of role playing in the classroom with handicapped students should refer to Buchan (1972) and Walker and Shea (1980).

SAMPLE LESSON PLAN 4.3

Author: Lynda Glascoe

Level: High School through community college

Situation: Resource setting or group meetings

Time Span: One class period

Objective: The student will be able to act out appropriate responses after he has received praise or criticism.

Activity: This is a role-playing activity that can simulate actual employment situations. Each situation is described on 3-by-5-inch cards. Each card should contain enough detail to allow the student to understand the situation yet still encourage him to use his creativity. Second, two or more students are chosen for each activity. After the students have read the situation and chosen their roles, they will decide what they will do and say during the play. Third, the class discusses the situation, responses, and possible alternatives.

Examples: (1) Your best friend quit his job and you are hired to take his place. After one week, your boss praises your work and begins to tell you about your friend's problems on the job. (2) You don't feel like working today and your boss notices it. He says "Unless you shape-up, you won't have this job much longer." (3) You worked late last night on the job and your supervisor tells you "Pretty good. But, you could have done better."

Evaluation: Students will be able to identify appropriate responses to each situation.

Related Subcompetencies   11.3   Accepting praise
                           11.4   Accepting criticism
                           19.4   Accepting supervision

Self-Concept Scales

Several self-concept scales are available to teachers and counselors at the elementary, secondary, and adult levels. Self-concept scales are primarily intended to measure the beliefs an individual has about himself. We have already discussed the difficulties encountered by researchers who have attempted to use the scales with populations of individuals with disabilities. At this stage of the discussion, we are more concerned with the use of self-concept scales or self-report scales as teaching devices rather than as measuring instruments.

The scales basically provide students with statements about themselves: "I am always happy." "I like to go to the movies." "My parents pick on me." The statements can reflect such things as physical ability, mental ability, appearance, favorable qualities, and skills and are usually rated on scales from "always" to "never," "excellent" to "terrible," and the like. Although the statements can include other people, they always reflect the student's feelings about what others do to him or think about him. Thus, teachers and counselors receive the student's interpretation of his present status, the attitudes and behaviors of others toward him, and the values he places on each ingredient. The obvious limitation of the whole process rests in the accuracy of the student's reports. What a student marks on a form may not be what he feels. But, this limitation in "measurement" provides teachers and counselors with the reason for using these kinds of instruments or reports for teaching purposes. The very fact that the student hesitates to complete a form or reports inaccurately indicates that this area should be investigated.[3]

Self-concept scales can be used as teaching devices in the following ways:

1. Statements on the report form alert the student to possible areas of behavior and attitudes that he needs to work on. In effect, the statements act as a stimulus for further discussions, in either small or large groups. These discussions can place greater perspective on the ranking of the student's status and the perception of various types of ability.

2. Many of the self-concept scales include statements reflecting the personal-social subcompetencies. Teachers and counselors would be able to gain an approximation of the student's ranking in such areas as self-awareness, socially responsible behavior, and communication. The use of the scales as a form of checklist would

---

[3]If teachers and counselors become aware that a student is refusing to disclose certain feelings on personal grounds, they should respect his privacy.

provide professionals with another means of marking the student's progress through the subcompetencies.

3. Responses on the report form can alert teachers and counselors to contradictions between the student's perception of events or attitudes and the perception of others, including professionals. Such contradictions can be matched against further observations and individual counseling sessions. Above all, the contradictions should not be left unattended. Numerous individuals with disabilities have maintained inaccurate views of themselves and the opinions of others toward their limitations merely because their views were not brought to a conscious level of discussion and inquiry that would have exposed the situation.

The following is a case report of a teacher's efforts to help fifth and sixth grade students learn how to identify emotions. The teacher, Nancy Strole, did not use a self-concept scale but did develop three sessions in which the students worked on the areas that could be measured by a formalized instrument.

In our first session, the class listed as many feeling words as they could think of. The students thought of about eight words. Then they were invited to describe different situations that made them feel happy, sad, mad, etc. Reaction cards were read to them and they filled in the feeling word such as "When I do something wrong and my parents find out, I feel _____." "When I have to read in front of the class and I don't know the words, I feel _____." At the end of the session, the class was divided up into teams, and the students were asked to think of as many feeling words as possible. At this time, the words were erased from the chalkboard.

At the second session, the class was divided up into pairs and each group was asked to give their feeling words. These were written on the board. The winning team thought of 35 feelings! A homework assignment was given to write sentences describing the feeling words. This was to be a contest. The sentence format was as follows: "When I _____, I feel _____." The assignment required the students to think about their emotions and served as a wonderful writing exercise. The class was very surprised and pleased to see how much they wrote.

We determined the "winner" by a group decision. The papers were read by the teachers without the names of the students. Students gave each paper a score on a 0–8 rating scale. They were told to vote on the amount of work put into the assignment, sincerity, and thought. Many students wrote 20–25 sentences. One winner was identified, but *all* were rewarded because of their hard work.

Values Clarification

Teachers and counselors have always worked in the realm of personal values, which includes their own, as well as those of the student. The way we regard ourselves and the level at which we prize our several attributes are composed of numerous smaller value choices. Values constitute the qualities and principles that the individual thinks are desirable. The valuing process is a means by which the individual balances the necessity of purposeful action with the idealized concept of himself and his direction. Within the past few years several authors have published discussions and techniques providing professionals with a means for enhancing student awareness of values, the valuing process, and the importance of both in developing the self-concept. Charles (1978) comments that these strategies help students clarify their values and become more aware of what they believe subconsciously.

Values clarification is a process that focuses on the student's particular mode of reaching decisions and the special importance of his actions and goals. One of the strengths of this approach is that it does not advocate a special set of values that supersede those of the student. The approach concentrates on the process so that the student becomes aware of the value, its relationship to other values, and fundamental aspects of change that the student could use if he decided to modify his beliefs. The process, according to Raths, Harmin, and Simon (1966), consists of three main behaviors and seven steps.

1. Choosing one's beliefs and behaviors.
   a. choosing freely.
   b. choosing from alternatives.
   c. choosing after thoughtful consideration of the consequences of each alternative.
2. Prizing one's beliefs and behaviors.
   a. prizing and cherishing one's choice.
   b. prizing and affirming one's choice publicly when appropriate.
3. Acting on one's beliefs.
   a. acting with purpose.
   b. acting with a consistent pattern.

An additional strength of values clarification rests on the numerous activities that have been suggested by advocates. The activities, games, or strategies would place students in all of the seven steps. Activities are applicable to classes for adolescent and adult groups and have been used with elementary grade students. We would recommend that teachers and counselors review the activities carefully if they attempt to engage certain individuals

145

with disabilities, as mental ability and emotional factors are variables in the anticipated results.

ACTIVITY TIP

The following is a game that can help students clarify values related to employment and personal goals: A former student has a comfortable job at Company A. He learns about an attractive job opening at a new Company B. The position at Company B pays more and provides training that the company will finance. But, if he decided to accept the position at Company B, he would have to travel a greater distance to work. The former student could cut the travel time by moving from his current dwelling, but his girlfriend would then be farther away. His relatives encourage him to explore the possible job. Some of his pals at Company A tell him to forget it since Company B may fold and besides, they need him for their sports team. What should he do?

CONCLUSION

The subcompetencies and teaching techniques for the personal-social skills are intertwined with each other. Self-awareness facilitates self-confidence, problem-solving skills leads students to greater independence, and adequate communication helps individuals to maintain interpersonal relationships. The subcompetencies also interact with the teaching techniques but at a level that we cannot fully measure and describe. Certainly, the personal-social skills are essential for obtaining and maintaining employment.

In order for the teacher and counselor to get the most out of any one technique or combination of learning strategies, he must establish a sense of trust that permeates the classroom. This fundamental sense of trust is important in those situations in which the individual with a disability has been integrated with normal students. We have identified enough instances in the everyday conduct of affairs for the reader to realize that some students are more vulnerable than others, merely because they manifest some behavior or physical sign that distinguishes them from the larger group. Any one injury or insult to the student's sense of integrity only serves to insulate him from those strategies that are intended to expand his awareness. Certainly remarks will be made, feelings will be hurt, and things will be misunderstood as the student progresses through the educational system. But, these events can be tolerated and used to broaden the student's perspective if the teacher and counselor can convey the feeling and understanding that the student is important, valuable, and necessary. Indeed, all the strategies and activities would be nothing without him!

The Occupational Skills

5

The previous two chapters have focused on many skills that are critical to independent living. Daily living and personal-social skills are also important for occupational success. All the competencies of the LCCE curriculum relate to occupational functioning as well as satisfactory community living whether they are in the areas of personal hygiene, communication, independence, or mobility.

The following lists six occupational competencies that are important to the career development of handicapped individuals:

> 17　Knowing and exploring occupational possibilities
> 18　Selecting and planning occupational choices
> 19　Exhibiting appropriate work habits and behaviors
> 20　Exhibiting sufficient physical-manual skills
> 21　Obtaining a specific occupational skill
> 22　Seeking, securing, and maintaining employment

This curriculum area includes those abilities that are necessary for effective job selection, satisfaction, and functioning. Occupational skills may often be defined as career education, and although we believe this curriculum area needs much more attention than it is presently receiving in most schools, it must be amalgamated accordingly with daily living and personal-social skills training to promote the individual's career development. Unless career education concepts are infused into the curriculum, a combination of academic and work-study training is simply not sufficient in today's complex society.

147

The six competencies comprising this curriculum area can be divided into three occupational *guidance* competencies and three occupational *preparation* competencies. Obtaining a specific occupational skill is the only competency that does not include an array of subcompetencies, since it depends on the area in which the individual is being trained. Attention will be directed toward this competency later in the chapter.

This chapter, like the two previous ones, will discuss each of the competencies and subcompetencies comprising our career education model. Narrative suggestions relative to objectives and instructional and guidance activities are presented. Activity tips and separate sections on specific occupational guidance and preparation techniques are given throughout the chapter as teaching examples. These techniques provide useful suggestions for teaching the student the occupational competencies. Once again, the

reader is cautioned that these are only suggestions and that the best technique depends on the unique situation and clientele of each helping person.

COMPETENCIES

17 Knowing and Exploring Occupational Possibilities

Individuals must have a broad perspective of the world of work before they can make satisfying and realistic occupational choices. This competency is closely allied to the career awareness and exploration stages of career education. Students should begin exploring the world of work and specific occupations almost immediately after beginning school. The more that students are

POINT OF VIEW

"Everyone's life could have a purpose if they could learn to accept themselves as they are and work with their abilities to make the world a better place." Mr. Muller was born in 1941 and was diagnosed as having cerebral palsy. His parents were told that he would never walk or talk, but they refused to accept the doctor's verdict to have him institutionalized for life. In 1966, Mr. Muller joined Steelcase Inc. in Grand Rapids, Michigan and is currently Administrator in the Marketing Department. He is also Adjunct Assistant Professor of Psychology at Aquinas College and has an Honorary Degree in Educational Psychology from the Free University in Amsterdam. In 1972, he received Michigan's Handicapped American of the Year Award. Mr. Muller has lectured at several national and international colleges and universities and has been invited to the White House by the President to participate in events concerning the disabled. Currently, he is a speaker, lecturer, and consultant for education and industry and works in human relations as a spokesperson for persons with disabilities. Mr. Muller's goal in life is to make sure that people with disabilities have the opportunity to make the most of their lives. He believes that disabled individuals have much more potential than they are given credit for and that they should be given proper personal, social, and educational opportunities so that they can become productive citizens and have a purpose in our economic society.

Robert Muller and his wife, Carol, live with their three children in Grandville, Michigan. Mr. Muller and his wife are writing a book entitled Every Life Has A Purpose.

aware of the reinforcing values of various jobs, the more likely it is that they will develop motivation and appreciation of the dignity of work and will identify with the occupational world. In conjunction with family and community resources, school personnel must provide an array of awareness and exploration opportunities (i.e., field trips, films, speakers, literature, summer work, and role playing) so that occupational possibilities are presented for the student's knowledge and exploration.

A variety of individuals should participate in making the student aware of occupational possibilities. The elementary teacher can relate various subject matter to job information. She can also elicit the assistance of the student's parents, employers, and employees who work in various settings throughout the community. Many pamphlets and other media can be used. As students progress in their awareness of occupational possibilities, actual exploration of jobs of interest can be offered in school, family, and community settings. Most persons who participate in awareness activities should ideally be involved in helping students explore hands-on experiences and special interest areas. Figure 5.1 illustrates what school, family, and community experiences might be provided to help the student acquire various subcompetencies involved in the competency, knowing and exploring occupational possibilities. The state employment service (job service), vocational rehabilitation agencies, community colleges, vocational schools, and newspaper ads can be important resources to adult learners.

17.1 Identifying the Personal Values Met through Work

Students should learn very early that many personal needs and values can be met by work and can become a personally meaningful part of their lives. At the same time, they must also learn that some personal needs and values may have to be gratified through leisure activities and other pursuits. One of the teacher's major goals should be to help students identify and choose a personally meaningful set of work values that foster their desire to become productive members of society. Values such as a sense of fulfillment, self-sufficiency, personal worth, positive self-concept, success, self-support, acceptance by others, satisfying social relationships, independence, and monetary gratification are examples of needs that students can meet through working. Field trips and classroom visits can give elementary students an opportunity to interact with various types of employed people and can expose them to ways in which these workers meet personal needs and develop values. Students can begin to identify the kind of personal values they presently possess and can visualize how to meet their needs through work.

Group discussions can give students an opportunity to hear how others arrive at their decisions. Parents can discuss the positive aspects of their jobs as well as ways in which they would like to change their jobs (e.g., more

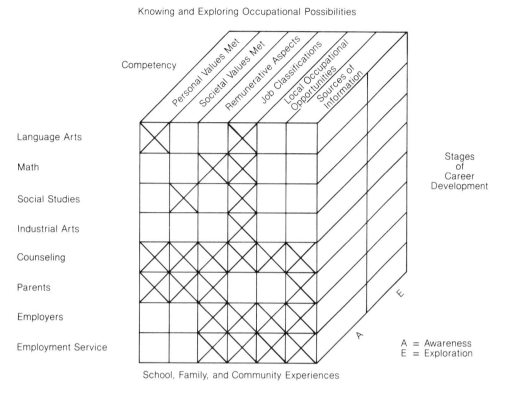

FIGURE 5.1
Examples of experiences related to knowing and exploring occupational possibilities (competency 17).

responsibility, variety, physical activity). They should explain how they meet these missing values and needs in their nonoccupational time. Secondary level students who are on job sites and former students who are employed can also discuss many features of their jobs. Adult learners can identify what personal values they met and didn't meet while working at various jobs. Other objectives that are related to this subcompetency are being able to help students recognize the importance of work for economic functioning and building self-esteem.

17.2 Identifying the Societal Values Met through Work

Students should be introduced to the ways workers affect society. Teaching activities can focus on specific ways individuals from various occupational categories contribute to the betterment of society (e.g., as police officers, fire fighters, food service workers, janitors, farmers, computer operators,

151

assembly line workers, clerks, and nurses). Teachers should cover an array of jobs, that require various amounts of skill and training. In this way, students can learn that everyone, no matter what she does, contributes meaningfully to society. Weekly field trips, speakers, or class discussions can highlight the social contributions of one or more jobs. Representatives from unions and industries, government, the Chamber of Commerce, and small businesses as well as parents should be extensively involved. Other objectives related to this subcompetency are exploring the ways that employees who have different jobs work interdependently and identifying the rewards of different occupations.

17.3 Identifying the Remunerative Aspects of Work

In general, elementary students seldom consider the differences among jobs in regard to pay. As students get older and their needs become more clearly defined, this subcompetency takes on added significance. Inherent in this process is the understanding that remuneration often depends upon such factors as the demand and supply of workers for the job, community needs for the services or goods provided by the worker, and the skill from training or formal education that students may need to perform the job. The student needs to understand reasons why people are paid to work and why there are different pay rates for different jobs. This understanding relates to several of the subcompetencies associated with competency 1, managing family finances, and can help students to calculate the amount of money they would receive from engaging in an occupation that interests them and relate this information to making wise and necessary expenditures and paying taxes. Other objectives should include identifying the different kinds of wages (e.g., piece rate or hourly, weekly, or monthly wage), and what personal needs can be met with a salary expected from jobs that interest them.

ACTIVITY TIP

Require each student to secure information on *one* job of interest per week for several weeks each semester. A "job information sheet" should be developed and then kept by the student. On the left side of a sheet of paper, students should record the name of each job they investigate. The following information is recorded for each job: company, salary, training required, hours worked, and job duties. (This information might be taken from the Job Analysis Form presented on p. 171 if it is used.) Parents can help the student investigate the jobs and complete the sheet. Weekly class discussions cover the jobs that the students have investigated and possible reasons for their salary level. A master list of community jobs can be developed to depict pertinent information relative to remunerative aspects.

17.4 Understanding How Jobs Are Classified into Different Occupational Systems

During the elementary years, students should be able to identify the rudiments of major categories of jobs, particularly those that are relevant to their specific interests. At first, jobs can be classified primarily as white or blue collar, skilled or unskilled, and according to type of work, training, or required education. Students in secondary and adult programs can use information about job and occupational clusters contained in the *Dictionary of Occupational Titles* (DOT), *Occupational Outlook Handbook, Guide for Occupational Exploration* (GOE), and other guides that can add more specificity to learning activities. Teachers should request a representative from the local employment service to explain how students may use major job categories and major criteria of other occupational classification systems. To observe how jobs are classified, students should be involved in organizing and participating with employers in a careers day program. Teachers can use bulletin boards, newspapers, and other media to illustrate different occupational systems. An objective associated with this subcompetency would be to identify education, training, and reimbursement related to various occupational categories.

17.5 Identifying Occupational Opportunities Available Locally

Students should learn about various jobs in their community. After identifying community sources of occupational information, they should secure information from one source for a period of time, write it down, post it on a bulletin board, and present it to the class. Newspaper advertisements, radio announcements, flyers, and community job surveys are examples of such sources. This exercise enables students to understand and use all community sources of occupational information while learning about jobs and their availability. Students could learn this subcompetency early in the school years. For example, students who are involved in a speech therapy program can conceptualize various community occupations while they learn respective speech sounds. The therapist and teacher can provide a variety of interesting games, role-playing exercises, and other activities that will increase the student's motivation and learning. Close inspection of available jobs can help students learn more about the world of work, job differences, and requirements. Other objectives associated with this subcompetency are for students to identify appropriate sources of occupational information and determine appropriate methods of securing and using such information.

17.6 Identifying Sources of Occupational Information

Identifying sources of occupational information is closely allied to the previous subcompetency. In addition to the community sources, students should

153

become familiar with such printed information as the *Dictionary of Occupational Titles*, *Occupational Outlook Handbook*, pamphlets from various businesses and industries, and government announcements. These materials provide a wealth of information that teachers can periodically review, discuss, and make available in the school counselor's office. Another excellent service is provided by commercial publishers who have developed a host of materials in the form of filmstrips, games, records and cassettes, and guides that require students to identify the kinds of information available from each source and how they can use these sources to obtain specific information about a particular job.

"For many of us who are handicapped individuals, we can remember vividly sitting in a career ed class and saying, 'Hey, that's great for all these other folks, but I never see any handicapped role models.' I assumed that the only people who worked in the work world were non-handicapped individuals. I think there is a real need for the adult handicapped individual to offer services to school programs and for school programs and career ed programs to actively seek out positive adult handicapped role models to enhance that whole career education process."

Wyeth (1981)

---

18 Selecting and Planning Occupational Choices

With a broad perspective of the world of work and the development of a positive set of work values, the student can begin to make preliminary and tentative occupational choices. Although elementary children may promulgate occupational aspirations as part of their career development, teachers should begin serious attempts to identify and direct secondary students toward relevant occupational choices. Many professionals become concerned about encouraging students to make occupational choices too early, believing that these students will get pigeonholed by selecting inappropriate work roles. However, we believe that young adolescents, who have explored occupational possibilities and have developed personal-social skills, are ready to think seriously about their future at about the ninth grade level. However, choices at this stage must be considered subject to change as students mature from further experiences. Making occupational choices gives the student's educational program more significance by revealing that the individual can contribute to society and function as an adult. In the case of adult learners, a considerable period of unemployment or failure may have occurred. Thus a substantial period of time may pass before students can make an occupational decision.

18.1 Identifying Major Occupational Needs

As students acquire personal-social skills of self-awareness, self-confidence, socially responsible behavior, interpersonal skills, independence, and problem-solving, they should be ready to identify those major occupational needs that are presently part of their work personality. They should be able to determine whether needs such as high pay, independence, achievement, praise, responsibility, authority, use of talents and abilities, advancement, security, social service, variety, and social status are of major importance in their future work life. Group discussions on the topic, supplemented with presentations given by persons working in various occupations, should be provided so that students can make these decisions and other choices related to an appropriate work environment (e.g., outdoor vs. indoor work, sedentary vs. active, urban vs. rural settings). These discussions can serve as a basis for lively and soul searching inquiry. Teachers can also attempt to have students identify the occupational needs that persons in occupations they are interested in tend to have.

ACTIVITY TIP

Have the class construct a list of occupational needs. Ask various members of the class to define and discuss each need. After the students have identified all possible needs, teachers should construct an "occupational needs inventory" and hand it out to the students. Each student should check which needs she feels are "high" and "low." Each need should be explained again before it is rated. The students should then identify their six most important occupational needs. Students will use this list later on when they begin to examine their occupational interests and aptitudes. (The *Minnesota Importance Questionnaire* would be a good instrument to obtain for this activity. Information about the *MIQ* can be obtained from the Department of Psychology at the University of Minnesota.)

18.2 Identifying Major Occupational Interests

By ninth or tenth grade, most handicapped students should have a basic idea of occupational areas that would interest them. These decisions are related more to what they think they would like to do, for example, "help people by working in a hospital as an aide or orderly," regardless of whether the job meets all or most occupational needs and aptitudes. If the jobs that the student identifies are not within her capability or need structure, she can explore related but more appropriate ones later on. What is important is that each individual is beginning to focus on specific occupational areas or jobs based on her knowledge of occupations and self. In some situations, interest inventories can be valuable, but for the most part, interests evolve

155

from experiences and explorations in the work place. Although occupational interests are unique to each individual, students can learn how others arrived at such decisions by engaging in group interactions. Other objectives that relate to this subcompetency are to help students identify occupations that permit the pursuit of personal interests and the occupational needs that can be met from these jobs.

18.3 Identifying Occupational Aptitudes

Use of extensive vocational assessment techniques can help students understand their vocational potentials and specific aptitudes. Prior to formalized vocational assessment, students will have had some indication of job areas that they are able to learn and perform successfully. Aptitudes or abilities in the following areas should be ascertained: verbal, numerical, spatial, form perception, clerical, motor coordination, finger dexterity, manual dexterity, and mechanical. *The General Aptitude Test Battery* (GATB) of the U. S. Employment Service is one instrument for identifying the strengths and weaknesses of some students. For others, work sample batteries can be particularly beneficial and provide a better indication of aptitudes than standardized test batteries, such as the GATB. A substantial number of vocational assessment systems are now on the market and will be discussed in greater detail in the occupational guidance techniques section. Another objective associated with this subcompetency should be to help the student identify ways of developing needed aptitudes for occupational interests.

18.4 Identifying Requirements of Appropriate and Available Jobs

With a knowledge of sources of occupational information (subcompetency 6) and their major occupational needs, interests, and aptitudes, students should be ready to review the specific requirements and characteristics of appropriate and available jobs. Publications such as the *Dictionary of Occupational Titles (DOT)* should be useful for individual and group sessions. The *DOT*, published by the Department of Labor, is a compendium of over 20,000 occupations representing the majority of jobs in the country. These activities can begin seriously during the tenth grade and can become a stimulus for independent job searching and decision making. Vocational assessment adds an important dimension to realistic decision making and planning, as does community resource personnel, who can give an in-depth personal analysis of the job's characteristics. A wide range of commercial games, materials, and packages are available for students. Another objective that should be attempted is to help students identify alternate, related occupations for which they are best qualified.

18.5 Making Realistic Occupational Choices

Experiences from the previous subcompetency will help students discover many jobs that really do not meet their occupational needs, interests, or aptitudes. For those that do, a second level of decision needs to be made relative to jobs of highest preference. The demand for the occupation, required education and training, and other factors are significant at this level. Students should learn the career ladder that the occupation offers and occupations for which they might qualify. These tentative occupational choices should be based on an analysis of the whole person and be systematically determined by students, parents, employers, and school personnel. Professional guidance and counseling is important for this subcompetency. Another objective that should be attempted is for the individual to be able to identify specific work sites where the job(s) of choice is available and to try out the job.

19 Exhibiting Appropriate Work Habits and Behaviors

The competency, developing appropriate work habits and behaviors, transcends the entire educational chain from the early elementary years through adulthood and can be taught by everyone responsible for the individual's career development. Work habits are more than study habits, although both have many similar features. School personnel should emphasize the necessity of developing the work habits and behaviors that all students will need when they begin responsible jobs. At certain times, teachers may simulate working environments in the school setting to illustrate the kinds of expectations employers have of competent workers. Field trips, class speakers, and parents can also play an important role in helping students to develop this competency.

19.1 Following Directions

Employers expect their employees to follow directions accurately. These may be given either verbally or in writing and will range from very simple one-step directions to those that are complex and require several steps that employees must remember and complete. Gaming and role-playing techniques can be particularly effective in helping students develop these skills. Exercises will need to begin early and be repeated intermittently throughout the grade levels so that all students, especially those who have a lower ability in this area, can learn and retain these skills. After students have learned the lower order steps, they should gradually learn how to follow more complicated directions. Another objective should be for the student to be able to perform a series of tasks in the home requiring simple to complex written instructions.

19.2 Working with Others

The inability to get along with co-workers and supervisors is one of the most common reasons people fail on their jobs. Students must learn work expectations, and the school can become a fertile ground for teaching these interactive and cooperative skills. Teachers should create an environment that promotes development of these work skills by encouraging students to practice interacting and cooperating with others. Field trips, role playing, and group discussions can also be used to illustrate and stimulate discussion on reasons for working with others and the individual's importance in cooperative efforts, and can help students identify positive and negative aspects of working together. Another objective might be to simulate actual work environments by developing projects that require students to interact and cooperate with others before they can complete a specific task.

ACTIVITY TIP

Set up an assembly line operation with the assistance of industrial workers from the community. The assembly line operation should be as realistic as possible. Have the workers explain their jobs, particularly as they relate to this competency area. Initiate the work and assess the students on their ability to work with others, accept supervision, and master other subcompetencies related to this competency. Some students may be supervisors or assume other roles associated with this type of work. At the end of the day, class discussions should ensue about the group's performance and future efforts. Rate each student on work habits and behaviors and provide individual feedback that will increase the student's awareness of strong points and areas where they need to improve. (Further discussion and ideas related to this type of activity are provided later in the chapter.)

19.3 Working at a Satisfactory Rate

It is important for the student to learn that people are employed to make money for the employer. This requires that students learn how to do work correctly at a sufficient speed. Teachers should require students to complete certain work activities within a specific period of time so that they form the habit as well as learn the concept. Time standards can be established for various work tasks in and out of the school, and teachers should chart the student's progress until she meets the criterion. Students should participate in establishing reasonable time standards so they can understand how and why time or piece rates are determined. Employers and workers can be useful in conveying the importance of this subcompetency, especially if these skills will help students earn more money. Other objectives associated with this subcompetency should be to help the student identify satisfactory rates required for various jobs of interest and reasons jobs must be performed at certain rates of speed.

19.4   Accepting Supervision

Although accepting supervision is related to previous subcompetencies, it is specific to various methods of supervision that are found in the work place. Supervision can range from being infrequent and indirect to very frequent and direct. Supervision can be constructive, critical, or unfair. It is important for the student to understand the various forms of supervision and how they should react to supervision under different conditions. Role playing is a viable method of presenting students with various situations and types of supervision so they can learn appropriate ways of responding. Role-playing activities can be followed by group discussions that focus on different responses that can help students develop other methods of handling the situation. The teacher can also use various methods of supervising class members and then get reactions to the method. Other objectives that can be attempted for students are for them to observe and discuss supervisory policies in several work places and identify various responses that can be used for various types of supervisory practices.

Learning appropriate work habits and behaviors in a realistic setting is an important aspect of vocational preparation.

159

19.5 Recognizing the Importance of Attendance and Punctuality

The classroom situation can be organized to emphasize the importance of attendance and punctuality in the work place. A classroom time clock is one method that can be used to promote this concept. The student should learn why attendance and punctuality are important to the employer (e.g., loss of production time, business income, and meeting deadlines). Students should learn acceptable and unacceptable reasons for lateness and absenteeism, and what the consequences are in both situations. Once again, employers and workers from various businesses and industries can be effective in presenting their own cases and company policies. Another objective that students should be required to meet is to identify appropriate actions to take if they need to be late or absent from work.

19.6 Meeting Demand for Quality Work

Students will need to know about quality standards for various types of jobs, particularly those that interest them. They should meet such standards on their work assignments, understand when and why such standards are not achieved, and work until they have met standards or until teachers have ascertained whether students are able to perform at that level. Elementary students should strive for quality while they are engaged in projects. Students can be assigned as checkers to ascertain whether work has met the job requirements and can participate in discussions conducted to point out problems. The secondary students' job explorations and try-outs establish the expected criteria that will be used to evaluate their performance. Another objective of this subcompetency should be to have the student perform simulated work tasks at minimum quality standards.

19.7 Developing Occupational Safety Skills

Many employers are afraid to employ handicapped people because they believe that these individuals will have more accidents. Thus, teachers should emphasize occupational safety skills to minimize the number of potential accidents that could occur and result in the individual's dismissal. Films, field trips, role playing, and class discussions are particularly important in helping students understand potential safety hazards and the necessary precautions they may need to take to avoid unnecessary accidents. Before placement on a community job site, students should be thoroughly prepared to handle all conceivable accidents that could occur at the work place. This subcompetency should be taught at all levels of the school program so that by the time the students leave school, they are well versed in safety practices. Other objectives associated with this subcompetency should require the student to identify major reasons for practicing safety on the job and potential safety hazards that exist in various types of occupations.

20 Exhibiting Sufficient Physical-Manual Skills

Occupations that the majority of handicapped individuals obtain require physical stamina, endurance, coordination, strength, and dexterity. The jobs that are available to the many students with handicaps require considerable fine or gross motor dexterity, standing, pulling, pushing, lifting, and carrying abilities. Development of adequate physical-manual skills should begin shortly after handicapped students enter school. Teachers can design class activities to promote the use and development of skills that will help students to experience a great deal of personal success, pride, and satisfaction. Thus a concerted focus needs to be made in this area.

20.1 Demonstrating Satisfactory Balance and Coordination

The physical education instructor could assume a major responsibility in evaluating and designing specific individual activities that can improve each student's physical capacities. Teachers may need to consult a registered occupational therapist who can design specific tasks that measure and develop an orthopedically handicapped student's balance and coordination skills. Students should keep a cumulative record of their performance in various activities. This can document progress in terms of functioning level and can help them target new goals. Competitive games and charts may motivate students by drawing attention to the importance of these skills. Other objectives that should be met are to have students identify the relationship between balance and coordination to the world of work and to job performance and requirements of various jobs.

20.2 Demonstrating Satisfactory Manual Dexterity

A number of manual dexterity tests may assist people who direct the development of the student's manual dexterity. The *Purdue Pegboard*, *Minnesota Rate of Manipulation*, *Daily Sensorimotor Training Activities*, *Wide Range Employment Sample Test*, and *Pennsylvania Bi-Manual* are examples of standardized instruments for evaluating and developing the student's manual dexterity. Evaluation of students should begin early and should continue to serve as a basis for determining what work tasks are within the physical capabilities of the student. Other objectives are to help students identify interests in occupations that require a fair degree of manual dexterity and reasons for developing a sufficient degree of dexterity for occupational and community life.

20.3 Demonstrating Satisfactory Stamina and Endurance

Most jobs require a given amount of physical and mental stamina and endurance. The physical education instructor can assume a significant role in designing special programs to develop the student's skills in this area. Students should chart their progress toward attainment of criterion levels of performance. This type of program can be used at home where purposeful tasks and responsibilities that relate to other subcompetencies can be designed. Several commercial programs are available for this subcompetency, but these would be unnecessary if the school personnel can develop the resources and activities within and outside of the schools that promote development of these skills. Other objectives that should be incorporated for this subcompetency are to require the student to identify jobs where stamina and endurance are absolutely critical and ways of building these skills to meet individual needs.

20.4 Demonstrating Satisfactory Sensory Discrimination

Many jobs require ability to distinguish sounds, shapes, sizes, and colors. The *Talent Assessment Program* is a work sample/task battery that relates the student's sensory discrimination skills to vocational potential. Many teachers have also devised their own methods by using everyday objects. Evaluation of those skills should occur early in the school program. Other objectives that we suggest are for students to be able to identify the need for sensory discrimination on jobs and the sensory discrimination they may need for jobs that they are interested in.

21 Obtaining a Specific Occupational Skill

Many professionals strongly believe that students do not need to leave the formal educational system with a saleable, entry level occupational skill. Their arguments are that training can be best provided later, that too many other types of learning are necessary, and that secondary students are too young for specific occupational training. Although these arguments may be valid, handicapped individuals need to acquire a skill before they leave the secondary school because

1. Training facilities for handicapped persons beyond the secondary level do not have enough specialists who can effectively meet the needs of handicapped individuals.

2. Many post-secondary programs are unattractive and dehumanizing or too long. Requirements for these programs are often stringent and unnecessary.

3. If the student can acquire a specific occupational skill before she leaves the secondary school, the student, parents, instructors, employers, and significant others will have more confidence in her ability to learn a saleable skill.

4. Training in a specific occupational skill results in development and improvement of other competency areas (e.g., self-confidence, socially responsible behavior, interpersonal skills, independence, problem solving, communication skills, occupational awareness, work habits and behaviors, and physical-manual skills).

5. Some handicapped individuals may need more intensive training in skills than other nonhandicapped workers.

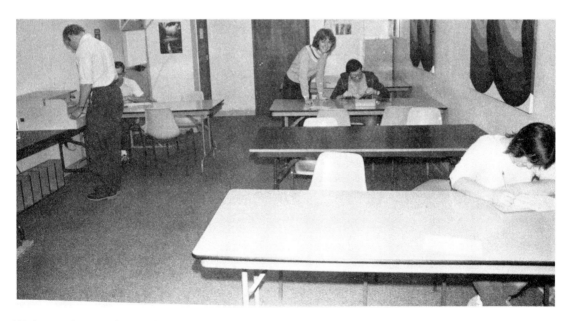

Work samples can be used to assess the student's specific aptitudes and skills.

6. Training results in a meaningful curriculum emphasis and makes other instruction relevant and reality-based.
7. Training provides handicapped students with an extra advantage over nonhandicapped individuals whom they will be competing against for similar jobs.
8. Attainment of an occupational skill can reveal higher order potentials that students can pursue after the secondary program.
9. It helps eliminate unrealistic occupational choices early enough so students receive training that is more appropriate to the individual's needs and abilities.

Although some students may receive training in post-secondary programs, they should try to obtain a specific occupational skill during the high school years. In addition to the other daily living, personal-social, and occupational skills that are important to the growth of a work personality, students should select a training area that fosters awareness of personal and occupational interests. Selection should be a carefully designed process of career development that student, parents, instructors, and significant others can agree upon.

Instruction in daily living curriculum areas may reveal the student's special interests and aptitude for occupations that are in the clerical, maintenance, personal care, food service, computer, service, recreation and leisure, or transportation fields. Personal-social curriculum areas should reveal the most suitable work environment for the individual (i.e., noisy, calm, pressured, interactive, flexible, restrictive, closely supervised, routine, reinforcing, and impersonal). The occupational curriculum area should also reflect the student's work values, needs, interests, choices, work habits and behaviors, and physical capacities. Thus, in the process of "becoming," a work personality emerges and forms to the extent that reasonable training choices can be determined.

22 Seeking, Securing, and Maintaining Employment

After leaving the formal educational system many students have difficulty seeking, securing, and maintaining employment. Apparently efforts at teaching this competency have failed to help many students retain this knowledge and ability over time. This is a major downfall of handicapped individuals in the community and is especially unfortunate for those who have been through an extensive educational program. Educators should begin teaching this competency in the tenth grade and should continue instructing their students in this area each semester thereafter. Many commercial materials are available for teaching this competency, although professionals may want to develop their own.

22.1   Searching for a Job

The ability to develop a logical step-by-step method of searching for a job is a crucial subcompetency. Knowing how to explore sources of information about possible jobs is a beginning. Teachers can help students develop this subcompetency by using bulletin boards to depict the steps that students can take to search for a job and explore various sources of information. Field trips to agencies that help people find jobs, role playing, games, and guest speakers can also help students to gain new perspectives in this area. Job descriptions and announcements, advertisements, and commercial materials on job-seeking skills are also available. The Singer Company has produced a job survival skills package and the Minneapolis Rehabilitation Center has developed a job-seeking skills kit that also merits consideration. Other objectives related to this subcompetency include identifying steps involved in searching for a job, researching a specific job, and following through on a job lead.

22.2   Applying for a Job

An important objective in vocational programming should be to prepare the individual to apply for her own job. Mastery of this subcompetency is another indice that reflects the student's ability and independence for vocational functioning. To demonstrate this, the student must become familiar with job application forms and procedures involved in applying for jobs. Beginning in at least the tenth grade, students should learn words that are typically used on application forms and interviews. Students should spend a great deal of time reviewing and completing application forms, learning job vocabulary, role playing, and collecting personal data needed for job applications. Another objective that students should be required to meet is to identify those factors they consider important to them in applying for jobs.

22.3   Interviewing for a Job

Interviewing skills are inextricably related to the other subcompetencies and should receive careful attention from educators. Employers, workers, and other community resources can help to prepare the student for an interview. The student must understand and learn steps involved in securing an interview, what to say and do when requesting an interview on the phone or in person, and how to handle herself in the actual situation. Role playing, group discussions, films, speakers and demonstrations, games and commercial materials, videotapes, and other techniques are all highly recommended. Other objectives for students should be to complete a simulated job interview in an actual business establishment and practice dressing for and transporting self to job interviews.

22.4 Adjusting to Competitive Standards

After students have secured a job, they must perform at the standard expected of other workers. If skills in adjusting to competitive standards are overlooked, former students may lose their jobs because of a misunderstanding of what is expected of workers and how they can advance their position and pay. Employers and workers present this kind of information and conduct on-site visits to various job locations so that students can observe what employers expect out of workers at various jobs and how this can be best achieved. Other objectives for students should be to identify jobs of interest and their expected standards and how improvements can be achieved by the individual.

22.5 Maintaining Post-School Occupational Adjustment

Occupational adjustment skills are concerned with how former students can resolve potential problems that they may encounter after they have obtained a job. Former students are a fertile source of information who can describe the most significant adjustments that students may need to make in a work environment. Role play depicting problem areas is a recommended technique that teachers can use to illustrate effective behaviors. Students should keep a notebook of techniques for future use. This subcompetency should be given considerable emphasis during the latter part of the high school program. Another objective for the student would be to identify sources of assistance for problems that students cannot personally resolve.

ACTIVITY TIP

The students should invite former students back to school to discuss their jobs (or lack of them) and should develop a set of questions relating to post-school adjustment. Discussions should include problems that former students encounter, how they handle those problems, what they feel the students need to do to be successful, and influences that affect their present career functioning. Later students should have the opportunity to observe former students working at their actual jobs. (The former students should be encouraged to bring in people who helped them adjust. Some former students may not cooperate in this activity because of their desire to no longer be identified with their past.)

OCCUPATIONAL GUIDANCE TECHNIQUES

Three competencies involved in occupational guidance activities are (17) knowing and exploring occupational possibilities; (18) selecting and planning occupational choices; and (22) seeking, securing, and maintaining employment. Students should know about and explore a variety of occupations before they select and plan appropriate occupational choices. Hands-on experiences will enable students to explore various occupations so that, by the time they reach high school, they will be prepared to make logical but tentative occupational choices. Students should also obtain skills that will help them to seek, secure, and maintain employment before they graduate from high school. School counselors can also contribute to the occupational guidance activities by helping students design and select appropriate types of occupational experiences. Special educators should work closely with the counselors on this task.

Attempts to generate lists of specific jobs that are appropriate for various types of handicapped individuals are generally fruitless. Blind people work in hundreds of different occupations at all levels and work as phone repair persons, welders, lathe operators, teachers, lawyers, and farmers. Homebound individuals have typically been engaged in small crafts and telephone answering or sales work, but with the advent of the computer, opportunities as programmers and data entry operators have become available (Kokaska, 1976). Phillips (1975) identified 515 distinct career opportunities for the deaf in three types of organizations: business and industry, professional and trade associations, and institutions of higher education for the deaf. Occupations such as scientist, teacher, accountant, clerk, salesperson, machinist, and bench worker are examples of the many possibilities that exist for this group. Robinson and Morrison (1981) report that mildly mentally retarded persons qualify for 6,033 out of 12,175 jobs contained in the *Dictionary of Occupational Titles (DOT)*. The U. S. Department of Labor (1983) has also found that manufacturing—led by such industries as computers and instruments—is expected to account for almost one new job in six between 1982 and 1995. Service industries will continue to generate most of the new jobs in the country, just as they have in the past. Strong growth of employment opportunities is projected in such industries as medical care and business and professional services.

There is probably no limit to what most handicapped individuals could achieve if they were provided with more opportunities to expand their occupational horizons and had more relevant and challenging training and employment opportunities. Students who have not acquired the three occupational guidance competencies will probably experience considerable difficulties after they leave school. Rehabilitation and other vocationally-oriented programs will probably be necessary to help handicapped individuals develop these competencies adequately. The rest of this section will present some of the techniques or strategies that will help handicapped students and adults learn more about their vocational potentials and make rational career decisions. Although vocational assessment is a major guidance technique, it will be discussed later in chapter 9.

"The physically disabled person experiences a career development process in much the same manner as the able-bodied. The careers pursued are based upon the direction and thrust of previous choices made throughout the individual's life."

Palmer (1980)

Counseling

Decision-making skills are the cornerstone of career education. If individuals can be provided with appropriate educational experiences, they should be able to make more effective decisions. Counseling may help individuals learn how to take risks, solve problems, select from alternatives, and explore their potentials in relationship to the occupational possibilities that are available in the real world. Counseling should be the responsibility of a variety of helping professionals who should use the same techniques in counseling handicapped individuals as they would use in counseling anyone else. Some basic principles for successfully providing this important service are the following:

- Trust is one of the most important elements in the counseling process.
- People can learn to make logical career choices and decisions.
- To build trust, helpers must be able to genuinely respect, accept, and empathize with the individual.
- Self-concept is one of the most important determinants of career and personal development.
- Individuals are capable of learning new behaviors and extinguishing inappropriate ones.
- Significant others influence the behavior and decisions that individuals make.
- An individual's psychological needs, beliefs, goals, and values are inextricably related to occupational decision making and satisfaction.
- Helpers should use a personalized, humanistic, systematic, and flexible approach in responding to the various characteristics and needs of handicapped individuals.
- A reciprocal relationship between counselor and client is necessary.
- Each person is a unique individual and may need a different counseling approach.
- Counseling is a learning process for everyone.

Major goals of vocational counseling are to help individuals learn about the world of work; identify appropriate experiences, courses, and persons who can assist in occupational awareness and exploration activities; choose more specific vocational aptitudes, interests, and needs; determine occupational training areas; and obtain job seeking and securing skills. Counselors should listen to what handicapped individuals say about their interests, needs, and abilities. However counselors should also consider the following:

1. Handicapped individuals generally have fewer work experiences than nonhandicapped persons and therefore, their concept of the world of work may be quite narrow.
2. Many handicapped individuals have a long history of failure and rejection and therefore, may underestimate their potentials and aspirations.
3. Some individuals may have difficulty understanding more complex verbal interchanges and may try to mask that they are not comprehending what is being discussed.
4. Many intellectually limited individuals can benefit from shorter but more frequent interactions in which specific assignments are given.
5. Audiovisual equipment, blackboards, role playing, and other non-didactic techniques enhance counseling efforts.

We believe that effective occupational guidance and counseling should provide the individual with more than occupational information, testing, and field experience. Occupational guidance and counseling should be a learning-oriented experience that involves an open, personal relationship between a well-trained counselor or special educator and an individual. Counselors should encourage the individual to explore her interests, needs, and abilities by actively listening to and empathizing with her feelings and thoughts. The individual should emerge from this experience with greater awareness of herself and confidence in her ability to take responsibility for herself. The counselor or special educator should try to direct the individual to make realistic occupational choices and training decisions. Counseling is a process that must be purposely built into the educational program so that it evolves over a period of time and is open to change as students gain new information and experience.

"If career education is to be a viable framework for American education and realistically prepare students to function as well-adjusted adults, vocational assessment must become the responsibility of the public schools."

Sitlington & Wimmer (1978)

Job Analysis

Job analysis and task analysis for occupational guidance may not seem necessary but in our opinion, they are effective methods of learning about work, specific jobs, and interest areas. A job analysis is a systematic way of observing jobs to determine what the worker does, how she does it, why she does it, and the skill involved in its performance. Jobs should be analyzed precisely as they presently exist, excluding temporarily assigned tasks. A detailed job description should include all tasks and requirements that contribute to successful performance. Task analysis is the process of breaking a task into smaller steps or skills that are required to complete the task.

Job analysis can become a powerful career awareness and exploration tool for handicapped students. When students take field trips to various work sites, they should fill out a simple job analysis form, such as the one depicted in figure 5.2, so that they can become aware of major characteristics and requirements of various jobs. The class and teacher should review each job analysis before the student includes it in her "Job Information Notebook." Students should be encouraged to ask each other questions relative to their separate analysis. Peers or teachers may need to help lower ability students gather and report the proper information. When a student becomes interested in a specific job, she can begin a task analysis. Once again, students become intimately involved in the task and learn a great deal about the nature of work by themselves and from other class members. In group counseling sessions, the analysis can become a focus of discussion and lively action. Once students have become more conscious and efficient in analyzing jobs, they should be able to use and understand occupational literature and other media. Job and task analysis is an important component of an occupational guidance program and should be part of elementary as well as secondary programs. It complements other career awareness and exploration techniques and, in our opinion, is a necessary and worthwhile endeavor for all students.

Simulations of Business and Industry

Establishing a simulated business in or out of the school setting can be a realistic, hands-on experience that can add considerable relevance to both occupational guidance and preparation efforts. Students can assume roles with varying degrees of responsibility so they can get a better perspective of what the job entails.

Career City developed by the Quincy Public Schools in Illinois, is an innovative example of a simulation. *Career City* consists of seven small buildings, which are located in the Resource Center of the elementary school. A greenhouse, grocery store, bank, bakery, photography shop, barber and

Job Title _____ DOT Title _____
Name of Firm _____ Code Number _____
Date of Analysis _____ Name of Analyst _____

A. Description of Work Performed _____
_____
_____

B. Job Requirements. Circle number of those required and comment if needed.

1. Adding _____ 11. Use telephone_____
2. Subtracting _____ 12. Lift, carry, push, pull _____
3. Multiplying _____ 13. Walk, run, climb, balance _____
4. Dividing _____ 14. Stoop, kneel, crouch, crawl _____
5. Make change _____ 15. Stand or sit _____
6. Use measuring devices _____ 16. Use hand tools _____
7. Read _____ 17. Operate machines _____
8. Write _____ 18. Other _____
9. Talk _____ 19. Other _____
10. Follow instructions _____ 20. Other _____

C. Working Conditions. Circle number that describes the job and comment if needed.

1. Extremely hot _____ 8. Good lighting _____
2. Extremely cold _____ 9. Good ventilation _____
3. Humid _____ 10. Tension and pressure _____
4. Wet _____ 11. Distracting conditions_____
5. Dry _____ 12. Hazardous _____
6. Dusty and dirty _____ 13. Work with others _____
7. Noisy _____ 14. Other _____

D. Training Required _____

E. Salary _____

F. Hours Worked _____

G. Good features of the Job _____
_____

H. Poor features of the Job _____
_____
_____

FIGURE 5.2
Example of a job analysis form.

beauty shop, and residential house are depicted in 5-by-5 foot structures, painted and decorated, and transported by special education students from the senior high school program. The major objective of *Career City* is to supplement the classroom curriculum by providing realistic, hands-on career experiences. This learning activity provides elementary school students with an array of career awareness experiences. Students learn to deposit checks in the bank, grow flowers and vegetables in the greenhouse, and use cameras and viewers in the photography lab. Each career has a packet with all the necessary information and equipment that students may need to participate in the many learning activities. Many nonspecial education students also take advantage of this career awareness opportunity. All students seem to have a better understanding of each career after they have participated in the career awareness activities of *Career City* (Bocke & Price, 1976).

Simulation of an assembly line operation is another example of an activity that can help early elementary students develop career awareness. Students can be provided with information about industry and manufacturing occupations while they experience the importance of cooperation among workers in production efforts and friendly competition and pride in doing quality work. Assembly line workers can visit the class, and field trips can be arranged to certain industries.

At an elementary school in Plainview, Minnesota, students in grades 4 through 6 managed a school store. Their first step in organizing the venture was to gain approval and suggestions from their Career Education Citizen's Advisory Board. The board suggested that students approach local businesses about their plan for a school store, which was wholeheartedly supported. One sixth grade class was responsible for ordering basic supplies—pencils, crayons, notebook paper, and erasers. A board of directors was elected to set up guidelines for operating the store. The board elected a store manager and personnel director, who developed job assignments and duties: sales people, stock people, and an advertising department. The advertising department consisted of several classes who competed against one another to see who could invent the best advertising gimmicks and promotions. A second venture by the school was a record shop. The school asked several radio stations to save records that were no longer in use. Students made purchases in cash from the record shop or traded used paperback books. A bookstore and travel bureau were other ventures that the school developed (Johnson, 1976). Haring (1978) described a successful teacher-designed career education program that took place in an economics class at Scottsdale High School in Arizona. Two hundred seventy-five students formed their own business enterprises that became part of a career education program called *Project Work*. The students created 89 companies that produced, advertised, and marketed products and provided services for fellow students or community members. Once operation was completed, the company divided the profits in various ways. Some business enterprises were corporations and paid their stockholders. Others were partnerships and sole proprietorships. Students paid appropriate taxes and licensing fees to the student government. *Project Work* was also conducted at a less sophisticated level in the lower grades. Students felt the project made them more aware of their interests and abilities and improved their attitudes and interest toward school and the teachers.

Business simulations are extremely effective in motivating students to learn academic material, become more knowledgeable about the world of work, and develop occupational interests and skills. School personnel can use simulations to integrate handicapped students into business operations and activities with nonhandicapped students. The potentials of this technique are limited only by creativity, time, and financial constraints.

Career Seminar

The two major purposes of career seminars are to help each student (1) recognize her individual strengths, interests, values, successes and goals, and (2) explore different careers that she may pursue. Career seminars can be semi-structured and meet once a week throughout the semester. Varelas (1976) recommends a modified human potential seminar group process approach that focuses on reinforcing the positive strengths and abilities of each student. During the seminar, the student describes three strengths, three successful experiences, and the three most important values in her life. Students also set short-term goals that they attempt to achieve each week.

A short paper is required covering five specific topics: (1) brief description of a career choice, (2) education required for the career choice, (3) expected salary of the career choice, (4) environment and location of the career choice, and (5) future outlook of the career choice. The key to success is to keep the group experience positive and reinforce individual strengths and abilities. The seminar can inspire students to ask "Who am I?" "What is my career choice?" and appears to be a successful method of helping students to grow socially, emotionally, and academically.

Teachers can encourage students to think about occupations by asking them to select an object and identify all the people whose work makes it possible for that object to come into the students' hands. The object may be in the category of food, shelter, clothing, toys, or equipment. For example, planters, irrigators, fruit pickers, and sorters, crate makers, manufacturers of trucks or planes, shipping personnel, delivery people, and grocers are all occupations that are responsible for delivering an orange into the student's

173

hand. The students could also list five or more occupations that they have seen on television and feel they might enjoy. The students then have to provide reasons for choosing them. Teachers may also ask students to identify two careers that they do not feel they would like and explain why (*Career Education Workshop*, 1977).

Field Trips and Speakers

We have repeatedly emphasized that students should visit a variety of work places because direct experience increases the student's comprehension and motivation. Teachers should make field trips part of the curriculum. Field trips should be planned carefully to represent various business establishments in the community. Prior planning with the company should permit the time for students to observe and record pertinent job analysis information and to speak with some of the people who perform various jobs. The jobs to be viewed should generally be those the group would most likely be able to assume themselves. Classroom discussions should cover the importance, characteristics, and opportunities associated with each job.

Class speakers are a valuable adjunct to field trips. In some cases, it may be advantageous to have someone from the business speak to the class prior to a tour. She may distribute information, show films, answer questions, identify points of interest, and explain what the students are going to see. In other instances, it may be more beneficial to invite the speaker into the classroom after the trip. Workers should also be invited to such presentations. Former students can also be effective in eliciting the student's interest in and understanding of the industry and its jobs.

Career Information Center

A career information center can be integral to an occupational guidance-delivery system. The center can provide students with a place to gather information about occupations and plan their occupational future with a counselor. This learning and planning should relate to what the student is receiving in classroom career-related activities. The center should also be a place where students can talk with other students about occupations. It should have a sufficient supply of materials so that students can find answers to career-related questions. Career information centers can be established at a fairly reasonable cost. Free materials are available from businesses, industries, and various organizations.

Mattson (1976) identified eight major considerations for establishing a career information center. The location of the center should be in the line of traffic so it is accessible for drop-ins, as well as appointments. It should be near the library but not part of the school's administrative center. The center should be large and quiet enough to accommodate material review, testing, student-counselor planning, parent conferences, and discussions with parents and employers. Staff should include vocational counselors, volunteers, student aides, and an identifiable budget for salaries, materials, publicity, equipment, and travel should be made. Some essential materials are *Occupational Outlook Handbook, Dictionary of Occupational Titles, Guide for Occupational Exploration*, subscriptions to career-related publications, *Encyclopedia of Careers*, a file of brochures on jobs, several regional newspapers, career-related library books, employment opportunity information, and audio-visual materials on interviewing and job seeking skills. Furniture and equipment should include copying equipment, bulletin boards, overhead projectors, projection screens, a microfiche viewer, conference and work tables, furniture for conversational settings, display racks, bookcases, files, and desks and chairs. Daily notices should appear in the staff and school newspaper, on flyers to parents, and bulletin boards, and announcements should be made at staff meetings and homerooms. The center could provide the following services: career counseling on an individual basis; career information to classes; career guidance material; administration and interpretation of aptitude, achievement, and interest tests; financial aid information; military information; information on employment trends, qualifications, and compensation; curriculum planning; resource center for faculty, staff, and parents; and liaison between the school and community, business, and other groups.

Many commercial career information systems have become available. The Career Information System (CIS) is a career decision-making program developed by the Appalachia Educational Laboratory (AEL). CIS is an organization and management system for career information resources and is based upon 12 areas and 66 work groups of the *Guide for Occupational Exploration (GOE)* written by the Department of Labor. AEL developed an educational version of the GOE and added a qualifications profile containing worker characteristics and traits that are common among the occupations contained in each group. Another example is the *Guidance Information System* (GIS) that is available from Houghton-Mifflin and Time Share Corporation. The GIS is a comprehensive, computer-based information system that has been used by several vocational rehabilitation centers for career information and exploration. Users search through the information files based on their personal needs and interests and can obtain print-outs about jobs or schools that best meet these needs. Many other career planning programs are also available to interested persons.

OCCUPATIONAL PREPARATION TECHNIQUES

Specific and formalized occupational preparation efforts should occur at all levels. The development of appropriate work habits and behaviors (19), sufficient physical-manual skills (20), and a specific occupational skill (21) are competencies that are related to occupational preparation. Teachers can use a variety of activities to prepare individuals for occupations. Elementary students should be assigned several different work projects and home responsibilities. Activities for students enrolled in junior high through adult education include complex work projects, on-campus jobs, business simulations, career exploration materials, work sample systems, and home training. Vocational education courses, on-the-job training, use of rehabilitation facilities, and a vocational and career development center within the school or community facility are additional sources of preparing senior high and adult education students for the world of work. Beginning at the elementary level, occupational activities should be designed in a systematic skill-building manner that combines a variety of methods for occupational preparation.

Work Tasks and Projects

Teachers can begin the occupational preparation aspect of career development by assigning elementary students to a variety of work tasks that include keeping the erasers and blackboards clean, posting and keeping bulletin boards in order, cleaning up and putting away materials, organizing chairs for various classroom activities, cutting out posters and other classroom materials, and a host of other prevocational tasks. In addition, stu-

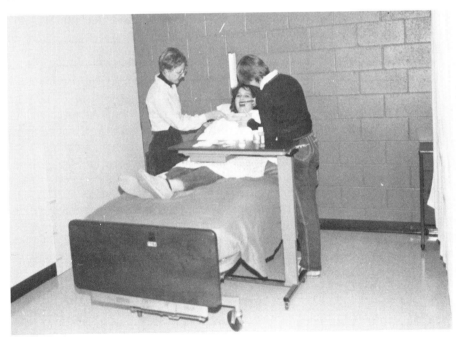

Some nurses' aid programs can provide high school and adult education students with an opportunity to develop occupational skills.

dents can become involved in various work projects during the year such as making collages, Christmas cards, and decorations; making presents for people in nursing homes; working with wood and learning other crafts; growing, collecting, and identifying plants; preparing stage sets and rehearsing for a class play; decorating Easter eggs; and building model stores and making products out of blocks to sell. Painting is also a particularly effective prevocational activity that helps students build physical-manual skills, work habits and behaviors, and personal-social competencies.

Most of these activities are generally conducted in elementary programs for handicapped and nonhandicapped students and should be emphasized even more for handicapped students in a purposeful manner. If the teacher emphasizes the relationship between these activities and the world of work, students will be able to judge how they feel about working at various jobs in the community. In this way, educators can plan a purposeful sequence of activities that are related to career education goals and objectives.

The family needs to be closely informed and involved in each series of prevocational activities for their children and can supplement the school's efforts with work activities in the home. Teachers should encourage parents to work with their children on school projects, both at school and at home, and help students to pursue specific interests and aptitudes when the school is no longer able to do so. Cooperation will help school personnel and family members to become closer and appreciate one another and, in the long run, will enhance the student's career development.

Simulations of Business and Industry. The simulated business approach mentioned in the occupational guidance section is also a specific occupational preparation technique. The students' experiences with *Career City* and the job analyses they have conducted should help them develop a relatively accurate idea of the job or jobs that they would be suited for within a simulated business. Thus the student can be "hired" to assume various employee roles within *Career City*. Creation of *Career City* or a simulated business will take considerable creativity, thought, time, cooperation among disciplines, and probably, money. However these activities attract and benefit students and involve the school and community in an innovative and effective educational technique. Business and industry can offer technical assistance and materials, and parents and school personnel can use their expertise to help students develop the skills they need to succeed at various jobs within Career City.

"Career development and work experience are critical and must go along with academic training. Young people with disabilities must have a chance to experience varying kinds of professions, as do other people in our society."

Roberts (1979)

On- and Off-Campus Training. The school cafeteria, library, gym, district warehouse, and housekeeping, clerical, and groundskeeping departments of schools are all resources that teachers can use in preparing handicapped students for various occupations. Students are generally placed on a work site according to their interest and ability and, in many cases, the job functions as a prevocational or career exploration experience. But if enough supervision and objectivity can be provided at the work place, these placements are also valuable in helping to identify student interests and training potentials. Care must be taken that the student is exposed to *all* aspects of the job and is not used primarily to do work that no one else wants to do.

Off-campus occupational preparation is one of the most realistic and competitive parts of the school program. Some students may need the services of a rehabilitation facility (or sheltered workshop) before they are placed at a real job site. Such a placement gives the student an opportunity to get away from the more academically-oriented atmosphere of the school so that she can learn how to get to the agency, meet and interact with other people, respond to the vocational nature and requirements of the facility, and realize that she is getting close to the time of leaving school and finding employment.

Off-campus training should begin as early as possible in the high school program, at least by the sophomore year, and will depend on the individual student and her level and needs. Based on the student's vocational assessment and educational background, reasonable decisions should be made regarding appropriate work sites and jobs. Vocational plans should be systematic and must meet the needs of the student. Teachers or counselors must carefully review the work site and have a clear understanding with those individuals for whom the student will interact. Career development at the work site must be assured; therefore, expectations for the student and procedures for reaching these goals must be outlined with the work supervisors.

Many placement personnel believe that the students should receive pay for the work they do on off-campus jobs. Although this is perhaps desirable, students may think that the primary purpose of their working experience is to earn money. They may select certain work experiences primarily because of the money they can receive rather than the intrinsic exploration and preparation values. If money becomes more important than the value of this experience, the students will eventually suffer. It might be better to conduct these placements as if the students were taking a vocational education skill-building course. Then if they become proficient and productive after a period of time, monetary benefits can be made available. Teachers should consider this controversial issue when designing a program.

178

Skill Development Systems

In recent years several commercially developed vocational development and training programs have been designed. Some examples of these skills development systems are presented in this section. Talent Assessment, Inc., has developed the *Talent Development Program (TDP)* primarily for the moderately mentally handicapped individual, although it has been used successfully with persons who have other handicaps. The materials consist of four box-shaped training modules that contain tools and hardware. The instructor provides progressive levels of training, from the simplest sorting and assembly of materials to complete assembly of the modules. The goal is to help the individual acquire basic work skills that they will need for future training and employment considerations—finger dexterity, eye-hand coordination, accuracy, work speed, size and shape discrimination, following directions, use of hand tools, spatial perception, working with others, work vocabulary, etc. Although this activity can be group administered, students or clients can proceed at their own pace.

Some special education students who are enrolled in vocational-technical programs can qualify for training in auto mechanics.

The *Prevocational Training Center*, developed by the Pleasantville Educational Supply Corporation, Pleasantville, NY, offers four training programs. Trainable students can use the Mail Sorting Training Program to learn job skills and work behaviors. An Instructor's Guide accompanies a Collating, Sort, and Filing Program that consists of several hundred job cards and program objectives relative to colors, shapes, alphabet, numbers, and essential vocabulary. The Small Parts Training Program teaches students how to work on an assembly line, sort nuts and bolts, assemble and bag products, remove staples and labels, and disassemble items using six work stations. The Time Incentive Program teaches students how to maximize the rate and accuracy of their work and the importance of arriving on time.

Project Discovery produced by the Southwest Iowa Learning Resources Center, Red Oak, is a series of hands-on training packages in such vocational areas as masonry, plumbing, wall covering, auto body repair, small engine repair, trucking, accounting and bookkeeping, filing, mail handling, sales, grocery clerking, banking and credit, waiter or waitress, artist, advertising, greenhouse work, law enforcement, religious service, meteorology, patient care, dental care, and many others. Participants are provided with work activity kits that contain hardware and software and individually written, illustrated instructions on how to do the work tasks. Instructions are written on a 5th and 6th grade reading level. A work evaluation component was added in 1980.

The *Building Maintenance and Repair Program*, designed by Ideal Development Labs at West Allis, WI, contains ten individualized vocational preparation units in carpentry and plumbing. Each unit has its own set of tools, training module, audiovisual cartridges, pretest and post assessment, academic enrichment exercises, instructor's manual, and trainee's manual. The Skills Orientation Series, by Singer Career Systems, Rochester, NY, offers 101 multimedia programs in four occupational clusters: building maintenance, manufacturing and processing, building trades, and distributive education. The programs are written on 3rd to 6th grade reading levels and are presented through full-color filmstrips, sound-synched audio-tape cassettes, lesson plan, activity sheet, and a program summary card. The skill units are geared to entry level job performance (Brolin, 1982). These systems and others like them are in a constant state of development. To find out the current status of these programs, interested readers should contact the publishers directly.

Behavioral/Task Analysis

Over the last several years, considerable activity has been generated by those concerned about the vocational skills training of the person with a more serious mental handicap (Bellamy, Horner, and Inman, 1979; Gold, 1976; Rusch and Mithaug, 1980). One example of a prevocational program that uses this approach is "Project Useful Hands" (Haines, 1982). Once appropriate training tasks and activities are determined for their students from a community survey, the staff conducts a three-step task analysis: (1) deciding how to perform the task; (2) breaking it down into components; and (3) constructing a task analysis data sheet so that the student can be trained in discrete steps.

Bellamy, et. al. (1979) view the purpose of vocational training ". . . to enable a worker to perform accurately and without assistance an operant chain specified in a task analysis" (p. 79). They outline a "step training procedure" that involves attending to behavior, providing assistance, reinforcing responses, assessing response accuracy, and correcting responses.

Research indicates that severely and moderately mentally retarded individuals can benefit from the behavioral or task analysis approach (Alper, 1981; Brown, 1982; Rusch & Menchetti, 1981; Wehman & Hill, 1982; Zohn & Bornstein, 1980). Exemplary projects such as Project Employability (Wehman & Hill, 1982), Employment Training Project (Rusch & Mithaug, 1980), Specialized Training Program (Bellamy et al., 1979), and, the Crisis Intervention Center Project (Karan, 1977) have used behavioral analysis technology to demonstrate the vocational training potentials of severely handicapped individuals.

Rusch and Mithaug (1980) list the following behavioral-analysis techniques that should be used in vocational training programs:

- Replicable training and management procedures (e.g., shaping to train new marketable skills)
- Individualized training that focuses on response deficits or excesses
- Emphasis on direct observation and measurement of vocational responses (e.g., speed of task completion)
- Repeated assessments (e.g., speed of completing tasks for several consecutive days)
- Objective analysis, including quantification of the behavior, that begins with a baseline measure of performance and determines what behavior needs to be changed
- Three training phases: acquisition, maintenance, and transfer
- Social and survival skills training
- Social acceptability for the overall effort

Interested readers can secure copies of the above publications and Brolin's *Vocational Preparation of Persons with Handicaps* (1982) for more detailed explanations of these occupational preparation techniques.

181

CONCLUSION

The occupational skills of handicapped individuals presents professional workers with an exciting and demanding challenge and a host of techniques depending on the interests, needs, learning styles, and abilities of each individual. Occupational guidance and preparation should begin shortly after the student enters the elementary program and should gain momentum as the student moves toward graduation and into adult programs. It requires the involvement of all the typical resources that career education demands: school personnel, family and community agencies, and business and industry. It requires innovativeness, time, and money, but most of all, the commitment and cooperation between a host of individuals and resources to assure the career development of the handicapped individual.

Chapter 10 will present a number of existing school and adult programs that have implemented the career education approach. Occupational skills is a major thrust of the career education concept. When combined appropriately with general academic, daily living, and personal social skills instruction, it will constitute a successful approach to meeting the life and career development needs of our handicapped citizens.

Family Contributions 6

Formulation of the **Individualized Education Program** (IEP) must involve cooperation and approval of parents and professionals. In the past, children who were diagnosed as blind, deaf, or physically handicapped were often placed in special schools or institutions so that they could begin their education as soon as possible. Although this concept of early education has expanded to include other areas of exceptionality, its effectiveness still depends upon the relationship between the three principal participants: student, parent, and professional. Cooperation must also extend into the area of career development so students can receive the fullest complement of experiences that will help the students develop views of themselves as producers, consumers, citizens, and parents.

Each participant (student, parent, and professional) benefits from the continued growth of the other. In other words, a reciprocal relationship exists between the participants, both in the smallest classroom and conference situation and in the larger contexts of group efforts and legislation. A lack of services for children caused parent groups to grow. Those expanding services drew new professionals who increased the number of success stories among children and adults with handicaps. The successes further encouraged efforts by parents and professionals; and thus the cycle is repeated but with greater consequences.

This chapter will examine how the family can contribute to the career development of handicapped individuals. Although the term *family* has wider connotations, principal attention will be focused on the parents. We will explore how parent groups have helped handicapped individuals to meet vocational needs, how parents have influenced the student's concepts, and how teachers and parents can work together to help students master the competencies.

183

POINT OF VIEW

Handicapped students leave our public school systems totally unprepared to do anything. These individuals have been inadequately prepared to enter college and have not received the vocational training that would equip them with a saleable skill. This translates into 12 wasted—often frustrating—years of the handicapped person's time and untold wasted taxpayers' dollars going for "pap programs" and glorified baby-sitting.

After high school, the handicapped person often faces a wasteland. Only a small percentage of persons are taken on by state Rehabilitation Services, and often, post-secondary education programs are as pallid and ineffective as the public school programs. The solution is simple, but professionals will not implement it for monetary reasons. *Parents* must take the initiative and demand that handicapped individuals have the rights guaranteed by PL 94–142.

Beginning with first grade, handicapped students should have a meaningful "career component" written into the the IEP. Licensed professionals should be hired to give 7th grade students vocational tests that will identify each individual's interests and aptitudes. From then on, each year's IEP should state at least two vocational classes that will ideally be offered to the student in a mainstreamed classroom. Concurrent with the program, students should be prepared for transfer to the next agency that will continue their education and rehabilitation.

Parents will probably have to work very hard to achieve each step of this program, but equipping handicapped students with saleable skills that will make them self-sufficient is well worthwhile.

Lillian Seymour was appointed to the California Advisory Council for Vocational Education and has served as a vocational chairperson to the California Association for Neurologically Handicapped Children and the Association for Children with Learning Disabilities.

PARENT POWER

Professionals can find a strong ally for career development in parents. Throughout the history of special education, parent groups have had to fight so many battles to ensure that handicapped individuals receive an appropriate education that parents have had little time to devote to improving other areas. However, with recent expansion in provisions for handicapped individuals, parents have been able to focus more of their attention on career development. Most of the interest has been in the narrower area of vocational training—work-study programs and job placement. However, some signs indicate that this scope will become wider as parents probe the full extent of career preparation. If they do pursue the daily living skills, personal-social skills, and occupational skills as it is believed they will, then professionals can expect several changes.

In his research, Brock (1977) has touched upon an increasingly important concept in special education: if parent groups can lobby for certification standards to be changed so that all teachers receive some training in the education of handicapped individuals, then parent groups can also impress training programs and state department personnel with the idea that career development should be an important component of that course work. Nichols (1977), a parent and executive director of a development center, provides an extensive discussion of the concept in the New Hampshire Association for Retarded Citizens *Newsletter.*

> The word 'advocacy' evokes fear in the minds of some, confusion in others and a sense of purpose in still others. Before we allow the word to fall into disrepute or oblivion, perhaps we should explore its meaning and function.
>
> Webster defines "advocate" as one who "supports the cause of another." Threatening? Confusing? On the contrary, the definition is very clear and relatively innocuous. Support can be financial, political or educational. One can advocate anonymously and silently or publicly and vocally. The support can be directed at very general issues (rights for the handicapped) or very specific ones (publicly funded training for handicapped children from birth to 21 years). Parents, educators, legislators, employers, public officials, private organizations and the handicapped themselves can be advocates.
>
> So, it seems, we have cleared up the initial question in two paragraphs—or have we? What about constructive versus destructive advocacy? Is there a way, in our zeal to support a cause, that we can ultimately do more damage than good?
>
> Legislation is often the answer to the problem of guaranteeing rights. But legislation without sufficient appropriation of funds can only serve to cloud the issue. Expensive court battles can follow, wasting energy and public funds and often the service goes unprovided, the rights unprotected.
>
> Constructive advocacy takes time, organization and a clear perception of the problem and the solution. First, we must be sure of what we wish to attain—do we only wish to bring attention to an injustice or do we want some action? Do we want new services or procedures or do we simply want to make better use of those that already exist?
>
> Next, we need to identify the barrier. Is it really a person or is it the policy he must enforce? Who or what is responsible for making the decision? Often we waste our time knocking on the wrong door or arguing with 'nonissues' (such as, 'your retarded child will never learn to read') and overlook the real barrier.

185

Third, we must strategize how to use existing precedents and other data to show that what we want is possible. We must be able to map out the solution, anticipating all the drawbacks and present it in a clear manner.

Finally, we must be willing to negotiate and compromise in the event of an impasse. Settling for half a loaf now may guarantee the balance in the future. Helping to effect the solution and monitoring that effect may mean temporary sacrifices and long-range commitments.

The handicapped and their parents, because of their unquestionable vested interest, have often been the most successful advocate. Their only purpose is to secure rights for themselves or their children—a purpose that cannot morally be challenged. But, because of the emotions involved, their advocacy is sometimes not constructive. Professionals, however, may remain unemotional about the issues but may jeopardize the constructiveness of their advocacy by directing it toward their own professional survival. We must be careful that partisan politics and personal ambition don't become part of the issue.

Advocacy means supporting a cause and we must advocate in an informative and constructive way that will provide dignity to the word and to those we support.

This discussion conveys the impression that some parents are highly skilled in changing systems of government and education. These parents have served on committees to organize write-in campaigns for legislation, lobbied legislatures, gained support from business and industry, and convinced celebrities from media and sports to appear at benefits and fund-raising drives. In general, they have formed successful organizations that implement and support common goals. Parents with these experiences and accomplishments will probably not accept future responses from school personnel to the effect that career development cannot be implemented, nor will they accept a secondary role in the formulation of the Individualized Education Program (IEP), which is the cornerstone of PL 94-142, The Education for all Handicapped Children Act. The provisions of this law, its safeguards for the rights of handicapped individuals and their parents, and the drafting of the IEP have already been discussed in chapter 1. Parent organizations are providing an ample amount of encouragement for parents to become acquainted with key provisions. Just about every publication that is designed with parents in mind has featured articles on the several components and safeguards and carry such titles as *Twenty Things a Parent Should Look for in an IEP, New Law for the Handicapped and Some Questions Parents Are Asking About It,* and *Ten Steps to Take When You Are in Conflict With Your School System.*

Parents have also become sophisticated in organizing coalitions to change public policy. Coalitions grow from the realization that the numerous separate organizations representing specific areas of disability (for example, individuals who are blind, physically handicapped, or mentally retarded) are, in effect, working to make similar changes in human care and education programs. These changes include institutions, school systems, state departments, local government, and all the regulations and delays that can be associated with the multiple layers of bureaucracy.

Coalitions have changed legislation, monitored implementation of mandates, and surveyed the needs of handicapped individuals. One successful combination of 18 organizations in the state of Minnesota, PACER (Parent Advocacy Coalition for Educational Rights) Center, Inc., was organized in 1976. PACER's numerous publications include parent training materials, awareness packets for school personnel and students, a newsletter, and other advocacy products that can be used in parent workshops. Additional information is available by writing PACER Center, Inc., 4701 Chicago Avenue South, Minneapolis, MN 55407.

One of the obvious goals for parent organizations and coalitions would be to change career prospects for handicapped individuals. Parents need very little prodding in this area because the children they sponsor soon grow into adolescents and adults. The preschool and mainstreaming issues soon give way to discussions about work-study and job placement programs. Numerous organizations have become involved with parent groups. For example the Department of Labor has awarded contracts to the Association for Retarded Citizens and the Epilepsy Foundation of America to train and place individuals with these disabilities. Since these organizations have been exchanging information and ideas with other parent groups, organizations that represent other areas of disability or coalitions of advocates will become involved in future applications. The contracts, efforts, and suggestions about how parents can become involved will continue to be disseminated through newsletters, information centers, and journals of individual organizations. One such organization was *The Parents' Campaign for Handicapped Children and Youth,* an information center that gave guidance and practical hints about special services and educational programs. The center prepared the following suggestions for parents:

1. Check local public schools for existing programs. These programs may include academic training and work-study situations.
2. Find out about the services offered through the local office of the state vocational rehabilitation agency. These agencies are responsible for providing aptitude testing, counseling, training, job placement, and other services.
3. Investigate programs offered by other organizations such as local chapters of the Association for Retarded Citizens or Goodwill Industries. Several of these organizations also have contact with school systems, vocational rehabilitation, and business and industry.

4. Inquire about work programs sponsored by sheltered workshops. Work programs can assist those individuals who need extra help to cope with their tasks.

5. Investigate day activity centers that may be sponsored by local parent organizations or mental health centers.

6. Get in touch with organizations that are composed of parents of handicapped individuals or are founded and directed by handicapped individuals. Check with your local chapter of the Easter Seal Society for Crippled Children and Adults for names and addresses of these organizations.

7. Apply for a "fair hearing" under regulations of the vocational rehabilitation agency if local services are inadequate. Be sure to compile a folder of accurate records that you can use to document your case. The folder should include the following information:

   a. name, address, telephone number
   b. school history with copies of pertinent records
   c. medical history with pertinent statement from physicians
   d. previous training and a list of occupations that are appropriate to the demonstrated skills
   e. any telephone calls or visits you have made in an attempt to gain access to education and training programs (the individual should keep a log of the calls and visits).

Other publications include suggestions and hints that parents and professionals can use in developing community interest and support for training workshops. The following topics and questions should be considered in developing a workshop.

1. Basic questions:

   a. Who is going to be the host?
   b. What are the costs?
   c. Where and when should it be held?
   d. Who is on the workshop team?

2. Organizing the format and speakers:

   a. What are the topics?
   b. How much time should be given for presentations, discussions, mini-sessions?
   c. Who will be the chairperson, feature speaker, panel members?

3. Exhibits:

   a. Who should be invited?

    b. Who may be interested?

    c. Where will they exhibit?

4. Advertising:

    a. Will the local radio station provide a public service announcement?

    b. Should the preconference information be mailed or hand-carried to schools and parent groups?

5. Odds and ends of conducting a workshop:

    a. Should there be a registration procedure?

    b. Who will draw signs and placards?

    c. Are there enough workshop packets?

Another parent organization, the California Association for Neurologically Handicapped Children (CANHC), discovered that there was very little effort on the part of agencies and programs to meet the vocational needs of individuals with minimal brain dysfunction or learning disabilities. A report presented by the organization's Vocational Committee (Anderson, 1976a) concluded with these observations:

> The battle for realistic vocational preparation for the neurologically handicapped has only begun. In every community, CANHC members and especially parents will have to work with local schools, Rehab Departments, colleges and other agencies to get help for their own adolescents and young adults. CAHNC cannot just *demand* services . . . for professionals and agencies do not yet understand or know what to do. Parents must be prepared to describe the needs, share information about resources and workable programs, encourage teachers and counselors in the efforts to serve our NH young people. Hopefully the materials prepared by the first Vocational Committee will help.

The committee was referring to their efforts in compiling a *Vocational Kit: Steps in Vocational Readiness for Adolescents and Adults with the Hidden Handicap* (Anderson, 1976b). The *Kit* includes 25 articles, written by teachers, parents, and other professionals that are related to activities in the classroom, counseling session, training program, or home. The several articles and suggested activities are organized under the following headings:

1. General information (including a glossary of terms and bibliography)

2. Tips for young adults, their employers and spouses

3. Remediation/any age (to facilitate job success)

4. Parents can help

189

5. Employment information (including resources for training and the use of vocational rehabilitation and job specifications)
6. Survival academics and vocational education.

Additional information is available by writing the California Association for Neurologically Handicapped Children, Box 4088, Los Angeles, California 90051.

The *Kit* represents an attempt by parents to influence classroom instruction and counseling. It grew from a frustration over the fact that students were not being prepared to enter the job market. This example was only true for the state of California, but we are sure that the *Kit* will be purchased throughout the country and used with other populations of individuals with disability. It is hoped that the *Kit* and this book will begin to have their effect upon professionals so that the impetus for change does not need to come from outside the school systems. The following discussions are intended to alert teachers and counselors to the role that parents can assume in career development.

Parent Influence

Long before the teacher or counselor ever encounters the pupil, the parents have influenced the student's approach to role models. Children begin to acquire opinions concerning the value of certain occupations when they hear some of the following comments:

> Look at the fire fighter, Johnny. Wouldn't it be fun to be a fire fighter?

> We're ready to board the plane to fly to Grandmother's. There's the captain. Doesn't he look grand?

> Your sister has to work late tonight at the store. It's really a hard job, and I wish she would quit.

The parents' inflections, interest, and estimation of importance clue the student as to the attractiveness of certain roles. Parents stimulate "fantasies" that influence the child's ideas about jobs, roles, responsibilities, and accomplishments. Although parents encourage "normal" students to think about a variety of occupations, less is known about whether parents of exceptional students express similiar attitudes. Prior selection probably takes place as parents screen various roles. The individual with cerebral palsy does not receive the same emphasis upon *being* a fire fighter or police officer as an individual with normal physical characteristics. The individual who is blind is not encouraged to become a captain or, for that matter, the pilot may not even be pointed out to him. The parent may reflect upon the sister's job, but he may not feel that his son or daughter who is mentally retarded could work in the same store.

190

"Your child's career choices will certainly affect your future as well as your child's. In this sense, you have a right, as well as a responsibilty, to be active in helping your child make career plans."

Office of Education (1978)

Elaboration about any one occupational role is determined by the parents' estimation and projection of the required abilities and behaviors. In some instances, students are not exposed to roles because parents imagine that their son or daughter will be unable to handle the responsibilities or meet prerequisites. But, parents are often not accurate as to what abilities are needed for a job. The great flaw in this delicate balance is that parents and educators are often relying upon their imaginations rather than using information. Both need a greater quantity and quality of information about occupations and other career roles, sexism, the student's abilities, what other individuals with handicaps have achieved, and the cooperative efforts of home and school in providing students with appropriate training.

Second, parents also maintain ideas about whether certain career roles are appropriate for the projected *status* of the family or student. These ideas are not major hurdles in the development of a training program for the majority of students, but they do occur enough times so that educators must consider parent opinions and attitudes in matching students, for example, to jobs. In a survey of work-study coordinators, Kokaska (1968) reports that high school students in classes for the mentally retarded were not placed in certain positions because these jobs did not meet the approval of the parents. Becker (1976) reports a large survey that includes training for 1,438 students in classes for the mentally retarded. The survey questionnaire was returned by 40 work-study coordinators from 35 school districts in 12 states and the District of Columbia. The purpose of the survey was to determine the types of jobs that were assigned to students during the 1972–74 school years. The coordinators were also asked to rank 10 statements that described problems they had in implementing the work-study curriculum. Obtaining cooperation from parents was ranked eighth.

Educators should be equally concerned about whether the home environment and classroom encourage students to think about various occupations. Some parents may assume that a student with an auditory impairment is not suited for the electronics field. However parents and educators should not eliminate this possibility during the student's early developmental years. If parents and educators assume that a certain role is unattainable, they will avoid presenting that model as a choice. The avoidance of discussions and illustrations will prevent the student from experimenting with and asking questions about roles. Students should receive as much exposure,

191

information, and interaction as possible with the full variety of productive activities that characterize work roles at all stages of career development.

"Parents should begin helping their child assess his aptitudes and work preferences at an early age."

Regan (1979)

The parent of an exceptional student is very different from the parent of a normal student. One of the first questions that these parents ask is whether the individual will be able to achieve independence as an adult. This is important to all parents, but those with a handicapped child have a very real concern as to whether the disability will hinder independent functioning. If the individual is unable to work, he will be dependent upon the parents or someone else for his physical and, in some instances, psychological support. The economics of this situation receives a considerable amount of attention. The systematic exploration of career roles and functions is one of the first attempts to prepare both parents and the student for later adult status. As such, educators can expect to encounter certain forms of resistance. Parents may make the following statements:

It is too early to concern ourselves with jobs.

My child will never be able to manage a home and family.

We're not particularly worried at this time.

The family should be an important factor in helping students to make the transition between dependence and independence. However the reluctance expressed in these statements may imply that the family has not fully resolved or accepted the fact that the student has a handicap. The parents' response may indicate that they have overestimated the effects of the disability upon the potential accomplishments of their son or daughter. Finally, educators must consider that the parents have to resolve their own feelings of guilt or pain, and that they may be trying to protect themselves until some future time when they will be able to deal with the problem. Although the teacher and counselor must consider the feelings of the parents, they should continue to pursue long-term goals that are for the benefit of the student.

Include parents in shaping educational objectives.

While services and programs for individuals with handicaps have been expanding, basic concepts of how these individuals encounter the realities of the modern world have also changed. The concept of the "dignity of risk" (Perske, 1972; Kokaska, 1974) has an important bearing upon the interactions between educators and parents concerning goals and programs for handicapped students. The dignity of risk emphasizes the fact that individuals develop a sense of value within themselves and in the eyes of their peers by encountering tasks commensurate with their functioning. Denying handicapped individuals of an opportunity to learn, venture, or try appropriate tasks is, in effect, devaluing and dehumanizing them. This is why legislation and regulations have emphasized the phrase "least restrictive environment." Educators and parents should choose those educational environments that are least restrictive to the development of the handicapped individuals' abilities *and* their sense of value.

Numerous advocacy organizations have repeatedly voiced that handicapped individuals should have the opportunity of working instead of receiving charity or welfare. The role of work, and the positive status of an employed individual are still woven tightly within the fabric of the American society. But, the actual physical process of work, which includes movement, dexterity, and endurance, places certain individuals in situations of risk. The social and interpersonal variables involved in other forms of work even dominate certain occupations and also function as other forms of risk. Teachers and parents sense these elements of risk. Even if risk is based on accurate information, parents and teachers may try to modify a handicapped student's intended goals.

If teachers, counselors, and parents are to work together in preparing students for various career roles that fulfill the handicapped student's need for dignity, then they must carefully examine their perceptions of tolerable levels of risk. The process of career development begins in the family, and the question of whether the handicapped individual should attempt a "risk situation" will occur at every stage of maturation. The question cannot be avoided, especially since more and more handicapped individuals are taking productive roles in society. Therefore, educators should encourage families to participate in helping handicapped students develop those competencies that will enable them to meet daily challenges and achieve a sense of value.

Thus, educators cannot afford to work apart from the parents. The authors of PL 94–142 and the Individual Education Program (IEP) recognized this by including numerous provisions that involve parents in shaping educational objectives. But aside from these guarantees, it would still behoove educators to actively include parents in decisions and activities that may shape students' future achievements and influence their socioeconomic status. These efforts by educators with parents are filled with rewards (and some disappointments) as can be seen in Fuhrman's (1982) commentary on programs in the State of Oregon.

First of all, an observation based on my limited experience (10 years) in working at various levels of career education with deaf students. Most parents of high school level deaf students tend to be 'burnt out' and are reluctant to get involved with any program of parent involvement that requires them to support, on a formal level, the career development of their son or daughter. . . . At the junior high level the interest is greater, thus the willingness to participate and assist career exploration programs is more evident. At the preschool-elementary level, the enthusiasm and participation is at its highest.

Our formal effort to have parents join us in the career development of their sons and daughters has been in two areas: a statewide career exploration program and the development of a statewide parent organization to help meet the needs of parents at all levels.

The career exploration program provided approximately 230 deaf students, ages 14–19, with vocational assessment, classroom training in job search skills, and three job samples in three different cluster areas for approximately 50 hours each. Parents were invited to go over the vocational assessment results with their son/daughter and the counselor. Parent approval was sought before the plans for the job samplings were organized. In many cases, parents had to arrange transportation which required coordination with their schedules, etc. Parents were asked to evaluate the total program and its benefits for their son/daughter. In many cases the program served isolated deaf students in the rural areas of Oregon. The result of three years of this program was a network of parents to begin some statewide organization. But again the implementation of the Oregon Association of Parents of the Deaf became a reality because of the energy and enthusiasm of the preschool-primary level parents.

Throughout the previous discussion, we have concentrated on parents who may be reluctant but yet interested in their child's future. The question may be asked: What can educators do with parents who are uninterested in their child's program? This question is not unique to career development for exceptional individuals. Regular and special educators may have to ask this question more frequently as the post-Korean War high school dropouts (uninterested students) become the parents of another generation of children. These children have been influenced by television and may have little tolerance for the classroom, especially if their parents see no value in education.

The educators' basic concern in confronting this problem has to be with the quantity and quality of communication between school personnel and parents. Educators cannot force parents to become interested against their will. But, educators can certainly make an eager attempt beyond the traditional parent-teacher conferences. The parents' lack of interest reflects a complex situation that may involve more than the student's progress with reading, writing, and arithmetic. Therefore, the amount of communication between home and school has to increase so that some of the elements of the situation may surface. The quality of communication refers to those face-to-face meetings between educators and parents that allow both parties to deal with problems and concerns.

One way of increasing parent interest is by involving them in an ongoing career education program. Parents can be used as speakers and resource persons and can become vital links to other members of the community who can contribute to a developing program. One publication, *Missouri Lincletter* (1982), suggests that teachers begin parent files on the following topics:

1. Parents who can share information about their occupations with students in training
2. Parents who have volunteered to accompany students on community visits to job sites, and
3. Parents who could provide tours of their businesses

The requirements of parent approval for the individualized education program actually provide educators with another tool for encouraging parent interest. Parents can become involved in responsibilities that are designated on the IEP form. But that spark of interest can be extinguished if parents are overpowered in meetings with three, five, or seven educators. In the final analysis, the educators must ask themselves such questions as

Have we repeatedly communicated our concern for the parents' and student's benefit through letters, notes, and telephone calls?

Have we used other means of encouraging parent interest, such as parent groups, volunteer aide programs, parent speakers, and community organizations?

Have we planned our meetings, newsletters, or announcements so that parents receive positive feedback about themselves and their child?

Have we attempted to meet parents in their homes or work areas at *their* convenience?

These questions and others allow educators to determine whether they have done enough to resolve problems that may possibly extend beyond their expertise.

Parent Training

While some parent organizations are providing information, workshops, and printed materials about career and vocational futures for handicapped individuals, educators have attempted the direct training of parents in career concepts and family activities.

Vasa and his colleagues have produced several publications based upon their experiences in the state of Nebraska (Vasa, Steckelberg, & Meers, 1979a; Vasa, Steckelberg, & Meers, 1979b; Vasa & Steckelberg, 1980a; Vasa & Steckelberg, 1980b). Two major topics run through their works. First the authors assume that the parents' concern for their child is greater than that of school personnel, parents have a right to know about and be involved in the student's program, and parents can be effective teachers in career education. Second an effective parent training program is characterized by definition of program parameters; needs assessment; feasable plans and forms of delivery; and evaluation of the parents' learning and behaviors.

All of these components are discussed further in several publications. For example, the forms of training (or delivery) included individual parent conferences, telephone conferences, mail correspondence, small group meetings, large group orientation meetings, and home visitations. The type of training has to be shaped according to the unique characteristics and availability of the parents who are participating in the program. In other words, educators need an individualized training plan to match the needs and time parameters of the family.

Lewis, Rimai, DiPalma-Meyer, and LeFevre (1981) reported on a training program for parents in career education. The project was made possible by a federally funded grant to Teacher's College at Columbia University and involved two groups of 50 parents over a period of three years. The children of the parents represented the full range of handicapping conditions. Both groups of parents passed through two phases of training (i.e. preservice training in career education and an internship). The publication does not include an elaboration on the internship but does provide the reader with numerous examples from the inservice component of the training.

Inservice workshops included such activities as role playing, values clarification, brainstorming, decision making, and interviewing. The activities were supplemented by guest speakers, media presentations, and other group exercises. The most valuable portion of the publication is the "lesson plan" and corresponding materials that accompany many of the following inservice topics for parent groups:

- the goals of the project, "Parents in Career Education"
- the concepts of career, career development, and career education
- home-based activities that promote career development
- the relationship of values, attitudes, and interest to work and career
- learning styles and the how-to of transmission
- the relationship of problem solving and decision making to work and career
- occupations, and how to find out about them

196

- the relationship of daily living skills to career
- task analysis and the teaching of skills
- legislation and handicapped individuals
- advocacy for handicapped individuals
- planning a workshop for parents
- conducting a local occupational survey of your community
- setting up a placement office
- setting up a library of occupational literature and training opportunities

The American Coalition of Citizens with Disabilities has also ventured into the area of parent training and published a resource guide which can be used in workshops (Razeghi & Ginyard, 1980). The guide is divided into five sections containing information that may lead to desired parent competencies. These competencies, in turn, would hopefully enhance career and vocational education programs and opportunities for disabled students. The competencies are not specified in the guide, and the reader will have to extract knowledge and behavior statements from the material. However, the publication contains basic information in an essay format with supplemental resources that could be duplicated for presentations to parent groups. The five sections include the following:

1. laws (steps in the identification process, the individualized education program, supplementary services, and interagency cooperation)
2. vocational education (qualifying students for employment, dimensions of vocational education, and vocational alternatives)
3. career education (definition, role of special educators, and benefits)
4. parent rights under due process (notification, evaluation, hearings, and appeals)
5. accessible systems (rationale, evaluation, and challenge)

These projects and their reports provide numerous suggestions for topics, activities, and materials that can be used in longitudinal parent training programs. Several themes in the literature coincide with our thinking. The following general suggestions are directed at involving parents and other members of the family in the student's career development. These suggestions include familiar activities, but educators should approach them with a desire to use the parents' influence upon student goals and behaviors.

Initiate an active information program for parents. The information may include suggested readings or reprinted articles about classroom activities, progress reports on former students who are employed in the community,

197

and reviews of guest speakers in the classroom. These resources provide parents with a perspective on the "career future" of the student. Some school districts have provided parents with suggestions about the kinds of questions that their children may ask concerning the parents' careers, jobs, previous education, duties, and rewards.

Provide parents with a brochure or handbook on classroom activities that can be replicated in the home. The handbook can contain lists of career terms, places to visit in the community related to career development, and household chores that develop the student's daily living skills. The handbook may also contain a checklist of the several competencies discussed in chapters 3 through 5. The checklist may be accompanied by suggested home and community resources related to the competencies. For example, the resources may include home study guides, manuals, community walking tours of industries or facilities, and guest presentations to organizations.

Present "career/vocational workshops" for parents. These workshops would include information sessions on family contributions to career development, possibilities for vocational training, work-study programs, sources of vocational information that can be acquired by parents, and other facets of career development. Former students and employers can also participate in these workshops by giving presentations on training and their experiences with the labor market.

Conduct parent field trips of training sites, placement facilities, and classroom activities related to career and vocational development. Field trips can give parents an opportunity to observe students who are in training and perhaps, working in selected roles. The observations are a vital link between what parents have read or been told and what they can experience through contact and conversation with students, trainers, and employers.

All of these suggestions can be modified to fit every educational setting. For example, field trips may not be appropriate for parents who work during the school day. These family members may profit best from a handbook on suggested activities in the home or a newsletter that informs them of weekly television programs related to careers, jobs, or the world of work. Other parents may respond enthusiastically to suggestions for a workshop. These parents may wish to engage speakers in discussions concerning training, perspective employment, and the role of the family. It is important to fit the suggested activity to the characteristics of the parents and the capacities of the professional staff. In some instances, as in the development of newsletters or printed matter, educators may enlist the services of professional writers and printers.

FAMILY INVOLVEMENT WITH THE COMPETENCIES

Throughout our discussions of the 22 career development competencies and their respective subcompetencies in chapters 3 through 5 we made numerous suggestions concerning activities that could be conducted in the classroom or home. Parents could be given a copy of this book or an even more extended listing of the activities accompanying each subcompetency. A review of each competency will soon reveal that parents and other family members can contribute significantly to the student's career development in almost all competency areas.

Because family members have not been trained as teachers or counselors, they may be discouraged when they are confronted with lists of competencies and activities. But we believe that the family can help students develop these competencies as they occur in the normal conduct of maintaining a home. For example, even before a child can read words, he can read pictures. A special recipe card with words and pictures can help the child develop reading skills. The child can learn to follow pictures and recognize packages such as canned goods, powdered sugar, flour, and salt. One way of teaching the child food concepts is by playing games that ask: "I'm thinking of something on your plate and it's white and square. Can you guess what it is?" Parents can give the child a sense of importance by assigning him tasks such as sponging the table top, scrubbing vegetables, or tearing lettuce into small pieces for a salad. Experience with preparing food can help children to learn safety rules, coordination and manipulation skills, and many other competencies related to their career development.

"The efforts of the school and the parents are, or should be, directed toward maximizing the handicapped individuals' career success."

Vasa, Steckelberg, & Meers (1979a)

The majority of activities in chapters 3 through 5 facilitate one or more of the skills involved in the competencies. These skills and competencies should serve as a basis for some of the conversations between teachers, counselors, and parents and can be included, for example, in the consultations relative to the objectives contained in the IEP.

Career-related topics and competencies can also form the basis of conversations within the family. The Mesa (Arizona) Public Schools (1976) published two brochures for parents entitled, *Talking with Your Child (Teenager) About Your Career*. The brochures included the following basic questions:

Why do you work?

When did you make your career choice?

Who benefits from your career?

What do you see in the future?

The publications also suggest appropriate moments in the day, such as during dinner, when parents can initiate conversations. The discussions will reflect the parents' career history and can prompt children and adolescents to think about their own career futures.

Once family members (father, mother, grandparents, brothers, sisters, and relatives) understand the long-term objectives and some representative examples of daily activities, they can create other activities that do not appear in booklets or textbooks. These ideas will be supported by family members and are particularly appropriate to the individual family, their life style, and the student's ability and limitations.

Regan (1979) identified a number of activities that parents could include in the home to expand the vocational possibilities for learning disabled adolescents. She wanted parents to help the adolescent assess his personal aptitude, work preferences, and ability to manage his own behavior. The home can be a miniature job analysis resource center where parents can shape experiences that help students evaluate strengths and weaknesses, solve problems, manage time, and acquire daily living skills. She also included suggestions for parents who are interested in the school's training program and employment possibilities in the community.

The following are 12 suggestions that we believe families should consider in helping their handicapped member to achieve the career development competencies contained in this book.

1. Emphasize the *development of coordination, dexterity, balance, and strength* by providing daily physical exercises or activities (sports, crafts, balance boards, chores around the house). The family should be aware of activities that involve both fine and gross motor functions. These skills can be transferred later to routines that are important for successful employment, daily living, and leisure.
2. Provide a *home workshop* so that students can learn how to use hammer, nails, saw, ruler, and drill press. Home workshops also help the individual learn to identify the names of tools, tasks, and consequences.
3. Assign *specific jobs/duties* to the individual. The duties should be completed to specifications and within a certain time frame. A second level of expectation is related to the individual's development of a plan of action to complete the job. This plan may include following a routine, maintaining a schedule, and returning tools or utensils to specified locations.

4. *Identify jobs* performed by various workers in the community, *visit job sites*, and *discuss them* in detail at home. Include the family in these discussions and observations. These discussions help the individual to express personal observations and ask questions about work. They also help build work values, interests, and long-term aspirations.

5. *Discuss the work of family members*, necessary training, difficulties, and rewards. If possible, arrange a visit to the work site or facility. This will add to the student's knowledge and perception of the family's role in the community.

6. Provide a variety of *family projects* and *activities*, such as camping trips, sports events, travel, and church events so the student can build leisure, recreation, and social skills. These family projects and outings also provide the handicapped individual with an opportunity to communicate ideas and feelings. These types of communications are important in helping the individual build positive concepts of himself and his role in society.

7. Insist that the individual *make his own decisions*, investigate alternatives, and understand the consequences. Problem-solving and decision-making abilities are essential to the development of the individual's independent status within the family and community.

8. Help the student to feel psychologically secure by *positively reinforcing* him for doing successful work and by giving him an opportunity to *participate in family decision making*.

9. *Work closely with school personnel* to achieve educational goals and objectives for the handicapped individual. Several classroom activities are richly supported by the cooperation of the family. For example, teachers often use classroom activities to teach students about their parents' occupations. The activities may include role playing, child-parent interviews, and class field trips to the work locations of the parents. The class functions would also support the family's attempts to build personal skills such as communication and problem solving.

10. Help school personnel develop *community experiences* that will expand curriculum opportunities, such as field trips, guest speakers, and work experience.

11. Encourage *part-time work experiences*, community projects, and hobbies that expose the student to various people and their careers.

12. Become involved in *school advisory committees* concerned with curriculum, development of resources, and other career education matters.

201

Home-school cooperation can make up for limitations in the teacher's activities. For example, because of financial constraints, many school systems only allow one field trip per year. However under the direction of the classroom teacher, parents can include their son or daughter in family outings to centers of work activity. This form of cooperation provides the educator with a greater array of experiences that can be incorporated into the curriculum.

Of course, the problem of maintaining continuity between the teacher's career development objectives for a particular field trip and the actual fulfillment of these objectives can be encountered by the cooperating parents or family members. This goal requires the teacher to provide the family with a basic understanding of the competencies, career development goals, and objectives for any particular field visit. Given these basic understandings, the teacher can tolerate variation in the family's emphasis upon the observed tasks and skills at a particular field site. Family involvement and effort increase the possibilities for exposing the student to many work settings.

Parents and teachers can use conferences to define student responsibilities in the home. These duties can be evaluated for the types of skills that students develop. Reports between home and school enable parent and teacher to appraise and reinforce each other's progress. This would continue to enhance efforts made by parents in the primary training site—the home—and the skilled individual in career development—the teacher. These "homework assignments" should not be taken lightly and help students to develop positive self-concepts. For example, Pollard (1977) suggests that the classroom teacher and students conduct a career education program for the parents. Students can display their projects and demonstrate activities. Parents can participate in the same career activities that students practice in the classroom. Pollard reports that parents of trainable mentally retarded adolescents were surprised to discover that the students could successfully complete a variety of work tasks. Once parents have discovered this, they will have more realistic expectations and will give the student more responsibilities at home.

The U. S. Office of Education has supported four models of the role the family and parent-teacher cooperation in achieving the overall goals of career education. The Home/Community Base Model is one of the four and has several implications for parents and teachers of handicapped individuals. First, the model emphasizes the home as a learning center (Simpson, 1973). The importance of values and activities has been previously discussed, but the concept of a *learning center* is not just theoretical. The learning center provides a means of communication between the home and an outside source of information via television, radio, or telephone and enables parents to obtain information and assistance relevant to training objectives that can be accomplished in the home.

Second, the model includes a designated area of the home where students engage in activities that further their understanding of careers and goals. This may involve a slide projector and cassette tape recorder or a designated program on a television channel. The model can be used to provide information relative to many of the subcompetencies.

Third, the model implies that the whole family is a career learning team. Parents and siblings are involved in furthering career pursuits and, thus, provide role models and experiences that influence the handicapped individual. Once the family understands the basic dynamics of the situation and the projected competencies, they can include the handicapped individual.

Finally, the home program seems most appropriate for individuals with certain types of handicaps because of their need for tutoring assistance beyond the scope of the ordinary school. Although outside the physical boundaries of the school, the home-based model would provide another learning environment that would be coordinated with the teacher's efforts toward mutually determined objectives.

WORKING WITH PARENTS

Working with parents of handicapped individuals is a crucial part of career development. The encounters between professionals and parents should include singular meetings or a determined series of sessions extending over a long period of time. For the professional, the purpose of these meetings is to

- exchange information related to student characteristics, achievement, program development, or instances in the home or classroom that may affect the individual's continued academic and social progress; and
- develop plans to solve problems that include cooperative efforts by school personnel and family.

Many articles that were published in the 1960s and 1970s discussed the role of the counselor with the family of the handicapped individual. Compendiums of several of these articles have appeared in publications by Noland (1971); Gowan, Demos, and Kokaska (1972); Browning (1974); Buscaglia (1975); and Stewart (1978). More recently, an insightful collection of essays by Murphy (1981) has been added to the storehouse of publications. He essentially identified the parent behaviors that helped the positive qualities of handicapped people and their families to emerge. Many of these publications have focused on

- helping parents to realize that their exceptional children and youth are more similar to than different from other children and youth. The exceptional aspects are important but secondary. That

Cooperative efforts between parents and professionals are crucial to successful career development and independent living for persons with disabilities.

type of orientation is not an easy accomplishment because parents have a great deal of psychological investment in their offspring. Parents have to reconcile damage, injury, and differences with their *image* of their sibling. Parents can adjust their goals and expectations by focusing on the individual qualities of the person. The numerous examples of success by individuals with handicaps in society, expansion of parent organizations, and technological advances have also helped parents adjust. Nevertheless, every family must move from such initial negative reactions of mourning, denial, guilt, rejection, shame, and frustration to productive actions on behalf of the exceptional individual. The professional in the counseling role is a vital ingredient to this transition.

■ helping parents work through their *feelings* about the many obstacles that stand between projected goals and daily accomplishments. Parents of exceptional individuals can be overcome by numerous medical reports and school evaluations identifying damage, limitations, or failures. This type of information can contribute to feelings of failure and resentment and serves as another obstacle that the family and school personnel must surpass. The professional's attention to the parents' feelings provides a basis of communication, understanding, and acceptance. The emphatic relationship between professional and parents has helped solve problems by allowing the latter to free themselves of concerns that interfered with the adequate solutions.

■ offering perspective on the total expanse of the exceptional individual's life so that parents can identify the relationships between stages of development. Of course, daily problems have to be solved, and each step in the developmental sequence has its own unique characteristics. The professional's contribution is to identify parental measures that can modify behavior or achieve success and attain future goals.

■ functioning as a resource to help parents and handicapped individuals achieve goals. Each year brings additional resources into the community on behalf of handicapped individuals and their parents. These resources include financial assistance, varied forms of instruction, medical and legal assistance, and vocational training. The average parent cannot be expected to be familiar with all the resources. However, it has been the experience of numerous professionals that parents can pursue appropriate avenues of support and assistance once they have become aware of community resources. At times, parent organizations have been instrumental in spreading such information through contacts with professionals in school systems and community agencies.

In addition to these broad themes for professionals, numerous publications contain specific suggestions for counselors who work with parents of handicapped individuals. One publication by Patterson (1956), a parent of a mentally retarded individual, was specifically intended to alert professionals about their own preparation for the parent conference. These pointers were expanded into 10 commandments for counselors by Jordan (1976). The two lists appear in table 6.1.

The pointers and commandments focus upon the attitude and procedures that enhance the relationship between counselor and parents. Parents need to express their feelings about their son's or daughter's handicap, gain confidence in the counselor, and attempt constructive planning. The counselor's concern, behavior, and techniques can contribute to the parents' overall success during the meetings. As parents become more accepting of their situation and the counselor's efforts, they can concentrate on the student's needs and accomplishments associated with the competencies that were

205

TABLE 6.1
Pointers and commandments for counseling with parents.

Pointers for Professionals	The Ten Commandments
1. Tell us the nature of our problem as soon as possible.	1. Be honest in your appraisal of the situation and explain it without unnecessary delay.
2. Always see both parents.	2. Deal with both parents, since they are a natural unit.
3. Watch your language.	3. Be precise, but do not be unnecessarily technical in your explanation.
4. Help us to see this is OUR problem.	4. Point out who must be responsible ultimately.
5. Help us to understand our problem.	5. Help the parents grasp the issues.
6. Know your resources.	6. Keep in mind the referral agencies that can be of assistance.
7. Never put us on the defensive.	7. Avoid precipitating ego-defensive reactions in the parents.
8. Remember that parents of retarded children are just people.	8. Do not expect too much too soon from the parents.
9. Remember that we are parents and that you are professionals.	9. Allow parents their quota of concern and uncertainty.
10. Remember the importance of your attitude toward us.	10. Try to crystallize positive attitudes at the outset by using good counseling techniques.
(Patterson, 1956)	(Jordan, 1976)

identified in chapters 3–5 as critical for career success. The mastery of competencies in the areas of daily living, personal-social, and occupational skills should constitute the long-range objectives for student instruction in the classroom and home. The parents' worries and questions chiefly center around the competencies:

Will my son be able to drive a car?

What shall we do when our daughter reaches the dating age?

Who will hire my son?

Will our child be cut-off from the rest of the students in the class because of the differences in appearance?

Although *all* parents in counseling and program planning sessions raise the same questions, they cannot all address the issues in the same way. The differences will depend upon the handicapped individual's physical or emotional ability to meet challenges. For example, all parents may wonder about their child's ability to hold a job in the adult years. But the parents of a blind or mentally retarded child will justifiably pursue answers to questions of employment at an early age in the developmental sequence. Some parents of handicapped individuals spend years helping their children accomplish certain competencies that normal students master in a semester.

The use of the competencies in the IEP provides a sound basis on which professionals and parents can meet to exchange opinions and plans. Parents may not be able to initiate measures within the home that prepare the student in all of the 22 competencies, but they should be able to understand the direction of the school program and identify competency areas that can be implemented immediately within the home. The student's attainment of the 22 competencies can be a reference point for teacher-parent conferences related to the individual education program. Both participants can start the IEP conferences with a common understanding about the short-term and long-term objectives for the student and the intended goals of school and home activities. Daily problems in adjustment or academic assignments take on a new measure of meaning when parents and professional are able to identify the relationship of these smaller parts to the overall direction of the curriculum.

"In order for the parent to be comfortable about asking for the child to be trained in Career Education, educators must be able to: (a) communicate with the parents in a nonthreatening situation, (b) understand the parent's concerns, (c) express the concepts of Career Education in 'language understandable to the general public.'"

Michaelis (1979)

The counselor or teacher should consider the following suggestions in conducting, planning, and evaluating activities related to the competencies and the IEP:

Evaluate the student's current status relative to the competencies to be achieved during the school year. Professionals must also be careful to identify variables that may prevent adequate appraisal of student competencies in the school, training, or home situation. Many of these limitations may be raised by parents who attempt to initiate activities and observe accomplishments. For example, a student may have the responsibility of "cleaning his room," but the parents may be unable to observe the student's progress because they may be busy with other responsibilities in the home. Although these problems cannot be classified as major stumbling blocks to progress, they should be resolved by teachers and parents.

207

Determine forms of reward for the parents. The simple attainment of a level of behavior by their child may be an ample reward for a parent. The first spelling test, colored picture, date, and driver's license often provide just as much positive feelings in the hearts of parents as in the students who achieved the goals. Nevertheless, the counselor should allow for instances in which parents receive direct recognition for their part in the process aside from the student achievements. The meetings at which teacher and parent review yearly progress on the IEP can be used for appropriate opportunities to provide parent rewards.

Involve as many family members as possible in the planning and progress of activities designed to train students in the competencies. Many of the student's experiences with competencies in the daily living skills and personal-social skills can be supervised by peers and relatives. This procedure involves a greater number of "teachers" in the training process of the student. There has been increasing emphasis upon the "team concept" in special and regular education, across different professions, and between the school and home. Activities and observations related to the competencies provide the family with more opportunities to become involved in a team effort.

Emphasize the importance of career development as a process that extends from childhood through adult years. Parents of young children will have difficulty visualizing the fact that all major competencies are worded in terms of adult experiences. Parents must realize that the student will need less training and instruction at later stages of development if he begins to acquire competencies at an early age. One of the objects of career education is to help students develop adult skills and competencies in the elementary grades; therefore, teachers and parents should not wait until high school to train and instruct students in important competency areas.

Encourage parent questions and suggestions. This procedure involves parents in helping the student master the competencies. It is also another indicator of the parents' involvement in competency training and IEP activities at home. If parents are attempting to conduct and supervise activities to achieve objectives on the IEP, then they will encounter problems. Professionals should prompt parents to discuss these problems in the planning conferences.

Present as much information as the parents can handle. Professionals can encourage parents to ask questions by presenting them with new information, such as new resources in the community or changes in school procedures. But, parents can be overwhelmed with the amount of information that is related to a particular disability, types of training programs, or activities that they can conduct in the home. If parents are presented with the right amount of information, they will be eager to hear, find information, and generate their own questions and suggestions instead of feeling overwhelmed and defeated.

Develop a schedule of activities that parents can follow and that coincides with the classroom lessons. This is another advantage to the IEP conference. Parents and professionals can plan coordinated activities to achieve common objectives related to the competencies.

Figure 6.1 is one example of a schedule of family activities for the same daily living skills that were presented in Figure 3.1 (see page 100). The schedule is specific to the individual student and family situation, whereas the curriculum check sheet in chapter 3 provides the teacher with an overview of the competencies that intersect with various curriculum areas.

FIGURE 6.1
Family activities.

Jane			Oct.–Nov.
Student			Week or Month
	DAILY LIVING SKILLS		

Competency	School Assignments	Family Activities	Family Comments
1. Identifying money	Arithmetic assignments will be sent home	Take Jane on weekly shopping at supermarket	
2. Using basic tools	Find examples of tools	Practice naming appliances; father and brother include Jane in repairing car	
3. Demonstrating physical fitness	Reading assignment on home safety	Practice safety measures for the home related to fires	

The parents' schedule provides them with an estimation of those classroom lessons, daily assignments, or exercises that students should complete at home. It also checks the parents' involvement and student progress in "out-of-school" functions, such as, for example, Jane's swimming lessons at the YWCA. It is not a perfect device but does provide another link in the communication between teacher and parents. The activities that the parents suggested during the IEP conference can also become a means by which the family can contribute to the student's development of the competencies. This element interjects a certain amount of accountability into the relationship of parents to the IEP.

CONCLUSION

This chapter emphasized the important role of the family in the career development of handicapped individuals. Parent groups have increased their attention and efforts in the broad career areas of daily living skills, while also focusing upon vocational training and placement. Parents and professionals should be able to turn to several of the national and state parent organizations for information and publications. These organizations will find willing companions in the quest for career development in those school systems and agencies that are initiating career education programs and expanding their efforts in vocational training.

The position of the individual education program in career development should be viewed as a centerpiece in the communication between teacher and parent. The IEP functions as a means through which the competencies can be translated into obtainable objectives and daily activities. It is hoped that teacher and parents will be able to devise activities that can be conducted in the classroom and home environments and, consequently, reinforce each others' attempt to obtain mutual objectives. This process of communication between teacher and parent should be ongoing and rewarding, which may explain why those who wrote the law and regulations that gave birth to the IEP specified that the participants were to establish objectives, as well as dates and time frames. In one sense, these requirements may be viewed as insurance that the school system and teacher will complete their part of the contract. We would rather view them as a way to bring teacher, parents, and students together to discuss, plan, and even dream about what *can* be accomplished.

Business and Industry 7

Cooperation between business, industry, and education has always been an integral consideration of leaders in career development. The benefits of collaboration have been explored in the professional literature of these fields. In his address to the Commissioner's National Conference on Career Education, Sidney Marland (1976) specifically mentioned how the business sector could collaborate with educators to improve the student's career education. He stated that business should be involved in

- developing better manpower for its own needs;
- creating an improved environment for the work force by reducing unemployment; and
- improving the purchasing power of the public.

Educators and their students can reap rewards by including the expertise and experience of individuals from business and industry who are involved in the production of goods and services. The question is not whether each sector could profit from one another's involvement in providing career education for America's public but rather how can these sectors work together toward mutual objectives?

Several noteworthy efforts have been conducted by business and industry that have direct bearing on the career education of handicapped individuals. Some of these efforts include the following:

- The *Chamber of Commerce of the United States* adopted career education as a major priority in 1971 and published a monograph entitled *Career Education: What It Is and Why We Need It* (1975). The Chamber of Commerce has helped local affiliates implement career education in their communities. Thus the local Chamber of Commerce can be an important resource that schools can use when they design their career education programs. Information can be obtained from a local Chamber of Commerce or by writing Chamber of Commerce of the U.S.A., 1615 H Street, N.W., Washington, D.C., 20062.

■ The *National Alliance of Businessmen* (NAB) is another excellent source for career education assistance. The NAB has tried to prevent the unemployment of disadvantaged individuals by sponsoring work-study programs for youth; a Youth Motivation Task Force Program involving successful businesspersons from disadvantaged backgrounds; and Career Guidance Institutes for high school counselors, which offer career education infusion materials developed by classroom teachers. Information can be obtained by writing NAB, 1015 Fifteenth Street, N.W., Washington, D.C., 20005

■ The *General Motors Corporation* (GMC) has become involved in a national career education effort to help students become better citizens by increasing their self-awareness and improving their decision-making capabilities and occupational skills. GMC has committed itself to providing classroom speakers and materials on specific careers, offering plant visits, cooperating with school personnel, and serving on industry-education advisory councils. Information can be obtained by writing GMC, Education Relations, General Motors Building, 3044 West Grand Blvd., Detroit, Michigan 48202.

■ The *Industry Education Council of California*, a statewide umbrella organization with 27 local affiliates, has coordinated efforts of businesses, agencies, and school districts to provide career guidance institutes, speaker's bureaus, labor market surveys, and career awareness programs that can be used to train and place handicapped students. The Council identifies and promotes promising concepts and practices related to career development by combining projects that can be shared across the state or nation.

General Electric Company, New York Life Insurance Company, and the Bell System are some examples of other large national companies that have or are developing career education programs. The Bell System has developed a multimedia program entitled "A Career is Calling," which consists of a 27-minute film concentrating on the specifics of several jobs in the system. A teacher's book, consisting of eight spirit master activity sheets, delves into the self-evaluation and self-knowledge that students must acquire before

POINT OF VIEW

The most salient feature of this chapter, in my opinion, are the many concrete examples of actual practices illustrating business/industry involvement in providing career education to persons with handicaps.

Two additional points seem important to me. First, it is important to differentiate among *cooperative*, *collaborative*, and *coalition* efforts involving the education system and the broader community. Cooperative efforts are easiest to establish but least effective in that they typically leave total accountability for success or failure of the effort with the education system. Collaborative efforts, involving *joint* authority/responsibility/accountability, along with *joint* interest and expertise, exist among both persons from the education system and persons from the broader community. While tougher to initiate than cooperative efforts, they are much more likely to be effective and sustaining. Coalition efforts are those involving the education system, the business/industry community, *and* a variety of other kinds of community agencies and organizations. In the case of meeting career education needs of persons with handicaps, coalitions seem to me most appropriate to consider.

It is also important to acknowledge that the term *business/industry* includes both (1) small business; and (2) organized labor as well as big business representatives. Many more examples containing one or both of these kinds of emphasis are badly needed.

Kenneth B. Hoyt is the former director of the United States Office of Career Education in Washington, D.C.

213

they can be happy and effective on a job in the Bell System or anywhere else.

A number of companies have also developed model programs to employ handicapped individuals. Pati, Adkins, and Morrison (1981) identify several companies in their text on human resource management. These include Continental Bank of Chicago, Minnesota Mining and Manufacturing, Control Data Corporation, McDonnell Douglas Corporation, and Sears Roebuck and Company. Each year several national organizations that work on the behalf of handicapped individuals identify more companies that train and employ disabled workers. Additional information can be obtained by writing to the President's Committee on Employment of the Handicapped for this year's "Employer of the Year" material.

This chapter contains three major sections related to the role of business and industry in the career development and employment of handicapped individuals. The sections will identify

- specific contributions that business and industry can make to programs for handicapped individuals;
- suggestions for involving members of business and industry in the career development of handicapped individuals; and
- procedures to follow when educators approach prospective employers of handicapped individuals.

CONTRIBUTIONS TO PROGRAMS FOR HANDICAPPED INDIVIDUALS

The resources and personnel within the sectors of business and industry are so extensive that educators must understand the objectives and means of collaboration. They should identify objectives and possible joint efforts before approaching members of business and industry. At the same time, they should be open to suggestions that are presented by these same members. In other words, educators should approach business and industry with an opening statement such as

I have an idea on ways that we can work together in the career development for handicapped individuals. Do you have additional suggestions?

This is contrasted with the question: "What should we do?" which may only serve to alert businesspersons to the fact that the educator has not done her "homework."

214

This section includes discussions of several ways in which business and industry can assist educational programs. The following list provides suggestions for building a collaborative effort between major sectors in career development.

- Identifying trends in the economy
- Furthering contacts with business and industry
- Becoming advocates for handicapped workers
- Serving as a classroom resource
- Providing program consultation
- Providing work experiences
- Participating in conferences and workshops
- Providing instructional and resource materials

Trends in the Economy

Educators are always interested in trends such as student fashions or birth rates that determine enrollments for years to come. Educators must be attentive to the overall condition of supply and demand in the labor market, as well as specific shortages within particular categories of employment that offer opportunities for handicapped workers. Reports on employment by categories, age groups, and industries are available through several government agencies, although the Department of Labor has the principal responsibility of providing the public with a continual assessment of the labor situation. For example, the Department of Labor is projecting a 32% growth in service-work jobs during the 1980's and 1990's. Job prospects for clerical workers, who are the largest part of the work force in America, will grow by 27%. Demand for craftsmen and skilled laborers such as carpenter, auto mechanic, and tool and die worker will also increase. Sales jobs in retail stores, manufacturing and wholesale firms will grow by 28%. Categories that will experience slow growth or no growth include production workers (those on assembly lines), unskilled laborers (freight and stock handlers, for example) and farm workers. This type of information constantly appears in such government publications as the *Monthly Labor Review* and *Occupational Outlook Quarterly*. Special reports and reprints can be obtained from the regional office of the Department of Labor, Bureau of Labor Statistics.

Community members of business and industry can translate major trends in the economy and labor force into the affects such movements may have upon job development and training for individuals with special needs. Businesspersons are often able to identify surges in demands for workers with particular skills, changes in job classifications, modifications of skill requirements due to the introduction of new machines or work routines, and growth or recession of the local economy. All of these factors affect the training, placement, and projected employment of handicapped workers.

Teachers, counselors, placement personnel, and other educators associated with the several aspects of career development may not be expected to be familiar with every machine and routine in the electronics or fast food industry. However, their familiarity with labor force data, general requirements for jobs within industries, and current conditions within the marketplace will improve communication between educators and local leaders in business and industry. This familiarity also provides a basic foundation for understanding the observations and recommendations from business people relative to changes in procedures and practices within the educational community.

Contacts with Business and Industry

Self-reliance is a major part of the collective American personality. Most Americans believe that a person's efforts account for her success or failure, whether she falls into the white or blue collar categories. Such terms as *clout, influence*, and *pull* to name a few, are used in a derogatory fashion to identify individuals who have advanced in the organization or achieved an objective based on means apart from their work skills.[4] Educators would be fooling themselves if they did not imagine that meeting people in business and industry for the purpose of securing contacts was a necessary function associated with developing jobs for handicapped workers. American workers would like to believe that their success on a job is due to their own efforts and ability, but individuals with special needs have stated that they would first like to have a chance at a job!

Individuals from one walk of life or profession ((education and rehabilitation) need an entree to another sector (business and industry) simply because the normal training and pursuit of professional goals does not bring members of one sector into frequent contact with those from the other one. Bankers are more acquainted with other bankers than they are with teachers because most of the working day and very often, their social life includes other bankers. Thus, it is a question of how an educator can meet individuals in business and industry who can help train or employ handicapped workers. One answer is to use all possible leads and contacts within business and industry.

Educators can use the resources of vocational rehabilitation, sheltered workshops, youth training programs, and just about any organization

---

[4]These terms, as well as the expression "It's who you know that counts," are not confined to the world of work.

that has contacts with business and industry. Such contacts are important because they

1. economize on the educator's time and energy that are needed to complete other responsibilities; and
2. provide an element of support for the employer interview.

An educator can approach an employer independently and achieve favorable benefits for the program. However, the chances for success are enhanced if the placement personnel are recommended or endorsed by another businessperson.

In their extensive review of rehabilitation and job placement of handicapped individuals, Zadny and James (1976) distinguish between formal and informal sources of job leads. Contacts with members of business and industry (employers) fall in the category of informal sources and are also characterized by Zadny and James as "underused." These underused channels may provide better results simply because the commonly used sources support greater numbers of job seekers. The two categories of sources appear in Table 7.1.

Professionals can use the information in Table 7.1 to place clients, students, or just plain job seekers. Underused sources of information can be categorized as *personal contacts* between professionals, workers, and businesspersons with prospective employers. As program personnel develop greater contacts with community organizations, advisory groups, and members of the business and industrial sector, they take advantage of underused

TABLE 7.1
Used and underused sources of job leads.

Commonly Cited Sources	Underused Sources
Newspaper want ads	Past employer
State Employment Service	Past clients
Private employment agencies	Counselor's acquaintances
Help wanted signs	Employers cited by employers who have
Yellow pages	hired clients
Trade publications	Counselor co-workers
Unions	Service persons
Civil Service bulletins	Client family and friends
Business pages of newspaper	Workers at business hiring clients
Employers who have hired clients	

Source: Jerry J. Zadny and Leslie F. James, *Another view on placement: State of the art 1976.* Portland, Oregon: School of Social Work, Portland State University, 1976, Tabel 4, p. 29. Reprinted by permission.

channels of information and avoid excessive competition from other applicants for jobs.

Advocates for Handicapped Workers

Representatives from business and industry have publicized the handicapped individual's success at employment by making statements such as the following:

> When the handicapped individual's abilities are matched with the requirements of the job, he is no longer handicapped . . .
>
> > Dr. Ralph T. Collins,
> > Eastman Kodak Company

> This is not a charity situation . . . it is a moneymaking part of our operation . . .
>
> > Laundry Owner

> There's no reason why a disabled person can't function, and there's no reason why it isn't good business . . .
>
> > Charles Vail, Jr.
> > Industrial Corporation

A second form of endorsement is gained through "Employer of the Year" awards presented by such organizations as the President's Committee on Employment of the Handicapped, Governor's Committee on Employment of the Handicapped, and Association for Retarded Citizens. Newspaper and magazine stories, interviews, and media coverage generated by these awards have also increased training and employment opportunities for handicapped individuals.

Some educators have followed the example of national and state organizations by developing their school programs. In an attempt to gain public awareness of their "Project Success," the Roland (California) Unified School District, a work training and placement program, used a public relations firm to prepare a sample speech that members of the Advisory Committee (including local businesspersons) could deliver to fraternal and business organizations in support of the project (Wright, 1973).

"It's no handicap to hire the disabled."

Advertisement, Rohr Industries, Inc. (1981)

Classroom Resource

Chapters 3 through 5 contain suggestions for using representatives from business and industry as classroom resources. These learning activities most often include the traditional field trips and class presentations given by skilled persons who explain techniques and demonstrate how to use materials and tools. Several school systems have provided teachers with a Community Career Education Directory. The directory contains information on local businesses and industry, including address, telephone number, major industry or work activities, suggested hours for field trips, availability of guest speakers for the classroom, and the name of the person to contact. Educators from elementary through secondary school can use the directory to enhance the student's awareness of the many careers and specific job functions in community industries.

Members of business and industry can also help teachers to select materials, training manuals, or instructional guides. For example, placement personnel may review application forms or provide suggestions on training students for interviews. Plant supervisors can suggest training procedures that teachers can use in school or workshop environments to prepare students for the world of work. Although vocational educators are usually familiar with changes and modifications in selected industries, personnel from various companies should continue to advise them on changes in materials, machines, or routines that should be reflected in the training program.

As one part of a comprehensive career education program for physically disabled students, Cohen and Stieglitz (1980) wrote a monograph that outlined the development of a "speakers' bureau." The bureau brought the experts to the students and helped to resolve some difficulties that physically disabled students experienced in exploring work sites and interviewing workers. The monograph can be used with all handicapped individuals and contains information on planning, implementation, evaluation, and suggestions for preparing students.

Prepare your resource person is one rule that educators should keep in mind whenever they ask a representative from business or industry to act as a speaker, consultant, or tour guide to groups of students, faculty, or parents. Preparation should include an interview with program personnel and presentation of printed or visual information about the resource person's role and importance in the development of the exceptional person's career. Preparation will give resource people an idea of what is expected of them and how they can use their time and resources more efficiently. This information will influence the resource person's decision regarding continued involvement with the school system.

Program Consultation

The scope of a career development program, including vocational training and placement, requires several skills on the part of educators. These skills are essential to such program components as student evaluation, program evaluation, management of resources, and cost analysis. In addition, these skills may be used to resolve specific problems relative to minimum wage laws and work-study assignments, cooperative agreements between the school system and other agencies, and placement evaluation of former students and their employers.

Opinions from members of the business and industrial sector may help educators to find solutions to mutual problems. One particularly useful resource to agencies, companies, and school programs is Mainstream, Inc. Located in Washington, D.C., Mainstream Inc. is a nonprofit firm that assists in the areas of affirmative action and compliance to federal laws. One of its publications on disabled people in the work world (Mainstream, 1981) identified six major problem areas that companies and training agents have to face. They should

- prepare company personnel to work with handicapped workers;
- use community resources to recruit qualified applicants;
- develop job training programs to match company needs with the applicant's abilities;
- establish guidelines for reasonable accommodation;
- return injured workers to the job; and
- help the applicant to "sell" her skills and qualifications.

The publication includes specific recommendations and resources for each problem area and is a valuable reference for program consultation.

Representatives from business and industry can also advise program directors about the competencies required by teachers or other personnel to prepare students for the job market. Jobs, skills, and work roles are in constant change, and those people who prepare students to enter such a fluid market must also command certain competencies.

Work Experience

If there is one ingredient that stands out as the prominent link between business and industry and the education system across the country, it is their cooperation in work experience or work-study programs for students. Business and industry have been active in collaborative efforts to develop field experience, student internships, summer employment, and on-the-job training. These programs provide students with hands-on experiences that test their interests in particular jobs; provide a source of evaluation for supervisory personnel; train students to use tools and complete tasks; and reward them for the amount of energy that they have invested in the experience. Although it may be a cliché to say "experience is the best teacher," every significant program for handicapped individuals involves the work experience situation.

Program personnel should consider two significant points in establishing a series of work experiences for their students. First, a sequence of experiences should be available so that individuals from elementary school through adult education can be involved in appropriate work positions meeting their level of maturity, interest, and ability. Work experience is not *the* final stage of a training program. Ideally, work experience should be an integrated element of the training program and should be available at various points in the student's career development. Such a series of experiences provide the individual and program personnel with several forms of evaluation relative to intended occupational roles. It also allows the student to experiment with work roles that may benefit her at later stages of development, as in the instance of a change of occupations.

Work experience is *not* the final stage of a training program . . .

Second, work experience is a training device. If program personnel permanently place a student in a work-study position, then they have lost it

Business and industry provide students with the training they need to achieve occupational goals.

221

as a training experience for other students. We are well aware of the temptation to place students in employment when the same firms indicate that there are openings. But, the real value of work experience is that a number of students can be cycled through a series of work tasks that have been identified and evaluated by supervisors and educators. This knowledge becomes a standard by which other students can be measured and trained. Eliminating a training site or series of experiences forces educators to repeat the laborious effort of locating another cooperative businessperson, establishing communication with supervisors, and investing additional time that could have been used to help more students find employment.

One variation on work experience is the involvement of faculty members in similar on-the-job routines. For example, Kern High School District, Bakersfield, California, financed the placement of its vocational instructors in work-study positions in community businesses. Since these instructors were to train students before placing them in the community, the district made sure that the teachers knew about the work routines and tasks that would be required of the students. The inservice training of the faculty allowed them to work on jobs that they would later teach to their students.

IBM Company conducts a summer work-experience program for deaf college students who are preparing for programming careers. It is felt that employers will be more receptive to hiring these individuals if they have proven themselves in a real work environment. They are paid a standard hourly rate. Managers and staff participating in the program are informed on such topics as residual hearing and hearing aids, speech difficulties, and language difficulties. The program is deemed successful by IBM, which employs a considerable number of trainees after graduation (Jamison, 1977a).

Conferences and Workshops

Conferences and workshops bring people together to discuss themes, problems, issues, or actions related to career development for handicapped individuals. These events can be used to explore such concerns as

- partnership of business/industry and education in career development for handicapped individuals;
- preparation of handicapped youth to meet the changing job market;
- education's role in retraining the employee who is disabled while on the job; and
- requirements imposed by legislation.

Various organizations within the business world, as well as individual companies, have sponsored conferences and workshops in the broad area of career education for American youth and workers. However, the 1977 White

House Conference on Handicapped Individuals made recommendations pertinent to extended cooperation by business and industry with education in career development of handicapped workers. Some of the delegates' recommendations also provided additional themes for joint conferences and workshops. The President's Committee on Employment of the Handicapped (1977a) reports the following recommendations:

- a national public awareness program should be developed to give recognition to employers who hire disabled people;
- training for supervisors should emphasize the utilization of handicapped workers;
- transitional employment programs should be developed (such as psycho-social centers for mentally restored people and occupational training centers for mentally retarded individuals); and
- vocational schools, sheltered workshops, and other places of training should teach the skills that really meet the needs of local employers.

Instructional and Resource Materials

Business and industry and education have cooperated for several years in the preparation of students for work roles. Although the cooperation has been greater in programs for normal and gifted or talented students, there are indications that the collaboration will expand to programs for handicapped individuals due to the encouragement of the President's Committee on Employment of the Handicapped, school personnel, and organizations.

Hensley (1977) reviewed the professional literature and cited numerous instances in which leading companies and business organizations have taken an active role in furthering career development in the work force, as well as students in community school systems. These activities include

- policy statements
- work experience
- tours and field trips
- continuing education
- projects that include business/industry and education
- conferences and workshops
- resources for classroom speakers and
- published instructional and resource materials

The latter activity includes such organizations as the American Society for Training and Development, National Association of Manufacturers, and the Business Industry Community Education Partnership, as well as such companies as International Telephone and Telegraph, General Electric,

223

Mountain Bell, and the Wells Fargo Bank of California. Readers interested in the original sources for many of the above activities should refer to the bibliography accompanying Hensley's review.

We need not elaborate on the kinds of materials related to career education that are provided by organizations and companies. Any description would soon be outdated as materials are changed or are exhausted. The important thing to remember is that these materials will exist as long as business/industry is involved in the career development of the American worker.

INVOLVING BUSINESS AND INDUSTRY

The previous section identified what members of business and industry could contribute to a career development program. This section suggests how educators can contact and involve members of business and industry in career development programs that benefit the entire community. The following list provides suggestions:

- Inviting business and industry to serve on a Community Advisory Committee
- Requesting input from Committee for Employment of the Handicapped
- Giving presentations to Civic Organizations
- Issuing publications about program (e.g., brochures, reports, news release items)
- Advertising in business publications
- Conducting job fairs, workshops, and institutes

Community Advisory Committee

The role of the Community Advisory Committee can be a significant factor in the success of the career development program. If school personnel anticipate that the community will accept the individual with special needs and support school programs, then the Advisory Committee must be more than a perfunctory group whose members' names enhance the program director's stationery. Campbell, Todd, and O'Rourke (1971) and Phelps (1976) state that the committee can provide valuable service by

1. reviewing program components, such as instructional materials, facilities, equipment, and cooperative training agreements;
2. identifying community contributions, resources, and effective measures of public relations; and
3. developing evaluation designs that will be included in the program.

There is no hard and fast rule as to how many members should be on the committee or for what length of time they should serve. Members of the committee would most likely include representatives from major industries that may employ graduates of the program. However, school personnel should not assume nor convey the impression that the members of the committee are obligated to find jobs for students or hire a certain number of graduates. The members' principal role is to assist the program and function as advocates for handicapped workers in the community. The following list of suggested members of the committee represents a cross section of the major groups of individuals who are interested in student success or who can directly influence training procedures:

1. personnel or employment managers who would be able to advise educators about application forms, interview procedures, and employment trends;

Participation in Community Advisory Committees is one of the many ways in which business and industry can contribute to the planning and implementation of career education programs.

2. supervisors who are in direct contact with handicapped workers and can identify potential difficulties for handicapped workers in work settings;

3. directors or managers of a firm that employs a number of handicapped workers who would speak to businesspersons about the company's successful experiences in employment or accommodation;

4. members of parent organizations who are strongly interested in the career development of handicapped people and could support school programs by forming coalitions of parents and handicapped workers;

5. members of community agencies involved in the training and placement of handicapped workers who could provide information on the challenges faced by the adult individual with special needs;

6. member of an insurance firm acquainted with the practices and rates for industries that employ handicapped workers;

7. individuals with handicaps who have succeeded in the work world and can provide unique insights into the program's training and placement components.

Even though committee members may have expertise in particular areas, educators should not assume that these members are familiar with the issues and problems involved in the career development of individuals with special needs. The members should attend a series of information sessions, informing them about the school program, community efforts, and the national scene. At times, members of the committee may conduct these sessions. But school personnel must initially plan the overall direction until the committee members have had time to identify their interests and request information on specific areas.

There are some unique examples of the extent to which community committees can become involved in the job success of handicapped individuals. Zuger (1971) reports the development and activities of a Committee for the Specialized Placement of the Handicapped, Institute of Rehabilitation Medicine, New York City. The committee consists of approximately 25 members, representing large and small companies, legal firms, banks, manufacturers, insurance companies, retail stores, and a daily newspaper. These community members regularly interview handicapped individuals who are ready to enter the labor market. But the committee members' strongest contributions come out of their suggestions for job leads and employment possibilities. This does not mean that the committee members are obligated to employ the candidates. Over time, this procedure may discourage members from active participation or exhaust employment openings. Zuger attributes the success of the committee to

1. availability of committee members for the regular meetings, discussions, and suggested actions that will help the individual reach employment objectives;
2. commitment of its members to provide employment leads; and
3. vigorous follow-up of committee members by institute personnel that will maintain communication on the progress of the committee, as well as individual workers.

"Handicapped workers are not handicapped when employed in the right jobs!"

Advisement, Employment Development Department, State of California (1981)

Committee for Employment of the Handicapped

The three levels of the Committee for Employment of the Handicapped are headed by the president, governor, and mayor. These committees are a powerful ally because members of business and industry serve on employment, education, communications, medical, and other subcommittees. The committee also provides educators with *contacts* to members of government agencies, labor, and civic groups. Some mayor's committees have cooperated with school systems and state agencies in the training and placement of handicapped workers.

The activities and influence of local committees will vary. Sometimes the first venture leads to tremendous rewards. For example, the South Bay (Los Angeles) Mayor's Committee sponsored the award winning film *A Different Approach*, which presented a humorous side to hiring handicapped workers. Success with the film contributed to the committee's partial financial support of the Media Office of the California Foundation on Employment and Disability. The Media Office, affiliated with the California Governor's Committee for Employment of the Handicapped, concentrates on getting disabled people hired in the communications and media industry. Hartman (1983) reviewed the Media Office's accomplishment in the few years of its existence. The Office has

1. conducted successful media awards banquets honoring members of the industry who have promoted positive images of handicapped people;
2. established a casting clearinghouse for an inter-guild committee of performers with disabilities;

227

3. sponsored "showcase" productions featuring the talents of performers with disabilities for interested writers, agents, casting personnel, and network and studio executives; and

4. provided technical assistance to writers and producers for script development and reviews that have accurately portrayed handicapped people.

The goals and future direction of the Media Office, as it works with the Screen Actors Guild and other guilds and unions, was summarized in the following excerpt from a letter to the editors of the *Los Angeles Times*:

> People's attitudes toward the world are shaped by their experiences. Some are firmly rooted in reality, while others are created by the illusions projected on their movies and TV screens. Therefore, we all have a responsibility to do the best job we can to enhance the humanism and integrity of the images we present. This is our goal as it relates to disability.
>
> Asner, Hartman, and Schallert (1982)

Civic Organizations

The term civic organizations is used broadly to include all groups that are interested in improving the well-being of members of the community. The organizations serve as fertile ground for contacts with members of the business community, simply because both the educator and businessperson share a desire to improve conditions for members of the community. This mutual respect provides educators with an opportunity to present the benefits of the training and placement program and pursue possible leads for further involvement with business and industry. Several program directors have said that some of their strongest supporters or employment leads have been discovered when a businessperson approached the educator after a presentation to a civic group.

We suggest that educators regard presentations to civic organizations as a major public relations project. The speaker should use any form of audiovisual technique or publication that would involve the audience. We also suggest that

1. the presentation emphasize major points so that the audience will not get "lost" in too many figures and details;

2. the speaker involve the audience by stimulating their desire to ask questions about career development, training, placement, or job success;

3. materials be available to members of the audience who wish to read at their leisure or contact other sources of information; and

4. former or current students of the program be included in the presentation to dispel the audience's possible misconceptions about the abilities of individuals with special needs.

Program Publications

The educator should always try to focus the community's attention on the students' goals and achievements. This can be accomplished through personal presentations, as discussed in the previous section, face-to-face meetings with civic leaders, and interviews with businesspersons and parents. However publications can be used as a ready reference when the educator is unavailable and can also be distributed to the public as well as to members of business and industry. The educator can use several kinds of publications to advertise career development and involve members of business and industry. These publications would include

1. an attractive brochure that provides an overview of the program, its intents, and the *advantages* that the program can offer to the reader. The brochure can help educators to make contacts and obtain interviews with employers. Brochures may include pictures of students at work to convey the impression that one of the goals and accomplishments of career development is successful employment.
2. several types of reports that provide "hard data" about the program. This information is necessary to justify expenditures and is valuable to administrators, teachers, members of the Community Advisory Committee, and members of the community who wish to know how their tax dollars are spent. The most frequent topics for these reports include successful placements by work titles; identification of business firms that have hired handicapped workers; and the amount of money that former students have earned over a period of time and the amount of tax dollars these students returned to the community.
3. news release items that can be used by the local media in direct reprints, broadcasts, or that can provide the basis for a feature story. The news release can advertise the availability of qualified workers, such as a "work wanted" advertisement. The advertisement may include the unique accomplishments of the student, such as the completion of a training program for mechanics or computer operators.

Business publications can also be used to publicize career development and involve business and industry. Several industries and companies publish their own materials. Anyone who has ever sat in a doctor's or dentist's office may have spent a long period of time paging through what are termed the *trade journals*. Articles about handicapped workers have appeared in many of these publications. Educators at the local and state level should be aware that such journals can help to advertise and inform potential employers about career development.

Job Fairs, Workshops, and Institutes

Several organizations (parent groups, associations formed by individuals with special needs, government agencies) have attempted to educate employers and other personnel in business and industry about the positive qualities of handicapped workers. These organizations have combined their talents, contacts, and efforts to

1. inform employers about ways they can meet recent changes in affirmative action laws for handicapped workers;
2. display the achievements of other employers who have hired handicapped workers;
3. provide a meeting place where employers can interview prospective employees with handicaps;
4. provide a forum to discuss common problems experienced by both employers and employees;
5. discuss local or regional job openings and projected changes in the demand and supply of labor; and
6. increase employers' knowledge about the abilities and skills of an untapped segment of the labor force.

These efforts may be presented over local or educational television and could be organized into the traditional conference or the increasingly popular "job fair." The job fair is a central location at which representatives from business and industry interview applicants. It benefits individuals with handicaps by providing several interview possibilities within one location. Job fairs have been conducted at the Annual Meeting of The President's Committee on the Employment of the Handicapped, regional and national conventions, and the International Abilities Unlimited Exposition in California which advertised two days of interviews with up to 100 major employers who were "searching for qualified applicants."

The Epilepsy Association of Central Maryland obtained a grant from the Department of Special Projects of the Maryland State Department of Education to increase job possibilities for individuals with neurological disorders (National Spokesman, 1977a). The association recruited employment specialists from private industry to conduct a series of 25 educational seminars designed to take the mystery out of neurological disorders and decrease the resistance to hiring individuals who have them. The seminars focused on meeting the needs of people who make policy decisions on employment, evaluate individuals, function as line supervisors, and interview prospective employees. These organizations will probably continue to use various training methods to increase the employer's understanding and improve employment possibilities for handicapped workers.

This section has focused on ways in which educators can contact and involve representatives of business and industry in career development activities. The following are some important considerations permeating the numerous attempts:

- *Involve members of business and industry as soon as possible in the career development of handicapped individuals.* There are several reasons for this recommendation. First, the active cooperation and commitment of members of business and industry may be stronger if they are approached in the formative stages of a program or project rather than serving as symbolic representatives. Second, they may be able to suggest important changes or ways of getting support while the program or project is in the developmental stages. This is especially crucial if the project actually includes provisions for cooperation with business and industry. Some educators have spent considerable time planning a project, preparing staff and students, identifying training experiences and appropriate industries, and then approaching business and industry with the expectation that employers, supervisors, managers, and businesspersons would just fit right into their plan. We do not recommend this course of action.

- *Maintain a continuity in communications with members of business and industry.* Business executives are accustomed to a certain degree of punctuality, and supervisors want precision. Both are especially discouraged when they are approached by several representatives of the same program or project. Just imagine what your response might be if three of four salespersons for the same product called you on the telephone during your office hours. The continuity of communication is also important once individuals are involved in the program, as emphasized in our discussion of the Community Advisory Committee.

- *Publicize the link between business/industry and education as much as possible.* Of course, any efforts at publicity should be approved by the principal agents involved in the program or project. Once publicity has been approved, educators should use as many resources as possible within the community, area, state, region, and nation. Successive stages of information contain a corresponding vehicle for communication with the public. For example, the community may have a small, neighborhood or local newspaper and radio station; an area may be covered by a large city newspaper, television station, and several AM-FM radio channels; a state would be covered by official publications written by members of the legislature or

---

231

speeches entered into the official proceedings; the region may be covered through professional publications that pertain to the particular industry; and the nation may release information through federal agencies that are concerned with education and employment of handicapped individuals. Such publication of an existing collaboration between business/industry and education can help to expand programs, as well as improve employment possibilities for handicapped individuals, as will be discussed in the following section.

- *Encourage the involvement of business and industry by using as many resources as possible.* The previous discussions of publications, presentations, and committees include references to the many agents within a community who can become advocates for training programs. These advocates, whether they be civic groups, parents' organizations, or influential citizens, will need the information and encouragement of educators. Furthermore, educators must be aware of the potentials for the involvement of the entire community and should coordinate activities with the goals of career development for handicapped individuals.

APPROACHING THE EMPLOYER

This section focuses on how educators can improve employers' attitudes toward handicapped individuals. Success of handicapped employees in a variety of occupational tasks is one important factor that has helped to change employers' attitudes. The professional and popular literature also report modifications and accommodations in work settings so that individuals in wheelchairs or with prosthetic aides may work in offices and on assembly lines. If one employer provides a handicapped employee with a chance to prove her ability then other expansions in job opportunities and successes will follow. Thus, the reader may encounter reports of electric welders who are blind, computer programmers who are severely handicapped or deaf, offset press operators who are mentally retarded, and physicians with cystic fibrosis.

Employers have always played an important role in the success of handicapped individuals, but it has only been within recent years that professionals in all disciplines associated with training and placement have developed more sophisticated approaches that influence the employer's decisions. Much of this sophistication has really been adapted from techniques used by members of the business community to market their products with the general public. McMahon and Spencer (1979) anticipated a certain resistence on the part of rehabilitation personnel to the concept of "selling" disabled workers to employers. They analyzed the system behind the professional and concluded that

What is being sold, rather, is a system—a system of services which the job creator provides to the employer in exchange for job opportunities. When perceived in this way, the legitimacy of using systems selling (not product selling) strategies becomes obvious.

McMahon & Spencer (1979, p. 69)

The idea of approaching a prospective employer with an array of supporting agencies, personnel, and placement strategies leads to a series of logical steps that can be taught to professionals. For example, Galloway (1982) reports a method through which a rehabilitation agency offers a package of services to a company in exchange for employment of the agency's clients. The method, called "The Employer Accounts Strategy," uses such major strategies as prospecting the account, assessing the agency's strengths prior to negotiations, establishing agency and client credibility, and preparing for the first appointment. Terms such as products, accounts, and negotiations used in reference to disabled people and their future contradict our efforts to establish these same people as first-class citizens. No doubt, you will be able to choose those methods that best represent your philosophy and personal style and thus, open up areas of employment for handicapped workers. The following list provides suggestions for approaching employers concerning job possibilities for handicapped individuals. Each suggestion is discussed further in this section.

Ways to Approach Employers:
- Study employers' apparent receptivity toward handicapped individuals
- Decide on the most appropriate method of contact
- Prepare a "sales" presentation
- Be able to counteract employer resistance
- Maintain employer contact after placement

Qualification of Prospective Employers

Placement personnel should research the potential employer's type of business, number of employees, current projections of the firm's earnings or success, size and complexity of the organization, and the extent of union involvement. Galloway (1982) also suggests that personnel acquire information on the firm's training programs, job opportunities, and internal career ladders so that disabled workers will not be placed in "dead end jobs." This information can enter into the conversations between employers and placement personnel and indicate to the former that the placement person is attempting to stay abreast of developments in the community and economy. However, this information can give the advocate an idea of whether she should even attempt a placement. For example, the firm may already be well-staffed in particular skill areas that match those of the prospective employee, or the firm may be experiencing an upswing in business and is about

233

to expand its labor force. This kind of information decreases fruitless attempts at placement.

Other clues that may indicate an employer's acceptance of handicapped employees include

1. the employers' participation in organizations or events that raise funds for exceptional individuals;
2. the existence of ramps at work sites to facilitate employee movements;
3. designated parking areas for handicapped drivers;
4. other architectural changes that indicate the firm's attempt to meet the needs of handicapped employees or prospective customers;
5. advertisements for career opportunities in publications that are directed at the community of handicapped people; and
6. articles in the local newspapers about the company's experience in placement of handicapped applicants *or* about the success of handicapped workers at a particular company.

The process of matching students to jobs, as well as influencing employers' opinions about hiring handicapped workers, requires a great deal of time and enthusiasm. An entire morning can be wasted on attempting to develop a job when some prior review of the considerations that were discussed in this section may provide better alternatives. Another way to eliminate wasted effort is to maintain a positive attitude toward job development. Visiting employers, attending civic functions, keeping abreast of the local economy and other activities can tax the placement person if her attempts have not resulted in increased opportunities for handicapped workers. The placement person must be aware of her success-failure ratio in order to prevent any decrease in enthusiasm and effort that may result from ignoring essential factors. These factors include knowledge about the employer, applicant, and interview techniques.

Contacting the Employer

There are several ways of contacting employers, but the success of these methods is measured by whether the placement person has gained an appointment to explain the merits of her program or trainees. Sigler and Kokaska (1971) identify four major means of contacting employers: (1) mail; (2) telephone solicitation; (3) personal visits; and (4) referrals.

The *mail* approach can be further divided into several forms of cover letters that introduce the program or sender with a statement of intent with the goal of establishing further contact with the employer. The letter can include a response form that the employer can mail to the sender. The disadvantage of the mail approach is that the employer may avoid any face-to-face contact with the sender. However, the letter can be combined with a referral from another employer, information about the program, and the honest intent of the placement person to avoid wasting the employer's time. This type of letter should be followed by a telephone call or personal inquiry.

Telephone solicitation can be combined with the cover letter and referrals and should precede personal visits. The essential part of this technique is that the placement person is assertive and positive and conveys much information in as short a time as possible. The following is an example:

Ms. Businessperson, my name is Mr. Placement person with Success School District. We have a program that trains individuals to work in companies like yours. I would like to see you for 30 minutes, at your convenience, to explain how our program and students can benefit you. Do you have an opening on your calendar?

Personnel should develop their deliveries to meet the requirements of the firm and practice "jumping" the various hurdles, such as telephone operators and appointment secretaries, who block contacts with employers.

Personal visits can be effective, since it is difficult for an employer to say she won't see the placement person when they are both in the office. Personal visits can also be dangerous if the employer considers it a definite intrusion on her schedule. Personnel must extradite themselves from such situations with assurances that they were in the neighborhood with other scheduled interviews and simply had the time and opportunity to call on this additional employer. Personal visits should be followed by an attempt to establish a definite time for an appointment.

Referrals are one of the most successful methods, since they can be preceded by a favorable work report or letter from the employer's associate or friend. In a sense, a referral obligates the employer to give the placement person a chance. However, it also obligates the placement person to present as strong and polished delivery as possible, since the employer can always inform her friend about the interview. The advocate who fails to make the appointed time, is ill-prepared, or blunders through the delivery may experience refusals for appointments, as well as loss of her initial source of referral.

Techniques for the Appointment

Business appointments are similar to classroom presentations in that the placement person must be well-prepared to accomplish her objectives through selected means. Several authors suggest techniques that can be used in the interview (Galloway, 1982; Payne, 1977; Payne & Chaffin, 1968; Payne, Mercer, & Epstein, 1974; Sigler & Kokaska, 1971). Payne (1977) suggests three categories of techniques that could be used with employers. The categories are derived from Graves' (1970) levels of existence, and the appropriate means of counseling and managing individuals who exhibit behaviors for a particular classification. The three categories include

1. the *saintly conformist* is a conservative pillar of the community who manages the business in an autocratic fashion;
2. the *materialist* is a production-oriented person who dresses and behaves like the "sharp" businessperson; and
3. the *sociocentric* is a people-oriented employer who judges success in terms of how well the employees get along with one another, but may be limited because she does not like to make unilateral decisions on hiring handicapped workers.

Knowledge about behavioral or managerial characteristics falls within our previous discussion of qualifying the prospective employer. Modifying the presentation according to the viewer has always been the mark of a "top" salesperson and is in no way unique to the field of job placement. But first of all, the presentation should include facts, figures, diagrams, and whatever means that will convince the employer that the handicapped worker is backed by a system of training and support. The following suggestions should be considered in preparing the sales presentation.

Develop rapport with the employer. Although the primary goal is to place students in an employment situation, every employer can benefit the program and the employment of handicapped workers in several ways. The employer may eventually become a member of the Community Advisory Committee, provide skilled advice for classroom activities, or allow her business to be a training site. Compatible relationships with employers facilitate actions that can benefit training programs.

Keep the presentation short and simple. Concentrate on developing a delivery that describes the basic elements of the program or individual. Charts, pictures, and audiovisual aids may be included, but the employer should not be overloaded with needless statistics and examples. The resource person should provide essential information that allows the employer to understand the *who, what, where,* and *why* of the program. A second type of information answers basic questions that the employer may raise about the program or applicant.

Speak in terms the employer can understand. Professionals must be certain to avoid medical or psychological terms that can only confuse the employer or that lead her to questions that divert from the objective of the presentation.

Emphasize the benefits for the employer. These benefits may be reflected in a specific training program that prepares the applicant for work tasks in the employer's firm, increases attendance, or expands production capacity. These benefits should be supported by information contained on the charts or other audiovisual aids.

"If the handicapped person will be an asset to the employer (as should be hoped and expected as a result of training), this must be conveyed in a convincing manner along with any statement about making follow-up support available if difficulties should arise."

Weisgerber, Dahl, & Appleby, 1981

Build employer responses in the affirmative. In other words, get the employer to say "Yes" to the questions you ask. Positive responses may cause the employer to be more receptive and may also provide the placement person with feedback. We would hope that the employer would find it very difficult to say "No" when you finally request her participation after a long line of "Yes" responses.

Stay with the objectives of your delivery. If you are asked a question, respond with a statement that may be near the answer that the employer wants but is closer to your purpose. For example if the employer asks you "How can you train those people?" you could respond, "You would be surprised at how rewarding it is. Our students have proven themselves to be dependable on such jobs as . . . ."

Emphasize success with the training and placement of handicapped workers. The employer has to be assured that she will hire a worker who is the product of a training approach or group of professionals that prizes success. Past and current achievements by other students provide a valuable source of information to answer employer questions about the program gains.

If you were referred to the employer, emphasize that the referral was based on the student's ability. This is consistent with the goals of attempting to place individuals who demonstrate the various work abilities that are important to the employer. Of course, if the employer is going to hire her first employee from the training program, that employee should be one of the best workers so that the employer will be encouraged to make other referrals.

Emphasize your availability for further discussion or assistance. Your primary responsibility is to the handicapped worker, but you should also try to maintain a positive relationship with the employer. The placement person can help the employer with other matters related to the hiring of handicapped workers, such as affirmative action policies.

Be truthful and objective about the worker's disability, but avoid initiating lengthy discussions if the limitation is not relevant to the performance of the work tasks. The regulations on affirmative action have decreased the tendency of employees or applicants to hide certain forms of disability and placement personnel to be defensive in their presentations to employers. Nevertheless, several questions should be considered in qualifying the employer.

- Has the employer hired other individuals with similar disabilities?
- What type of work tasks will the employer expect of the applicant and will the disability prevent completion of the tasks?
- Does the employer think that personality factors are important to the completion of work tasks?
- Will the applicant's failure to reveal the disability disqualify her if the employer discovers it at a later date?

The final answer as to whether the employer should *always* know about the employee's special status is certainly a personal issue that the placement person and the applicant should resolve before either enters the interview or completes an application for employment.

Employer Resistance

Securing employment or training opportunities for individuals with special needs requires that placement personnel identify the employer's

- particular needs and requirements for employees, and
- doubts and misconceptions about handicapped employees.

The first element will vary according to the particular industry or occupational task. For example, the owner of a fast food service may stress speed of delivery, appearance, and a pleasing manner in dealing with customers, while the production manager of an electronics firm will be concerned with the employee's accuracy and ability to withstand fatigue. These unique requirements will surface during the interview between the placement person and prospective employer and are also linked to the employer's questions and doubts about the handicapped worker's ability to meet the established criteria.

The employers' objections to hiring handicapped workers have been discussed in the professional literature (Sears, 1975), speeches (Jamison,

1977b), and publications by the President's Committee on Employment of the Handicapped and the Department of Labor. The objections may include specific references to the applicant's lack of ability or reflect stereotypes about certain forms of disability. The placement person should use her experience or the professional literature to anticipate the employer's possible negative responses or attitudes. Most objections can be traced to the employer's misunderstanding of words used to describe exceptional individuals and a lack of exposure to the abilities of individuals with special needs. The placement person should meet the employers' objections or puzzled expressions with honest and firm answers and should continue to emphasize the applicant's ability to accomplish work tasks.

Some of these doubts and misconceptions will be examined in the following paragraphs. Professionals and researchers in the fields of special education, vocational placement, and rehabilitation have heard employers express these statements in various ways. These are not the prevailing attitudes of employers but rather reflect requests for better information and insight.

```
I need somebody with initiative.
```

In a survey of 200 community employers in Baltimore, Maryland, Stewart (1977) concluded that employers in certain industries are more interested in the applicants' work attitudes and motivation than their technical skills. Employers often picture the handicapped worker as being unable to learn new things, take responsibility, or cope with pressure. In some instances, these demands may be outside of the person's present capabilities, but the school personnel should determine the kinds of initiative that may be required for each job. One employer's concept of initiative may be another's idea of recklessness!

```
Could somebody like that really handle this job?
```

The employer's knowledge of a worker's disability can create doubts about the applicant's skill in certain situations or competence. The placement person has an advantage in these situations if she is familiar with the job specifications, confident of the applicant's abilities, and capable of matching the two to the satisfaction of the employer. Work experiences or a trial period on the job may convince the employer that the handicapped worker is able to meet job requirements.

> Our supervisors aren't counselors or therapists.

Although employers may recognize that the individual has the physical skill for the task, they may wonder if the applicant has the social-personal skills to get along with other employees. The employer's concerns may be justified, as in the placement of individuals with a history of personal problems. In these instances, the placement person will have to identify the amount of support that the employer can expect from outside sources that will insure the individual's success and decrease the concerns of the employer and fellow workers. This objection may also be countered if the applicant does not need any special supervision or help but simply has the skills for the job.

> My insurance company won't let me hire handicapped people *because* my workmen's compensation rates will skyrocket.

There are several ways of responding to this statement. Placement personnel can use specific instances to point out that the handicapped employee has not adversely affected the safety record of a particular business or industry. In fact, neither workmen's compensation nor group insurance rates are affected by the employment of handicapped workers. One of the best discussions of this artificial barrier to employment is by Brantman (1978) who was a rehabilitation counselor for CNA Insurance Company. Two factors that determine an employer's insurance rates are the nature of the business, and the accident record of the individual employer.

The President's Committee on Employment of the Handicapped or your state's Governor's Committee may be able to provide you with reprints of the above article as well as other examples in which employment of handicapped workers has not adversely affected safety records or insurance rates.

Two widely quoted surveys of the work performance of handicapped individuals were conducted at E. I. du Pont de Nemours and Company, America's seventh largest employer (Sears, 1975; E. I. du Pont de Nemours, 1982). The first survey gathered data on 1,452 employees who have disabilities such as blindness, heart disease, impaired vision, paralysis, epilepsy, impaired hearing, total deafness, and orthopedic problems. The second survey increased the number or respondents to 2,745 and added the categories of allergies, mental function, respiratory, and other impairments. The latter group of respondents included 429 workers with a second disabling impairment and 81 with a third. The major findings were that

1. disabled employees maintained a high standard of *safety* of 96% compared with 92% for nonimpaired employees.
2. disabled employees improved their *performance* of job duties from 91% to 92% over the two survey years as compared to 91% for nonimpaired employees.
3. disabled employees improved *attendance* records to 85% in 1981 compared to 91% for nonimpaired employees.

Sears also stated that there were no increases in compensation as a result of hiring disabled workers at du Pont. The two studies should be required reading for professionals who are working with prospective employers.

"The evidence is clear: disabled people are qualified and are meeting the criteria by doing their jobs with typical or better-than-typical attendance records, safety performance, and work attitudes."

The President's Committee on Employment of the Handicapped (1981)

I'll have to change my entire operation.

The imagined change is often far greater than the real one. For example, Krents reports on the results of a survey that found that it took 1 cent per square foot to make a building accessible to handicapped individuals, while it cost 13 cents a square foot to clean the floors. Berkeley Planning Associates (1982) surveyed 367 firms to determine the extent and types of accommodations that federal contractors initiated. About one-half of the accommodations cost employers nothing. Another 30% of the accommodations involved expenses ranging between $1.00 and $500.00, and 8% cost over $2000.00. In the same survey, 79% of the employers did not think accommodations were prohibitively costly. If the employer resists making changes in the work site to accommodate the needs of handicapped workers, she may be violating affirmative action regulations established by Section 503 of the Rehabilitation Act of 1973. Placement personnel can provide employers with the latest publications on affirmative action and information on several attempts that employers have made to alter job sites. The report by Berkeley Planning Associates contains numerous practices and incentives

241

for making accommodations. Other publications are available from Mainstream, Inc. and the President's, Governor's, and Mayor's Committee on Employment of the Handicapped.

> I want to know that the employee I hire will stay with me.

An employer can never be certain that any employee, able or disabled, will complete a certain period of employment. People find other forms of employment and experience numerous changes in their living conditions that can affect how long they stay with any one firm. Placement personnel can refer to the applicant's previous record of attendance in school or training programs.

> I've had some negative experiences with handicapped applicants.

This response is the most difficult to combat because it is based on fact rather than myth. With the development of advocacy groups, federal legislation, and interagency programs, employers have come in contact with more handicapped applicants *or* their representatives. A research study by Ellner and Bender (1980) identified some techniques that employers use to comply with federal regulations. The survey and interview results also identified several critical comments about the marketable job skills of the applicants and the performance of professionals in agencies that attempt to place handicapped people. One of the major criticisms rested on the employers' experiences with applicants who did not have the prior training, interview preparation, and motivation to warrant employment. These three critical components should provide placement personnel with the keys to success. The placement person *and* applicant should demonstrate the individual's skill, interpersonal abilities, and determination to secure the job.

This section has highlighted some of the major objections by potential employers. However the opposite to resistence is commitment, and one researcher (Petzy, 1979) presented a valuable discussion for placement personnel who want to engender positive responses. He described *the employer interaction process model* and the following six stages that reflect increasing levels of employer commitment to hiring disabled workers.

1. The employer fulfills his commitment in a brief interview by giving general information about his company.
2. The employer gives specific information about the company or position.

3. The employer allows site visits.
4. The employer accepts work experience placements within the company structure.
5. The employer changes the work environment to assist the individual.
6. The employer changes work assignments which is the most difficult stage to master.

Steinmiller and Retish (1980) elaborated on the above discussion to include a seventh stage (i.e. the employer as a teacher). They stated

> The employer's job is to provide the dimension of the skilled worker who knows the job expectations and appropriate behaviors. The special educator's job is to incorporate this material in the classroom so that the student can be successful in both the classroom and on the job. Again, it is a cooperative effort at the early stages in the student's education that will affect future employment.

Maintaining Employer Contact

Assuming that the educator has established contact with employers, developed the Community Advisory Committee, and recorded successful placements of students, the next major step should be maintaining a purposeful relationship with employers. The educator's contacts with employers can lead to benefits to the program, such as employer endorsements or suggestions for modifications and improvements. Follow-up contacts further integrate the experiences of the employer with handicapped workers into the overall training program and, therefore, assist placement goals for future students.

Program directors can contact employers through a consistent method of inquiry via the telephone, through the mail, or by visiting the employer. The inquiry need not be extensive but should provide the employer with an opportunity to elaborate on particular problems or concerns. Program directors should begin the inquiry with the following array of questions or topics that prompt the employer and allow for discussion.

Responsibilities. What kinds of duties are assigned to the employee? This information can be used in future advertising to attract potential employers and the general public. It also alerts program personnel to jobs, duties, and abilities that former students have mastered after they have completed a sequence of training experiences. Follow-up studies have helped to alter the placement personnel's perspectives on the students' abilities and potentials in the work world.

243

Success. What is the level of achievement of the employee? Is the employee more successful at some tasks than others? Employers are aware of production rates and success factors that determine the costs involved in the final product. Program personnel must continually strive to develop performance rates in their students that are compatible with employed individuals in a given business or industry.

Needs. Does the employee need to improve in specific areas? These areas may include the vocational, personal, or social skills of the worker. However, the interviewer must know two things about these needs once the employer has identified them. First, is the employee's status in jeopardy? Employers may recommend improvement but will not dismiss an employee just because she does not fraternize with other workers. Second, can the training program help the employee achieve new goals? This assistance may include additional training, if the employee wants to renew a relationship with her former teachers and counselors, or a referral to another community agency.

Communication. Is the employee successfully communicating with supervisors and co-workers? Communication is necessary for understanding tasks and, therefore, is a vital element in successful employment. Note that the emphasis in this area of inquiry is on *successful* communication and not on the form of communication.

Acceptance. Is the employer pleased with the work performance of the employee? This constitutes the proverbial "bottom line" to the entire follow-up process. Employers should not be forced into predicting whether they will continue to employ certain individuals because several forces act upon an industry or business that determine those decisions. A secure job one day may be changed a few months later, regardless of the employer's satisfaction with the employee. If the interviewer is able to obtain information on the five basic areas of inquiry, as well as obtain further insights from the employer (which may include projections on the economy, industry, or business), then program personnel will be able to determine if the employer is satisfied with graduates from the training sequence.

A second benefit from a continuous involvement with employers relates directly to the length of employment of the former student. The more interest that the placement person has in the training program, the more likely it is that the individual will remain on the job. There are several situations in which the worker may need some initial assistance by program personnel and tolerance by the employer. These situations may occur when the worker is

- being employed for the first time;
- changing occupations or employers;

- increasing the amount of responsibility;
- changing the kinds and sequence of tasks due to the introduction of new machinery or routines; and
- dealing with other problems outside of the job that nevertheless influence performance.

Counselors, educators, and rehabilitation personnel influence these situations and function as valuable references and sources of support. They may suggest alternate forms of behavior on the part of worker and employer or involve other professionals in the adjustments needed to maintain the worker in an employee status.

In addition, handicapped individuals can experience difficulties justifying post-placement attention by program personnel. These difficulties can include

- teasing and other disrespectful remarks by fellow employees;
- lack of social sophistication;
- environmental or structural impediments;
- adjustments to work schedules, routines, and overall surroundings;
- levels of anxiety promoted by personal desires to succeed on the job;
- transportation difficulties;
- adjustments in the individual's nonwork life to facilitate personal health and energy while on the job; and
- initial difficulties in communication with supervisors or fellow employees.

There are undoubtedly more difficulties and situations that program personnel can identify and resolve in their attempts to maintain former students in successful employment. General problems occur across all groups of workers; others are specific to industries or characteristics of the individual. These factors can only be identified if program personnel maintain a vigorous and consistent follow-up effort with employers. The benefits of such a policy accrue for the program, employer, and exceptional individual.

CONCLUSION

The actual involvement of business and industry in career education for handicapped individuals is in the very first stage of development. Business and industry has been hiring handicapped workers for many years and will undoubtedly increase that practice due to Sections 503 and 504 of The Rehabilitation Act of 1973. But employment is only one important part of career development. Although business and industry has been actively involved in career education, the vast majority of instances have been with students in regular education. Once again, handicapped individuals are near the end of the line in this aspect of career development. It is hoped that the suggestions contained in this chapter will provide educators with both the skills and enthusiasm for bringing business/industry, and education into numerous collaborative efforts in career development for handicapped individuals.

III
Implementation

Part three presents information for implementing career education. Career education is a carefully planned process that requires commitments from a large number of persons who desire to change educational practices for handicapped learners. This part explains how career education can be planned for students and adults and how community resources can become involved. The book concludes with an overview of issues and future directions in career development for handicapped individuals.

Chapter 8 illustrates and discusses a suggested process for planning and implementing career education in a school district. A 16-step process is recommended and explained. A Career Education Special Needs Committee, working with a District-Wide Career Education Steering Committee is suggested for providing the organizational leadership. A detailed organizational structure for career education committees is presented. A model Career Education Plan that can be used within education agencies is also presented.

Chapter 9 reviews four major areas of implementing career or vocational assessment. The chapter opens with a discussion of the contrast between traditional norm-referenced testing and criterion-referenced assessment. The second section elaborates on the Competency Rating Scale (CRS) that assesses the student's progress with the Life-Centered Career Education (LCCE) Curriculum. Vocational assessment is the third section and constitutes four components: clinical assessment, work evaluation, work adjustment, and job-site evaluation. The chapter concludes with a review of several attempts to apply vocational assessment to severely handicapped individuals.

Chapter 10 provides suggestions on how career education can be structured in a program by emphasizing academic, daily living, personal-social, and occupational instruction and their interaction. This is followed by reviews of school systems that have implemented Life-Centered Career Education (LCCE). A successful Experience-Based Career Education project in Iowa is described and depicts the potential of this approach in rural areas.

Chapter 11 presents an innovative Lifelong Career Development (LCD) model of comprehensive services for adults with handicaps. The LCD model is based on the competency approach as described in previous chapters and includes goals and objectives for programs at the community college level. The chapter elaborates on the roles of LCD team members in the following service areas: training, instruction, career assessment, career development planning, resource collection, information, and advocacy. Several practical examples of the application of services in each area are included. The chapter concludes with a discussion of the LCD Program Model and its Service Flow Design.

Chapter 12 identifies *some* of the major agencies and organizations available at the local, state, and national levels that are important to the career development of handicapped individuals. Community resources such as service organizations, vocational-technical schools, rehabilitation facilities, and sheltered workshops are particularly important local sources of assistance. The chapter also identifies major informational systems for materials and references on career development.

Chapter 13 briefly summarizes some of the major problems, needs, and issues in career education for handicapped individuals. The authors identify several future directions and areas of interest which are illustrative of the expanding interest in career development. Much has been accomplished; however more remains to be done if the career education needs of persons with handicaps in this society are to be served appropriately. If people are willing to change and work together, we will meet these needs.

Planning Career Education Programs 8

The **overall goals** of education and rehabilitation are to prepare the individual to live and work in society. If individuals with handicaps are to meet these goals, they must develop and integrate the necessary daily living, personal-social, and occupational skills into a rewarding and satisfying lifestyle. This includes learning about personal interests, needs, abilities, potentials, and the realities of a modern world. These understandings can help individuals to make appropriate decisions about their careers. The implementation of the career education concept should be infused throughout the entire curriculum. Thus, if career education is to become a reality for handicapped individuals, professionals will need to make changes to implement a meaningful and purposeful career development program.

Until recently, most school systems have provided students with a content-oriented curriculum in which students learn a specific body of knowledge. This approach may not directly suit the individual's needs. We recommend that educators adopt a process-oriented educational philosophy. Process education emphasizes the acquisition of specific skills that are necessary for community living and working and requires professionals to decide upon desired outcomes that can be defined in precise, measurable terms. This does not negate the importance or need for general education. We believe that the *program must include both general and career education* to maximize the student's career development.

If significant and positive changes in curriculum are to occur for handicapped individuals, the program should be carefully planned. It is not easy to convince people to substantially change the teaching, counseling, or services that they provide to students. They will need to believe in the need to change, be involved in making changes, and be recognized and rewarded

251

for their efforts. Normalizing the educational and rehabilitation process for handicapped individuals is an important concept that will need administrative support.

A career development program will most likely succeed if education for all students is directed toward similar goals. However this may not always be the case, since the curriculum focus for handicapped individuals is sometimes different from the programs that are planned for their nonhandicapped peers. When this occurs, fewer school personnel will be involved in the handicapped student's education program than if the entire student body was receiving a career development focus. We strongly recommend that career education be developed from a broader perspective that encompasses career development for all students within the school system.

This chapter will discuss the salient aspects of career education planning and implementation. We define *career* in its broader context, as illustrated in figure 8.1. The chapter is divided into three sections: the process of curriculum change; LCCE planning and implementation; and guidelines for the development of a career education plan. We hope that this chapter will help you understand the means through which career education can become a reality in school districts and in post-secondary settings.

THE PROCESS OF CURRICULUM CHANGE

Career education requires the active participation of the entire school community, parents, and various segments of the community. Interestingly, the current plea for educational reform calls for cooperative effort and collaboration between these three educative forces. Although education of our young people is everyone's responsibility, collaboration simply has not taken place

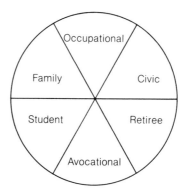

FIGURE 8.1
The various life roles comprising a career.

in this country. Perhaps the message has finally gotten across to the American people.

Change does not come easily. As the saying goes, "Everyone's for change unless they have to do it!" In their two-year federal project, *Promoting Collaborative Planning of Career Education for Disabled Students*, the

POINT OF VIEW

As we near the close of the twentieth century, the complexity of the world in which we live and work continues to increase. Far-reaching changes are occurring in the nature and structure of our social system. More people are looking for meaning in their lives, particularly as they think about the work they do, their situations as family members or as individuals, their involvement in their communities, their roles in education, and their involvement in leisure activities. The task of education and rehabilitation is to prepare young people and adults for this changing society by providing them with educational programs that will help them obtain the necessary skills to live and work effectively today and tomorrow.

However, effective educational programs don't just happen. A sound philosophical base and an effective planning process are necessary. This chapter provides readers with both of these elements. It involves career development orientation in an educational program that features life roles. The chapter also provides an effective step-by-step planning process to change existing programs into meaningful and purposeful career development programs.

Norman Gysbers is a professor in the Department of Educational and Counseling Psychology at the University of Missouri-Columbia (formerly president of the American Association for Counseling and Development).

Technical Education Research Centers (1980) identified several barriers that prevent collaboration from succeeding: time constraints, red tape, communication difficulties, turfdom and ego barriers, reluctance to share "power," disparate organizational goals, and coordination of efforts where typical line authority management techniques cannot be exerted.

Hoyt (1983) points out that before school and community interaction can truly take place and be successful, educators, parents, and other members of the community must agree on the purpose of education. They will need to clarify the basic purpose, goals, and objectives of the school if students are to have an organized and acceptable system of learning. The question of who the schools are for must also be answered. Changing curriculum will not occur unless educators pay considerable attention to these and many other issues. Two major problems are getting the community to accept responsibility and for the schools to loosen their hold. If members of the community are going to get involved, they must believe that they will get something in return. The proposal for involvement must make conceptual sense, and educators should be confident that what they propose will work. Otherwise they will probably never be able to involve the community again.

The key to successful career education for handicapped students is to involve school and community personnel who can help plan, implement, and evaluate programs. Career education should be part of the special education programs from elementary to high school (Taymans, 1982). Malouf (1982) identifies seven important questions to consider in starting or improving career education programs:

1. Is a full spectrum of career/vocational instruction provided to the handicapped, including development of: (a) career knowledge, attitudes and preferences; (b) marketable vocational skills; and (c) personal skills needed to find and keep jobs?
2. Is there a continuum of placement and service alternatives in the career/vocational education of handicapped students, with placement being made in the least restrictive settings?
3. Is there a continuity of curriculum across age levels—elementary to secondary and post-secondary—to allow systematic career/vocational development?
4. Are services provided to facilitate transitions—elementary to secondary, comprehensive to vocational-technical school, self-contained to integrated setting, school to work experience, and school to post-school life?
5. Are instructional goals adaptable to individual student career/vocational capacities?

6. Are evaluation procedures used appropriately?
7. Are non-school resources fully utilized, including: (a) rehabilitation and other agencies; (b) employers and private businesses; (c) professional and labor organizations; (d) parents and volunteers?

Although it may not be possible to introduce all of these elements immediately into a career development curriculum, they should serve as a major goal in moving toward a comprehensive career education program.

Handicapped adults are a neglected community resource for career education. Ward (1982) reminds us that "Inservice education programs . . . rarely involve handicapped people. Able-bodied people talk to other able-bodied people about how they should relate to handicapped people, but no one brings in the warm bodies" (p. 31). He recommends contacting handicapped members of consumer groups who can serve as trainers, small group facilitators, and workshop participants. Their involvement can give educators another perspective on the need for implementation approaches that will break down traditional stereotypes. Being severely handicapped himself, Ward speaks from experience. He has been involved in a unique program located in the Washington, D.C. area called *career orientation rap sessions* for handicapped adolescents.

Various school personnel, vocational rehabilitation counselors, parents, and business and industry will need to collaborate so that curriculum change can occur. MacArthur (1982) identifies several inservice education strategies that have proven to be effective in producing change. First, training should be directed at groups of people who can work together as a team in a given school building, agency, or district. Second, the staff should be involved in a planning process that will help them identify their needs, develop or find solutions, and implement program changes. Third, the administration, particularly principals, should support and commit themselves to changing the program. Fourth, trainers will need to provide information and serve as consultants to the planning teams. Fifth, many exemplary programs have been developed that can be adapted to fit a variety of settings (for example, the National Diffusion Network, U.S. Department of Education, Washington, D.C., has identified 28 programs in career and vocational education that work).

This is an opportune time for schools to redirect their curricula so that parents, handicapped citizens, service agencies, and business and industry become a community in partnership with the school. But the school personnel must make the first move. We believe that career education provides the mechanism for doing this, and in the next section we will describe a process that can achieve this end.

LCCE PLANNING AND IMPLEMENTATION

The process of planning and implementing comprehensive career education in a school district involves considerable time, work, and resources by a number of dedicated individuals from the school and community. Almost half of the school districts in this country report that they have some form of career education in their schools. But a closer perusal of these programs often reveals an expanded vocational education or guidance program rather than a totally infused career education program. The same situation generally exists for handicapped students, although as noted in other chapters, outstanding programs do exist.

Figure 8.2 illustrates some of the major steps that we believe are necessary for planning and implementing career education in school systems. Each of these steps is discussed next.

Step 1: Enlist Support of School District Leadership Personnel

The initial step in planning a career education program requires that interested staff become involved in an organization committee that will be supported by top level administrators in the school district. With the current pressures to educate handicapped students in the least restrictive environment, which is usually the regular classroom, most administrators will be willing to listen to how career education can meet the mandates of appropriate educational programming for these students.

At first the educator may need to approach the administration with a proposal that will involve only a small part of the staff and student population until the program has proven to be successful. Overwhelming proposals for educational change may produce a resistance reaction in some school districts. In others, administrators may be willing to restructure present practices and support the concept in its entirety.

The career education concept should be promoted as an agent of change that can respond to the many criticisms schools are receiving about their curriculum. Career development will link the gap between theory and practice so that students can apply the curriculum to living and working in this society. However career education should not be presented as a panacea for all the ills in education and society.

In addition to administrators, certain other decision-making groups may need to support career education programs. Teacher and community groups may be necessary for endorsement before top level administrators approve a career development orientation. Schools often need an outside stimulant to bring about a change.

FIGURE 8.2
Steps in planning and implementing career education.

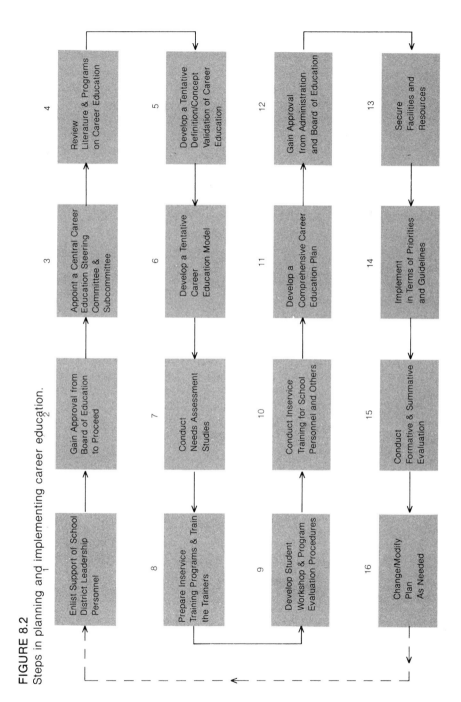

Source: *Trainers guide for life centered career education* (Brolin et al., 1978).

Step 2: Gain Approval from Board of Education to Proceed

Once the school district leadership personnel have endorsed the proposal, educators should seek similar support from the Board of Education. At this point, the educator should ask the Board of Education to endorse a career development-oriented curriculum in the district or in pilot schools. Figure 8.2 illustrates the proposed steps that program planners should present to the board so that they understand the process. Board members may indicate where they feel they should be involved and make administrative decisions (e.g., career education definition and conceptualization, career education model, inservice training program, and evaluation efforts). Educators should assure the board, as well as the top level administrators, that they will be kept informed of progress by the implementors. A timetable for the accomplishment of the various steps would also be helpful. To insure success, it is recommended that the organization committee gain a commitment from the board relative to the kind of activities that will be conducted. This commitment should also be requested of the administrators and other groups identified in Step 1.

Step 3: Appoint a Central Career Education Steering Committee and Subcommittees

A District-Wide Career Education Steering Committee should be organized to plan, implement, and manage the curriculum development activities. Such a committee may already exist, but it may not fully meet the needs of handicapped students. The committee's activities may need to be expanded to include a competency-based program for handicapped students.

The committee should consist of at least 12 people, including the person in charge of instruction, Director of Guidance, Director of Vocational Education, Director of Special Education, Director of Career Education (if any), principals, classroom teachers, one or two students, and community representatives. Community representatives should include parents, as well as persons from the business and industrial sector. Program planners should resist the temptation to put numerous people on this committee. It would be best to limit the size of the Steering Committee but increase the number of participants on the subcommittees.

The District-Wide Career Education Steering Committee chairperson should be knowledgeable about career education, should be influential enough to get people to work together, and should have the time and inclination to serve in this responsible position. Members should also be selected with care and should be informed of their responsibilities. Typical responsibilities of this type of committee are to decide upon goals and objectives; identify tasks and task force groups; set timetables; coordinate, communicate, and evaluate the work of the various subcommittees or task forces; and secure funds and resources.

The Steering Committee may decide to appoint a special subcommittee for the career development curriculum. We suggest that this is a viable procedure and will refer to such a subcommittee as the Career Education or Special Needs Committee. The chairperson and at least two other members of this committee should also be members of the District-Wide Career Education Steering Committee. This Special Needs Committee will be responsible for developing and promoting the school district career development program and each school building's career education plans for handicapped students. It may assume several of the responsibilities that were listed previously for the Central Steering Committee. The Special Needs Committee should work closely with the Steering Committee in formulating policies and procedures relative to the development of career education activities. The structure of the committees, critical to career education planning, is illustrated in figure 8.3.

If the district has a Career Education Steering Committee for all students, it will or should probably have several subcommittees, as described in figure 8.3. The Special Needs Subcommittee should in turn have task forces that would report to the respective subcommittees of the larger Steering Committee. They can provide these subcommittees with various information on handicapped students that relates to their area and the Special Needs Subcommittee. The Building Level Special Needs Committee implements career education in each of the schools. These committees should have four to six members, including special education, vocational education, and guidance personnel, administration, and perhaps one or two students. These committees work with the task forces and the Special Needs Subcommittee to implement ideas, identify needs, arrange for staff development training, and communicate with parents and other community representatives. Some of these individuals should be on a task force of the Special Needs Subcommittee.

The Special Needs Subcommittee must delegate the needed activities to the proper task force or building level committee. The following is a list of activities of the Special Needs Committee.

1. Review literature and programs that are pertinent to the career development of handicapped individuals;
2. conceptualize and define a career education model relative to handicapped students that is consistent with district policy;
3. compose a preliminary list of career education goals and objectives that can be categorized into three areas: instructional, community involvement, and administrative;

259

FIGURE 8.3
Organizational structure for career education committees.

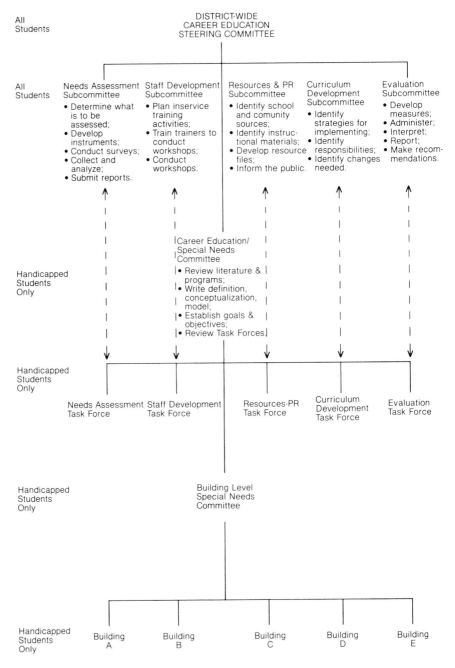

Source: Adapted from *The Missouri career education delivery system handbook*, (Arni, Magnuson, Sparks, & Starr, 1977).

4. present the philosophy, goals, and model to the District-Wide Career Education Steering Committee and the central administration to gain their support and suggestions;

5. approve the needs assessment studies proposed by the Needs Assessment Task Force;

6. review and approve the inservice training program proposed by the Staff Development Task Force;

7. review and approve student assessment, workshop evaluation, and program evaluation procedures proposed by the Evaluation Task Force;

8. review and approve the resources development and public relations proposals of the Resources and Public Relations Task Force;

9. review and approve the curriculum development proposals and activities of the Curriculum Development Task Force;

10. use the information submitted by the various task forces to compile, analyze, and prepare written reports that, in turn, should be submitted to the appropriate administrative channels and the Steering Committee;

11. write the career education plan for the district with information provided from various task forces and building committees;

12. present the career education plan to the Steering Committee and/or administration and the Board of Education for approval;

13. secure facilities and resources so that a comprehensive career education program becomes available to handicapped students;

14. implement the curriculum model in various school buildings according to priorities and guidelines;

15. supervise program evaluation efforts to ascertain curricula effectiveness and changes; and

16. instigate changes and modifications needed to deliver career education to handicapped students.

Step 4: Review Literature and Programs on Career Education

The Special Needs Subcommittee should act quickly so that members learn about career education and their specific responsibilities. These efforts and responsibilities should be publicized so that other faculty and interested community members may anticipate future activities.

Before the committee can formulate their career education definition, conceptualization, and model, members should become familiar with the various philosophies and opinions of leaders in the field and should visit school districts that have adopted the career education approach. They need to discuss their observations to determine the most appropriate philosophical basis and model design for their district. As can be determined from the previous chapters of this book, there are a great number of sources of information about current needs and practices. A telephone call to the state coordinator for career education and other state department of education officials may identify other programs in the state that merit review.

Based on this, the committee should be able to reach a consensus on the career education philosophy and model that suits their particular needs. They can formulate a tentative position statement requiring administrative and teacher or counselor reactions before the committee renders a final decision.

Step 5: Develop a Tentative Definition and Conceptualization of Career Education

Definitions and conceptualizations of career education range from a work-centered to a life-centered approach. A career consists of occupational, social, leisure, and interpersonal roles and is more than just an occupation or vocation. Career education is a multifaceted approach and should be distinguished from vocational education. Career education is a life-centered approach to education that is infused into all aspects of education and should prepare individuals for *all* aspects of community life that involve work.

If the Special Needs Committee chooses this conceptualization of career education, then their definition may be:

Career education is the process of systematically coordinating all school, family, and community components together to facilitate each individual's potential for economic, social, and personal fulfillment.

Step 6: Develop a Tentative Career Education Model

Many models of career education will be uncovered as the Special Needs Committee members review materials and visit projects and programs. The school district or state may already have their own model. It is not our intent to review these. Rather, we shall use the LCCE model as an example of the infusion of career education into the school curriculum.

The three-dimensional model illustrated in figure 2.1 (p. 45) is designed to provide the student with the competencies necessary for most of the roles, settings, and events comprising his life. It requires basic subject matter to be taught in relation to these competencies and forms the basis for developing the career education plan, which we will discuss later in this chapter.

The committee should review the definition, conceptualization, and model of career education with top level administrators, as well as the District-Wide Career Education Steering Committee. All interested parties should have the opportunity to react, contribute to, and endorse the program. The Board of Education should also review and endorse the proposals of the Special Needs Committee.

Step 7: Conduct Needs Assessment Studies

Needs assessments may be designed to measure a number of different aspects of the educational program. Gysbers (1973) describes three types of needs assessments required for sound program development: (1) the needs of students; (2) the status of the current program; and (3) the professional needs of the staff. These three types can be described by the following questions:

1. What do students, educators, parents, and community members see as important education outcomes?
2. Is the current program delivering the desired student outcomes?
3. What does the professional staff need to produce the desired outcomes?

Students should be encouraged to contribute to the curriculum planning process.

The answer to these questions will guide educational planners toward a person-centered rather than content-centered curriculum (Arni, Magnuson, Sparks, & Starr, 1977).

The District-Wide Career Education Steering Committee and the Special Needs Subcommittee should establish the objectives of assessment studies. However, the Needs Assessment Task Force will probably need to assume most of the duties associated with this activity and should inform the Special Needs Committee of its activities and request their suggestions. The task force will need the endorsement of the Special Needs and Steering Committees, as well as top level administrators, before the needs assessment instruments can be distributed to the respondents. An example of a needs assessment instrument that can be used to measure school personnel's knowledge, attitudes, and commitment toward career education and retarded students is presented in figure 8.4. The data obtained from this survey helps to measure student and school personnel needs and growth after inservice training and program implementation.

FIGURE 8.4
Needs assessment survey (partial).

DIRECTIONS: The following statements are designed to identify beliefs you have concerning career education and/or retarded students. There are no right or wrong answers. Just circle the response which best describes how you feel about each statement. Circle only *ONE* response for each item.

KEY: SA—STRONGLY AGREE WITH STATEMENT
    A—AGREE WITH STATEMENT
    U—UNDECIDED, NO OPINION, NEITHER AGREE NOR
       DISAGREE WITH STATEMENT
    D—DISAGREE WITH STATEMENT
    SD—STRONGLY DISAGREE WITH STATEMENT

1. A student is classified as retarded because he/she lacks ability in the areas of general intelligence and adaptive behavior.   SA A U D SD

2. Selective integration is an effort to move these students into regular classes in an effort to be more accepted by "normal" peers.   SA A U D SD

3. Selective integration will eliminate special services, classes, and programs for these students.   SA A U D SD

4. Career education should systematically coordinate the school, family, and community   SA A U D SD

resources to facilitate each individual's career potential.

5. There are few appropriate community resources available to assist teaching career competencies to these students.　SA　A　U　D　SD

6. It is unlikely that these students will be thought of as contributing to society.　SA　A　U　D　SD

7. Mainstreaming is an effective way to provide career education to these students.　SA　A　U　D　SD

8. These students would benefit if a greater emphasis was placed on career education.　SA　A　U　D　SD

9. Being labeled "Mentally Retarded" causes these students social and academic problems.　SA　A　U　D　SD

10. School personnel should make the decisions regarding proper classroom placement of these students.　SA　A　U　D　SD

11. Counselors should be allowed to make career choices for these students.　SA　A　U　D　SD

12. Competency training in occupational skills is not important for these students.　SA　A　U　D　SD

13. Generally, these students do not look any different than other students.　SA　A　U　D　SD

Source: *Trainers guide for life centered career education* (Brolin et al., 1978).

The Needs Assessment Task Force may have to seek additional people to administer the instruments. These individuals should be well-trained in the procedure. Some parents and other community representatives should be involved in the study. The ideal assessment is conducted in a face-to-face situation. Some instruments may be administered to a group of individuals under the instruction and supervision of one administrator. In all cases the respondents should receive clear explanations about the reason the needs assessment is being conducted, what will be gained from it, and their responsibility in the process. They should also know how and when they will be informed of the results (Arni et al., 1977).

The decision makers (administrators, Board of Education, Steering Committee, and Special Needs Subcommittee) should receive the specific results of the needs assessment studies. Certain information can be released to the general public and faculty, so that everyone is informed of the progress and findings.

Needs assessment is the cornerstone for a career development-oriented curriculum. Considerable care and thought must be devoted to the conceptualization of the respondents, questions, the interviewing variable, analysis, and final report.

Step 8: Prepare Inservice Training Program and Train the Trainers

Inservice training of personnel is critical to the success of any innovative interventions, especially those of the magnitude that are included in career education. If permanent change is to occur, teachers must be able to participate in the decisions that directly affect their work role. Inservice education provides this opportunity and uses new knowledge and competencies in the career education of handicapped students. Teachers and counselors involved in inservice education are important individuals who should influence the inservice atmosphere (Mohr, 1971).

Inservice training is the most effective when the instruction comes from personnel within the school district. As inservice training packages become more available and transportable, school systems will need to depend less on the outside expert who has limited knowledge about the unique circumstances existing in the school environment. But dynamic and effective trainers will be needed if inservice training is to be successful. Trainers must be knowledgeable and motivated enough to conduct the programs. The Staff Development Task Force must identify individuals who will be able to work effectively in this capacity.

Step 9: Develop Workshop and Student and Program Evaluation Procedures

Conducting successful workshops requires considerable preplanning, effective trainers, and appropriate training materials for the participants. The first step of the workshop should be to determine the attitudes and obtain knowledge of the participants before they receive any training. Participants should complete an evaluation sheet at the end of each session and/or workshop day. If the workshops last for several days, evaluation of the total inservice program should also be conducted.

Evaluation forms should be short but as effective as possible in gathering worthwhile data. An example of a daily evaluation form is presented in figure 8.5.

Until recently, little attention was given to evaluating the effectiveness of programs for handicapped individuals. Formative and summative evaluation procedures are needed to assure that students get a quality educational program that appropriately meets their needs. Formative evaluation, or process evaluation, provides information at intervals so that additions, deletions, or modifications can maximize program success. Summative evaluation, or outcome evaluation, provides information about a program's

FIGURE 8.5

Example of evaluation worksheet.

Please rate the general effectiveness of the second workshop by checking one response for each item. Then complete the unfinished sentences expressing your personal reaction toward the workshop.

1. The organization of the workshop was (_____ excellent; _____ good; _____ average; _____ fair; _____ poor).
2. The objectives of the workshop were (_____ extremely evident; _____ evident; _____ moderately evident; _____ slightly evident; _____ vague).
3. The work of the LEA/Trainers was (_____ excellent; _____ good; _____ average; _____ fair; _____ poor).
4. Attendance at this workshop should prove to be (_____ extremely beneficial; _____ beneficial; _____ moderately beneficial; _____ slightly beneficial; _____ not beneficial.

Today's workshop was:	Strongly Agree	Agree	Undecided	Disagree	Strongly Disagree
5. Relevant;	_____	_____	_____	_____	_____
6. Successful;	_____	_____	_____	_____	_____
7. Clear;	_____	_____	_____	_____	_____
8. Practical;	_____	_____	_____	_____	_____
9. Interesting;	_____	_____	_____	_____	_____
10. Excellent;	_____	_____	_____	_____	_____

Unfinished Sentences

11. The strongest factor of the workshop was . . .

12. The weakest factor was . . .

13. Overall, I feel that . . .

14. I would like to include . . .

General Narrative Reactions/Comments:

Source: *Trainers guide for life centered career education* (Brolin et al., 1978).

267

outcomes so that decisions can be made regarding the continuation, rejection, or modification of the product or program.

Step 10: Conduct Inservice Training for School Personnel and Others

We believe that educational practices will not be altered significantly unless a strong and substantial inservice training component is built into the design. Many fine curriculum guides and other publications have elicited needed changes in educational practices, but few have provided the necessary inservice education to make any difference in most school districts.

Based on several years experience of conducting inservice activities, we have found the following to be particularly important for successful training endeavors:

1. Obtain firm administrative commitment and support to maximize workshop attendance, cooperation, involvement, and subsequent implementation;
2. notify school personnel in advance of the educational innovation and the eventual inservice that is going to be offered;
3. select and train a cadre of school district personnel to do as much of the training as possible. They should be dynamic, energetic leaders who have a strong interest and commitment to career education and handicapped students. They must be prepared effectively and are the key to inservice success. A well-developed *trainer's manual* is essential;
4. select initial participants who are actually willing to work with handicapped students. There is no sense in "forcing" training on those who will not change their attitudes and methods of teaching;
5. provide special incentives for participating in the workshops (e.g., salary credits, college credits, and special recognition);
6. conduct the training outside of the school in a pleasant setting where there are few distractions from everyday business. Eating facilities should be available;
7. limit workshops to 5 or 6 hours per day. Participants become fatigued with a concentrated training program. They should have the opportunity to move around and relax;
8. vary workshop sessions with a few lectures, warm-up activities, gaming techniques, participant involvement, media, hands-on experiences, and coffee breaks;
9. focus on building a teamwork relationship and a cooperative, positive attitude among the participants;

268

10. provide a variety of instructional materials that are attractive, short, easy-to-read, and well-organized. Transparencies, slide or cassette presentations, films and other media can enhance the workshop immeasurably;

11. limit the number of handouts, particularly if they are lengthy and cumbersome. Concise and highly relevant information should generally be disseminated. Participants should be able to easily refer to the material during the workshop sessions;

12. avoid making many assignments between workshops unless participants are paying for the workshop, taking it for college credit, or serving on one of the task forces;

13. emphasize how the workshop will achieve its objectives so that participants understand their roles and appropriate conduct;

14. publicize the inservice workshop activities and results in a school bulletin, newsletter, or newspaper article, thus providing people with recognition and credit for their efforts; and

15. use Advisory Committees and consultants to give necessary input to designing an inservice training program that can be evaluated for its effectiveness.

Educational change is a slow process. Innovators must realize that they are not going to dramatically change the system or its major parts in a short period of time. Although resistance to new ideas is normal, people must be convinced that change is needed and that they can devise a manageable method for accomplishing their goals.

Thus, inservice education that involves the entire school staff must be offered so that all individuals are given the opportunity to invest themselves into planning and implementing career education into the school curriculum. The more people are involved in changing educational practices, the more they will contribute to a worthwhile educational endeavor. It is important to capture the interest of the faculty and provide them with the knowledge and skills they will need to implement career education successfully.

Step 11: Develop a Comprehensive Career Education Plan

Inservice training should include the drafting of a career education plan for the school faculties involved in the workshops. This must be developed at the grass-roots level if there is to be any real hope of implementing a comprehensive plan within the curriculum. The career education plan should be designed to focus on curriculum modifications, instructional strategies and materials, and infusion and collaboration techniques. A separate section in this chapter is devoted to details of developing a comprehensive career education plan.

269

Step 12: Gain Approval from Administration and the Board of Education

Various comprehensive career education plans developed by the participating school faculties should be submitted to top level administrators and the Board of Education for final endorsement. A great deal of written material and verbal input will be generated during the workshops, but after they are completed, the Curriculum Task Force and Committee, in concert with the Special Needs Subcommittee and Building-Level Special Needs Committees, will be responsible for recording their plans in final form. In addition to the individual building plans, the Special Needs Subcommittee will need to write a district-wide career education plan. A considerable amount of work may need to be accomplished after the workshops and task force meetings to produce the final career education plan, or plans.

We suggest that the plan be presented to the workshop participants for review, suggestions, and ultimate approval before it is forwarded to the administration and Board of Education for approval. Although these groups have been informed, they may ask some of the following questions before they render a final decision. Can this plan be realistically implemented? What must be done with the budget? Is this what the students, school personnel, parents, and community want? How does this curriculum for handicapped students interface with programs for nonhandicapped students? If these and other questions are properly answered, the administration can seek the support of the Board of Education.

Step 13: Secure Facilities and Resources

The Special Needs Subcommittee should take the following actions upon receiving approval of the plan: order materials and equipment; establish cooperative relationships with business, industry, community organizations, and agencies; inform parents and the community of the final plan and their responsibilities; conduct inservice training for staff members who will be involved with handicapped students; and secure additional space and/or renovations for those areas identified as having this need.

Step 14: Implement in Terms of Priorities and Guidelines

The pilot or comprehensive program should begin at the start of the school year, beginning of the second semester, or during a summer session. The program cannot be implemented in its entirety if funds, staffing, and resources are unavailable. Thus, priorities must be established. The Building-Level Special Needs Committee will be necessary to insure action, monitor progress, serve as a liaison with the Special Needs Subcommittee, and identify new needs.

Step 15: Conduct Formative and Summative Evaluations

The Building-Level Special Needs Committee should coordinate all evaluation efforts with the help of the Evaluation Task Force of the Special Needs Subcommittee. This includes the implementation of the program and the extent to which students are attaining the competencies and subcompetencies.

Step 16: Change and Modify Plan as Needed

The Curriculum Development Task Force of the Special Needs Subcommittee and the Building-Level Special Needs Committee should meet periodically with faculty and others who are involved in program implementation. They can change and modify the original plan based on their experiences with implementing the goals and objectives of the plan. They should note changes and modifications that will require future inservice and curriculum development activities. The career education plans should be flexible enough to allow for changes but should not be disregarded unless the curriculum group has found a better alternative.

This section has presented a comprehensive process of planning career education within a school curriculum. Two vital ingredients to the success of this endeavor are the inservice training of personnel and the cooperative efforts in the development of a comprehensive career education plan by school personnel, parents, and community representatives. The impact and significance of inservice training will be minimal unless the participants apply their definitive objectives (Brolin, McKay, & West, 1977a). The career education plan provides the vehicle by which participant input and commitment can be put into motion and career education implemented.

The process of developing a career education plan begins well before inservice workshops are conducted. The plan should be developed during three major time periods: (1) prior to the inservice workshops; (2) during and between the workshops; and (3) after the inservice has been completed. An overall district-wide model may be developed, but each school implementing career education will have to adapt the model to meet its own circumstances or develop its own plan based on guidelines that they have agreed upon.

The Special Needs Committee of the larger Career Education Steering Committee and its task forces (Needs Assessment, Staff Development, Resources and Public Relations, Curriculum Development, and Evaluation) are responsible for developing and implementing the career education plan. The process is set in motion when the Special Needs Committee and its task forces begin reviewing the literature and programs on career education, developing a tentative philosophy and model for career education, conducting district-wide needs assessment studies, preparing an inservice training program, and deciding upon evaluation procedures for the workshops and the career education program that is developed.

Inservice workshops provide school personnel, parents, students, and community representatives with the opportunity to react to the work of the committee and task forces and to help identify needs and activities necessary to infuse career education into the curriculum and the community. This grass-roots input and commitment is important in determining a go/no-go situation in the various schools. Inservice personnel should generate a multitude of ideas about directions that will have to be taken if career education is to be implemented. The committee will need members and leaders who can contribute to the development of the career education plan.

After inservice workshops are completed, the committee and task forces must combine the input, investigate other matters that emerge from the workshops, and begin to write the final career education plan or plans. Building committees should write their own plans with assistance from the Special Needs Committee. A suggested outline for writing the plan is presented in figure 8.6.

Career education goals and objectives should be consistent with the school district's philosophy and definition or conceptualization of career education. We suggest identifying at least three types of goals: instructional, community involvement, and administrative goals. Participants from the inservice workshops should help determine and agree to these goals to gain a shared commitment. Examples of each type of goal are as follows:

- *Instructional Goal:* Provide all handicapped students with the opportunity to learn the 22 competencies; integrate handicapped students more appropriately in regular classes; encourage teachers to emphasize career concepts in their subject matter; and provide career awareness, exploration, preparation, and placement experiences.
- *Community Involvement Goals:* Involve community groups on career education advisory committees and task forces; increase community career education sites; and develop home training materials for parents to teach competencies.
- *Administrative Goals:* Secure adequate staff facilities and resources; select inservice staff and community representatives; and conduct frequent assessments of student competency attainment and IEP needs.

The last component of the career education plan, implementation, reflects the steps or actions needed to incorporate career education into the

FIGURE 8.6
Suggested outline for career education plan.

CAREER EDUCATION PLAN OUTLINE

Name of School _____ City, State _____

A. School district philosophy

B. Definition or conceptualization of career education for handicapped students

C. Career education goals and objectives

    1. Instructional
    2. Community involvement
    3. Administrative

D. Instructional goals and objectives

    1. Strategies, methods, and responsibilities
    2. Competency instruction responsibilities: school personnel
    3. Courses changes or additions
    4. Instructional materials needed
    5. Assistance needed from special educators
    6. Other

E. Community involvement goals and objectives

    1. Strategies, methods, and responsibilities
    2. Competency instruction responsibilities: community personnel
        a. Family
        b. Agencies
        c. Business and industry

F. Administrative goals and objectives

    1. Strategies, methods, and responsibilities
    2. Staffing requirements
    3. Facilities or resources
    4. Staff development
    5. Student assessment
    6. Program evaluation
    7. Budget
    8. Other

G. Implementation

Source: *Trainers guide for life centered career education* (Brolin et al., 1978).

school. Timetables and responsibilities should be determined so that personnel, facilities, public relations, and other provisions can be provided accordingly. Once the central administration approves the plan, materials and equipment will need to be ordered, cooperative efforts secured with various community groups, further inservice programs developed, and public relations efforts conducted.

Once the plan is put into operation for students, formative and summative evaluations will determine how well the program meets student needs. Feedback on the effectiveness of instructional experiences at school, home, and in the community will determine any needed modifications.

The West-Allis-West School District in Milwaukee, Wisconsin implemented the LCCE curriculum. This district was involved in the special project that developed the LCCE curriculum model in the mid 1970's. Excerpts from their career education plan developed in 1979 are presented in Appendix B. We are grateful to Robert J. Buehler, Director and Supervisor of Special Education for providing the plan and other information about the LCCE curriculum activities. The Bellevue (Washington) School District has also infused the LCCE curriculum into its existing special education curriculum in order to provide a systematic approach for their students. A committee of teachers representing programs that serve a variety of grade levels and handicapping conditions reviewed and revised the curriculum to reflect local concerns. They also determined the appropriate grade level(s) for instruction in each of the subcompetencies, listed programs in the district that were already teaching each subcompetency, and cross-referenced each of the subcompetencies with the *Brigance Inventory of Essential Skills* (see page 403). This cross-reference helped each school make the transition to a career education curriculum.

Work sessions provided teachers with (1) an introduction to the curriculum; (2) an opportunity to determine which parts of the curriculum were appropriate for their programs and which areas of their programs needed further curriculum development; and (3) time and technical assistance for writing competency packages. Competency packages written during these sessions were compiled and given to other teachers within the district. Additional school districts that have implemented the LCCE curriculum are described in the next chapter.

CONCLUSION

Career education planning and implementation is a comprehensive process that requires the involvement of school, parents, and community resources. Administrative decision makers should solidly support career education if it is to be successful. In addition, a competent and committed core of organizers, process of development, needs assessments, inservice training, and career education plan must all interact effectively to result in a change of educational practices and a dedication to career education. If a major impact is to be forthcoming, a large number of individuals must be involved in planning career development programs. Change will occur only if these people believe that they have had an impact on what is proposed.

Career and **9**
Vocational Assessment

Student assessment is one of the most difficult tasks that classroom teachers face. Misuse of tests and recent discoveries regarding the inappropriateness of some tests have led to a general distrust of their results and usefulness. Some states have passed legislation against the use of traditional tests in public schools. However literally thousands of tests are still on the market that purport to measure practically anything.

For certain groups of individuals, such as handicapped students, tests may require differential interpretation or revision before results can be useful. Performance below the average only means that testing revealed what a person cannot do when compared to the general population. Thus, alternative evaluation activities will be needed to obtain information that will more accurately assess the performance and progress of students and their career development.

DOMAIN AND CRITERION-REFERENCED ASSESSMENT

Psychoeducational assessment has traditionally used standardized tests to measure the student's ability and achievement. The results of testing are used to *predict* a student's success or failure during school and after graduation. Norm-referenced tests use composite scores to compare one student with other students and have few direct implications for instructional intervention. Therefore norm-referenced tests classify students according to handicap but reveal little about the type of educational plan that can meet the student's needs (Hofmeister & Preston, 1981).

277

POINT OF VIEW

The assessment of potential has long been recognized as a component in the vocational rehabilitation of persons with handicapping conditions. Vocational assessment has been used to discover the interests, aptitudes, and abilities of individuals so they can be appropriately placed in the competitive job market. Vocational tests, work samples, and situational assessment can help to guide persons with handicaps into jobs and training that would be consistent with their interests and abilities.

Since vocational assessment has proven to be a viable tool in working with adults with disabilities, public school systems have recently begun to recognize that it may benefit students with special needs. Traditionally, students with handicaps did not participate in vocational training classes, or they were placed in classes based only on their interests or for other reasons. Within the last 5 to 6 years, vocational schools have been working diligently to provide special needs students with access to vocational training. Many secondary vocational education centers have established vocational assessment laboratories to help them place these students in more appropriate classes. These vocational units are responsible for assessing a student's interests, aptitudes, abilities, skills, and learning modes and recommending vocational classes consistent with the results of the evaluation. Because a large majority of special needs students are not college bound, vocational assessment and training at the secondary level is the best alternative to insure that students learn marketable skills and become employed.

Arden Boyer-Stephens is a vocational resource educator at the Columbia Career Center in Columbia, Missouri.

Traditional assessment practices are changing. Norm-referenced tests are no longer an acceptable approach for education. Reynolds (1975) has called attention to the changing nature of special education and its assessment practices by stating

> We are in a zero-demission (rejection) era; consequently, schools require a decision orientation other than simple prediction; they need one that is oriented to individual rather than simple prediction; they need one that is oriented to individual rather than institutional payoff. In today's context the measurement technologies ought to become integral parts of instruction designed to make a *difference* in the lives of children and not just a *prediction about* their lives (p. 15).

Halpern, Lehmann, Irvin, and Hiery (1982) noted that traditional assessment assumes that measures of a student's aptitudes, interests, and traits can be used to predict subsequent learning, performance, and adjustment. However the authors recommend that educators use more contemporary assessment that directly measures the student's attainment of actual competencies and has direct implications for program planning. Halpern, Lehmann, Irvin, and Hiery identified three general approaches to applied performance assessment: (1) direct assessment of criterion behaviors in real or simulated settings; (2) measurement of knowledge on those criterion behaviors; and (3) evaluation of how students learn new competencies. Their excellent publication identifies 51 domains of measurable behavior and describes 23 assessment instruments.

As Reynolds and Birch (1982) have pointed out

> Testing is only one way of obtaining information about an individual; assessment involves far more. It may include such aspects, for example, as examination of school and health records; a case history prepared by a social worker; interviews with parents, teachers, or other persons; observations of the child in the classroom or in other settings; the use of educational or other tests; and special examinations conducted outside the school by specialists. Nothing is taken for granted. Every factor that could reasonably affect how the child learns is examined and its possible influence is evaluated. (p. 61)

Earlier, Reynolds (1975) listed the following critical assessment needs in special education that are relevant today:

- We need information to help guide young people into their adult roles in society, to make sure that the race for the top (for which the schools clearly serve as one of the referees) is as fair as possible.

- When children are to be removed from or returned to the mainstream or regular classroom, we need information to justify those actions.

279

■ When children are provided with special curricula or support services, we need information to match the children with the services.

■ We need measures to record progress and evaluate efficiency of training in specific skills and competencies. These measures must reflect progress toward productive, individual goals, apart from the measures that reflect relative success in the race for the top.

■ We need measures that make it possible to account for the productiveness of educational programs in terms of individual progress toward diverse individual goals, rather than in terms of numbers of children-in-category or grade-level-equivalent standings (p. 6).

He concluded that predictive instruments and rejection decisions are not enough in those instances of unfavorable prediction. If educators are really concerned about each child and if educators commit themselves to making no rejection decisions, they must obtain more information about children and their life situations. The answer is to use domain and/or criterion-referenced testing procedures. In carefully sequenced and individualized instruction educators should use tests that represent various domains of knowledge or skill so they can make meaningful decisions without norm-references (Reynolds, 1975, pp. 22, 26).

The Education for All Handicapped Children Act of 1975 (PL 94–142) requires appropriate educational placement, equality of educational opportunity, and the student's right to ethnic dignity and respect. To prevent unfair stigmatization of students, the Act mandates that (1) the testing and evaluation materials and procedures will be selected and administered so as not to be culturally discriminatory; (2) the materials and procedures are provided in the child's native language or mode of communication; and (3) no single procedure or test can be the sole criterion for determining the appropriate education program for the child. Under PL 94–142, the pupil's needs and not a district-wide testing program should determine the instrument and associated assessment processes (Hofmeister & Preston, 1981).

Assessment is more than testing. It is the systematic process of using information from all possible sources so that educators can make informed decisions about their students. Hofmeister and Preston identify six assessment methods: (1) inspection of the child's record files; (2) informal consultation with others who know the child; (3) structured interviews; (4) observation; (5) norm-referenced tests; and (6) criterion-referenced tests. The need to develop Individualized Education Programs (IEPs) for special education pupils requires reconsideration of norm-referenced procedures because most norm-referenced tests do not provide enough information for teaching specific skills. Most do not relate directly to a specific curriculum sequence. Although numerous standardized diagnostic tests provide both norm-referenced and criterion-referenced information, student achievement is directly related to the content of instruction, and measured progress is highly influenced by congruence between test and curriculum (Hofmeister & Preston, 1981).

Criterion-referenced tests evaluate the students on learning tasks at some absolute standard that is independent of the performance of others. However, the quality of a criterion-referenced test depends on how well a skill area is operationalized. Thus some criterion-referenced tests are poorly constructed. Hively (1974) has introduced the concept of "domain-referenced" as one approach to criterion-referenced testing to insure that performance on the test items represents the specific curriculum area or domain more accurately. Hively notes that "transfer and generalization are the underlying ideas in the domain-referenced testing model because domains of items are composed to serve as targets for instruction . . . the whole idea is to 'teach for the test' and, at the same time, to design the testing system so that it includes all the basic ingredients that make generalization to the abstract universe possible" (p. 5). The whole effort behind domain-referenced testing is aimed at: (1) defining concrete domains of competence to serve as the goals for instruction and (2) testing out and demonstrating the transfer from those immediate goals to related or subsequent instruction (Rosner, 1975).

Norm-referenced tests that compare a student's performance against the norm are not the most appropriate method of assessment to ascertain the individual's competence. In our opinion, a type of criterion-referenced test that assesses the student's mastery or competence in specific areas is more useful. The focus of criterion-referenced tests is on *what* the student knows and/or can do. There are no comparisons with how many individuals possess the knowledge or skill (Popham & Husek, 1969). Assessment provides information on a student's level of proficiency in a particular subject skill. The individual's strengths and weaknesses can be discerned so that the IEPs and the Individualized Written Rehabilitation Plans (IWRP) can be written, the immediate curriculum can be planned, and individual and group progress can be monitored.

CAREER ASSESSMENT

This book conveys that career education is a broader concept than vocational education. Therefore career assessment is also more encompassing because it focuses on the individual's interests, needs, aptitudes, and abilities that relate to productive work activity in the home, community, vocation, and avocation. Thus as we have previously indicated, career education is an eclectic approach to the individual.

However, the most available career assessment tests measure vocational variables even though they use the term "career." Therefore the professional worker should use a combination of measurement scales to do a career assessment (e.g., independent living, adaptive behavior, personal-social, and avocational). The LCCE curriculum uses the competency rating scale (CRS) described in the next section.

The LCCE Competency Rating Scale (CRS)

The assessment approach devised for the LCCE curriculum uses a Competency Rating Scale (CRS). It provides a systematic approach to organizing and standardizing the assessment of each student's career development competency level. The 102 subcompetencies are the actual CRS items of the scale. A part of the daily living skills scale is presented in figure 9.1 to illustrate how the CRS is constructed. The complete scale and its manual is contained in *Life Centered Career Education: A Competency Based Approach* (Brolin, 1978 & 1983) which is available from the Council for Exceptional Children.

A competency rating scale manual presents several behavioral criteria that educators can use to judge the student's mastery of each competency or subcompetency. The ratings are performed by those most knowledgeable about student performance in a specific area. The manual contains information on how to select criteria for rating students, how to interpret numerical values, who should do the rating, when the rating should be done, what forms to use for recording and summarizing data, as well as how to record demographic data. The rating forms are divided into the three career education areas: daily living, personal-social, and occupational skills. The evaluator may use at least three criteria to derive the rating for each subcompetency: (1) immediate personal observation of student performance and behavior; (2) personal records or notes on student performance; and (3) written or verbal reports from other persons. The latter is considered the least valid source of information but may be necessary to substantiate the other information. When sufficient information exists to rate a subcompetency, the following rating scale is used: 0 (not competent); 1 (partially competent); 2 (competent); and NR (not rated). Each of the three domains can be administered independently. It is recommended that one individual rate all subcompetencies of a particular domain. The CRS results can then be related to the student's Individualized Education Program (IEP) as indicated in Appendix A.

Although the CRS can be useful as a general rating measure, it is not a precise measure of the 102 subcompetencies or skills. Professionals have indicated a need for a criterion-referenced measure (a criterion-referenced measure is currently being developed by Brolin). Until such a measure is developed, professionals may consider using such existing measures as the

FIGURE 9.1

Daily living skills.

Student Name _____ Date of Birth _____ Sex _____

School _____ City _____ State _____

Directions: The following items are skills identified as being important for successful career education. Please rate the person according to his/her mastery of *each* item using the Rating Key below. Indicate the ratings in the column below the date for the rating period. Use the "NR" rating for items which cannot be rated. For subcompetencies rated "0" or "1" at the time of the final rating, place a check (√) in the appropriate space in the yes/no column to indicate his/her ability to perform the subcompetency with assistance from the community. Please refer to the CRS manual for explanation of the Rating Key, description of the behavioral criteria of each subcompetency, and explanation of the yes/no column.

Rating Key: 0 = Not Competent   1 = Partially Competent   2 = Competent   NR = Not Rated

To what extent has the person mastered the following subcompetencies:

Subcompetencies	Rater(s)								Yes	No
	Grade Level									
	Date(s)									
I. Managing Family Finances										
1. Identify money and make correct change										
2. Make wise expenditures										
3. Obtain and use bank and credit services										
4. Keep basic financial records										
5. Calculate and pay taxes										
II. Selecting, Managing, and Maintaining a Home										
6. Select adequate housing										
7. Maintain a home										
8. Use basic appliances and tools										
9. Maintain home exterior										
III. Caring for Personal Needs										
10. Dress appropriately										
11. Exhibit proper grooming and hygiene										
12. Demonstrate knowledge of physical fitness, nutrition and weight control										
13. Demonstrate knowledge of common illness prevention and treatment										
IV. Raising Children, Family Living										
14. Prepare for adjustment to marriage										
15. Prepare for raising children (physical care)										
16. Prepare for raising children (psychological care)										
17. Practice family safety in the home										
V. Buying and Preparing Food										
18. Demonstrate appropriate eating skills										
19. Plan balanced meals										

Subcompetencies	Rater(s)								Yes	No
	Grade Level									
	Date(s)									
20. Purchase food	—	—	—	—	—	—	—	—	—	—
21. Prepare meals	—	—	—	—	—	—	—	—	—	—
22. Clean food preparation areas	—	—	—	—	—	—	—	—	—	—
23. Store food	—	—	—	—	—	—	—	—	—	—
VI. Buying and Caring for Clothing										
24. Wash clothing	—	—	—	—	—	—	—	—	—	—
25. Iron and store clothing	—	—	—	—	—	—	—	—	—	—
26. Perform simple mending	—	—	—	—	—	—	—	—	—	—
27. Purchase clothing	—	—	—	—	—	—	—	—	—	—
VII. Engaging in Civic Activities										
28. Generally understand local laws and government	—	—	—	—	—	—	—	—	—	—
29. Generally understand federal government	—	—	—	—	—	—	—	—	—	—
30. Understand citizenship rights and responsibilities	—	—	—	—	—	—	—	—	—	—
31. Understand registration and voting procedures	—	—	—	—	—	—	—	—	—	—
32. Understand selective service procedures	—	—	—	—	—	—	—	—	—	—
33. Understand civil rights and responsibilities when questioned by the law	—	—	—	—	—	—	—	—	—	—
VIII. Utilizing Recreation and Leisure										
34. Participate actively in group activities	—	—	—	—	—	—	—	—	—	—
35. Know activities and available community resources	—	—	—	—	—	—	—	—	—	—
36. Understand recreational values	—	—	—	—	—	—	—	—	—	—
37. Use recreational facilities in the community	—	—	—	—	—	—	—	—	—	—
38. Plan and choose activities wisely	—	—	—	—	—	—	—	—	—	—
39. Plan vacations	—	—	—	—	—	—	—	—	—	—
IX. Getting Around the Community (Mobility)										
40. Demonstrate knowledge of traffic rules and safety practices	—	—	—	—	—	—	—	—	—	—
41. Demonstrate knowledge and use of various means of transportation	—	—	—	—	—	—	—	—	—	—
42. Drive a car	—	—	—	—	—	—	—	—	—	—

*Total Possible Score
(TPS) = N × 2 _____

*Total Actual Score
(TAS)   — — — — — — — — —

*Average Score
(AS) = TAS/N   — — — — — — — — —

Comments:

Source: *Life centered career education: A competency based approach* (Brolin, 1978).

284

Brigance Inventory of Essential Skills (Curriculum Associates) which has been cross-referenced to the LCCE competencies by at least one school district (see Appendix C) and *The Social and Prevocational Battery* (California Test Bureau, McGraw-Hill). At the present time, implementers of LCCE need to use a variety of measures depending on the type of individuals served. There is no quick and easy path to evaluating competency attainment. But evaluations can be done fairly well with currently existing instruments and evaluator ingenuity. Several rating scales and tests that can be used to assess various career competencies appear in table 9.1.

TABLE 9.1
Examples of rating scales and tests that assess various career competencies.

Rating Scales
1. Adaptive Behavior Assessment (Woodcock-Johnson Psycho-Educational Battery)
2. AAMD Adaptive Behavior Scale
3. Adult Basic Literacy Assessment
4. Behavioral Characteristics Progression
5. Brigance Diagnostic Inventory
6. Camelot Behavioral Checklist
7. Career Assessment Inventory
8. DALE System
9. Dial Behavioral Rating Scale
10. Florida International and Diagnostic-Prescriptive Vocational Competency Profile
11. MDC Behavior Identification Form
12. Progress Assessment Chart of Social and Personal Development
13. San Francisco Vocational Competency Scale
14. TMP Performance Profile
15. VALPAR #17 Pre-Vocational Readiness Battery
16. Vineland Adaptive Behavior Scales
17. Vocational Assessment and Curriculum Guide
18. Vocational Behaviors Checklist
19. Work Adjustment Rating Form

Tests
1. Independent Living Behavior Checklist
2. Micro-Computer Evaluation and Screening Assessment
3. Mid-Nebraska Mentally Retarded Services Three Track System
4. Social and Prevocational Information Battery
5. Social and Prevocational Information Battery—Form T
6. Street Survival Skills Questionnaire
7. Tests for Everyday Living
8. Trainee Performance Sample
9. VALPAR #17 Pre-Vocational Readings Battery

VOCATIONAL ASSESSMENT

The need to have better organized and comprehensive methods of evaluating the handicapped individual's vocational interests and skills is becoming more widely recognized by schools and agencies. Vocational assessment units have recently emerged in many junior and senior high schools as well as in numerous post-secondary settings. Peterson (1980) revealed that more than 80% of Texas educators felt that comprehensive vocational assessment was crucial in developing an appropriate educational program for secondary handicapped students.

Despite the recognized need and increased emphasis for vocational assessment in schools, its actual utilization by school personnel is questionable. Nacson and Kelly (1980) and Wright, Padilla, and Cooperstein (1980) have concluded that placement in vocational education is seldom based on

Wayne Tiritrilli and Bill Quinones conduct vocational assessments for the Dallas, Texas Independent School District.

the students' assessed vocational interests and competencies but rather depends on their level of basic academic skills. A study by Cobb (1983) found that vocational assessment reports are placed in cumulative folders but are seldom used in terms of IEP annual goal specification, present levels of performance, or classroom placement. He also found that vocational assessments were overwhelmingly informal and observational.

Ianacone et al. (1982) and others report the need for more and better vocational assessment practices in the schools if appropriate vocational potentials and the training needs of handicapped individuals are to be adequately identified. The question is who should do it and when and how should it be done. Who should conduct vocational assessment depends on how it is defined. In our opinion, vocational assessment can be defined as *a comprehensive process involving an interdisciplinary approach to assessing*

The Dallas Independent School District

The Dallas Independent School District (DISD) offers several vocational programs for special education students.[5] These include Work Activity Centers in each of the three school subdistricts and two district-wide programs that involve a Vocational Assessment Center and a Multiple Careers Magnet Center. Students from secondary special education programs throughout DISD attend the Vocational Assessment Center to help them identify their individual interests, skills, and potential for vocational training and placement programs.

Vocational assessment includes an evaluation of vocational interests, vocational aptitudes, work habits, personal and social adjustment skills, and physical capacities. Assessment tools include commercially developed work samples and tests, locally developed work samples, and observational rating techniques and scales. The students

are at the center for a half-day for five days. Throughout the assessment the vocational evaluators provide feedback to school personnel and the student so they become more aware of each person's vocational strengths and weaknesses.

The Vocational Assessment Center is housed in the same facility as the Multiple Careers Magnet Center. This exposes students to new training programs as well as gives them the opportunity for situational assessment. The Assessment Center is a major asset in providing vocational planning information for students needing extensive observation before placement as well as those needing supplementary career planning and vocational exploration.

Information provided by Wayne Tiritilli, Special Education Department.

[5] The DISD reports that the LCCE competencies are integral to their program for students in its Work Activity Centers.

an individual's vocational potentials and training and placement needs. This means that trained vocational evaluators are necessary as well as a wide array of teachers, counselors, and work supervisors who are in a position to observe and conduct various assessment activities in their school or agency.

In our opinion, vocational assessment should begin early (i.e., during the latter part of the elementary grades). Career awareness and exploration experiences will uncover student interests, aptitudes, work habits, behaviors, and other student characteristics that can be related to instructional planning. Vocational assessment should not pigeonhole the students but should help them develop a work personality and shape future course alternatives. Educators should initiate a more formalized vocational assessment process for junior high students by using vocational interest inventories, some aptitude measures, work samples, job tryouts, classroom projects, and the like. At the senior high level, many schools are instituting vocational evaluation labs that are directed by trained vocational evaluators who work with other vocational personnel. Vocational-technical schools, community colleges, and rehabilitation facilities have also become quite sophisticated in vocational assessment methodology and generally offer extensive programs in this area. Besides the assessment function, vocational assessment can also increase students' career awareness by engaging them in actual work activities and career exploration experiences.

How should vocational assessment be carried out? We recommend a comprehensive vocational assessment program consisting of four major components: (1) clinical assessment; (2) work evaluation; (3) work adjustment; and (4) job site evaluation. Figure 9.2 illustrates these four components relative to when they can begin and how they can relate to eventual vocational education and training. The four components are not necessarily conducted in a specific order but rather are interwoven together according to each individual's particular characteristics and needs.

- *Clinical Assessment* is conducted primarily by physicians, social workers, psychologists, teachers, counselors, and others who are able to assess vocational aspects from a medical, social, psychological, and educational standpoint.
- *Work Evaluation* consists of assessments from work evaluators, vocational educators, special educators, occupational therapists, vocational instructors, or vocational and rehabilitation counselors with input from clinical workers.
- *Work Adjustment* is conducted by work adjustment specialists, vocational counselors, psychologists, special or vocational education teachers, and work supervisors who attempt to determine if work behaviors and experiential deficiencies can be modified.

FIGURE 9.2
Grade levels for implementing the vocational assessment components.

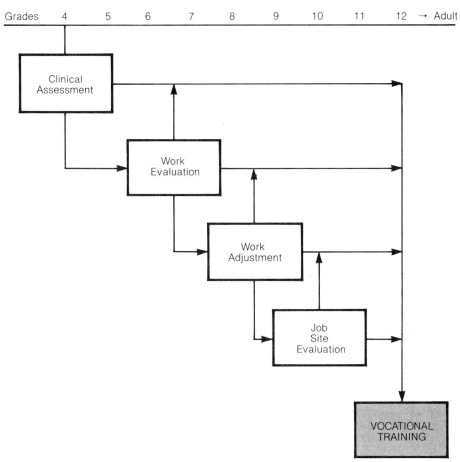

- *Job-Site Evaluation* or *Job Tryouts* is conducted by work evaluators, work-study/experience instructors, vocational educators, vocational counselors, work supervisors, and/or employers. It is a reality-based vocational evaluation process (Brolin, 1982).

Components of Vocational Assessment

Clinical Assessment. Clinical assessment consists of four major types of evaluations: medical, social, educational, and psychological. *Medical assessment* involves evaluation of the person's physical capacity, general health, vision, hearing, speech, perceptual-motor functioning, coordination, dexterity, and

289

any other suspected anomalies precluding optimal health and physical functioning. Special examinations, physical therapy, occupational therapy, and speech therapy may also be required for some individuals. *Social assessment* can include review of the individual's and family's background, interviews with family members, independent living skills assessments, and social and adaptive behavior inventories. This assessment is important in understanding the family relationships and expectations and the person's social skills, interpersonal skills, personal needs, and ability to use leisure time. Social assessment also gives important cues about occupational interests, aptitudes, and future possibilities. *Educational assessment* should include an analysis of the students' academic history as well as functional academic skills. The evaluator needs to discern the person's particular likes and dislikes, techniques that worked best, and school behavior and motivation. *Psychological assessment* is the fourth type of clinical assessment. Caution is advised in using these measures. Although some tests can give valuable bits of information, educators should not rely upon them too heavily in vocational planning for persons with handicaps. Personality assessment data should always be considered tentative.

Work evaluation. Work evaluation assessment is unique in its focus on work. Four types of work evaluation activity are intake and counseling interviews; standardized vocational testing; work and job samples; and situational assessment. *Interviews* can help school and rehabilitation personnel identify the person's interests, work history, and future goals and needs. Interviews with the family can provide educators with greater understanding of the student's home environment, the family's aspirations, pressures, and ability to assist the person in her vocational development. *Standardized vocational tests* are of two primary types: aptitude and interest. Some measures are presented in Appendixes D and E. *Work and job samples assessment* are gaining popularity. Work samples are simulated tasks for which there exists no industrial, business, or other counterpart. Job samples are models or reproductions of a job or part of a job that exists in an industrial, business, or other setting and involves the use of tools of the trade and the standards and norms associated with that job (Sankovsky, Arthur, & Mann, 1971). Work and job samples appear more like real-life jobs and can be motivating to the person taking them. They are somewhat time consuming and expensive to develop but have the advantage of assessing local labor possibilities—something the commercially developed samples discussed later in this chapter can't do. *Situational assessment* involves providing a group of persons with a real or simulated work environment so that various aspects of the person's "work personality" can be observed, recorded, and modified, if necessary. Situational assessment can be performed in a classroom setting, sheltered work program, or in the actual labor market.

Work samples such as this small motor assembly relate to actual jobs and are becoming an increasingly important vocational assessment technique.

Work adjustment. Work adjustment is a purposeful behavioral change process by which individuals can learn acceptable work behaviors and employability skills. Educators can assess work adjustment by using different approaches that are integrated into the vocational assessment process. These are engineering techniques; counseling; instruction; and situational work. The *engineering approach* focuses on modifying the worker and the work place. This includes modifying the physical layout or location of the work environment; providing assistive devices for the worker; restructuring job processes; and modifying machines and equipment. Work simplification procedures such as motion economy are used to determine how a job can be best done by the individual. *Counseling* is an important technique for helping individuals view themselves appropriately, relate better with others, and change inadequate work behaviors. *Instructional work adjustment* training involves

291

a small group of students or clients who meet regularly to learn better work attitudes and work personality characteristics. Applied behavior analysis or modification techniques can be used with more severely handicapped persons. The *situational work* approach focuses on modifying deficient behaviors by using a work environment like a sheltered workshop or job laboratory. This technique provides an opportunity for work conditioning whereby work requirements relative to quantity, quality, and speed can be gradually increased. Work tasks can progress from simple to more complex tasks.

Job site evaluation. Job site evaluation is the only realistic way the individual can be evaluated against regular employees and working demands. Educators should carefully scrutinize the work environment and its job requirements to insure that the student receives appropriate instruction and supervision and has contact with co-workers. Figure 9.2 illustrates what we consider to be approximate grade levels at which the vocational assessment components should begin. As indicated earlier, vocational assessment is part of the career development process that can help educators make vocational training decisions. The diagram depicts a feedback loop (i.e., students may be re-evaluated on every component several times as they move through the process, depending on their particular needs). For example, the work evaluation may be cut short because a student may need a considerable period of work adjustment (conditioning) before she becomes motivated and displays actual vocational interests and aptitudes on the various tests, work samples, and work activities contained in the work evaluation phase. Once this is attained, the student may then receive a more formalized work evaluation before job site evaluation is considered. Figure 9.2 also illustrates that after comprehensive vocational assessment is completed, the next step in the student's career development is a vocational training program. Given this comprehensive assessment approach, more appropriate and successful vocational training should occur.

Systematic and long-term vocational assessment is a significant part of the student's educational plan and involves various school personnel. We suggest that a Vocational Profile be developed for each student so that interests and abilities can be recorded and monitored as they change throughout the school years. Data derived from vocational assessment activities can be used to write IEPs for each elementary school student. The following publications contain more detailed information on how to conduct comprehensive vocational assessment: *Vocational Preparation of Persons With Handicaps* (Brolin, 1982); *Vocational Evaluation and Assessment in School Settings* (McCray, 1982); and *Vocational Assessment of Students With Special Needs: An Implementation Manual* (Occupational Curriculum Laboratory, 1982). In addition, the publication *Vocational Education for the Handicapped: Perspec-*

tives in Vocational Assessment (Ianacone, et al., 1982) is an excellent reference on trends, issues, and personnel development. Several national organizations are developing position statements and guides on vocational assessment for persons with handicaps reflecting the wide concern and need that special educators, vocational educators, counselors, and school psychologists have about its place in school settings.

The Severely Handicapped Individual

Although a great number of standardized vocational assessment measures are available, the more severe the handicap, the fewer the number of tests that are applicable. This is particularly true for persons with visual, hearing, and intellectual handicaps. In many instances, educators should modify tests for certain individuals (e.g., instructions, time frames, scheduling, individual rather than group administration, rapport and reinforcement emphasis, and motivation building). Any time a test is modified, caution must be exercised in its interpretation and validity. Educators should give handicapped individuals special consideration in vocational testing endeavors. Many *visually handicapped* individuals have never experienced shape, color and other visual concepts. Therefore, their set of experiences is quite different from other persons. They often lack the typical set of learning experiences and materials that most individuals take for granted. Large print tests can be ordered from the American Printing House for the Blind, 1839 Frankfort Avenue, Louisville, Kentucky 40206.

Assessment of persons with *severe hearing impairments* also presents problems. It will be necessary to determine the individual's communication skills and method(s)—sign language, lip or speech reading, or finger spelling. Deaf persons may have been isolated and, consequently, have a limited range of social and educational experiences. Language development may be very poor; thus, tests requiring only a basic reading level and nonverbal test are most appropriate. An interpreter may be needed to translate the instructions.

Most *severely mentally retarded* individuals have had limited experiences and concomitant physical handicaps, such as vision, hearing, speech, coordination, and/or cultural deprivation. Vocabulary level, attention span, frustration tolerance, anxiety, self-concept, and expectancy to fail are some possible problems that must be accounted for before and during testing.

Bernstein and Karan (1979) believe that inadequate vocational assessment practices are a major obstacle in the mentally retarded individual's vocational normalization. They report that these evaluations predict failure and consist of tools that have questionable validity and usefulness with severely mentally retarded individuals. Wehman (1981) recommended the following five skills that are critical to the severely mentally retarded individual's success at employment: proficiency, rate, quality, perseverance, and

293

Missouri and many other states have organized Vocational Evaluation and Work Adjustment Association (VEWAA) programs that provide professional assistance.

endurance. Thus, educators who use the behavior analytic approach to train these individuals utilize what they consider to be summative and formative assessment. Rusch and Mithaug (1980) describe summative assessment as data that reflect the individual's abilities and behaviors from past intelligence tests scores, prior education, and family history. Formative assessment consists of quantitative behavior that is reassessed to obtain an in-depth view of the individual's skills in a single area. One example of an organized method to implement this approach is the Prevocational Assessment and Curriculum Guide (Mithaug, Mar, & Stewart, 1978). The instrument is a summative assessment of the trainee's deficits that prescribes training goals and evaluates the individual's progress toward those outcomes.

CONCLUSION

Many leaders in the field recognize the need to focus instructional and assessment activities on the critical skills that students will need in today's complex society. However concise and comprehensive career assessment is not a particularly easy matter. Criterion-referenced assessment is recommended over norm-referenced approaches because it is more useful in discerning students' proficiency level and in writing IEPs and Individualized Written Rehabilitation Plans (IWRPs). Although a number of rating scales and tests are available, no one measure of critical career skills presently exists. The LCCE Competency Rating Scale (CRS) can be helpful but should be supplemented with other criterion-referenced instruments.

Vocational assessment is a major component of career assessment that is rapidly becoming an important dimension in career and vocational planning. However many issues need to be resolved relative to when and how vocational assessment should be done and who should do it. We anticipate that these issues will become resolved as more school personnel learn to understand and appreciate its contribution to better instructional planning and career development.

Conducting Career Education Programs 10

Life-centered career education (LCCE) is necessary if handicapped individuals are to successfully assimilate into today's rapidly changing and demanding society. Although the development of occupational skills is critical to competing and surviving in the labor market, the individual must also possess personal-social, daily living, and academic skills. Career education provides the individual with the opportunity to pull it all together by considering the whole person.

Special educators have always been concerned about the adjustment of the adult handicapped individual in the community. Kokaska and Kolstoe (1977) indicate that the vocational aspect of career education has often been emphasized but that the totality of the student's life is also a valid area of instruction within the curriculum. In their opinion, career education concepts are particularly important for handicapped individuals since they often need longer periods of intensive teaching. Thus, "career concepts can be used to maintain a continuity to a curriculum that extends from early childhood through the adult years" (p. 5).

In chapter 2 we discussed the many concepts of career education and our conceptualization of a career education-oriented curriculum. We emphasized the need for students to obtain the 22 career development competencies that our research has found to be critical to the student's community and occupational success. We advocated a competency-based curriculum approach that involves school, family, and community representatives and incorporates the elements of career awareness, exploration, preparation, and placement and follow-up into its design.

Each of the 22 life career development competencies can be broken down into subcompetencies that should be taught at the elementary level. Many subcompetencies should be emphasized throughout the student's educational program, particularly those that relate to the various personal-social and occupational skills.

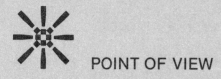

POINT OF VIEW

A growing concern about the unemployment rate for handicapped persons is resulting in rapid changes in attitudes toward the content of the curriculum. This concern will lead to major curriculum changes in the school system and personnel preparation programs.

Future curriculum planners and implementors will need to focus on career education programs. Life-centered career education will be a required component of each student's individualized educational program and will be the theme around which content will be taught. Career development will no longer consist of the splintered efforts of a few educators, but will involve the family, community and other agency personnel. The ultimate goals of programs will be to prepare handicapped individuals for employment and independent living.

The 22 Life-Centered Career Education (LCCE) competencies that research has found to be critical to community and occupational success is an excellent framework for developing a K–12 program for handicapped students. Program planners should relate teaching objectives and activities to these competencies with ongoing assessment of the student's attainment level. The programs described in this chapter provide many ideas for those who will be developing or improving upon a comprehensive, ongoing career education approach.

Iva Dean Cook is an associate professor at the West Virginia College of Graduate Studies in Institute, West Virginia (formerly president of the Division on Career Development, The Council for Exceptional Children).

There is no simple recipe as to how career education can be structured in a K–12+ program for handicapped students. In this chapter we will give suggestions, but the reader should keep in mind that every school situation is different. What is important is that school personnel shift from a *content-based* to *process-based* curriculum. Students should understand how the content is related to their career development, both as future workers and as functioning members of society.

CURRICULUM CONSIDERATIONS

The learning climate is a primary factor in determining the success of career education programs. Professional workers should facilitate a democratic rather than autocratic atmosphere that optimizes each person's development in all areas. Magnuson (1974) suggests the following steps that can be used to create a facilitative atmosphere: (1) Take an honest look at the present climate; (2) Ask if each person who will sit in the classroom throughout the year would enjoy being there; (3) Ask, "What can I do to insure each person's success?"; and (4) Ask "How do my students see me?" and "How would I like for my students to see me?" Once these questions have been honestly answered, the instructor will be able to establish a systematic, facilitative environment that should include the following beliefs.

I BELIEVE:
—It is my responsibility to strive to love, accept and understand each student as a unique human being with unique needs.
—It is my responsibility to plan for creating a psychologically safe learning environment for every student trusted to me.
—It is my responsibility to serve as an adult model who demonstrates compassion and empathy.
—I do have time in my day to encourage success in each student.
—Human interaction between students and students, and students and teachers is an essential part of growing.
—How I teach is as important as what I teach.
—I, by nature of my position as an educator, have power over human lives. It is my responsibility to remain cognizant of this fact and utilize my power in ways that will maximize human growth.

Magnuson, 1974

Some ideas Magnuson lists for improving the learning climate are: *interact* with your students and be available; *talk* with other teachers about ideas for implementing career education activities; *plan* an all-school project to get everyone involved; work toward making your *faculty lounge* an enjoyable place to be; and agree on some common ground rules relating to *noise* level.

299

Roger and David Johnson of the University of Minnesota have promoted and studied application of a cooperative learning approach (Johnson, Johnson, & Rynders, 1981; Johnson & Johnson, 1982; Johnson & Johnson, 1983; Nevin, Johnson & Johnson, 1982). For several years they have investigated procedures that regular classroom teachers can use to insure successful mainstreaming. Educators should maintain the following three assumptions: (1) it is unnecessary and unrealistic to ask regular classroom teachers to become experts in special education since expertise on special education is already in the school; (2) any teaching strategy implemented in the regular classroom to facilitate the integration of handicapped students should benefit the education of all students, not just those with special learning needs; and (3) the first priority of mainstreaming is to build positive relationships between handicapped and normal-progess students. Johnson and Johnson believe that when handicapped students are liked, accepted, and chosen as friends, mainstreaming has a positive influence on the lives of both handicapped and nonhandicapped students. They state that placing a handicapped student in the corner of a classroom and providing her with individualistic learning experiences is not effective mainstreaming. Their studies have revealed that students who have been placed in a cooperative learning environment have a higher self-esteem, interact more, feel accepted by teachers and nonhandicapped students, achieve more, and behave more appropriately in the classroom than those students who have been placed in competitive and individualistic conditions. It seems that the career education approach lends itself nicely to the cooperative learning model.

Through the process of conducting inservice workshops and developing a career education plan for the school, the partnership between all possible school personnel, in addition to family and community representatives should become established. As we indicated in chapters 2 through 5, career education transcends the entire curriculum and requires competency and subcompetency instruction at all levels. Curriculum emphasis will vary from school to school and student to student, depending on the school's resources, philosophy, and preparedness. Based on our experience, career education instruction in academic, daily living, occupational, and personal-social skills follows the breakdown over the K–Adult curriculum period as depicted in figure 10.1. Each of these four curriculum areas is discussed next.

Academic Skills

During the elementary years, handicapped students must learn functional academic skills, such as reading, writing, and arithmetic. This must be the primary emphasis during these years because academic skills lay the foundation for subsequent learning of the daily living and occupational skills needed for community living and working.

At the junior high school level, a decrease in teaching academic skills should begin although much of this instruction can be directed to teaching

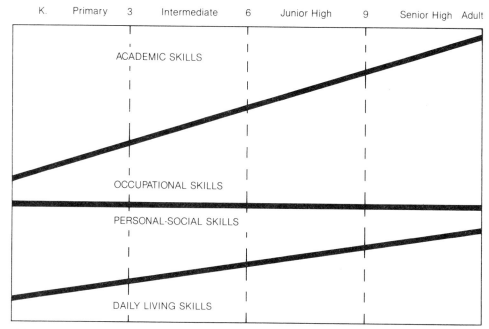

FIGURE 10.1
Suggested curriculum for career development at various grade levels.

specific daily living and occupational skills. Of course, this will vary with the handicapped student and her potential and need for academic skills instruction. However at this age, students begin questioning the relative value of what they are learning compared to what they will do later in life.

At the senior high school level, academic instruction should focus on subjects that the student has not yet mastered well enough and are critical to community functioning and subjects that are of high interest to the student. Otherwise, daily living and occupational skills should form the greater part of the student's course of study.

Adult programs will need to assess the extent to which the individual has acquired the academic skills needed for community living and working. For the latter, the emphasis should be on those academic skills needed for job goals. Variance in the number of academic skills that the student learns will depend on the quality of public school services.

Daily Living Skills

Several subcompetencies can be taught during the elementary years in addition to basic academic skills. Daily living skills include: identifiying money and making correct change; making wise expenditures; dressing appropriately; developing grooming and hygiene skills; developing eating skills; understanding local laws and government; participating in basic leisure and recreational group activities; and understanding traffic laws and safety practices, which are subcompetencies that handicapped students can learn, or can begin to learn.

At the junior high level, a much greater emphasis on daily living skills should occur. Learning about bank and credit facilities, home maintenance, adequate housing, use of basic appliances and tools, physical fitness, nutrition, and weight control practices, marriage and child care practices, meal planning, preparation and purchasing, clothing purchase and care, citizenship rights, recreational planning, traffic rules, and use of various means of transportation are subcompetencies that can begin to be learned and perhaps acquired by the time students enter the high school program.

At the senior high school level, the student should have learned the subcompetencies that were taught earlier and also those that have not yet been taught or emphasized. Learning how to keep financial records, calculate and pay taxes, maintain a home interior, prevent and treat common illnesses, respond to questioning by the law, plan vacations, and drive a car are higher order subcompetencies that some students may never learn adequately. Students unable to learn certain competencies or subcompetencies will need to know how they can receive assistance. Adult programs should provide training for students who have not acquired these subcompetencies but have the potential to acquire these skills. This needs to be carefully and systematically discerned.

Personal-Social Skills

The elementary years are particularly important to handicapped students for developing adequate personal-social skills. The first few years of life are vital to personality development. Handicapped children in particular are vulnerable to the attitudes and behaviors of others toward them, that in many instances, may be manifested by ridicule, hostility, rejection, or physical abuse. Thus, they must learn how to handle these negative behaviors and should discover enough about themselves so that they feel they are worthwhile persons. This area needs much more attention if handicapped students are going to benefit from educational efforts and attain optimal career development. All seven competencies and their subcompetencies should become part of the instructional program at the elementary level. All school personnel teaching the handicapped student should include personal-social development as part of instruction.

If educators attempt to help the handicapped student develop personal-social skills during the elementary years, emphasis on these subcompetencies may be decreased during the secondary programs. This is not meant to de-emphasize the importance of personal-social skills. Rather, we mean to imply that if educators help students learn enough about themselves, develop self-confidence, and display socially responsible behavior, the need to learn other personal-social skills may be reduced. On the other hand, certain students who have not acquired these skills will need to spend a substantial amount of time in this area. All school personnel and guidance and counseling persons should use their special expertise to help students ovecome unusually deficient behaviors. Rehabilitation counselors can also offer work adjustment services in a rehabilitation setting to help adult students acquire the personal-social skills needed for career development.

Occupational Skills

Career education highlights the need for elementary programs to provide much more attention to the student's occupational development at this level. Young children are interested in the world of work and actively seek to find out what their parents and significant others do to make a living. We believe that educators should emphasize many of the following subcompetencies in this curriculum area during the student's elementary years: work attitudes and values; remunerative aspects of working; work habits (following directions, work with others, accept supervision, good attendance and punctuality, quality and quantity performance, safety); and physical-manual skills (balance, coordination, dexterity, stamina).

As the student progresses through the educational system, the occupational emphasis needs to become even greater. At the junior high school level, students should be exposed to industrial arts, home economics, and other vocational subjects so they can develop prevocational skills and motivations. Career exploration experiences in the community become important, and the opportunity to try out various jobs in the classroom and community (besides in the home) will enhance the student's concept of herself as a productive member of society. Educators should initiate occupational guidance activities such as those discussed in chapter 5 to assist the student in her career development and decision-making skills.

During the high school years, occupational skills should form at least half of the curriculum for most handicapped students. A Career Information and Assessment Center will help students learn more about jobs, specific vocational aptitudes and interests, and job-seeking skills and procedures. Such a center should be open at any time for the student, teacher, parent, and community representative and should be integral to the student's weekly program. Vocational subjects, work or job samples, on-the-job work experiences in the community, and other activities of this nature should be provided. The entire school faculty should work toward the goal of helping the student prepare for community living and working requirements, and economic, social, and personal fulfillment.

Most of the daily living, personal-social, and occupational skills comprising the competency-based curriculum approach can be taught in regular subject matter courses at the post-secondary level. Educators can use math, social studies, music, art, physical education, English, home economics, home mechanics, driver's education, business, and special education courses to teach daily living skills.

All teachers can teach personal-social and occupational skills with additional help from school counselors and special educators who can work together to assist each student. Occupational preparation is particularly dependent on vocational teachers from home economics, industrial arts, agriculture, auto mechanics, and other special programs that the educator has established in the school and community. Well-established work-study programs (vocational adjustment, work experience) developed by special

LESSON PLAN			
Student _____ Subject _____		Teacher _____ Grade _____	
Curriculum Area	Objectives	Activities/Strategies	Resources or Materials
Academic Skills			
Daily Living Skills			
Personal-Social Skills			
Occupational Skills			

FIGURE 10.2
Example of form that could be used by teachers to indicate their career development instruction.

educators can be used for the occupational preparation needs of handicapped students but should not constitute the only source of such training. (See Chapter 11 for an Adult Model.)

The form presented in figure 10.2 can be used to identify the benefits of each course the handicapped student takes as it relates to her career development. This form can be used with the Individualized Education Plan that we have mentioned frequently. The IEP not only assures that the student receives the typical content transmitted in a regular classroom but also insures that the teacher relates the subject matter to its implications for career development (daily living, personal-social, and occupational skills).

LIFE-CENTERED CAREER EDUCATION (LCCE) PROGRAMS

The LCCE curriculum model has gained considerable acceptance and adoption in many schools, rehabilitation facilities, and residential centers across the country and elsewhere. The publication, *Vocational Preparation of Persons with Handicaps* (Brolin, 1982), presented several of the following facilities: Special School District, St. Louis, Missouri; West-Allis-West Milwaukee Public Schools, Wisconsin; San Diego City Schools, California; a Willmar, Minnesota rehabilitation facility; and two community colleges that have implemented the LCCE Lifelong Career Development Program for Adults which will be presented in the next chapter. The community colleges were Brainerd College which is located in Minnesota, and Iowa Central Community College in Fort Dodge. The preceding chapter included the process a school district could use to plan and implement the LCCE and other career education approaches. This section will present some schools that have implemented LCCE.

Pine Plains Central School District No. 1, Pine Plains, New York

The Pine Plains Central School System subscribes to the policy position of the Council for Exceptional Children (CEC) and the Division for Career Development (DCD) regarding career education for handicapped students. It is believed that a *satisfying career lifestyle* is the potential and desirable outcome for every student who may obtain a competitive position in the work force or a satisfying position in a sheltered workshop or who may function as a volunteer or resident in a sheltered setting. The outcome is a reflection of each individual's talents and attributes, and is not based solely on the work ethic, but rather on the individual's human potential.

It is difficult to separate the career education from the special education program. Career education is the umbrella under which all other activities fall. All handicapped students are mainstreamed in the least restrictive environment possible. Depending on in-

305

dividual needs (i.e., learning rate, social or emotional needs, management needs and physical development) students may be placed in special classes or attend resource rooms for the amount of time deemed necessary by the Committee on the Handicapped. If needed, students may attend these special classes or resource rooms from kindergarten through high school. Handicapped students are encouraged to stay in school until they are at least 21 years old.

Specific career education information and curriculum are infused into the students' activities as part of their normal program. This *infusion model*, based on a program developed for the state of Michigan, matches career education objectives with content area objectives, fuses the two into a single learning goal, and achieves both objectives in the same lesson.

The LCCE curriculum is used as the career education guide. All teachers are encouraged to appropriately include LCCE in their curriculum and teaching strategies. Special education teachers determine which subcompetencies they will teach throughout the students' K–12 program. The individual's career choice can be extremely varied and depends on the type of handicap and individual abilities.

During the elementary years, students develop career awareness and self-assessment skills. As students progress through junior and senior high school the emphasis changes to include career exploration, decision making, and career preparation. Most of the students choose a vocational path; however with the increasing number of college programs for learning disabled individuals, more students are expressing interest in professional careers.

All students are mainstreamed into regular prevocational classes (shop, home economics, art) that are modified to meet the individual's educational needs. Special classes (modified programs) in content areas such as English, math, social studies, and science are also available to students. These special education classes contain no more than 12 students who receive the minimum state required curriculum for earned credit toward graduation. Students who are unable to function at a level necessary for a high school diploma may be mainstreamed in areas where they have particular strengths or may be involved in a more practical life-centered curriculum in either a special class or resource room.

After students have completed prevocational courses at approximately the ninth grade level, they can make a number of choices for further training. They may enroll in college preparatory curriculum with the special modified program option, a work-study program, or a vocational program within the district or they may choose a combination of programs. A preliminary follow-up study of educable mentally retarded graduates indicates that these students with work-study experience do better on a number of adult adjustment variables than comparable students who attended a vocational/technical school or who were mainstreamed for vocational training at their home school with resource room support. As students consider their options, they are encouraged to assess their skills and the job requirements of various employment opportunities and may begin to make decisions regarding appropriate career directions. Work-study provides students with the opportunity to sample a number of different jobs and helps them make career choice and vocational training

306

decisions. Work-study gives some students the opportunity for on-the-job training in a vocational area of interest; and for others, it provides students with the opportunity for a smooth transition from school to the world of work. Probably of greatest value, the work-study program helps students to develop the personal and social skills necessary for success in communicating with co-workers.

However even after vocational training and/or work study, some students still are not prepared and perhaps might never be ready to obtain completely independent or competitive employment. Our goal is a *satis-*

Frank Peroti provides job training experiences for students in his community.

fying career lifestyle for each of our students. These students are referred to private agencies for continued training and sheltered placements that offer the greatest amount of independence and freedom for each student. These services are available locally through the New York State Office of Vocational Rehabilitative Services, The Association for Retarded Citizens, Gateway Industries and Rehabilitative Programs, Inc. Essential to the success of the Pine Plains program is the commitment by the local school board and its administration to educate *all* of their students and provide them with an equal opportunity to succeed.

Information was provided by Dr. Frank S. Peroti, Jr. who is a work-study coordinator and the director of Special Education for the Pine Plains Central School District No. 1, Pine Plains, New York.

Holly Hill Junior High School, Holly Hill, Florida

The LCCE program was used as a reference when the objectives for the Special Partnership in Career Education Project (SPICE) for junior high school students were revised. The emphasis of the junior high program shifted from the students' development of self-help skills in the elementary school to development of occupational skills and career and educational awareness. The program also emphasized that students learn how to make informed decisions, develop awareness that doing a good job results in self-satisfaction and recognition from others, and identify where they may find skill training.

Project SPICE and the LCCE model stress that career awareness activities can be infused into the curriculum by using a variety of delivery systems. Each project SPICE module contains objectives for language arts, math, science, social studies, home economics, and art. The project SPICE components of peer facilitation, on-site visits, community career consultants, classroom instruction, and parent participation correspond to the roles of the special educator, regular educator, family, and community in the LCCE model.

Project SPICE and the LCCE model view the special educator as a consultant or advisor who coordinates activities with regular educators, parents, and community organizations. Both programs advocate integration of home, school, and community activities to provide the most effective career awareness experiences for handicapped students.

Techniques for mainstreaming handicapped students are an important part of project SPICE and the LCCE program. Project SPICE proposes that peer facilitation or the pairing of handicapped with nonhandicapped students in structured and supervised school and community activities presents a method for mainstreaming handicapped students without the undesirable effects that often occur in traditional mainstreaming attempts. The small group settings and continual support by project staff and school personnel insure that handicapped and nonhandicapped students will achieve success in fulfilling project goals and developing positive attitudes toward each other.

Information was provided by Deborah Rouse who is the facilitator for Project SPICE, Holly Hill Junior High School.

Oakland County Schools, Pontiac, Michigan

Daily living skills, personal-social skills, and occupational skills are compatible with the Michigan Code requirements insuring that students receive prevocational and personal adjustment education. Curriculum based on the life competencies was developed to implement programs for handicapped students who were not succeeding in general education programs. The emphasis has been on hands-on experiences rather than traditional paper and pencil exercises. The goal of the LCCE program is to prepare persons for all of life roles as workers, family members, citizens, and people who engage in leisure activities. These competencies could not be attained in the high school years alone, but rather had to be an ongoing developmental process starting in the preschool years and continuing throughout the adult years.

Special education students can use the following three avenues to achieve these competencies: (1) The student who is mainstreamed could achieve the competencies in general education courses with supportive services from a special education teacher or consultant. (2) The student who is mainstreamed part of the day could accomplish these objectives partly in general education and partly in special education. (3) The student who cannot benefit from mainstreaming would achieve these objectives in a self-contained special education program. Two unique programs have been developed in Oakland County for students in this last category. These are the Marta Jardon program in Hazel Park, and the Northwest Oakland Skills Center program in Waterford. Although the goals and objectives of each program are the same, each program has a unique character.

Marta Jardon, Hazel Park. The present program at the Jardon School began in 1966, but its roots go back to 1934 when Marta Jardon, a special education teacher, began to teach her students life role skills. The program has evolved over the years into a comprehensive junior and senior high school for 12-to-26-year-old students who come from districts throughout Oakland County. The basic philosophy of the school is learning by doing.

The focus in grades seven through nine is on prevocational classes that emphasize practical experiences. In addition to English, math, and science, the students are involved in industrial arts, home economics, greenhouse, and crafts. While developing work skills, they are also acquiring appropriate work-related behaviors that they can use in all life roles.

The students are placed in vocational classes during the high school years. The vocational training available at Jardon includes auto mechanics, horticulture (greenhouse and flower shop), air conditioning, heating and refrigeration, prenursing, woods (general and construction), cosmetology, welding, mechanical drawing, child care, commercial foods, and sewing and needlecraft. Students in these programs are supported by the teaching staff, teachers' aides, and the community. Jardon teachers and administrators strive to coordinate the academic courses with the vocational classes.

After they have finished their vocational training, every student enrolled in Jardon must complete 40 weeks of part-time or 20 weeks of full-time work prior to graduation. Although the Michigan law states that the student must have vocational training, work

experience is also required for graduation from the Jardon School.

The Jardon program has been successful for students who have difficulty in regular classes and has served as a basis for the development of the Northwest Oakland Skills Center program in Waterford. The philosophy of these two programs is the same—to prepare the student to take on all of life roles.

Northwest Oakland Skills Center, Waterford. This program was started in the fall of 1980 to provide hands-on prevocational experience for junior high school students who were not succeeding in regular classes, even with special education support. Many of these students were not succeeding in vocational programs because they did not have the proper or necessary prevocational experiences such as use of common tools, measuring skills, or safety rules. Students attended this program one-half day for a full year and had their academic subjects in their home schools. It soon became evident that a full day program was necessary if the program was to have an impact on these students. Starting with the fall of 1983, the program expanded to a four-year prevocational and vocational program covering ninth to twelfth grades. This program is based in a high school that also houses the adult community education program.

The program offers courses in industrial arts (wood and metal shop), life skills (foods, sewing, and human growth and development), business, health, small engine repair, and career exploration and includes vocational assessment. English and math classes are taught in relation to the prevocational and vocational programs. Additional programs such as custodial services and horticulture training will be added to expand the program. When students are ready for voca-

309

tional programs, they enter a program in their local district or attend one of the area vocational schools. Each area vocational school has a special needs program in which the regular vocational programs are modified to meet the needs of handicapped and disadvantaged students. Students who are not able to succeed in vocational education classes even with special assistance are placed in community-based Individualized Vocational Training (IVT) programs. In IVT programs, the employer functions as the trainer, and the special education person serves as the program coordinator. The IVT programs have been effective with more severely limited students because the training site can be selected to meet the individual needs of the student. Nursing homes, restaurants, and hospitals have been used frequently because they provide a variety of learning experiences. Although job placement is not required for graduation at this time, it is highly recommended that the student have some paid or unpaid work experience before completing high school.

Adapted physical education is a unique feature of this program. The students receive one hour of physical education each day. It is recognized that physical education is important for personal well-being and leisure activities. The development of physical endurance is a necessary part of the curriculum since most of these students will enter jobs that require physical stamina.

The Marta Jardon program and the Oakland Skills Center have been successful because they have been designed to meet the specific needs of the students, rather than forcing the students to fit into existing programs. The goal of these programs is to prepare students for independent living. Using the LCCE curriculum increases the chance that graduates of this program will have met

this goal. An instruction continuum is provided for both the student and teacher; the individual's progress can be monitored, and adjustments can be made in the program to insure that the student has the opportunity to achieve independence.

Information was provided by Dr. Herman Dick who is the director for curriculum management and Dr. Gretchen Thams who is the career education consultant for handicapped students in Oakland Schools, Pontiac, Michigan.

Leavenworth Special Education Cooperative, Leavenworth, Kansas

In the fall of 1980, the Educable Mentally Handicapped Department of the Leavenworth County Special Education Cooperative agreed to accept LCCE as a curriculum model. The overall goal of the program is to teach each student the academic, social, and vocational skills required to become adults who function independently in the community. The first task was to relate teaching objectives and supporting activities to the 22 LCCE competencies. Each teacher listed the specific special education and mainstreamed courses offered to students. Next they identified at which level the LCCE competencies would first be modified, introduced (I) and then reviewed and enriched (R/E). This involved identifying what each student needed. Then the faculty indicated in which content area each subcompetency would be addressed. They next developed goals or objectives for each subcompetency and then selected activities and strategies for delivery.

The *Brigance Diagnostic Inventory of Essential Skills* was used to assess students' progress, and *Competency Rating Scale* (Brolin, 1978 & 1983) was completed for each student. Throughout the work-study program all senior high students are given sections of the *Social and Prevocational Information Battery* (SPIB) and the *Program for Assessing Youth Employment Skills* (PAYES). A student's IEP is developed according to this and other selected data. For example at Level IV, for a student who is weak in the area of following directions, the long-term goal might be to improve in the area of occupational skills while the short-term objective would be to follow the rules and regulations of the student's employer as evidenced by an average rating on a quarterly evaluation that will be completed by the employer.

Interest inventories are administered to sophomores toward the end of the year so students can be placed in an area of their interest. Juniors enter a community based work-study program that will place them at a job site. The daily living, personal-social, and occupational skills acquired up to this point will help the student make a smooth transition from school life to community life. This placement becomes a measure of the student's readiness to assume an adult, independent life in the community.

Once a job site has been agreed upon, a *Cooperative Work Experience Agreement* form is drawn up and signed by the cooperating employer, the student, and the work-study coordinator. This agreement clarifies the specific requirements involved in the job. Also it alleviates any question concerning when and how much the student is to be paid, and if applicable, the terms of employer reimbursement. The final step in placing the student is getting the parents' approval. This states that the parent or guardian approves of the job site and has been notified of who the supervisor is, what the job entails, and, if applicable, how much it pays.

The work-study coordinator develops job possibilities, observes the student at her work site, and conducts counseling sessions that can be used to discuss problems or concerns of the student or employer. The work-study coordinator meets with new students prior to the fall semester and explains the work experience program. The student can gain credit by working as a volunteer or paid employee. Occasionally, a student who works part-time and goes to school part-time may begin to miss her classes, yet will continue to work, particularly if she is paid for her work. To justify removing a student from a job, a *Student Agreement Form* is signed obligating the student to report for both classes and work or be dropped if she does not live up to these terms. Students are graded each week and employers submit quarterly evaluation reports.

The Leavenworth County Special Education Cooperative agrees that the LCCE concept of coordinating all school, family, and community components facilitates each individual's potential for economic, social, and personal fulfillment. The LCCE model makes what students are learning more relevant to what they will need for their future.

Information was provided by Mr. Randi Williams who is the work-study coordinator for Leavenworth Senior High School, Leavenworth, Kansas.

Huron Residential Services for Youth, Inc., Ann Arbor, Michigan

The LCCE curriculum has also been implemented in residential treatment facilities. One example is Huron Residential Services for Youth, Inc. (HRS). This agency is a private nonprofit residential treatment organization that serves troubled adolescents who are between the ages of 10 and 18.

HRS has adapted the LCCE curriculum to fit their existing behavior modification program. Much of the curriculum was already in use; however, the competency rating scale (CRS) provided staff with a tool that will help them assess the student's progress in LCCE. During the summer of 1983, HRS staff broke down the LCCE model into its three components: personal-social, daily living and occupational skills. With minor changes they implemented the LCCE curriculum into their program using the treatment modalities of individual counseling, small group workshops, and actual coursework in a class called Survival Skills in the Community. These last two areas were implemented and revised with LCCE in mind.

Small group workshops at each home were used to discuss occupational skills. HRS staff devised a pre-employment training manual that home counselors could use. This manual described ten workshops that covered specific issues relating to the world of work, as well as numerous strategies that can be used to facilitate a group workshop. One particular counselor at each home, the employment liaison, acts as the facilitator of the group and uses the CRS to rate the client's progress.

Daily living skills are taught through Survival Skills in the Community, a class offered to clients as they make final preparations prior to leaving the HRS program. This course requires that students become involved in the community. Students take weekly field trips to those organizations that they must rely upon such as utility companies, the Internal Revenue Service, the Secretary of State office, rental agents, etc. Weekly class discussions help students to conceptualize the information that students obtained on the field trips. This course was revised to encompass more of the Ann Arbor community, instead of focusing on the classroom alone. With a few additions, the CRS allows the instructor to rate the student's progress in each subcompetency.

HRS also helps youth develop personal-social skills needed for a successful transition to an independent life in the community. The program provides the support and consistency necessary to review the events of the school day. All clients attend either a public or in-house school to enhance academic skills, work toward high school completion, and develop appropriate social skills. After the school day, clients return to their respective HRS homes. Upon arrival, the youth works with a counselor in the area of personal-social skills. Each client maintains a one-to-one relationship with the counselor who helps the student refine these skills. An effort is currently underway to modify the LCCE curriculum so that it fits individual clients' needs. Because the LCCE curriculum is so critical, HRS staff breaks down subcompetencies to even more specific skills. The CRS can be used again to describe each client and can help counselors develop new objectives according to their client's progress.

All in all, LCCE has been a cookbook. With much time and energy the recipes can enhance any program in this field. The CRS is especially useful in quantifying the progress of youth in this type of program.

Information was provided by Patricia Przygodski who is the community resources coordinator for the Huron Residential Services for Youth, Inc., Ann Arbor, Michigan.

Gault Junior High School, Tacoma, Washington

Junior high students can be the worst in the world and the best in the universe. The students at Gault Junior High School are earthy, sometimes rude, and socially unskilled; however once they have established a trusting relationship, they are caring, thoughtful, and accepting of their teachers and peers.

Gault is a school with a declining enrollment; most of the students are underachievers who have obtained the lowest CTBS scores in the district. The general staff is skilled and makes every effort to work effectively under difficult circumstances. They expressed a need for support personnel and alternatives so they could cope with the unique population at Gault. Resource students were especially in need of alternatives that would defeat the failure syndrome. The low self-concept of each student blocked the achievement of her potentials.

When the staff decided that "the way it has always been" was not enough and that changes were necessary, they sought alternative methods that would resolve the problems. They scrutinized traditional instruction-drill-homework models in search of the answer. A closer look at the situation revealed the following ideas:

1. *Traditionally, resource students have been over-individualized.* Every student worked in a corner on her own level, memorizing and completing extensive homework assignments without behavioral incidents; but none of the students could get along in a group setting. Anger in the form of verbal and physical abuse toward peers and supervisors and

JoAnn Balmer shows her class how basic math relates to life skills and career development.

313

inability to share or work together on a project was the rule rather than the exception. This environment was not conducive to optimal learning so the structure of the classroom was changed to a group process format.

2. *Students could not apply their knowledge.* Every student had been drilled on fractions and decimals, but none of them could double a recipe or make correct change. Every student was able to add, subtract, multiply, and divide, but if they were required to apply this information most students drew a complete blank. Using math and English to solve problems in life was impossible. Memorizing facts in social studies and science was confusing because most students could not remember what they learned.

3. *Students had difficulty understanding cause-and-effect relationships.* The use of reason by the teacher in the form of communication, values clarification, and positive reinforcement was the key toward building desired student self-control. Skill building was necessary in dealing with peer-adult conflict, if self-defeating behavior was to be erased from the student's repertoire. The students responded positively to a "soft glove" over a "hard-nosed" approach. Such an approach helped them move in the direction of a trusting relationship with the supervisor. At the onset of the semester the students were informed that there would be no E's or "hacks," their performance in the class would be reviewed bimonthly, and their behavior would be discussed with the class group when necessary. We all cared about each other because each individual was important (1) as a person, (2) for her contribution to the learning environment, and (3) to the group as a whole. Individual conferences

and parent student conferences were held as needed for the Individual Education Planning process and when general goal evaluation seemed appropriate. The teacher's behavior was also open for discussion. The class had a democratic structure.

4. *The learning resource center atmosphere should be a supportive, trusting, and interesting environment where students could find themselves and be themselves.* Pencils, paper, and emotional support were available to each student at all times through the day. A snack was in the cupboard if the student was hungry (better attention and work comes from a full stomach).

5. *School is the job of the student.* Most of the students lacked work skills, realistic employment goals, and employed role models in their community. Attendance, punctuality, task completion, appropriate behavior toward supervisors and peers, good grooming, acceptance of constructive criticism, and willingness to attempt all assigned jobs were used to help students develop work skills.

Students set three types of employment goals: (1) overshoot ("I want to be an attorney, and if I can't read or write, my secretary will do all that stuff for me."); (2) middle hugger ("Who needs a job? I have welfare."); and (3) undershoot ("I don't know what I will do because I can't do anything anyway"). Self-awareness and self-analysis had to be a major force in the curriculum. It was never expected that junior high students would know exactly what they wanted to do, but the students needed to set some goals if they were to start thinking about work and make the associaton between school and future work. Exploration of the job clusters and the academic, physical, and personality strengths needed in each area were infused into the program.

After two months of on-the-job study and a teacher who had a career/vocational background, career infusion was the logical model to follow. The major categories of the LCCE competencies and their incorporation into the general and resource curriculum are outlined in Table 10.1.

Information was provided by JoAnn N. Balmer who is a teacher at Gault Junior High School, Tacoma School District, Tacoma, Washington.

TABLE 10.1

Life-centered career education competencies and instructional areas at Gault Junior High School.

Competency Category	Instructional Area
1. Managing family finances	*Math*
	Identifying coins and making change
	Verifying a bargain
	Writing and keeping a budget
	Writing checks; keeping and balancing a checkbook
	Understanding payroll deductions, income tax, social security
	Recognizing a bargain; reading and verifying advertisements
2. Selecting, managing, and maintaining a home	*Basic skills* (contact) *health*
	Decorating and maintaining the classroom
	Making basic home repairs
	Cooking and planning balanced meals
	Eating proper foods and controlling weight
	Understanding vitamins and minerals for basic health
3. Caring for personal needs	*Basic skills* (contact) *health, physical education* (contact)
	Developing hygiene and grooming skills
	Understanding the need for physical activity (health and weight control)
	Learning rules for common games as a participator and spectator
	Learning first-aid skills
	Obtaining knowledge of common illness and when to seek medical attention
	Obtaining knowledge of over-the-counter and prescribed medication
4. Raising children—family living	*Health*
	Babysitting
	Learning home and school safety practices
	Identifying marriage responsibilities and appropriate dating behavior

315

TABLE 10.1 (continued)

Competency Category	Instructional Area
5. Buying and preparing foods	*Math, basic skills* (contact)
	Developing table manners
	Planning and preparing nutritious meals on a budget
	Obtaining knowledge of the supermarket (sales, impulse buying, selection of a market, advertising)
	Storing food and using leftovers
	Recognizing the importance of kitchen cleanliness
6. Buying and caring for clothes	*Basic skills* (contact) *English, math*
	Reading and following label directions
	Using a washer and dryer (using settings, soap, bleach, fabric softner)
	Ironing
	Selecting clothes (choosing colors, styles, and bargains)
	Mending
	Sorting clothing for laundry
7. Engaging in civic activities	*Social studies*
	Understanding school government (student, administrative structure, school board function)
	Registering to vote and fulfilling responsibilities
	Understanding city, county, state, national government function, and responsibility and service to constituents
	Understanding personal rights as a citizen
	Developing awareness of world problems and issues (malnutrition, conflict, nuclear proliferation)
	Gaining knowledge of the political process
	Mapping, charting, and reading graphs
	Developing basic knowledge of U.S. history (events, people)
8. Recreation and leisure time	*Physical education* (contact), *health*
	Developing knowledge of community recreational facilities (contact person, eligibility requirements, cost)
	Understanding need for recreation
	Understanding spectator sports
9. Getting around the community (mobility)	*Math, English*
	Reading transportation schedules
	Developing awareness of requirements and responsibilities of being a licensed driver of a car, motorcycle
	Obtaining knowledge of insurance
	Reading maps
	Understanding the function of the police traffic division

TABLE 10.1 (continued)

Competency Category	Instructional Area
9. (continued)	Planning a trip (cost of ticket, gas, miles per gallon)
	Developing awareness of bicycle safety practices
10. Achieving self-awareness	*Health, physical education* (contact), *English, social studies*
	Identifying values and emotions
	Identifying conflict and coping with stress
	Expressing feelings (anger, joy)
	Understanding and experiencing group interaction
	Developing awareness of body and its interaction in space
11. Acquiring self-confidence	*Health, social studies, English, math*
	Analyzing levels of competency performance and engaging in self-analysis
	Understanding potential level(s) of performance
	Developing awareness of strengths and weaknesses
	Developing awareness and understanding of personal behaviors
	Coping and identifying with conflict and ability to identify ownership of the problem
	Accepting praise and criticism
	Accepting teasing
	Listening actively to others
	Analyzing and providing feedback to others
	Recognizing stress and when to seek assistance
12. Achieving socially responsible behavior	*All contact and resource classes*
	Developing acceptable field trip, assembly, and speaker behavior
	Knowing strengths and weaknesses and developing an active plan to build on strengths and correct or accept weaknesses
	Understanding behavior in various situations (school, home, job)
	Recognizing the rights of self and others, the evils of assault, vandalism, abuse
	Recognizing a feeling of self in the world of school, family and future employment
	Expressing realistic ambitions and hopes for the near and far future
	Understanding school as his or her job
13. Maintaining adequate interpersonal skills	*All contact and resource classes*
	Developing ability to define, acquire and maintain friendship

317

TABLE 10.1 (continued)

Competency Category	Instructional Area
13. (continued)	Identifying different levels of friendship and acquaintanceship
	Understanding dating behavior
	Clarifying personal values in heterosexual relationships
	Establishing and maintaining close relationships
	Developing awareness of strengths and weaknesses in self-organization on a variety of tasks (class, social, family)
	Developing ability to listen, ask questions, and respond appropriately
	Gathering facts and setting realistic goals
14. Achieving independence	*All contact and resource behavior*
	Completing assigned responsibilities (see 13)
15. Achieving problem-solving	*All contact and resource classes*
	Gathering facts, discussing alternatives, and reaching conclusions
	Understanding the need for goals in a variety of situations
	Becoming aware of the concept of cause and effect
	Accepting consequences for personal actions
	Seeking out the assistance of advisor, counselor etc., when a need for problem solving arises
16. Communicating adequately with others	*All contact and resource classes*
	Recognizing and appropriately responding to emergency situations
	Realizing the need for academic abilities (reading, writing) to fulfill future goals
	Understanding the need for commercial types of communication in our daily lives (newspapers, TV, magazines)
	Developing knowledge of the psychology of advertising
	Completing forms
17. Knowing and exploring occupational possibilities	*All resource classes*
	Understanding the need for value such as self-concept, acceptance of others, independence, self-sufficiency
	Realizing and meeting the responsibility of completing assignments, making up assignments after an absence
	Realizing the advantages of work
	Obtaining knowledge on career clusters and the requirements of each
	Developing knowledge of unions, community industries
	Developing knowledge of steps in seeking employment and/or training

318

TABLE 10.1 (continued)

Competency Category	Instructional Area
18. Making appropriate occupational choices	*All resource classes* Obtaining knowledge of various types of jobs Identifying job categories Identifying appropriate types of work (outdoor vs. indoor) Identifying strengths and abilities (verbal, numerical, coordination, mechanical) Identifying possibilities for entry level jobs (first part-time job)
19. Exhibiting appropriate work habits and behaviors	*All contact and resource classes* Following written and verbal instructions Understanding the team concept (following and leading) Developing ability to take turns Developing ability to agree or disagree appropriately Developing awareness of the importance of attendance, punctuality, quality of work, and productivity
20. Developing appropriate work habits	*Physical education* (contact) *health* Realizing the importance of exercise and diet to physical well-being Understanding and fulfilling a need for physical activity for optimal success toward future work and community living

EXPERIENCE-BASED CAREER EDUCATION PROGRAM

Experience-Based Career Education (EBCE) is a major nation-wide project that helps students explore the world of work. EBCE is an alternative program for students in early high school that provides them with an opportunity to explore occupations while taking academic subjects for graduation. In this section, we will discuss the Appalachia Educational Laboratory Model and its dissemination for special education students.

In the mid 1970s, Iowa Central Community College developed a pilot EBCE program for 33 local schools who needed assistance with secondary career and vocational education. Teacher training, curriculum adaptations, and implementations were supported by federal monies.

As a result of the successful three year EBCE program for students in general education, the Special Education Department, a branch of the Department of Public Instruction, asked the EBCE staff at Iowa Central Community College to help them prepare a dissemination project for special students. In the late 1970s, a team of trainers held workshops and provided

319

technical assistance for special education classroom teachers, work experience instructors (WEIs), and special education consultants from over 45 school districts. EBCE was thereby delivered to students who were classified as learning disabled, mentally disabled, and emotionally disturbed.

The Iowa Special Education EBCE project rewrote materials for various populations of students. The document contained sixteen sets of teacher, students, and community books that were revised to meet the needs of learning disabled and mentally disabled students. The necessary vocabulary, graphic, and worker activities levels were changed in the document to accommodate the special students. Adaptations in time and task level were made for emotionally disabled students.

Finally, the staff at Iowa Central Community College developed a training system. Teams were identified in each of the merged areas of the state, and clusters of teachers, consultants, and work experience instructors were trained to conduct their own training workshops. They were required to participate in five days of training before they could become fully certified EBCE learning coordinators, and it became necessary to expand the training base from central Iowa to other regions of the state.

EBCE programs are:

1. Community-based: Students explore various job sites developed by a learning coordinator.
2. Voluntary: Students or resource persons in the community do not receive salaries.
3. Experiential: Students receive hands-on exposure to the world of work.
4. Exploratory: Programs are the students' first contacts with the world of work *before* they enter the skill preparation stage.
5. Academic: At the work site students complete math, English, or other assignments that show how the worker uses each subject to complete a specific task.

After they have attended an EBCE orientation program, the students are placed at a job site for one to thirteen weeks. Although there are various modifications in the schedule, most students are in the mainstream or special education resource room for one-half of the day. A specially trained learning coordinator (or a team consisting of a classroom teacher and a job site developer) writes weekly activity sheets that specifically describe the student's career and academic assignment. The orientation, placement, and evaluation follow-up stages are outlined in Figure 10.3.

Local schools help Area Education Agencies (AEAs) identify disabled learners who need to receive this kind of training. In Iowa, Area Education Agencies provide special education support services to local schools within their geographical boundaries. Without the cooperation of the public schools

FIGURE 10.3
EBCE Process Flow Chart.

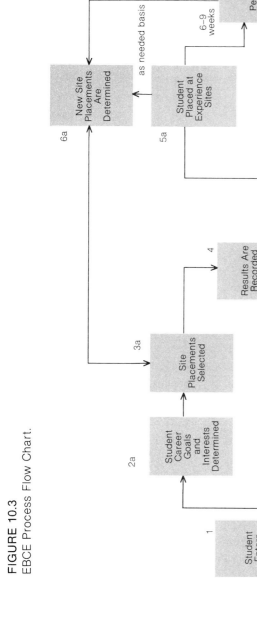

321

and the local community business and industry, the program would not be able to serve disabled learners.

Arrowhead AEA employs work experience instructors (WEI) who are trained to provide and effectively implement EBCE programmming for disabled learners. The local school district is also responsible for providing appropriate special education programming for disabled students. Therefore cooperation between the local school and the AEA is essential to providing students with the appropriate programs.

Annual reviews of special education students' programs occur consistent with the provision of P.L. 94–142. This annual review becomes the first step in serving the disabled learner through EBCE. Local school personnel, including special education teachers, area education personnel, and parents and/or students meet to review each student's special education program and decide on an appropriate educational plan. This annual review staffing must determine the following:

1. Is an exploratory career education experience needed?
2. Will the EBCE program model appropriately meet the needs of the student?
3. What programming will be provided through EBCE?
4. When will programming occur?

Once these questions have been answered, the WEI assumes responsibility for implementing EBCE for the student. The following steps are taken:

1. Orient the student.
   a. Determine student's career interests and aptitudes
   b. Identify worker trait groups
   c. Select experience sites
   d. Review EBCE curriculum and student program outline
   e. Evaluate basic skills and academic needs
   f. Choose EBCE courses
2. Place the student at a community site.
   a. Develop activity sheets
   b. Evaluate activity sheets
3. Evaluate the student.
   a. Evaluate the student's performance at the community site
   b. Evaluate the appropriateness of the learning experience

The WEI, AEA, special education teacher, and the local school work together to develop a highly coordinated program for each disabled learner. This coordination assures the student that her program is designed to meet unique educational and career goals.

The outcomes of EBCE can be defined in quantitative and qualitative terms. Third party evaluations were written on each of three major years of the special education pilot program. As AEL, students, teachers, parents, and community resource people design the EBCE system, they are polled several times for their opinions and comments about student progress and the program effectiveness. Some of the major outcomes for students include

1. development of a positive self-concept
2. exploration of actual occupations at a noncontractual, no-risk basis
3. development of employer-employee relationships
4. development of positive worker behaviors such as promptness, courtesy, and proper reporting of problems
5. increased awareness of what students like *and* dislike about the world of work
6. realization of how basic skills such as math, English, and social science are used in the job world

Although many students in the 45 pilot programs explored jobs traditional for special education students (custodial, kitchen, laundry), many new experiences were "opened up" for them (see Table 10.2).

The learning coordinator provides in-depth guidance using EBCE materials.

TABLE 10.2
Examples of experience sites and occupations for students in Iowa EBCE project.

Site	Occupation
Bakery	Baker
Outdoor nursery	Plant care worker
Supermarket	Carryout clerk, stockperson
Plumbing, heating, and refrigeration	Repairperson, plumber
Newspaper	Photographer, layout designer
Garage	Lubeperson, car clean-up worker
Grocery	Produce person, carryout person, stock-person
Job service	Job placement clerk
Conservation (county)	Conservationist
Catalog store	Sales person
Drugstore	Clerk, buyer
Beauty salon	Hair-dresser stylist
Carpet store	Warehouse worker, carpet installer
Lumber store	Yard person, delivery person
Service station	Mechanic, attendant
Body shop	Body repair person
Service and repair shop	Mechanic, mechanic's assistant
Cleaners	Presser
Cafe	Short order cook, busperson
Heating and cooling company	Sheet metal repairperson
Manufacturing company	Sewing machine operator
Flower and candle shop	Flower designer
Water treatment plant	Water treatment operator
Concrete company	General light construction worker

CONCLUSION

In this chapter we have suggested curriculum and instructional activities for handicapped students within a career education context. This instruction should begin in the student's early years and should involve a variety of school and community resources. Various programs using LCCE and other career education approaches were presented to give you an idea of the several possibilities for curriculum change. The Experience-Based Career Education (EBCE) model is also discussed as an approach that has considerable promise. EBCE can easily become a component of the LCCE Curriculum during the career exploration stage. We are grateful to the educators who provided us with information about their efforts so we can share them with you.

Career Education for Adults 11

The concept of career education has provided educators with a vehicle that can alleviate some of the problems in preparing their students for adult functioning. But it is not a panacea for all of the problems associated with "preparation for life." It has become increasingly clear to us that career education concepts and approaches such as Life-Centered Career Education (LCCE) must also be implemented in adult programs. Basically, career education is a lifelong process. Thus an adequate delivery system must be available so persons with handicaps can have access to services that will meet their career development needs throughout various life stages.

Very few follow-up studies have been conducted to determine how well the over 500,000 special education students, who leave the educational system each year, have adjusted to adult life. However 28 of the 35 million Americans with various handicaps are adults. Are most successful? Do they find employment? Do they make a living wage? Do they get married and raise families adequately? Is there considerable failure and dependency? These are questions we must continually ask ourselves and try to answer.

The studies that have been conducted over the last 10 years indicate that a large proportion of individuals with handicaps have a low employment status. Biklen and Bogdan (1978) reported that 85% of these individuals had yearly incomes of less than $7,000 and that 52% of these made less than $2,000 a year. According to Levitan and Taggart (1977), only 40% of individuals with handicaps are employed compared with 74% of the nondisabled. Viscardi (1976) reported that only 4 out of 11 million capable adults with handicaps were actually working. Bowe (1978) reported that two-thirds of all adults with handicaps are at or near the poverty level. Schoepke

(1979) found a 35% rate of employment in a survey of 161 persons in the Midwest.

More recent figures published by the Social Security Administration reveal that employability and independence are critical problems. The researchers reported that 4.1 million adults with handicaps earn less than $3,000 yearly, 7.8 million have no income at all, and of the approximately nine million who are employed, average earnings overall are $2,000 less than the income of nondisabled workers (*Programs for the Handicapped*, 1983a).

Why do these conditions exist? Are the majority of persons with handicaps really that incompetent and unable to be trained to work at a competitive level? Is the unemployment rate so high that they cannot compete with their nondisabled counterparts for available jobs? Do educators lack the know-how to prepare them for adult functioning? We believe the answer to all these questions is an unequivocal *no.* In our opinion, four major reasons for the high unemployment rate are (1) inadequate career preparation; (2) negative attitudes and lower expectations; (3) lack of a well-coordinated and cooperative delivery system that is responsive to the career development needs of these individuals; and (4) inadequate training to prepare individuals to cope with the day-to-day problems that are not related to employment.

A study of members of the American Management Association (Ruffner, 1981) identified lack of marketable skills and poor job preparation as factors hampering the employment of persons with handicaps. They cited the lack of training in technical areas as a limiting factor. One executive (Papke, 1980) revealed that members of business and industry are suspicious about referrals from educational and rehabilitation agencies. They fear that the persons referred will not be "job ready." Hippolitus (1982) has reported that the proportion of handicapped students in various training programs is unnecessarily low: 3% are enrolled in community colleges, 3.5% in universities, 2.5% in vocational education programs, and 3.5 % in public employment and training programs. In addition, the state vocational rehabilitation agency serves only 50,000 handicapped youth between the ages of 16–24, which is a small proportion of the 500,000 graduating each year.

Negative attitudes, stigma, and stereotypes toward people with handicaps poses a second major obstacle to their normalization. Despite a concentrated effort to eliminate the stigma associated with disability, only minimal positive impact has been made on the general public. A pervasive prejudice still exists toward persons with handicaps and even professionals are sometimes guilty of inappropriate attitudes. They may consciously or unconsciously reinforce their clients for dependent behaviors while "helping" the individual to deal effectively with problems and needs. The human service worker must constantly evaluate his or her actions to avoid the tendency to interact in a prejudiced or devaluating manner. Handicapped individuals also have to cope with the attitudes of their family, friends, and relatives. Although the attitudes of relatives are generally positive and accepting, some have certain resentments, rejection, or guilt feelings that affect their relationship. Many employers avoid hiring handicapped individuals because they feel they will pose a problem to their operation.

The service-delivery system is the third major deterrent to the adult adjustment of individuals with handicaps. Recently, a major news analyst remarked that the reason many foreign countries have gained industrial supremacy is that administrators and their workers cooperate with other

POINT OF VIEW

The LCD Model has contributed to the development of a service-delivery system that enables people to receive needed services. The literature clearly identifies the need for effective programming. Once society has provided the appropriate services, individuals can make the transition between employment and independent living and can live meaningful lives. Without the needed support system and programming, many disabled persons will continue to be dependent upon society for survival which will result in continued pressure on our tax dollars. Taxpayers pay the the bill whether they provide appropriate services or not. An LCD approach will enable us to spend the tax dollars in a positive manner for the benefit of disabled persons and society. LCD is flexible enough to allow communities to adapt and modify the program to meet their specific needs.

Carl Larson is an assistant superintendent at the Iowa Central Community College in Fort Dodge, Iowa.

groups to produce a quality product. This sense of purpose and comraderie seems to be lacking in American society. The President's Committee on Employment of the Handicapped (1979) has identified major barriers to interagency coordination such as "turfmanship," overlapping services, lack of knowledge about implementation of interagency cooperation, differing agency regulations, and lack of cooperation among advocacy and consumer groups that represent the rights of individuals with handicaps. Handicapped individuals would benefit from greater interagency cooperation. Fortunately, there is now a movement occurring that indicates that agencies are beginning to work together. In the next section, we will examine services in more detail.

SERVICES TO ADULTS WITH HANDICAPS

Various public and private programs try to address the career development needs of adults with handicaps (see Chapter 12). However George Conn, Commissioner of the Rehabilitation Services Administration, has revealed that

> Within the world of disability, at the federal level, we are presented with an amazing panorama, for there is no single focal mechanism of compelling purpose (p. 18).

Conn describes the fragmentation and duplication that occurs in the Departments of Health and Human Services, Education, Labor, Housing and Urban Development, Interior, Justice, Transportation, and the Veterans Administration. He reports that there is "great difficulty in developing agreements between existing departments and agencies for the purpose of developing a coherent, rational, positively directed, and substantial generic program that calls for the provision of a continuum of services to disabled persons from the onset of the disabling condition, and wherever and whenever appropriate, provide access to such services throughout that person's lifetime" (p. 19).

Comprehensive programming and cooperation among human service organizations have been promulgated for decades. Federal education and rehabilitation legislation in the 1970s mandated development of a locally coordinated service-delivery system to meet the needs of disabled people over their life span. Each state is required to develop a plan to promote cooperation and minimize duplication of services. Although some states such as Maryland have responded to this mandate after years of struggle, coordination of lifelong support services has been difficult to implement in most states. Conflicting viewpoints between disabled persons and service providers has also contributed to this problem. The dependency-inducing features of the professional-client relationship is seen as part of the problem and not the solution (DeJong, 1981). Many disabled persons dislike the "treatment" philosophy of service providers who assume that they should "treat" the disability because the problem lies within the individual. A rising number of disabled people believe this is demeaning and dependency-inducing. They believe that the problem is their environment, and given appropriate supportive services, accessible environments, and information and skills, they can exercise self-determination and participate in all aspects of society (Frieden, Richards, Cole, & Bailey, 1979).

Thus in the late 1970s, the government passed the Rehabilitation, Comprehensive Services, and Developmental Disabilities Amendment of 1978 (PL 95–602), and a substantial Independent Living movement (IL) was established. A major purpose of these nonprofit Independent Living programs is to locate and coordinate existing resources and to develop and provide services that are not offered in the community. Brolin (1982) listed these to include

- housing and attendant care
- information and referral about goods and services
- transportation
- peer counseling
- advocacy
- independent living skills training
- equipment maintenance and repair
- social and recreational services

Initially the IL movement has focused on adults with physical handicaps. But the application of its basic tenets is apparent for other handicapped individuals. Any comprehensive community-based delivery plan must include such a program of services into its design if it's available.

Many agencies provide handicapped adults with career development services. The following agencies provide vocational services: state vocational rehabilitation agency; state employment service; public and private rehabilitation centers, facilities, and workshops; and some community colleges and vocational-technical schools. Persons in institutions will usually have vocational training opportunities. Daily living skills, personal-social skills, and other training needs can be met at some of these agencies, IL Programs, social and health agencies, various disability voluntary organizations, and adult education programs. These will be discussed in Chapter 12.

Although agencies provide important services to many adults with handicaps, too many people remain unserved or receive inadequate service. Research reveals that too many adults with handicaps do not know how to spend leisure time and lack interpersonal, independent living, personal maintenance, management, community integration, and vocational skills (Schoepke, 1979; Foss & Peterson, 1981; Melstrom, 1982; Schalock, Harper,

329

& Carver, 1981; White, Alley, Deshler, Schumaker, Warner, & Clark, 1982). An alarming finding is that 42% of youth in correctional institutions meet the criteria of handicapped as defined in the federal special education legislation, PL 94–142.

Education and training is a lifelong process. Career interests and needs change as people grow older and progress through adulthood. A continuum of lifelong learning services is as important to these individuals as it is to anyone else (Brolin & Elliott, 1984). Students should be able to return to an educational agency whenever they feel motivated to remedy early educational deficits, upgrade current vocational skills, acquire new vocational skills, and learn more about themselves and the society in which they live (Brolin, 1982).

Many adults with handicaps are not acquiring the Life-Centered Career Education (LCCE) skills that were outlined in Chapter 2. In addition, they do not have access to a well-coordinated delivery system where they can go for career guidance, training, and referral. Haraguchi (1981) suggests that a coordinated delivery system with a central location could initiate appropriate services for these individuals.

Such a system is based upon the results of a three-year federal project from the U. S. Department of Education, Special Education Programs between 1978–1981 and was called the Lifelong Career Development (LCD) project. The project selected the community college as the centralized setting for conducting a coordinated service-delivery system for adults with handicaps who requested career development information and/or services. Special recognition and credit should be given to Iowa Central Community College, Ft. Dodge, Iowa and Brainerd Community College, Brainerd, Minnesota for their full-fledged support in developing and field-testing the project's concepts and materials.

LIFELONG CAREER DEVELOPMENT (LCD) MODEL

The Lifelong Career Development (LCD) Model is a life-centered approach based on the competencies described in Chapter 2. It was a field-developed program that used the community college as the central coordinating agency for career development services. Community colleges provide service to all people who have educational needs. Most offer various specific job training, guidance and counseling, and community service programs.

The community college acts as a catalyst within the community and unites various agencies that serve persons with handicaps. Community outreach and service, visibility, positive image, close commuting distance, and facilities make the community college an ideal setting for linking and providing lifelong career development services. Thus the community college is a multifaceted program that has a wide geographic base of operation and employs a diverse population of lay persons and professionals who can respond to the career development needs of adults with handicaps (Larson, 1982).

Combining service, training, and career education in a natural setting opens new vistas for these persons and replaces old stereotypes and a dearth of opportunities with valued role models, accurate information, and occupational alternatives vital to their aspirations and careers (Wolfensberger & Tullman, 1982; Dahl, 1981). Hartley (1980) observed that the open door/open exit policy of most community colleges is ideal for averting admissions criteria that often exist in other agencies and hamper adults with handicaps.

In contrast with other human service agencies, the community college provides the handicapped individual with a sense of dignity and respect. The opportunity to receive services at a community college "like everyone else" can give people with handicaps more self-confidence and motivation to benefit from other community services. However other agencies can implement the LCD program if it is more relevant for that community. These programs could include IL, vocational rehabilitation, developmental disabilities, vocational-technical schools, and colleges and universities.

Life-centered competency development requires the cooperation of the disabled individual's family, community agencies and organizations, and business and industry. Thus, the LCD approach requires that each of these groups actively participate in the program to better insure that individuals acquire those skills that are necessary for successful career development.

Goal and Objectives of an LCD Program

Lifelong career development is a systematic approach to acquiring skills and services needed by handicapped individuals to achieve and maintain an optimal degree of independent functioning throughout the life span. The program is designed to include the following four characteristics that most human services lack:

1. *The community college is in a normalized setting.* The community college provides handicapped individuals with a normal setting for discussing and resolving problems and needs relative to daily living, personal-social, and vocational functioning.
2. *The community college is a liaison between service providers.* The community college provides a location and method by which community agencies can work together to meet the needs of adults who are handicapped.
3. *The community college focuses on career development.* The community college provides handicapped individuals with opportunities to acquire all of the skills necessary for a successful career

331

(i.e., as an employee, homemaker, volunteer, or participant in a productive avocation).

4. *The community college provides services throughout the life span.* The community college provides a central location where handicapped individuals can seek services throughout adulthood.

LCD is a multifaceted program designed to serve several target groups. The following chart lists the LCD program's goal, objectives and methods to accomplish each objective.

Goal: To improve the opportunities for adults with disabilities so they can achieve a satisfactory level of career development.

Objectives	Methods
■ Improve delivery of services to adults with handicaps	■ By organizing a network of community services and community colleges
■ Meet needs of adults with handicaps so they can master the Life-Centered Career Education (LCCE) competencies	■ By providing career assessment, life-centered career development planning, information, referral to existing services and development of additional programs at community colleges and other settings
■ Improve skills of able-bodied persons for interacting with and better meeting the career development needs of handicapped individuals	■ By providing training and information services to professionals and others

---

A conceptual model of LCD is presented in figure 11.1. As the model portrays, handicapped individuals and those concerned about their career development need one or more of the seven services that are provided by a LCD Coordinator, Team, and Advisory Committee who utilize various community resources so that successful career development can be achieved.

The LCD Coordinator and Team

The Lifelong Career Development (LCD) program is a team approach. The team provides seven career development services to handicapped individuals in community settings.

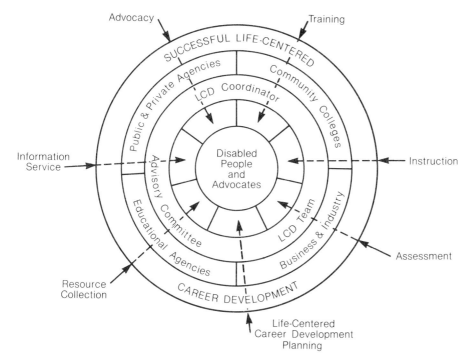

FIGURE 11.1
LCD conceptual model.

The LCD Coordinator. The coordinator is responsible for facilitating personnel and providing LCD services to adults with disabilities and others in the community. She works closely with community agencies, other groups, and individuals who are concerned about the career development of adults with handicaps. The coordinator, who is skilled in the areas of leadership, communication, facilitation, and public relations, guides program development and contributes considerable energy to program activities. The LCD Coordinator should be a member of the community college staff who is experienced and knowledgeable about community resources, systems, and persons with handicaps.

The LCD Team. The LCD Team, a group of 6–10 people, is central to development and implementation of the program and provides the core of expertise required to conduct the program.

The team is composed of handicapped consumers, family members, community college staff, and agency personnel. This cross-section of knowledge, experience, and interests maximizes the team's ability to implement

333

an effective program. The team, under leadership of the coordinator, conducts a service that fills seven distinct roles. These roles are

1. *Training.* The team develops and conducts various training services that help individuals and groups provide better services to persons with handicaps.
2. *Instruction.* The team increases the availability of learning opportunities for adults with handicaps by developing support courses and other resources in the community.
3. *Career Assessment.* The team evaluates the individuals' skills and learning interests relative to life skills.
4. *Life-Centered Career Development (LCD) Planning.* The team works with the individual to develop an individual career development plan based on the training interests, needs, and options available at the college and in the community.
5. *Resource Collection.* The team provides all interested community members with a central location that contains information about disability and resources that can assist handicapped individuals in lifelong career development and functioning.
6. *Information Service.* The team provides information and suggestions to community college faculty and staff, agency personnel, employers, handicapped individuals, their families, and others concerned about career development.
7. *Advocacy.* The team facilitates effective advocacy by preparing handicapped individuals to become self-advocates, serving as a resource to disabled persons, and becoming advocates for persons with disabilities.

The extent of each team member's involvement will depend on release time and the person's other job responsibilities. The goal and objectives of the seven roles will be more completely described in the next section.

ROLES OF THE LCD TEAM

Training

The overall goal of the LCD team is to train others to interact with and provide more appropriate services to persons with handicaps. The team should conduct five major tasks: (1) determine training needs in the community relative to disabilities; (2) facilitate existing training resources; (3) develop appropriate forms of training as needed; (4) conduct various training services including workshops, seminars, panel discussions, media presentations and speakers; and (5) evaluate effectiveness of training.

Team members develop and conduct inservice training and awareness-building experiences for community college faculty, staff and students, agency personnel, employers, disabled people, and others in the community. This LCD educational outreach helps professionals and others to interact effectively with disabled people and, in turn, benefits disabled individuals by preparing others to interact with them more successfully. Some important points to consider in initiating and implementing training activities are the following:

- Use all available manpower and resources to implement training. For example, recruit a team of disabled citizens willing to participate in panel discussions and serve as speakers when opportunities arise.
- Evaluate training efforts. Plan each training event, obtain and *use* input and feedback from trainees.
- Use evaluation data to improve future training and document effectiveness of services.

Development of training programs depends on the community's needs, the team's resources, and available opportunities. The following training activities are some examples of services that the LCD program can provide.

- Inservice training for community college faculty and staff that focuses on adaptation of the curriculum and instructional methods to accommodate disabled students.
- Presentations and question and answer sessions conducted by disabled adults to increase children's awareness of disabled people.
- A seminar for employers who wish to learn more about legislation related to disabled people in the work force.
- A workshop for disabled adults on the topic of accessible housing.
- A speaker for the luncheon meeting of a community civic club to address topics related to adult living and employment.

Instruction

The LCD Team should also try to increase the availability of learning opportunities that will meet the career development needs of adults with handicaps. The team has three major objectives: (1) determine availability of instructional resources for handicapped individuals in the community and at the community college; (2) facilitate the individual's use of existing learning opportunities; and (3) develop and conduct programs to fill unmet learning needs of these individuals.

335

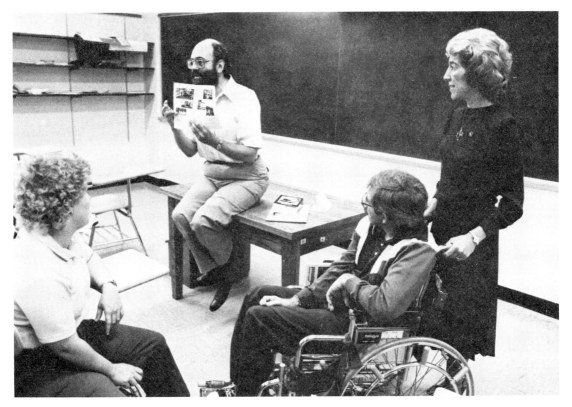

Neva Williams, the LCD coordinator at Brainerd, Minnesota Community College, provides disabled students with specialized services.

The LCD team should focus on two major instructional goals: (1) facilitate use of existing learning opportunities and (2) assist in development and implementation of instruction to serve the individual's needs that are unmet by current resources. Team members gather information about resources available in the community and refer handicapped individuals to them as needed. When appropriate instruction is not available, the team may develop support courses or individualized learning opportunities to meet specific needs. Courses may be organized around the 22 LCCE competencies or the three domains of daily living, personal-social and occupational skills.

Some important points that the LCD team should consider in initiating and implementing instruction are the following:

- Handicapped individuals are the target group for the LCD team's instructional services. However the target audience for the LCD team's training services are professionals, family members, and employers as well as handicapped individuals.

- In planning support courses, the LCD team can offer courses through established programs like adult or continuing education or the community college. This may decrease the work involved in planning and increase the course's visibility to prospective students.
- Relatively inexpensive curriculum materials are available to teach many of the 22 competencies and may greatly simplify course planning.
- The LCD team may wish to recruit volunteers to teach some of the support courses developed through the LCD program.
- Agencies may wish to refer clients to support courses offered by the LCD program.
- Advisory committee members may be able to arrange individualized instruction opportunities in the community.

The following lists some examples of group instruction that the LCD team can conduct.

- A course on cooking skills for people with limited use of their hands.
- An activity-oriented class on recreation opportunities for mobility-impaired people in the community.
- A structured growth group that will help disabled individuals to build self-awareness and self-confidence.
- An interpersonal and communication skills course for disabled individuals.
- A career exploration group for disabled adults.
- A job-seeking skills course specifically geared for adults with mental retardation.

In some cases, the person's needs are best met through individualized instruction. The following services exemplify this type of instruction.

- One-to-one instruction is arranged for a woman with cerebral palsy to learn to swim at the YWCA.
- An opportunity for on-the-job career exploration is arranged with a local architectural firm for an orthopedically disabled person interested in drafting.
- A blind instructor at the community college provides campus orientation to a new student who is blind.

Career Assessment

The goal of career assessment is to evaluate the handicapped individual's skills and learning interests relative to the 22 life-centered competencies. The team assumes four major objectives or responsibilities: (1) obtains background information; (2) selects and administers the Career Development Inventory (CDI) and other appropriate assessment instruments; (3) prepares a profile of results and confidential file for the person; and (4) discusses results with the individual.

During career assessment, a member of the LCD team uses a cumulative record file called the Career Development Record (CDR) to gather background information, administer the Career Development Inventory (CDI), and prepare a career development profile. If appropriate, the LCD team member should administer additional assessment instruments and may need to seek records of previous evaluations.

Some important points that the LCD team may wish to consider in performing career assessment include the following:

- An individual's first contact with the assessment process should involve person-to-person interaction, not paperwork. Forms and instruments can be completed later.
- Explain that records are confidential.
- Don't pressure the person. Be flexible and responsive to the needs of the individual you are assessing.
- Administer the CDI and other appropriate assessment instruments such as *Tests for Everyday Living, Social and Prevocational Information Battery,* and other vocational evaluation instruments.
- Obtain records from other sources *only* when there is a specific need. It should not be a routine measure. Always get the individual's or guardian's written permission.

The following lists some examples of how the LCD team can use career assessment.

- A team member uses the Background Information form in the Career Development Record (CDR) to identify and collect information on the handicapped individual's development needs and goals.
- A team member administers the Career Development Inventory (CDI) and the Social and Prevocational Information Battery to identify training needs of an adult with mental retardation who plans to move into a group home.
- A team member reads the Strong-Campbell Interest Inventory or other interest measures to an individual who is blind and wants to explore her career interests.
- A man with cerebral palsy and a team member discuss areas of training needs suggested by CDI results.

Life-Centered Career Development (LCD) Planning

The team's role or function is to develop a workable Life-Centered Career Development (LCD) plan. In performing this role, the team should meet five major objectives: (1) involve the handicapped individual in planning; (2) generate options for services to meet the person's needs; (3) identify and use the individual's strengths and weaknesses in LCD planning; (4) write an LCD plan that is responsive to the individual's goals; and (5) interview the individual periodically to assess her progress.

LCD planning is an important service to individuals with handicaps. The team member uses this process to analyze assessment data and information, generate service options, and establish specific goals and plans. A member of the team follows the individual's progress toward these goals through ongoing contacts with the person.

Some important considerations that the team must consider when implementing this role are the following:

- The team's role is to plan with, not for, the individual. Actively involve the person in planning. In some cases, the team member may include the family in the planning process.
- In planning sessions, the team member should work directly with the handicapped individual rather than relying on family members or friends. This should be a general policy although exceptions may arise.
- The LCD planning process may require several meetings with the individual. The length of time required to establish a workable LCD plan will vary.
- The team member should consult with the team, advisory committee or other resource people if she encounters difficulties in LCD planning. The handicapped individual should remain anonymous during such interactions with advisory committee members or resources outside the LCD program.
- The entire team should not meet with the handicapped individual during the LCD planning process because she might feel intimidated. However for some persons a group meeting may be feasible and useful. Select the process that best accommodates the individual.
- If appropriate resources are not available to meet the person's needs, the team member may wish to establish an individualized service or training opportunity as described under the team role of instruction.
- The team member responsible for follow-along interviews should have a good rapport with the handicapped individual. This can be facilitated by including the follow-along person in LCD planning meetings with the person.

- Interviews should occur once a month, preferably in person.
- The team member responsible for follow-along interviews should conduct the exit interview when the person is ready to conclude participation in the LCD program. A format for this interview is provided in the CDR.

The following steps are involved in the LCD planning process.

---

1. One or two team members meet with the disabled person to discuss the individual's goals and options available to help achieve them.
2. The individual and team member(s) write an LCD plan using the format provided in the CDR.
3. The team member should consult the team if additional input is needed.
4. As the LCD plan is implemented, a team member monitors the individual's progress by contacting the individual and service providers on a regular basis.

Resource Collection

The overall goal of resource collection is to make disability-related information and resources available to interested individuals. The team should assume four major functions: (1) collect and organize resources so that information is easily accessible; (2) respond to requests for information available in the resource collection; (3) acquire and organize information about local and state resources that the team could include in the resource collection; and (4) update and revise resource collection.

A centralized and accessible collection of disability-related information is an essential resource to the team as well as to other interested persons. The role of resource collection includes communication of disability-related information in response to requests and collection and organization of information about local and state resources.

The resource collection should include information that has already been obtained as well as new resources acquired specifically for the collection. Updating and revising the collection are ongoing responsibilities of the team. Some important points that the LCD team should consider when implementing the role of the resource collection are the following:

- The LCD team should make sure the resource collection is housed in a facility that is accessible to disabled people.
- The team members should build the resource collection early in the developmental stages of the LCD program. It will serve as a resource to the team in implementing other roles.

- The LCD team should establish a resource collection to provide information for use in conducting each of the seven roles, if the community chooses to implement a modified LCD program model that does not include all seven team roles.
- All team members should become familiar with the organization and contents of the collection so they can locate materials easily.
- Team members should survey local resources as soon as possible and include the information in the collection.
- The LCD team should ask members of the LCD Advisory Committee to share information about new resources and materials. This may be included as a regularly scheduled activity during committee meetings.

The following activities are some examples of the responsibilities involved in resource collection.

- The LCD team organizes a collection of books, newsletters, and pamphlets about disability-related information and local resources in a section of the community college library or in a room outside the LCD coordinator's office.
- A member of the LCD team orients students from a community college course in human services about how to use the resource collection.
- A LCD team member shows the disabled individual how to use the resource collection to locate information about local vocational training opportunities.
- A LCD team member can show a local advocacy group how to use the resource collection to identify other advocacy organizations in the state.

Information Service

The overall goal of information service is to provide appropriate information and referrals in response to requests from individuals in the community. The team should assume three major tasks or functions: (1) clarify the request for information; (2) formulate and communicate the information or referral in response to the request; and (3) follow-up to determine whether information or referral was satisfactory.

Through the role of information service, team members respond to requests from individuals who have questions or problems related to the career development of handicapped individuals. Requests may come from community college faculty and staff, agency personnel, employers, persons with handicaps, their families, and others. The role of information service may be as simple as referring a person on the phone to an appropriate resource or as complicated as a consultation on indepth program planning.

341

Team members obtain information about circumstances surrounding the request and formulate recommendations to meet the needs of the individual who has requested assistance. The process ends with communication of the information or referral and follow-up to determine if results are satisfactory. Some important considerations in implementing this role are the following:

- The team members should be sure to understand a person's request before attempting to provide recommendations.
- The team members' interviewing skills influences whether they can provide the appropriate information.
- The team members should use the resource collection to address requests.
- The team members should conduct a follow-up with the person to determine whether their recommendations resulted in a satisfactory outcome.
- Team members should keep records of their activities within this role. Without these records, day-to-day services that demonstrate effectiveness of the LCD program may not be documented.

Activities that fall within the realm of information service may seem elusive for several reasons. Information service differs from some of the other program-related tasks because team members do not initiate the action. The team does not plan their information service activities as they might plan the development of the resource collection or a training workshop. Instead team members respond to issues and problems that others bring to them. Also, it is easy to forget that day-to-day problem solving often falls within the realm of information service. Some examples of an information service are presented below.

- A community college instructor asks for help in modifying instructional techniques to meet the needs of a disabled student.
- A business firm asks for assistance in planning a convention that is accessible and convenient for participants with disabilities.
- The spouse of a disabled person requests help in locating a local support group for families of disabled people.
- A wheelchair user attending the community college asks the LCD coordinator for help when the elevator in the classroom building is out of order for an extended period of time.

Advocacy

Another goal of the LCD team should be to facilitate effective advocacy involving individuals who have handicaps. Three important functions that the team should fullfill for this role are the following: (1) prepare the individual to become a self-advocate; (2) serve as a resource to handicapped individuals pursuing advocacy; and (3) become advocates for individuals with handicaps.

Through this role, team members become involved in various types of advocacy and prepare disabled individuals to be effective self-advocates. Team members who are well-versed on relevant legislation, bargaining techniques, and resources work with disabled people who wish to solve specific problems or improve self-advocacy skills. Some important points that team members should consider are the following:

- As an advocate, the team member's primary objective is to help others help themselves.
- Whenever possible, team members should use the following strategy: (1) help individuals solve problems or pursue issues on their own; (2) act on the person's behalf if other avenues are unsuccessful. In some cases, this approach may be inappropriate, but team members should try to implement this strategy whenever possible.
- Knowledge and expertise of team members is especially important to success in the role of advocacy. The following are key areas: relevant legislation, bargaining and negotiation techniques, and advocacy resources.

The following presents some examples of advocacy activities.

- Team members conduct a seminar for disabled people on bargaining and negotiation techniques.
- The team helps to organize a self-advocacy group composed of disabled citizens in the community.
- At a disabled person's request, a team member provides feedback about the wording of a grievance to be filed with the Office of Civil Rights.
- The team conducts a workshop on legal rights for disabled individuals and advocates.
- A member of the team who is disabled joins the city transportation committee to represent concerns of disabled citizens.

The seven roles constitute the services provided by the LCD team. The target audience for each role is highlighted in the following chart.

LCD roles that serve
   Disabled Adults
- Instruction
- Career assessment
- LCD planning
- Advocacy

LCD roles that serve
Disabled and Non Disabled Persons
- Training
- Resource collection
- Information service

LCD ADVISORY COMMITTEE

The LCD advisory committee, composed of community college, agency, and consumer representatives, is an information resource to the team who develops the LCD program. An enthusiastic committee, well-versed in LCD's goals and activities, expands the program's resource and knowledge base and secures the LCD program a place within the community.

Typically, advisory committees develop in one of two directions: (1) members operate as a token committee who attend meetings to hear about program developments and offer minimal commitment of time, energy, or support; or (2) members participate as a working committee who evaluate the program's progress, recommend improvements, and share their ideas, expertise, and time whenever possible. Within the framework of the LCD program, the active involvement of the committee is vital to achieving maximum impact in the community. The following points should be considered when forming and refining the LCD advisory committee:

- Select members carefully. Look for people who are open-minded about the program and willing to expend effort as committee members.
- Be sure the committee represents a cross-section of the community. Include representatives from consumer groups, business and industry, local government, and civic organizations as well as school, college, and agency personnel.
- Clearly explain to prospective committee members the goals and organization of the LCD program, the committee's function, and the level of involvement expected.
- Establish an attendance criterion to "weed out" inactive members. For example, members who wish to remain on the committee must attend at least two out of every four meetings. Inform prospective members about the criteria for establishing a term of membership.
- Schedule meetings well in advance. Give members at least a month or six weeks notice.
- Mail an agenda to members before the meeting and specify the topics that the committee will cover.
- Mail minutes of meetings to members, especially to those who were unable to attend.
- Periodically evaluate the committee and make membership changes as needed.

More specifically, the advisory committee participates in activities related to five areas: linkage of service, consultation, manpower and expertise, resource information, and community support. *Linkage of community services* is one of the committee's most important contributions to the LCD Program. An active committee composed of a cross section of representatives from agencies, consumer groups, business and education can function as a loosely organized network of services. Participation in a committee gives members an opportunity to meet and communicate with other people in the community who are interested in the concerns of disabled individuals. The committee can establish channels of communication that can better coordinate existing services.

Advisory committee members serve as *consultants to the team* regarding different aspects of the LCD program. Committee members may provide input to the team about program plans and recommend changes. The committee may help the team identify referral options for handicapped individuals in the program.

The advisory committee can also expand the availability of *manpower and expertise* to implement program activities. A member may speak at an LCD-sponsored workshop or teach a support course to adults with handicaps. The team should encourage advisory committee members to share their expertise by conducting selected program activities.

The advisory committee is a valuable *source of information* about local, state, and national resources of information on disability. Members can help the team keep the resource collection up-to-date by bringing new books and materials to committee meetings to show the team and participating in efforts to document local resources.

Through their contacts with disabled individuals, professionals, and others in the community, advisory committee members also can *increase community support* by conveying information and expressing favorable attitudes about the LCD program. Committee members should be encouraged to inform their colleagues about the program and should participate in public relations efforts.

THE LCD PROGRAM MODEL

If the disabled individual is interested in improving her competency level, she should be evaluated on the 22 competencies and learning needs (career assessment). Afterwards, the team can meet with the participant to work out career development plans. Figure 11.2 is a graphic representation of the LCD program. This model depicts the services provided to target groups and demonstrates interrelationships between elements of the LCD program. The model should help the team implement the program and can introduce others to the LCD concept. Figure 11.3 can be used to interpret the model.

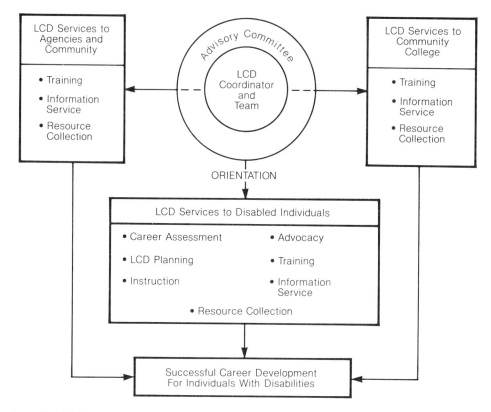

FIGURE 11.2
LCD program model.

Vertical Flow

The vertical flow of figure 11.3 depicts LCD program services that are available to individuals with handicaps. An adult seeking career development services talks with a team member or designate who should describe the LCD program, respond to questions, and provide a program brochure. Thus, the handicapped adult becomes oriented to the LCD program. Depending upon the individual's needs and goals, the team member may recommend or provide one or more of the seven LCD services: career assessment, LCD planning, instruction, advocacy, training, information service, and resource collection.

Horizontal Flow

The horizontal flow of figure 11.3 depicts LCD services that are available to the agencies, community, and the community college. Services that the team provides to agencies and community include training, information service,

FIGURE 11.3
Flow chart depicting how disabled persons and others can use the LCD service.

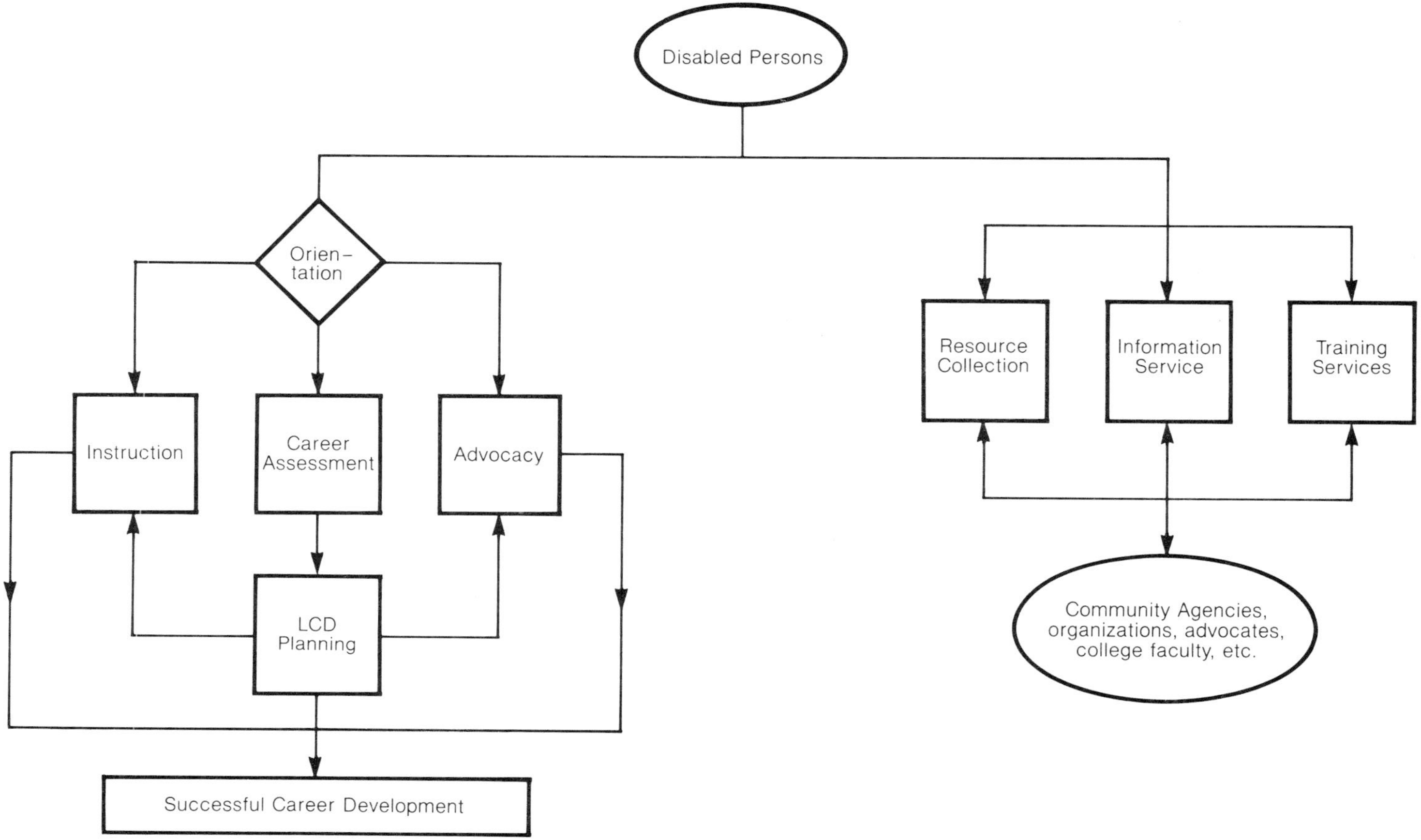

and resource collection. The team also provides training, information service, and resource collection to community college faculty, staff, and students.

As shown by the vertical and horizontal flow of figure 11.3, the LCD program involves two areas of service. The vertical flow identifies the services that were designed for individuals with handicaps. The horizontal flow depicts the services that are available to professionals, family members and others. These services benefit the handicapped population by preparing others to interact successfully with them and meet their career development needs. The LCD program focuses on two target populations for the program's various services.

Finally, we want to clarify what has been said about the LCD model by focusing in on the prospective uses of services. When a handicapped individual encounters the program, she immediately hits a fork in the road. The direction she goes in is determined by the person's most pressing needs. Depending on the service needs, the person is referred to an appropriate agency or undergoes an orientation and receives services directly from LCD team members. Figure 11.3 portrays this process in graphic form.

CONCLUSION

The LCD program is a model for achieving the elements of service improvement discussed previously—delineation of necessary life skills and linkage of community services. This multifaceted program emphasizes coordination and provision of services for handicapped individuals relative to 22 life-centered competencies. These competencies serve as the focal point for many program activities.

The organization of the LCD program is specially designed to generate ongoing communication between service providers in the community. A team approach and active involvement of a community-based advisory committee allows consumers and service providers to work together, identify available resources, and implement the program.

The LCD concept is an innovative model for providing a coordinated and comprehensive array of services that meet the career development needs of persons with handicaps. The program involves the community college in the linkage and provision of career development services to these individuals. The community-based program, housed at the community college, derives maximum benefit from the community college's resources and unique role in the community. In addition, the program could also be coordinated out of such agencies as independent living programs, vocational-technical schools, rehabilitation agencies, and perhaps other settings if needed.

Agencies, Organizations, and Instructional Resources 12

One of the major contributions of the career education concept has been the involvement of numerous community agencies and organizations in the career development efforts of the school. In addition to drawing upon considerable expertise not readily available in the school setting, there are several particularly significant reasons for involving community agencies and organizations. First, these agencies and organizations have funds, equipment, contacts, and a constituency far beyond the resources of the school. Second, the agencies and organizations are able to assist in the improvement of the school's curriculum and courses. Third, the agencies and organizations sometimes lend financial support for pressing needs the school encounters in implementing career education. Fourth, the general public's negative attitudes and misconceptions toward handicapped individuals will be counteracted as these agencies and organizations become partners in career development efforts.

Numerous civic, professional, and private nonprofit organizations and government agencies are located in most middle-sized and large communities. Besides the many local avenues for career development, there are several state and national resources that local personnel should use for additional information, literature, contacts, funding possibilities, and, in some cases, direct services.

This chapter identifies and describes some of the major agencies and organizations at the national, state and local levels that can be included in career development efforts for handicapped individuals. Information about most of the agencies and organizations is presented in Tables 12.1 and 12.2. The chapter also briefly discusses some of the major informational systems that are useful for materials and references on career development.

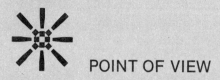

POINT OF VIEW

Each phase of career education (awareness, orientation, exploration, and preparation) is essential to all individuals who wish to improve the quality of their lives, their education, their independence, and their employment skills. Career education is a life-time process; its occupational information base and occupational skills are always changing with the development of technology and growth of knowledge and information.

No one agency or organization can provide all the resources needed to supply these lifetime experiences. At no time in American history and education has the challenge been greater than now to centralize information bases and coordinate local, community, state, regional, national, and international resources.

Collaboration of local school and community resource persons, agencies, and organizations is needed to ensure that handicapped individuals have access to the supportive services and the many career experiences that will enhance their capabilities. A partnership of education and community leadership is key to integrated and cost-effective career education experiences for handicapped children, youth, and adults.

Lorella A. McKinney is a project director for the National Center for Research in Vocational Education at the Ohio State University in Columbus, Ohio.

350

GOVERNMENT AGENCIES

Numerous government agencies are important in promoting and supporting career development programs for handicapped individuals. Personnel at the local level should be aware of the relevant information, professional literature, funding, and technical assistance that is available from each of these agencies. Table 12.1 outlines federal agencies important to the career development of handicapped individuals.

The *Office for Special Education and Rehabilitation Services* (OSERS) administers and operates the federal program for educating the nation's handicapped students. It is responsible for identifying national priorities and implementing the Education for All Handicapped Children Act (PL 94–142).

TABLE 12.1
Federal agencies important to career development of handicapped individuals.

Agency	Branch or Department
Administration of Developmental Disabilities	Office of Human Development Services/ Department of Health and Human Services
National Council on the Handicapped	Department of Education
National Institute of Education	Office for Educational Research and Improvement/Department of Education
National Institute of Handicapped Research	Office of Special Education and Rehabilitative Services/Department of Education
Office of Special Education and Rehabilitative Services	Department of Education
Office for Vocational and Adult Education	Department of Education
Office of Information and Resources for the Handicapped	Office of Special Education and Rehabilitative Services/Department of Education
President's Committee on Mental Retardation	Office of Human Development Services/ Department of Health and Human Services
Rehabilitative Services Administration	Office of Special Education and Rehabilitative Services/Department of Education
Veterans Administration	Veterans Administration

Sources: Charles B. Brownson (Ed.) *Congressional Staff Directory.* Mount Vernon, VA: Congressional Staff Directory, Ltd., 1982.
Federal Organization Service. Washington, D.C.: Carroll Publishing Co., 1981.

351

The *Office for Vocational and Adult Education* (OVAE) administers the mandated vocational education monies that must be matched in amount by the states. The *Rehabilitation Services Administration* (RSA) administers the state-federal program of vocational rehabilitation, including a network of regional offices and state agencies that receive matching federal funds based on an established formula. RSA also has funds for research and demonstration projects that provide effective rehabilitation services to handicapped individuals, including school populations needing better career development services.

The *Administration of Developmental Disabilities* (ADD) is responsible for helping states plan and implement programs for developmentally disabled individuals (autism, mental retardation, dyslexia, cerebral palsy, and epilepsy). Project grant funds are available to public agencies and nonprofit organizations who are developing new and improved techniques. The *Office of Information and Resources for the Handicapped* publishes a valuable document entitled *Programs for the Handicapped*, that reports events, techniques, programs, legislation, publications and other important matters for handicapped individuals. The *National Institute of Education* (NIE) conducts and funds research and development activities in career education. It has produced curriculum modules, the Experience-Based Career Education models, materials to eliminate sex bias in career counseling, and materials assessment documents.

The *National Council on the Handicapped* (NCH) is composed of 15 members appointed by the President of the United States with the advice and consent of the Senate. The council reviews the operations of the National Institute of Handicapped Research, evaluates programs and activities conducted by federal departments and agencies that represent handicapped individuals, and recommends ways to improve programs or establish research objectives. The *National Institute of Handicapped Research* (NIHR) has long range plans to conduct research on prevention, restoration, maintenance, quality of services, employment, and daily living activities. Its objectives are to disseminate information and stimulate the development of technological devices by the private sector in addition to research and demonstration projects.

The *Veterans Administration* (VA) is an important federal agency that offers a broad range of programs, including medical care, rehabilitation, education and training, income support, and other benefits for eligible disabled veterans and their dependents. VA regional offices and centers are situated throughout the country.

A historic "memorandum of understanding" between RSA and the then U.S. Office of Education was released in October 1977, with the intent of pursuing methods by which the two delivery systems could achieve greater cooperation and provide complementary services. The commissioners of these agencies transmitted memorandums to their state directors, requesting them to seek a coordinated service delivery for handicapped persons. Since both agencies require written programs for each handicapped individual, the groundwork has been laid for coordinating the delivery of services among these systems. The directive read:

> In order that education and vocational rehabilitation agencies may integrate the goals of the IEP and the IWRP, the plans should reflect short-term and long-range objectives for career development, vocational skill training, personal adjustments and job placement. To effect this integration, education agencies must provide guidance to those preparing IEPs and establish local contact with VR agencies. And VR agencies must similarly assure that appropriate IWRPs—e.g. for persons who should complete their plans for special and vocational education—are developed in conjuction with education agencies.

Thus, the wheels began to turn in favor of consolidated and cooperative efforts within and between agencies, so that the many pressing needs of handicapped citizens could be met. But, the wheels of change move slowly and often reluctantly. It is hoped that this will not be another meaningless and momentary declaration by those people who are responsible for its implementation.

At the state level, several agencies are available to assist in the career development needs of handicapped individuals. Most of the agencies are extensions of the federal agencies discussed previously and are accessible to the practitioner. Their titles and identity in the department structure will vary from state to state. Some of the important agencies are the following:

- *Special Education.* Administers the state program for the education of exceptional children; offers technical assistance to school districts and programs; conducts seminars and workshops; disseminates information; conducts student identification and needs studies; promotes the development of professional services; and promotes, writes, and enforces legislation.
- *Vocational Education/Handicapped and Disadvantaged Program.* Administers the federal/state legislation that relates to vocational education for handicapped and disadvantaged individuals (called *special needs*); promotes the development and funds programs in secondary/post-secondary educational settings; works closely with universities in developing personnel training programs, conducting special projects, developing and disseminating materials, and other activities of career development.
- *Vocational Rehabilitation.* Administers the program of assisting physically and mentally disabled persons to become gainfully employed. To be eligible, a person must have (1) a physical or mental disability that interferes with getting or holding a job, and (2) a

reasonable chance of being able to work. Services include (1) medical evaluation, including mental and emotional status; (2) evaluation of vocational potential, training, and placement needs; (3) medical, surgical, psychiatric, and hospital care if the individual needs these services to maintain or secure employment; (4) artificial limbs, braces, wheelchairs, and hearing aids if necessary for work; (5) vocational training, including tuition and fees, books, and supplies at universities, colleges, commercial and trade schools, rehabilitation facilities, or on-the-job training; (6) maintenance for daily living costs and transportation for medical treatment or vocational training; (7) job placement equipment, such as job-related tools and licenses; (8) individual guidance and counseling; (9) coordination of services; (10) help in finding employment; and (11) on-the-job follow-up. Although there is no age limitation, most vocational rehabilitation clients are between 16 and 65.

■ *Bureau for the Blind.* Administers the vocational rehabilitation program for blind and visually handicapped persons of all ages. Services include mobility training; communication skills, such as braille, talking books, tape recorders, telephone; daily living activities, such as grooming and hygiene, social etiquette; physical conditioning; and prevocational skills.

Persons working with handicapped individuals should know about and interface with these state agencies to develop and conduct meaningful career development services. In addition, the following agencies may be helpful: (1) state employment/job service provides direct employment and counseling services, appraises the client's employment capabilities, prepares the client for interviews; develops and modifies jobs; and obtains information on vocational training programs; (2) the Governor's Committee on Employment of the Handicappped conveys to the governor and general public the pressing needs and desires of handicapped citizens.

At the local level, many of these agencies and organizations have offices in moderate- to large-size cities. Agencies such as vocational rehabilitation, public health, employment service, mental health centers, social services/welfare, and diagnostic services provide an array of daily living, personal-social, and occupational assistance. In addition, local government officials and political parties can promote adequate career development services for handicapped citizens.

ORGANIZATIONS

Numerous private, nonprofit, volunteer, and other organizations are dedicated to providing handicapped individuals with the appropriate services. Many of these organizations were started by parent groups and other concerned citizens who felt that specific areas of need required special attention.

Some special national committees and centers that promote the career development of handicapped individuals are the following: (1) *The President's Committee on the Employment of the Handicapped* has over 600 volunteer organizations and individuals representing business, handicapped persons, industry, labor, media, medicine, education, rehabilitation, religion, veterans, and youth, and other groups promoting education, rehabilitation, and employment opportunities for handicapped individuals; (2) *The President's Committee on Mental Retardation* (PCMR) advises and assists the president on all matters pertaining to mental retardation and disseminates public information; and (3) *The National Committee, Arts for the Handicapped* (NCAH), an educational affiliate of the John F. Kennedy Center for the Performing Arts, operates as the national coordinating agency for the development and implementation of arts programs for handicapped children and youth.

Table 12.2 identifies *some* of the major professional organizations that are particularly important to the career development of handicapped individuals. Several of the national organizations listed in the table have state chapters that implement their philosophies and policies. Particularly significant are the state associations of the Association for the Severely Handicapped, Council for Exceptional Children, National Easter Seal Society, United Cerebral Palsy Association, Association for Retarded Citizens, and National Rehabilitation Association. Each of these organizations has a large constituency of professional workers and parents who focus on the improvement of services, professional standards, legislation, workshops and conferences, informational bulletins and newsletters, and many other matters significant to the career development of handicapped citizens. Some of these organizations have their own executive director and, perhaps, a small staff that works with communities, including their local affiliates, to meet the objectives established for their agency.

Some cities will have local affiliates of the state and national organization. The Association for Retarded Citizens and United Cerebral Palsy are such examples. These organizations receive considerable guidance and support from the state and national organizations to carry out their policies and objectives. Both the ARC and UCP have sponsored day-care facilities, sheltered workshops, and other direct service programs at the local level. If you do not know whether any of the organizations listed have state or local chapters in your area, write the national office for information. They may also provide other resources that can be of assistance to you.

Resources at the local level will vary according to the size, location, and particular circumstances of each indiviudal community. Figure 12.1 illustrates possible resources and services that can be used at the local level for career development.

TABLE 12.2
Professional organizations important to career development of handicapped individuals.

Organization and Address	Publications	Features
Alexander Graham Bell Association for the Deaf 3417 Volta Place, N.W. Washington, D.C. 20007	*Volta Review, Newsounds*	Provides information services to parents, educators, libraries, hospitals, clinics, and others.
American Association of Workers for the Blind 1511 K St., N.W. Washington, D.C. 20005	*Blindness, News and Views*	Renders assistance in promoting, developing, and improving services to blind persons and publishes proceedings of international meetings.
American Association on Mental Deficiency 5101 Wisconsin Ave., N.W. Washington, D.C. 20016	*Mental Retardation, American Journal of Mental Deficiency*	Promotes legislation, seminars and conferences, services and standards for facilities, and professional standards.
American Coalition of Citizens with Disabilities 1200 15th St., N.W. Washington, D.C. 20005	*ACCD News Net*	Promotes advocacy, referral services and information, and publication distribution. An umbrella organization of and for handicapped individuals.
American Deafness and Rehabilitation Association 814 Thayer Ave. Silver Springs, MD 20910	*Journal of Rehabilitation of the Deaf, Deafness Annual,* newsletter	Promotes services, research, professional training, legislation, and information on careers.
American Foundation for the Blind 15 West 16th St. New York, NY 10011	*Journal of Visual Impairment and Blindness, Washington Report*	Serves as a clearinghouse for information on blindness, and promotes research activities, talking books, aids and appliances, public education, a lending library, legislation and action programs.
American Printing House for the Blind P.O. Box 6085 Louisville, KY 40206		Provides literature and appliances to blind people on a nonprofit basis, publishes and distributes embossed books and other educational materials.
American Psychiatric Association 1700 18th St., N.W. Washington, D.C. 20009	*American Journal of Psychiatry, Hospital and Community Psychiatry*	Promotes medical education and career development, services, research and development, professional education, public information.

TABLE 12.2 (continued)

Organization and Address	Publications	Features
Association for Children and Adults with Learning Disabilities 4156 Library Rd. Pittsburgh, PA 15234	newsletter	Disseminates information, provides assistance and publications
Association for Retarded Citizens 2501 Ave. J. Arlington, TX 76011	*OJT Information, The ARC*	Focuses on public education, family counseling, research, demonstration, and employment opportunities
Association for the Severely Handicapped 7010 Roosevelt Way, N.E. Seattle, WA 98115	*Journal of the Association for the Severely Handicapped*	Advocates quality education and vocational training methods and programs.
Boy Scouts of America P.O. Box 61030 Dallas-Ft. Worth Airport, TX 65261	*Boys' Life,* manuals on various disability areas.	Promotes involvement in same activities as nonhandicapped, including cubbing, scouting, exploring, camping, civic activities recreation, job preparation.
Council for Exceptional Children 1920 Association Dr. Reston, VA 22091	*Exceptional Children, Teaching Exceptional Children,* journals and newsletters from 12 divisions	Distributes materials, provides technical assistance, conducts training institutes and conferences, promotes legislation, provides 12 divisions of special interest groups.
Disabled American Veterans 3725 Alexandria Pike Cold Spring, KY 41076	*Disabled American Veteran's Magazine,* newsletter	Promotes welfare of service connected disabled veterans and their dependents through several special programs.
Division on Career Development 1920 Association Dr. Reston, VA 22091	*Career Development for Exceptional Individuals,* newsletter	Works with other CEC divisions and various organizations to promote research, legislation, professional training, techniques and training materials.
Epilepsy Foundation of America 4351 Garden City Dr. Landover, MD 20785	*National Spokesman*	Offers numerous programs in medical, social, and informational service areas.

TABLE 12.2 (continued)

Organization and Address	Publications	Features
Girl Scouts of the U.S.A. 830 Third Ave. and 51st St. New York, NY 10022	*Girl Scout Leader Magazine,* several publications on handicapped individuals	Provides typical girl scout services with needed adaptations.
Goodwill Industries of America 9200 Wisconsin Ave. Washington, D.C. 20014	newsletter	Provides vocational rehabilitation services for employment and personal growth.
Muscular Dystrophy Association 810 Seventh Ave. New York, NY 10019	*Muscular Dystrophy News*	Promotes research for curing and treating, patient services, recreation, and clinics.
National Association of Rehabilitation Facilities P.O. Box 17675 Washington, D.C. 20015	*Rehabilitation Review*	Conducts educational seminars and conferences, assists members in developing and improving their services.
National Association of the Deaf 814 Thayer Ave. Silver Springs, MD 20910	*Deaf American, Broadcaster,* newspaper	Serves as clearinghouse for information, provides experts, conducts studies and workshops to improve services and resolve problems.
National Association of the Physically Handicapped 76 Elm St. London, OH 43140	newsletter	Promotes legislation, employment, barrier-free design, publicity, housing, education and research, recreation and sports, transportation.
National Association of Vocational Education Special Needs Personnel c/o American Vocational Association 2020 N. 14th St. Arlington, VA 22201	*Journal for Vocational Special Needs Education* (newsletter)	Promotes legislation, technical information, staff development, and special workshops to help vocational educators.
National Braille Association 654-A Godwin Ave. Midland Park, NJ 07432	*Bulletin*	Produces materials in braille, including special vocational materials for blind workers.
National Easter Seal Society for Crippled Children and Adults 2023 West Ogden Ave. Chicago, IL 60612	*Rehabilitation Literature, Easter Seal Communicator* (newspaper)	Conducts extensive program of service, education, and research at national, state, and local levels, including public awareness workshops and conferences.

358

TABLE 12.2 (continued)

Organization and Address	Publications	Features
National Federation of the Blind 1800 Johnson St. Baltimore, MD 21230	*Braille Monitor*	Promotes research into legislation for blind individuals, and advocacy and public education groups, provides assistance to local employment projects.
National Industries for the Blind 1455 Broad St. Bloomfield, NJ 07003	*Opportunity*	Coordinates production activities of 100 workshops, researches and recommends new products, procures subcontract work, and promotes evaluation and training programs for blind persons.
National Industries for the Severely Handicapped 4350 East-West Highway Bethesda, MD 20814		Provides technical assistance to workshops in producing commodities or services for sale to federal government, researches and develops commodities that can be produced in sheltered workshops.
National Mental Health Association 1800 North Kent St. Rosslyn, VA 22209	*Focus/In Touch*	Sponsors research, social action, education, and service to improve the care and treatment of mentally ill.
National Organization on Disability 2100 Pennsylvania Ave., NW Washington, D.C. 20037	*Report* (quarterly newsletter) and *Update*	Advocates community partnership programs to improve attitudes, expand access, and promote opportunities in education, housing, recreation, and employment.
National Rehabilitation Association 633 S. Washington St. Alexandria, VA 22314	*Journal of Rehabilitation*	Promotes legislation, provides a forum through publications and conferences, research, and stimulates professional training endeavors.
National Society to Prevent Blindness 79 Madison Ave. New York, NY 10016	*The News, Wise Owl News*	Promotes community services, publications, public information, lay and professional education, research, census information, and educational program descriptions.

TABLE 12.2 (continued)

Organization and Address	Publications	Features
National Spinal Cord Injury Association 369 Elliot St. Newton Upper Falls, MA 02164	*Paraplegia Life,* newsletter	Dedicated to direct service and advice, medical and scientific conferences, and educational seminars and publications.
National Therapeutic Recreation Society 1601 N. Kent St. Arlington, VA 22209	*Therapeutic Recreation Journal,* newsletter	Promotes recreation and leisure services.
National Wheelchair Athletic Association 2107 Templeton Gap Rd. Colorado Springs, CO 80907	newsletter	Formulates rules governing wheelchair athletics, rule changes, keeps records, and sanctions meets.
Paralyzed Veterans of America 4350 E. West Hwy. Suite 900 Bethesda, MD 20814	*The Paraplegia News, Sports-N-Spokes*	Promotes elimination of architectural barriers, special housing, litigation, sports and recreation.
United Cerebral Palsy Associations 66 East 34th St. New York, NY 10016	*Word from Washington*	Provides professional service program assistance in regard to research and professional training, infant care centers, vocational programs, governmental activities, and public information/education.
Vocational Evaluation and Work Adjustment Association 633 J. Washington St. Alexandria, VA 22314	*VEWAA Bulletin,* newsletter	Promotes standards for vocational evaluators and work adjustors, disseminates and publishes information, promotes training efforts of field personnel.

Source: Excerpted from ENCYCLOPEDIA OF ASSOCIATIONS, Vol. 17, edited by Denise S. Akey (copyright © 1959, 1961, 1964, 1968, 1970, 1972, 1973, 1975, 1976, 1977, 1978, 1979, 1980, 1981, 1982, by Gale Research Company; reprinted by permission of the publisher), Gale Research, 1983.

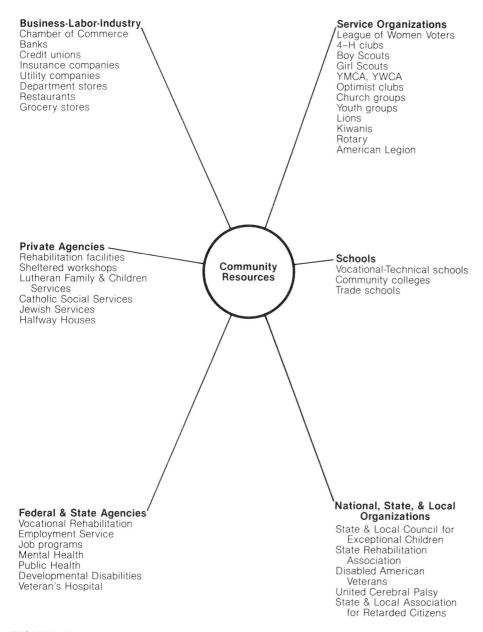

Business-Labor-Industry
Chamber of Commerce
Banks
Credit unions
Insurance companies
Utility companies
Department stores
Restaurants
Grocery stores

Service Organizations
League of Women Voters
4–H clubs
Boy Scouts
Girl Scouts
YMCA, YWCA
Optimist clubs
Church groups
Youth groups
Lions
Kiwanis
Rotary
American Legion

Private Agencies
Rehabilitation facilities
Sheltered workshops
Lutheran Family & Children
  Services
Catholic Social Services
Jewish Services
Halfway Houses

Community Resources

Schools
Vocational-Technical schools
Community colleges
Trade schools

Federal & State Agencies
Vocational Rehabilitation
Employment Service
Job programs
Mental Health
Public Health
Developmental Disabilities
Veteran's Hospital

National, State, & Local Organizations
State & Local Council for
  Exceptional Children
State Rehabilitation
  Association
Disabled American
  Veterans
United Cerebral Palsy
State & Local Association
  for Retarded Citizens

FIGURE 12.1

Some community resources important to career development of handicapped individuals.

As indicated in chapter 7, *industry, labor,* and *business* resources can provide students with community work experiences and observations; help develop career-oriented curricula; assist in job placement efforts, provide volunteers for the school; and elicit support for career education throughout the community. Many community resources such as banks, credit unions, insurance companies, utility companies, department stores, restaurants, and grocery stores can give students information and experiences in the daily living skills area. These sources are also a powerful influence for obtaining additional and needed funds from the government and private sectors.

Service organizations and other *civic* groups can help to develop viable career education programs. The League of Women Voters, church groups, youth groups, Lions International, and others generally look for projects that will benefit the community. These organizations can also provide schools and agencies with the talents of their members. *Rotary International Magazine* (1976) features a special section on the relationship between education and work. The American Legion adopted career education in 1976 as a priority and has continued to emphasize ways in which members can assist school efforts in career development (The American Legion, 1980 & 1983).

Private social service agencies such as Lutheran Family and Children Services, Catholic Family Services, and Jewish Services are available in some communities to help families and individuals resolve personal adjustment problems, interpersonal conflicts, and social and emotional difficulties. Trained social workers, using individual and group methods, help the student to find ways of fulfilling personal-social needs.

Vocational-technical schools, community colleges, rehabilitation facilities, and sheltered workshops provide vocational training, counseling, and job placement services. In response to the federal legislation, vocational schools are increasing their capacity to help various handicapped persons develop competitive skills, although much work is still needed in this area. Many community colleges have developed meaningful programs for handicapped individuals. Rehabilitation facilities and sheltered workshops are particularly important for the more limited handicapped person who needs intensive instruction to develop work habits, vocational skills, and personal-social skills. These facilities generally have a variety of professionally trained counselors, evaluators, teachers, and supervisors who provide work opportunities as both a treatment and training medium. Sheltered workshops may provide employment for individuals who are incapable of working in a competitive setting but who can work productively in a semicompetitive environment, at least for a period of time.

Halfway residential houses are available in some communities for individuals who need some supervision while receiving vocational training and other career development services elsewhere. Some halfway houses provide daily living and personal-social instruction, particularly if they are affiliated with a rehabilitation or sheltered workshop. A small staff may be available for individual and group counseling.

In general, the list of community resources for career development is extensive. The list in Figure 12.1 is not all inclusive but represents the many resources that are available to help handicapped persons.

INSTRUCTIONAL RESOURCES

Identification and discussion of instructional resources can never be complete. Information and materials are being created at such a rapid pace that it is difficult for both researchers and practitioners to keep up. A few years ago the dominate question was: "Is there anything available?" However within recent years this question has been changed to: "What information resources should I use from the number of items that are available?" We will not be able to supply the answer to the second question because the use of materials, devices, and assessment tools is dependent on the intended goals and characteristics of the individual learner. However, we do hope to provide a broad base of understanding about sources of information. Many products and publications developed for nonhandicapped individuals can also be used in teaching handicapped learners.

Instructional resources can be divided into four categories: information systems; books; career education projects that have resulted in publications; and films, audiotapes, learning devices, and other instructional materials available from commerical publishers. Journals related to career development are listed in Appendixes F and G. We have not attempted to review or list any films, audiotapes, or learning devices because these resources can readily be obtained from the information systems.

The first step is to use an information system that contains current information relative to a given topic. The usual term given this condition is *the state of the art*. The primary goal of an information system is to enable the user to determine the state of the art at a given moment. An information system usually provides the following functions:

- Collects materials such as reports, papers, documents, guides, bibliographies, books, instructional devices, and dissertations;
- abstracts and indexes references and descriptions of the collected items and/or references;
- provides access to abstracts through printed copies or visual display; and
- distributes information such as bibliographies, position statements, and copies of items in hardcover or microfilm.

363

The potential user should identify the system that collects appropriate information or materials, contact the system to gain access to the collection, and present the request according to the system's specific instructions.

Information systems that we believe can best provide materials and references related to aspects of career development are listed in Table 12.3 and are described in the remainder of this chapter. Each of these systems defines its own mission and procedures. These systems exist for the purpose of providing information; sometimes just a simple letter of inquiry will be answered with a packet of material.

TABLE 12.3
Information systems for materials on career development for handicapped individuals.

Organization	Location
Educational Resources Information Centers (ERIC)	
ERIC Clearinghouse on Adult, Career, and Vocational Education	Ohio State University
ERIC Clearinghouse on Handicapped and Gifted Children	Council for Exceptional Children
National Clearing House of Rehabilitation Training Materials (NCHRTM)	Oklahoma State University
National Network for Curriculum Coordination in Vocational-Technical Education	
• Northeast Curriculum Coordination Center	Trenton, NJ
• Southeast Curriculum Coordination Center	Mississippi State, MS
• East Central Curriculum Coordination Center	Springfield, IL
• Midwest Curriculum Coordination Center	Stillwater, OK
• Northwestern Curriculum Coordination Center	Olympia, WA
• Western Curriculum Coordination Center	Honolulu, HI
National Resource Center for Materials on Work Evaluation and Work Adjustment (Materials Development Center)	University of Wisconsin-Stout
The National Center for Research in Vocational Education	Ohio State University
The Council for Exceptional Children Information Services	Reston, VA
Wisconsin Vocational Studies Center	University of Wisconsin-Madison

You are encouraged to review issues of *Programs for the Handicapped* that have included reviews of data banks and clearinghouses and the *Directory of National Information Sources on Handicapping Conditions and Related Services* (1980). Some systems that appeared in the first edition of this text no longer exist although their publications may still be available. Other centers have been curtailed due to restraints in the federal government's financial support. Therefore we have listed those systems that have been available for several years even though longevity is not an assurance that these systems will continue to be funded.

INFORMATIONAL SYSTEMS

Educational Resources Information Centers (ERIC)

ERIC is a national computerized network of centers that acquire significant educational literature, select the highest quality and most relevant materials, process (i.e., catalog, index, and abstract) the items for input to a data base, and disseminate information upon request. Their services include functions such as abstracts, computer searches, document reproduction, indexes, and production of microfiche (a small printed negative that must be read with a special viewer). The educational literature may include things such as articles, bibliographies, books, conference proceedings, curriculum, materials, guides, and reports.

The educational information is disseminated through two publications: *Resources in Education* (RIE), and *Current Index to Journals in Education* (CIJE). RIE is a monthly journal that includes abstracts of documents, research, and programs, with an index to the abstracts. CIJE is a monthly publication that includes the annotations and indexes of articles from over 750 professional education journals.

The *Thesaurus of ERIC Descriptors* contains the ERIC subject headings used to index and retrieve documents and articles. Two ERIC Clearinghouses sponsored by the National Institute of Education (NIE) will be of particular interest if you are searching for information on career development for handicapped individuals.

ERIC Clearinghouse on Adult, Career, and Vocational Education. The focus of the ERIC clearinghouse is formal and informal career education at all levels that encompasses attitudes, self-knowledge, decision-making skills, general and occupational knowledge, and specific vocational and occupational skills; formal and informal adult and continuing education relating to occupational, family, leisure, citizen, organizational, and retirement roles; vocational and technical education that includes new subprofessional fields, industrial arts,

365

and vocational rehabilitation for handicapped individuals. The center has several bibliographies and information analysis papers on career development. More information about this program can be obtained by writing The National Center for Research in Vocational Education, The Ohio State University, 1960 Kenny Road, Columbus, OH 43210.

ERIC Clearinghouse on Handicapped and Gifted Children. The ERIC clearinghouse on handicapped and gifted children provides materials and publications in the areas of aural, visual, physical, speech, learning, and behavior disabilities and students who are gifted and talented. Other areas of focus include administration of special education services; preparation and continuing education of professional and paraprofessional personnel; and information on learning and development of exceptional children and youth. More information about this program can be obtained by writing The Council for Exceptional Children, 1920 Association Dr., Reston, VA 22091.

National Clearing House of Rehabilitation Training Materials. The National Clearing House of Rehabilitation Training Materials is a nonprofit organization, funded by the Rehabilitation Services Administration, that identifies, collects, catalogues, annotates, duplicates, and distributes training materials developed for rehabilitation personnel throughout the United States. The organization will assist personnel in locating materials for basic instructional purposes, address unusual or complex training needs, and provide inservice training for practicing rehabilitation professionals. More information about this program can be obtained by writing National Clearing House of Rehabilitation Materials, Oklahoma State University, Stillwater, OK 74078.

National Network for Curriculum Coordination in Vocational-Technical Education

The National Network for Curriculum Coordination in Vocational-Technical Education contains six regional centers that are responsible for identifying information and materials relative to vocational-technical education. An individual teacher or researcher can initiate a curriculum search that usually proceeds through the local education agency to a state liaison representative who contributes to the regional and national network in the following ways:

- *Communication.* The state liaison representative (SLR) provides information to the national network on new materials, developmental activities, and needs for the state and distributes materials and information to the local education agencies within the state. Thus, the SLR stands as a key link between the needs and changes within a state and the capabilities of a national network to assist and profit from local efforts.

■ *Administration.* The SLR helps the national network and local education agencies identify priorities for material and curriculum development. The decisions on priorities are based on data collected within the state relative to needs. This requires various strategies of assessment and evaluation, which is another crucial responsibility of the SLR.

Once again, educators are encouraged to contact the state liaison representatives for the network since most of the exchange of information will be between the state and local levels.

National Resource Center for Materials on Work Evaluation and Work Adjustment (Materials Development Center)

The Materials Development Center is the national resource for the collection, development, and dissemination of literature, materials, and procedures on work evaluation and adjustment. It mainly provides services to personnel who work with handicapped individuals in rehabilitation facilities and sheltered workshops. Among its many publications are updated annotated bibliographies, special monographs, and media packages on work evaluation and adjustment. Information can be obtained by writing Materials Development Center, Institute for Vocational Rehabilitation, University of Wisconsin-Stout, Menomonie, Wisconsin 54751.

The National Center for Research in Vocational Education

The National Center for Research in Vocational Education's mission is to increase the ability of diverse agencies, institutions, and organizations to solve educational problems relating to individual career planning and preparation. Some of the center's major divisions include development, research, evaluation and policy, personnel development, field services, and information systems. The last division houses the ERIC Clearinghouse on Career Education and publishes *Abstracts of Instructional and Research Materials in Vocational and Technical Education (AIM/ARM)*. This publication reports relevant articles and materials in abstract and index form from a wide range of topics in vocational and technical education.

The center offers an extensive collection of products on such specific topic areas as career education, career guidance, and disadvantaged and handicapped individuals. Information can be obtained by writing The Ohio State University, 1960 Kenny Road, Columbus, Ohio 43210.

The Council for Exceptional Children Information Services

As the major professional organization in the education of exceptional individuals, CEC publishes materials in both print and nonprint formats that facilitate continued improvement in services. A list of the products include the following:

- *Exceptional Child Education Resources (ECER)*. This resource contains documents and articles listed in the basic ERIC publications *Resources in Education and Current Index to Journals in Education*. In addition, ECER contains information about commercially published books, films, tapes, and dissertations;
- topical bibliographies based on the references in ECER;
- professional books and tape cassettes on instructional methods and materials, administrative procedures and programs, training of personnel, legislation and legal procedures, and projected changes in education and training of handicapped and gifted individuals;
- the several journals and newsletters related to the 12 divisions within CEC. The two prominent journals are *Exceptional Children* and *Teaching Exceptional Children*; and
- custom computer search of the ERIC data bank upon individual requests.

The Council has expanded its offerings to professionals and the general public through a Center for Information, Technical Assistance, and Training on the Exceptional Person. The center offers the following services:

- *Information.* These services range from publications to customized searches and products.
- *Technical Assistance.* These services include short- and long-term consultation on specific problems and projects.
- *Training.* These services may include institutes, workshops, self-instructional packages, and presentations by qualified speakers.

Information can be obtained by writing The Council for Exceptional Children, 1920 Association Drive, Reston, Virginia 22091.

Wisconsin Vocational Studies Center

The Wisconsin Vocational Studies Center uses the special resources of the University of Wisconsin to solve problems to deliver information on vocational, technical, and career education to citizens of all ages in communities of the state and nation. In recent years, the center has conducted training workshops and published reference and instructional materials related to the modification of regular vocational programs to meet the needs and abilities of handicapped individuals. Several products include the filmstrip cassette programs *Better Than I Thought* and *Whatever It Takes* and the catalog *Tools, Equipment and Machinery Adapted for the Vocational Education and Employment of Handicapped People.* The products focus on the handicapped individual's abilities and the kinds of academic and support services that are needed for successful integration with regular students. Information can be obtained by writing University of Wisconsin-Madison, 964 Educational Sciences Bldg., 1025 W. Johnson St., Madison, WI 53706.

CONCLUSION

Community interest and involvement in career education is not new. As Hoyt (1976b) stated, "it seems more legitimate to ask whether the education system will work with the broader community in career education than to ask whether the community is willing to work with the formal education system" (p. 25). Those who have professed that career education lacks resources and community support are mistaken. The resources are there if the time and attention is given to developing the necessary contacts, relationships, and methodologies for using them appropriately.

In communities with limited resources, state and national organizations may become more important. It is hoped that these organizations are available to assist if they are contacted for relevant purposes. The amount of free technical assistance, materials, and referrals to other helpful sources by these associations and organizations is often overwhelming. A substantial number of different organizations serve as advocates for handicapped individuals and are extremely receptive to assisting community personnel.

Career education requires school personnel to collaborate with those outside of their internal structure. It requires certain individuals to assume a coordinating role if all the necessary resources are to be appropriately orchestrated. Although this is no easy task, it is indeed a necessary one if we are to offer the comprehensive and relevant curriculum that handicapped learners deserve.

We are encouraged by numerous articles, projects, books, reports, guides, instructional materials that are presently available. However we are concerned by how little this literature is read and used by those who work with handicapped persons daily. Those of you who become familiar with the resources presented in this chapter and the appendixes will hopefully identify and secure useful information and tools for your work.

Issues and Future Directions

$\mathbf{W}$e've attempted to present a total approach to conceptualizing, developing, and conducting career education for persons with handicaps. The central focus has been on the 22 career development competencies that we firmly believe that these individuals must learn to be successful in community living and working experiences. The available evidence on the adjustment of handicapped persons clearly reveals that the majority of handicapped individuals are presently either unemployed or considerably underemployed and have had to settle for jobs below their levels of potential.

A central theme of this book has been our broad conceptualization of the term *career*. We define career as the constellation of the various, major roles that individuals are expected to assume in their lifetime, including an occupation. Thus, career education consists of helping individuals learn the skills needed for productive work activity in the home, occupational, community, and avocational settings. Although this concept may be difficult for some people to understand and accept, it distinguishes career education from vocational education. An adequate way to distinguish the two terms is by describing *career education as preparing people for productive work activity* and *vocational education as preparing people for an occupation*.

We have attempted to identify and explain what we believe constitute the components of a comprehensive and appropriate career education approach for handicapped persons. This includes the following:

1. competency-based instruction, focusing on the daily living, personal-social, and occupational skills needed for successful community living and working;

371

2. involvement of all possible school personnel in providing services in the least restrictive environment and designing subject matter to include career implications;
3. considerable parent and family involvement in curriculum and instruction building, competency teaching, and community resource development;
4. extensive use of community agencies and professional and civic organizations having personnel and resources for career education;
5. use of an array of business and industrial resources both in and out of the school setting;
6. systematically planned and sequenced career awareness, exploration, preparation, and placement and follow-up opportunities that are available throughout the individual's lifetime;
7. cooperative curriculum and instructional planning by a variety of educators, students, parents, agency personnel, and members of business and industry;
8. extensive inservice training of school, community, and family members in attitude, knowledge, and skills development so that cooperative efforts can be implemented and maintained;
9. use of more instructional resources and materials that are now available for career education; and
10. frequent and appropriate student evaluation to determine competency achievement and plan instructional procedures.

The 22 competencies advocated in this book include daily living, personal-social, and occupational skills for career development. Close inspection of these competencies will reveal their relation to and development of occupational interests and skills. This should have been apparent in our discussion of the competencies in chapters 3 through 5.

SOME MAJOR ISSUES

Several issues still need to be resolved if career education is to be effectively implemented and conducted in schools, agencies, and institutions.

1. Should career education be primarily job-centered or life-centered? Career education is generally viewed in the following three ways: It is vocational education; it is an expansion of vocational education; or it is a complete educational approach focusing on the various roles, settings, and events in which productive work activity occurs for individuals. In our opinion, the latter view is most appropriate. For many handicapped individuals, their career

POINT OF VIEW

For individuals to succeed in a world that increasingly values information as a commodity to be produced, packaged, transmitted, and translated, they must have access to the world that performs those functions. If handicapped individuals are to participate in these circles, they must first have the opportunity.

At first automobiles were not designed so that handicapped individuals could drive them. However, gradually devices were developed to help overcome this barrier.

The future seems filled with machines as unmanageable by handicapped individuals as automobiles once were. Robots now do much of the mechanical, intricate work formerly reserved for persons with fine motor skills or strength. Genetic engineering occurs at a microscopic level—a stratum reserved for sensitive machines. These two areas are examples of machines that not only work for humans but also are directed by humans. Hopefully design improvements will occur in new machines as they did in automobiles. Perhaps, career education may become the key that unlocks the entrance to the high tech era for handicapped individuals—a circumstance from which we may all benefit just as we have from the improvement of cars.

Oliver P. Kolstoe is a former professor in the Division of Educational Studies at the University of Northern Colorado in Greeley, Colorado (past President of the Division on Career Development, The Council for Exceptional Children).

may consist exclusively of avocational, family, and civic work activities if they have limited vocational abilities and opportunities. They are still able to lead a satisfying, meaningful, and productive life by functioning in this manner.

2. Should career education be a separate program or should it be infused into the regular curriculum? Many professional workers believe that career education is a separate course that should be taught for one or two hours each day. The other position advocates that career education concepts and materials should be infused throughout the curriculum and that all school personnel should modify their courses to incorporate career education into the curriculum. It is probably much easier to develop a separate course than to adopt the infusion approach. In our opinion, however, career education for handicapped students is almost everyone's responsibility, and it must be in-

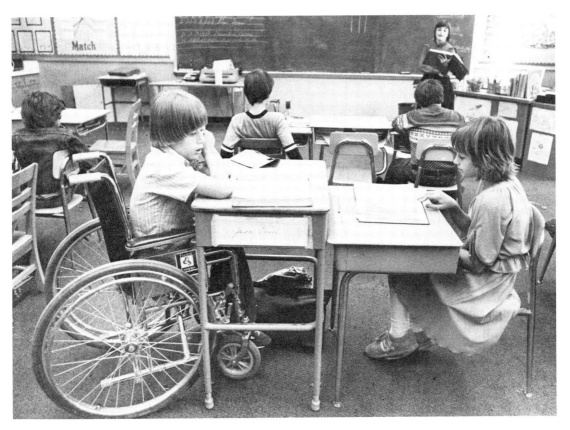

Mainstreaming enriches the lives of both handicapped and nonhandicapped students.

fused into school, home, and community settings. Although it is not the only education the students receive, it should be a very significant and pervasive part of what is taught.

3. Who has the responsibility for handicapped students? Although many special educators may find it difficult to abrogate their responsibilities to these students, the career education approach and the Individualized Education Program requirements clearly specify shared responsibility. The IEP requires that other school personnel and the student's parents collaborate and monitor the program. Since other school personnel are becoming so involved in the program, special educators may now be able to concentrate on other important areas (e.g., parents, community, severely handicapped individuals, career assessment). In our opinion, special educators should not readily abandon their responsibilities to these students. Someone knowledgeable about handicapping conditions and the individual's needs must be available to monitor progress and see that the needs of these students are met.

4. Does career education aid or hinder mainstreaming efforts? Although research in this area is limited, it would seem that career education enhances the assimilation and achievement of handicapped students since they learn best when instruction is related to the real world and hands-on experiences. In our opinion, career education is the vehicle by which successful mainstreaming can take place.

5. What should be done with present courses, materials, and teaching approaches? Career education requires school personnel to take a hard look at what they are doing and ways that courses can be modified, materials added or eliminated, and new teaching methods used. It does not call for a wholesale abandonment of present practices. Rather, career education adds greater relevance to the curriculum and requires a more democratic environment. In our opinion, school districts must develop more systematic and comprehensive career education plans so that courses, materials, and instruction are presented in an effective scope and sequence.

6. How can personnel be trained? Will universities and colleges and other training resources be able and willing to adequately prepare special educators, general educators, counselors, administrators, and others who need instruction about career education for handicapped persons? What constitutes an effective delivery system, how will it be carried out, and who will do the training? These are major concerns of those in the field. When these concerns are coupled with changing school enrollments, teacher layoffs, and budget crunches, we encounter major obstacles in implementing effective career education. In our opinion, staff development training is the key to career

375

education. Local school districts must provide their own inservice trainers to teach their faculty. State and local administrators must convince universities to prepare their graduates for this responsibility. Although there has been remarkable progress in addressing some of these issues, many serious deficiencies reflect needs that must be given more attention today. Some of the major problems, needs, and unresolved issues are presented in the following sections.

Problems and Needs

1. Implementation of career education has been poorly conceived and too limited in most schools. Although over half the school districts throughout the United States claim to have implemented career education, inspection of most of these programs reveals that very little has changed since the introduction of career education. A process of relabeling has occurred, but the content and intent of instruction are not much different from what they were previously. There is a need to provide school personnel with clearer methods and materials that they can use.

2. There is minimal administrative support for career education. Federal, state, and local administrators claim to endorse career education but, in practice, do little to integrate it into the mainstream of the educational system. The reasons for this are not clear, though some of what has been mentioned probably accounts for much of the lack of responsiveness. There is a need to focus more attention on administrators and to provide them with better reasons and means for implementation.

3. The lack of cooperation among many professional disciplines and agencies is disturbing. Despite many efforts to link services and enter into cooperative agreements, many agencies still refuse to work together. Each agency seems more ready to defend its existence and protect its reputation than to show concern for the people it serves. Many post-secondary agencies that should provide education and training services refuse to accomodate handicapped individuals as the law mandates. There is a need to apply more pressure on agencies to cooperate and understand their role in the career development process.

4. Numerous curricular and career development projects have not had enough of an impact on education. Many projects and their products end up having little effect on the system. For this reason, adult handicapped persons have organized their own advocacy agencies and independent living programs. They advocate services that are in direct contrast with the bureaucratic con-

cept practiced by most agencies. These individuals promote an *environmental change concept* rather than the *person change concept* of most traditional agencies. There is a need for agencies to respond to the advocate philosophy and determine how they can provide more client-centered service.

5. Many career and vocational assessment practices in the schools are poorly conceived and operated. Although this area has become recognized as very critical to educational planning, few trained evaluators have been employed to improve assessment services. There is a need to train more and better evaluators as well as to design and validate career or vocational assessment models that meet the needs of students and various school personnel.

6. Many professional workers continue to inappropriately stereotype and label people with handicaps. Demeaning labels and names of services continue to stigmatize and devalue these individuals. We foster dependence and childlike behavior when we tag people with labels. There is a great need to minimize negative stereotypes. Dehumanizing labels must be dropped.

7. Many teacher training programs have been unresponsive to the career development movement. They continue to label students and teach how to use behavior modification and other limited techniques instead of providing these individuals with a challenging, motivating, and practical learning experience that will lead to adult success. Many special education teacher training programs continue to use a categorical approach. There is a need for education agencies to apply pressure to these training programs to make them more responsive to teaching career development principles and processes.

Unresolved Issues

1. *The issue of the need to change.* The majority of special education graduates (and dropouts) fail to succeed as independent and productive adults. Recent statistics reveal, for example, that 42% of the residents of youth correctional institutions meet the criteria of handicapped as defined in PL 94–142 (*Programs for the Handicapped,* 1983b). This tragic situation exists despite all the social interventions (special instructional techniques, behavior modification, vocational technology, legislation, and new agencies) that have evolved over the past two decades. Educators cannot blame the poor economy as the major culprit. We are still not doing enough to prepare students for "life-after-school."

377

We must change by more closely examining our curricula, instructional approaches, and perhaps, most of all, ourselves. Are we receptive to change? Do we promote dependence? Do we consider the long-term needs of our students? Are we making education relevant and exciting? Are we emphasizing the individual's personal development? Career education proponents believe that schools can meet the needs of their students if they teach skills needed for adult functioning.

2. *The issue of definition.* Professionals and the general public still tend to view "career" as a job. Although major career development theorists have clearly pointed out that a career is more than a job, a majority of responses to the term "career" continue to be of a vocational or occupational nature. Although vocation is certainly one important component of career education, *career education also concerns itself with unpaid work.* The key words are *productive "work" activities* that people do in the various settings where they live. The three career arenas where people engage in productive work activities are (1) in the home; (2) in the community; and (3) on the job. Career education focuses on the entire person and his productive living and working skills. It provides an educational framework that focuses on the critical aspects important to working. Career education is not the only education students receive, but it should be a substantial part.

3. *The issue of when career education should begin.* Too many educators still consider career education as a secondary or high school concern. Career education advocates point out that the work personality develops early. Effective work habits, aptitudes, and interests can develop during the early years if the student is in a stimulating home and school environment. Psychologists point out that 80% of an individual's personality is formed during the first five years of life. The same is probably true for an individual's work personality. Each individual's unique set of abilities begins forming shortly after birth and is highly susceptible to reinforcers in the environment. An environment that provides learning and growth reinforcers will promote the specific aptitudes and career maturity necessary for a healthy work personality. Thus, the elementary years are perhaps the most important years for career education and are a major determinant of later vocational education efforts. When students understand why they should learn math, English, and other academic subjects, they will be more motivated to succeed in the classroom. Career education, through a variety of awareness activities and hands-on experiences, provides students with the re-

ality base they need to become motivated. Students begin viewing themselves as future workers, and in the process, develop healthy self-concepts.

4. *The issue of responsibility.* Many educators believe that career education is not "their" responsibility. But career education should be everyone's responsibility. The special educator is important in orchestrating the career education effort for exceptional students. Special educators must meaningfully involve parents, professionals in the community, regular class teachers, and counselors. Career education is an infusion strategy, not a separate program. If the special educator is highly motivated to assume this important coordinative effort, career education will succeed. Career education also lends itself to mainstreaming. If regular class teachers and counselors use career education concepts and processes, successful integration of handicapped students can occur. Career education promotes cooperation by involving educators, parents, and community resources in the teaching process. If this cooperative endeavor can be put into operation, career education will succeed.

5. *The issue of implementation.* Implementation is a very complex area that has not been well-addressed. A substantial inservice education effort that takes considerable time is necessary for career education to be adequately implemented. Administrators blame the lack of funds, other priorities, inadequate materials, limited inservice time, teacher indifference, and other factors as reasons for delaying implementation of career education. In addition, they have a difficult time justifying it as cost-effective. However, teachers believe that the administrators must back the concept completely before they will commit themselves. They cite larger class sizes, lack of inservice training and time, and other pressures and priorities as reasons for not implementing it adequately. However, implementation will occur only if career education is given a strong push from top administrators. A well-designed staff development program that supports and rewards teachers and counselors for their extra efforts will pay off in the end.

FUTURE DIRECTIONS

Major societal changes do not occur overnight. Support from administrative decision makers, time to redirect curricula, attitude changes, cooperative efforts, and a recognition of the direction of change are but a few of the many needs existing in most communities. We have just begun to make significant strides in providing handicapped individuals with a free and appropriate education. However, if career education is to become a reality that allows handicapped learners to reach their optimal level of career development, dramatic changes in our service-delivery system are still required.

The following lists the developments that we believe will occur in career education and are of an absolute necessity if career education is to move forward in the 1980s.

1. *Applied Research.* Career education must establish its efficacy, but presently there is a paucity of available empirical research. Critical research needs were the topic of a national conference sponsored by the Bureau of Education for the Handicapped at the Educational Testing Service in Princeton, New Jersey, from January 17–19, 1975. Eighty-six special and vocational educators, rehabilitation workers, and researchers identified the following as top priority research topics:

   - Attitudes that impede the handicapped person's opportunities for career development and employment (families, employers, labor unions, peers, educators, community, and the handicapped persons themselves);
   - critical incidents or factors that lead to maintenance, improvement, or loss of jobs;
   - development of decision-making, problem-solving, and coping skills;
   - development of better communication among all people involved in services for the handicapped;
   - how handicapping conditions limit career potentials;
   - how teachers can be motivated to implement career education;
   - how parents can be trained to work effectively with their child;
   - post-placement counseling effectiveness;
   - personnel development needs;
   - retention techniques for job-seeking, readiness, maintenance, and mobility skills;
   - effectiveness of such teaching technologies as television and audiovisual aids;
   - teacher competencies needed to integrate leisure-education;
   - effective counseling techniques;
   - who should deliver counseling services; and
   - how leisure time complements the career development process.

The conference participants viewed career education as a developmental process, beginning from the early identification of the handicap, through preparation and intervention programs and into retirement. They considered living and leisure skills as important adjuncts to preparation for work. A state of the art paper by Brolin and Kolstoe (1978) revealed only minimal research activity occurring in these areas. By the mid-1980s, only a moderate amount of substantive research activity in these areas has been reported.

2. *Cooperative Efforts.* We are seeing more cooperative efforts between various agencies, organizations, business and industry, and the parents of handicapped learners. Certainly, directives from the U.S. Department of Education and the Rehabilitation Services Administrations have stimulated cooperative planning between education and rehabilitation agencies. Also, another USOE statement issued in 1978 promulgating "an appropriate comprehensive vocational education for all handicapped persons" has helped to secure more and better services from vocational educators. If the various agencies continue to work together in greater harmony and respect for each others' contributions, these services will meet the career development needs of individuals with handicaps. Territorial rights, professional jealousies and rivalries, theoretical differences, and many other long-standing problems must be eliminated.

3. *Expanded Agency Services.* Community colleges, vocational-technical schools, rehabilitation agencies, and workshops are becoming more accessible to handicapped individuals. A continuum of services should become a greater reality for these individuals as agencies start working more closely with secondary programs to provide transitional services and lifelong learning opportunities for those leaving and who have left the school setting. The importance of independent living skills, training, and other lifelong learning needs is being recognized in basic academic, personal-social, and occupational skill areas.

4. *Community Learning Experiences.* There is an increased recognition of the contribution of the learning laboratory that is available in the local community. The Experience-Based Career Education (EBCE) Model is an excellent example of the use of the community for relating career development needs to the classroom. As educators become familiar with business and industry and other resources, community personnel are more likely to become involved with the school.

381

5. *Accountability.* Service providers still experience various degrees of accountability for their services and its failures. The handicapped person is often blamed for these failures even though the service provider may be at fault. Employers have not been closely monitored to determine their response to Sections 503 and 504 of the Rehabilitation Act of 1973 and the regulations passed in 1977. The Office for Civil Rights (OCR) has not had enough staff to become a vital force for this purpose. Nevertheless, handicapped people and their advocates will continue to press for the rights and privileges that are contained in the laws and court decisions. Thus, career education efforts will need to provide more of an accountability component to demonstrate its effectiveness with handicapped learners.

6. *Individualized Education Programs.* Some IEPs are still not written with comprehensive career development goals and objectives in mind. There is considerable concern from career education proponents indicating that more attention will be directed to this important area.

7. *Parent Involvement.* Educators need to include parents in decision-making and curriculum procedures by providing information programs (readings, reports, newsletters) and training parents to work with students at home to achieve school objectives. Educators will need to develop appropriate materials for parents to use with the student.

8. *Personnel Preparation.* Effective inservice and preservice models continue to be developed for training school, family, and community personnel for career education. Every educator should be required to complete a specified inservice and/or preservice program in career education for handicapped individuals. School districts will have to assume a greater responsibility for training their personnel.

9. *Severely Handicapped.* There should be a considerable increase in career education services as educational technology becomes more precise and effective with severely handicapped individuals. The Association for the Severely Handicapped has increased attention to this area. The technology is being developed, and a substantial number of researchers and practitioners are giving their full attention to career development practices.

10. *Professional Constituency.* A large constituency of advocates and promoters of career education for handicapped individuals has evolved for persons who work in the schools. The Division

on Career Development (DCD) of the Council for Exceptional Children and the National Association of Vocational Education Special Needs Personnel (NAVESNP) of the American Vocational Association are two such groups. They represent special and vocational educators who are particularly interested in supporting legislative priorities and funding for meeting the career development needs of handicapped persons. By working together with rehabilitation, advocacy groups, and professional organizations, these two organizations can maintain the focus of career education as a national need and strategy.

11. *Career Guidance and Assessment.* School and rehabilitation counselors must become more involved in career counseling and assessment services. Career assessment systems need to be validated to prove their usefulness. If that can be done, they should provide an excellent vehicle for identifying career interests and aptitudes so appropriate instructional procedures can be designed. Schools are employing more career educators and vocational evaluators.

12. *Placement and Follow-Up.* Employment opportunities should increase because of legislation, business and industry involvement, public awareness, and the efforts of various advocacy groups. However the key to opening employment opportunities is the school's ability to implement and conduct effective career education services that are consistent with the demands of the work society.

Numerous career education materials have been marketed and will continue to be developed. More refinement and field testing is needed to establish those materials that are particularly effective. New scientific inventions are making it possible for handicapped individuals to be mobile and communicate effectively with their environment. Reading machines and low vision aids for blind and visually impaired individuals, electronic aids to help physically handicapped individuals manipulate and function within their environment, teletypewriters, hearing aid adapters for deaf and hearing impaired individuals, and other dramatic breakthroughs are helping handicapped individuals become independent, productive members of society.

CONCLUSION

Career education has made its mark on the field of education and will continue to prepare persons with handicaps for satisfying and productive lives. It has been difficult for many to accept the broader view of "career," but we

383

believe that it truly reflects our major educational and rehabilitative goal for these individuals (i.e. to be able to engage in satisfying paid and/or unpaid work roles as adults).

The vast majority of handicapped individuals in this country can become productive, contributing members of society. For some of these individuals, paid employment may not be their major role. But the individuals' career potentials should be maximized to the fullest. Employment need not be

Colleges and universities need to be even more responsive to the educational and personal needs of persons with handicaps.

the sole criterion for successful outcomes of educational efforts with handicapped students if these individuals can be productive and satisfied in such roles as family member and worker, citizen, and active participant in leisure and recreational pursuits.

Career education is the hope and promise for the handicapped citizens who reside in our society. It is an eclectic educational concept that brings meaning to curriculum efforts by making individuals aware of themselves, their potentials, and their educational needs. It does not replace present educational practices but rather helps make all instructional material personally relevant by restructuring it around a career development theme. Thus, we recommend the use of the term *career education* rather than basic skills, life skills, vocational education, or other names that do not reflect the total span of our major goals for these individuals.

The mandate for changing our educational approaches is clearly upon us. Educational reform groups are calling for change in the way that education prepares students to take on life's challenges. Competency attainment, as we have proposed with the LCCE curriculum, is one way that education can help students meet this challenge. We simply cannot continue to provide educational and rehabilitative services that do not meet the person's needs. We have the knowledge and technology to meet all the needs of children, youth, and adults with handicaps. Special educators, rehabilitation workers, and others have done much to help handicapped persons develop these capabilities. But, there is much yet to do; we must integrate our technology, refocus the curriculum, and involve the community. Colleges and universities that train professional workers must take the lead and be more responsive.

As we decide how to respond to the many educational needs of our handicapped citizens, let us remember the words of Bill Yore. Bill was a 19-year-old senior at Lakeshore High School in Michigan who was considered to be mentally and physically impaired. He was one of three students selected as a commencement speaker. His mother and teacher had both tried to discourage him from speaking, but he worked for weeks on his speech. He had been in special education programs all of his life, and he had a message he felt impelled to communicate. It is a message that all of us need to hear.

> Mr. Reilly, honored guests, ladies and gentlemen and members of the graduating class of 1974. I want to take this opportunity to convey appreciation to you for allowing me to express my feelings this evening.
>
> Tonight represents a dream come true for my parents, friends and relatives. Tonight also represents the attainment of a goal for many interested and concerned teachers, counselors and staff. Tonight also represents the downfall of a diagnosis that was made over 15 years ago. Let me explain.
>
> In 1958, a 4-year-old boy was taken to the University Hospital at Ann Arbor for neurological examinations. After many hours of examinations,

385

tests, x-rays, and waiting, a verdict and sentence was handed down by the University doctors. The parents were informed that their son was mentally handicapped and the best place for him was in an institution. "Your son, at best, may some day be able to sell papers on a street corner," the doctors informed the stunned couple. On the convictions of these parents, through the efforts of devoted teachers and the legislation of interested taxpayers like yourselves, this would-be resident of Coldwater's Home for the Mentally Handicapped was placed in our local school system.

This boy was loved and cared for not only at home, but also at school. Sure, there were hard and rough times. It isn't easy competing with other kids, even when you are normal much less handicapped. But, the love and the patience were there for 19 long years. And, tonight I am proud to stand here and say that I am that boy—almost condemned to an institution. True, I am not an "A" student. But neither am I a dropout. I may never go to college but I won't be on the welfare roles either. I may never be a great man in this world, but I will be a man in whatever way I am able to do it.

For tonight, I say thanks to my parents who prayed and worked so hard. I say thanks to you, my instructors and the staff of Lakeshore High who had the patience and dedication to see me through. I say thanks to this audience for your work, your dollars, and your concern in providing me with an opportunity for my education. And, to you, my classmates, I also say thanks. I will always remember our years together and I hope that you will also.

Remember me as you search for a place in life, for there will be youngsters needing your help as you select a vocation in life. Remember me as you become paying members of our communities because there will be children needing your financial support. And, remember me and others like me in your prayers because in some cases there are not always parents, teachers, and classmates like I have had at Lakeshore High School. Thank you.

He hesitated, lost his place, stuttered, but he went on. No senior in the assembly moved.

Life Centered Career Education A

Individualized Education Program Form[5]
(Use attachments as needed for each student)

Student's Name: _____ School: _____ Grade: __10__ Date: __9/1/84__

SECTION I: Present Level of Educational Performance

Reading Level:	4.2(CAT)	(8/25/84)
Math Level:	3.1(CAT)	(8/25/84)
CRS Cumulative Average Score:	0.88 (Maximum = 2.0)	(9/1/84)

SECTION II: Annual Goals

This student will progress toward acquiring functional behaviors in the following competency areas. (Check the appropriate annual goals.)

__X__ 1. Managing Family Finances
____ 2. Selecting, Managing, Maintaining Home
____ 3. Caring for Personal Needs
____ 4. Raising Children, Family Living
____ 5. Buying and Preparing Food

____ 6. Buying and Caring for Clothing
____ 7. Engaging in Civic Activities
____ 8. Utilizing Recreation and Leisure
____ 9. Getting Around Community (Mobility)
____ 10. Achieving Self-Awareness
____ 11. Acquiring Self-Confidence

[5]Source: Brolin, D. E. *Life centered career education: A competency based approach.* Reston, VA: The Council for Exceptional Children, 1978, 1983.

387

___ 12. Achieving Socially Responsible Behavior
___ 13. Maintaining Good Interpersonal Relationships
___ 14. Achieving Independence
___ 15. Achieving Problem Solving Skills
_X_ 16. Communicating Adequately with Others
___ 17. Knowing & Exploring Occupational Possibilities

___ 18. Selecting & Planning Occupational Choices
___ 19. Exhibiting Appropriate Work Habits & Behaviors
_X_ 20. Developing Physical-Manual Skills
___ 21. Obtaining a Specific Occupational Skill
___ 22. Seeking, Securing, & Maintaining Employment

For additional annual goals, attach another sheet.

SECTION III: Specific Educational Services Needed

Goal Number	Special Services Needed	Special Media/Materials and Equipment	Individual Implementors
1.	Individualized curriculum including student group activities, community input, and class presentations.	Real or simulated money, checks, magazines, tax forms, clothing labels, price tags.	Special education/math/home economics teachers, IRS representative, bank representative, parents, peers.
16.	Individualized curriculum involving student group activities, community input, field trips, and class presentations.	Audio and videotape equipment, audio and videotapes, bulletin board, transportation, telephone, telephone book, cookbook, job applications.	Special education and language arts teachers, civil defense representative, police/fire/ambulance representative, movie manager, switchboard operator, pharmacist, personnel representative, TV personality, parents, peers.
20.	Individualized curriculum involving field trips, class presentations, student group activities, and community input.	Bulletin board, transportation, work samples, color vision tests.	Special education, physical education, vocational education teachers, physical therapist, occupational therapist, vocational rehabilitation and employment service counselors, school nurse, personnel representative, graduates.

SECTION IV: Short-Term Individual Objectives

This student will receive assistance focusing on the following short-term individual objectives. (Check specific behaviors and use an attachment for this section if these objectives are developed independently by the implementor. The numbers in parenthesis indicate the annual goal, listed on the previous page, under which these behaviors will be used.)

X 1. Identify money & make correct change (1)	___ 37. Use recreational facilities in commun. (8)
X 2. Make wise expenditures (1)	___ 38. Plan and choose activities wisely (8)
X 3. Obtain & use bank & credit services (1)	___ 39. Plan vacations (8)
X 4. Keep basic financial records (1)	___ 40. Know traffic rules & safety practices (9)
X 5. Calculate and pay taxes (1)	___ 41. Know various means of transportation (9)
___ 6. Select adequate housing (2)	___ 42. Drive a car (9)
___ 7. Maintain a home (2)	___ 43. Attain a sense of body (10)
___ 8. Use basic appliances and tools (2)	___ 44. Identify interests & abilities (10)
___ 9. Maintain home exterior (2)	___ 45. Identify emotions (10)
___ 10. Dress appropriately (3)	___ 46. Identify needs (10)
___ 11. Exhibit proper grooming and hygiene (3)	___ 47. Understand physical self (10)
___ 12. Physical fitness, nutrition, weight control (3)	___ 48. Express feelings of worth (11)
___ 13. Common illness prevention & treatmt. (3)	___ 49. Tell how others see him/her (11)
___ 14. Prepare for adjustment to marriage (4)	___ 50. Accept praise (11)
___ 15. Prep. raising children (phys. care) (4)	___ 51. Accept criticism (11)
___ 16. Prep. raising children (psycho. care) (4)	___ 52. Develop confidence in self (11)
___ 17. Practice family safety in home (4)	___ 53. Character traits needed for acceptance (11)
___ 18. Demonstrate appropriate eating skills (5)	___ 54. Know proper behavior in public (12)
___ 19. Plan balanced meals (5)	___ 55. Respect for rights & prop. of others (12)
___ 20. Purchase food (5)	___ 56. Rec. authority & follow instructions (12)
___ 21. Prepare meals (5)	___ 57. Recognize personal roles (12)
___ 22. Clean food preparation areas (5)	___ 58. Know how to listen and respond (13)
___ 23. Store food (5)	___ 59. Make and maintain friendships (13)
___ 24. Wash clothing (6)	___ 60. Establish heterosexual relationships (13)
___ 25. Iron and store clothing (6)	___ 61. Establish close relationships (13)
___ 26. Perform simple mending (6)	___ 62. Understd. impact of behavior on others (14)
___ 27. Purchase clothing (6)	___ 63. Understand self organization (14)
___ 28. Understand local laws (7)	___ 64. Develop goal seeking behavior (14)
___ 29. Understand federal government (7)	___ 65. Strive toward self actualization (14)
___ 30. Understd. citizenship rights & respon. (7)	___ 66. Differentiate bipolar concepts (15)
___ 31. Understd. regis. & voting procedures (7)	___ 67. Understand the need for goals (15)
___ 32. Understd. selective service procedrs. (7)	___ 68. Look at alternatives (15)
___ 33. Rights & resp. when questioned by law (7)	___ 69. Anticipate consequences (15)
___ 34. Participate in group activities (8)	___ 70. Know where to find good advice (15)
___ 35. Know activities & community resources (8)	X 71. Recognize emergency situations (16)
___ 36. Understand recreational values (8)	X 72. Read at level needed for future goals (16)

X	73.	Write at level needed for future goals (16)
X	74.	Speak adequately for understanding (16)
X	75.	Understand subtleties of communication (16)
___	76.	Personal values met through work (17)
___	77.	Societal values met through work (17)
___	78.	Remunerative aspects of work (17)
___	79.	Classification of jobs (17)
___	80.	Local occupational opportunities (17)
___	81.	Sources of occupational information (17)
___	82.	Identify major occupational needs (18)
___	83.	Identify major occupational interests (18)
___	84.	Identify occupational aptitudes (18)
___	85.	Identify job requirements (18)
___	86.	Make realistic occupational choices (18)
___	87.	Follow directions (19)

___	88.	Work with others (19)
___	89.	Work at a satisfactory rate (19)
___	90.	Accept supervision (19)
___	91.	Attendance and punctuality (19)
___	92.	Meet demands for quality work (19)
___	93.	Demonstrate occupational safety (19)
X	94.	Demonstrate balance & coordination (20)
X	95.	Demonstrate manual dexterity (20)
X	96.	Demonstrate stamina & endurance (20)
X	97.	Demonstrate sensory discrimination (20)
___	98.	Search for a job (22)
___	99.	Apply for a job (22)
___	100.	Interview for a job (22)
___	101.	Adjust to competitive standards (22)
___	102.	Postschool occupational adjustments (22)

For additional short-term individual objectives, attach another sheet.

SECTION V: Date and length of time relative to specific educational services needed for this student

Goal Number	Beginning Date	Ending Date	Goal Number	Beginning Date	Ending Date
1.	9/15/84	9/15/84			
16.	11/16/84	2/15/85			
20.	2/16/85	4/15/85			

SECTION VI: Description of extent to which this student will participate in the regular educational program

	Percent of time		Narrative Description/Reaction
Language arts	15	%	CAT results 8/25/84
Math	5	%	CAT results 8/25/84
Science		%	
Social science		%	
Vocational	15	%	Student reads well enough to follow simple directions.
Physical education	15	%	Student has no physical limitations.
(other) _____		%	
(other) _____		%	

SECTION VII: Justification for type of educational placement of this student

Overall CRS evaluation and results of California Achievement Test.

SECTION VIII: Individual Responsible for implementing the individual education program

Name   Role/Responsibility

Special ed., home ec., vocational ed., language arts, mathematics
    teachers
Graduates
Civil defense representative
Police/fire/ambulance representative
Movie manager
School nurse
Switchboard operator
Pharmacist
Personnel representative
Banker
TV personality
IRS representative
Physical and occupational therapists
Voc. rehab., emp. service counselors
Audiologist

SECTION IX: Objective Criteria, Evaluation Procedures, and Schedule for assessing short term objectives

Objective Criteria can be found in the Competency Rating Scale (CRS). Criteria listed reflect the short term individual objectives checked in Section III of this form.

Evaluation Procedures can be determined by the IEP Committee reviewing the Competency Rating Scale Manual.

Schedule for Assessment should include time, date, frequency, place, etc.

    CRS Rating   5/1/84   Should be reevaluated yearly

SECTION X: Estimated Date, Location, and Time for next IEP Committee Review Conference

    1/15/84 at 10:00 A.M.

School District of West Allis-West, Milwaukee, Wisconsin

B

Career Education Plan

A. INTRODUCTION

Traditionally, career education has been an integral part of the philosophy and practices in providing programs for handicapped children and youth. It is the opinion of the writers that an organized and consistent approach to career education is essential to the total development of each student.

The *Life Centered Career Education Curriculum—A Competency Based Approach* was adopted as a vehicle for bringing relevancy into the classroom for all students with exceptional educational needs (EENs). The curriculum has been adapted to meet specific career education needs unique to the School District of West Allis-West Milwaukee, et al.

The Life Centered Career Education Curriculum was adapted to provide all persons involved in the education of handicapped students with a consistent and relevant approach to career education.

B. PHILOSOPHY

The School District of West Allis-West Milwaukee, et al. is committed to the infusion of career education into all levels of the curriculum. The District views career education as a total set of experiences through which every student is given the opportunity to learn and prepare for engaging in work as a part of living in today's society. This philosophy, adopted by the District, is used in planning all school programs.

---

[6]Information provided by Dr. Robert Buehler, director of Special Education at the West Allis-West Milwaukee School District in Wisconsin.

Public Law 94–142, The Education of All Handicapped Children Act of 1975, mandates career and vocational training for all students with exceptional educational needs (EENs). The School District of West Allis-West Milwaukee, et al. is committed to providing career and vocational opportunities, giving each EEN student a realistic opportunity to be a contributory and functional member of the work force.

The School District of West Allis-West Milwaukee, et al. is striving to coordinate all school, family, and community components to facilitate each individual's potential for economic, social, and personal fulfillment.

C. GOALS AND OBJECTIVES

1. To make all instructional subject matter more personally relevant through restructuring and focusing it around a career development theme when possible.
2. To provide all persons the guidance, counseling and instruction needed to (a) develop self-awareness and self-direction, (b) expand occupational awareness and aspirations, (c) develop appropriate attitudes about the personal and social significance of work.
3. To assure all persons an opportunity to gain an entry level marketable skill prior to their leaving school if termination is necessary or a desirable option.
4. To prepare all persons completing secondary school with the knowledge and skills necessary to become employed or to pursue more training.
5. To provide placement services for every person in his preparation for a career, whether it be placement assistance in employment or further education.
6. To build into the educational system greater involvement and coordination of all possible resources in the community.
7. To facilitate entry and re-entry, either into the world of work or the educational system, for all persons through a flexible educational system which continually reviews and expands educational and occupational options.

Specific objectives as they relate to the implementation of the Life Centered Career Education Curriculum are presented below:

Instructional Objectives
1. To provide all students with the opportunity to develop the 22 Life Centered Career Education competencies.
2. To facilitate the integration of handicapped students into regular classes and services for career development.
3. To increase the number and kinds of hands on activities within various subject areas.
4. To encourage all teachers of handicapped students to emphasize the career implications of their subject matter and provide for career awareness, exploration, guidance, and preparation opportunities.

Community Involvement Objectives
1. To involve the family more appropriately in career education planning and services.
2. To involve community agencies more appropriately in career education planning and services.

3. To involve business and industry more appropriately in career education planning and services.

Administrative Objectives
1. To monitor each student's competency level and progress more appropriately and relate it to an individualized education program.
2. To determine ways in which special educators can be more adequately used by regular teachers, counselors, and community personnel.
3. To secure additional financial support to implement an effective career education program for handicapped students.

Other goals may be added as necessary since these only represent some essential goals which have been identified during the development of this curriculum.

1. Explanation of Curriculum Considerations for EEN Students
   A. *Academic Skills.*—Emphasis on functional skills (reading, writing and arithmetic) during the elementary school years establishes the foundation for subsequent learning appropriate for daily living, and occupational skills for community living and working. At the junior high school level and teaching of academic skills decreases as the teaching of specific daily living and occupational skills increases. Academic instruction at the senior high level aims to remediate those academic skills necessary for daily living and job placement.
   B. *Daily Living Skills.*—At the elementary level certain basic daily living skills can be taught in addition to the above mentioned academic skills. These skills include, but are not limited to, economic education, the need for leisure time activities, personal hygiene, and the need for local laws and government. An increased emphasis on teaching basic daily living skills plus the introduction of those subcompetencies that can be learned should occur at the junior high level. These could include information regarding personal finance, physical fitness, home and personal care, citizenship rights, and traffic laws. Senior high school students should learn as many of the subcompetencies that have not yet been taught/learned, and the procedures by which they can receive assistance for those competencies/subcompetencies they were unable to learn.
   C. *Personal-Social Skills.*—During the elementary school years students' personality development is important especially with regard to dealing with the attitudes and behaviors of other non-handicapped students. Instruction in developing self-confidence, displaying responsibility, acceptable behavior and other personal-social skills is important. Instruction in these skills should continue throughout the junior and senior high school.
   D. *Occupational Guidance and Preparation.*—Occupational development begins at the elementary level with an introduction to proper work habits, attitudes and values, and physical-manual skills. At the junior high school level occupational guidance and preparation continues with an emphasis on vocational subjects that develop pre-vocational skills and motivations. At this stage career exploration experiences in the community (e.g.; job try-outs, shadowing) assist students in their career development and decision-making.

395

During the senior high school years, occupational guidance and preparation in the form of vocational subjects, on-the-job experiences, etc., should comprise at least half of the students' weekly program. Additionally, access to a Career Information and Assessment Center will assist students in their quest for vocational/occupational information, vocational aptitudes/interests, and job seeking skills/procedures.

D. COMPETENCY UNITS

In addition to its identification, each competency unit contains three sections: objectives, activities/strategies, and adult/peer roles, designed to assist teachers and counselors in providing students with experiences to develop and demonstrate each competency. No specific grade or developmental level is suggested for the teaching of each competency unit (subcompetency)—this is left to the discretion of the individual school and its career education plan. Obviously, some competency units could be taught during the elementary years, whereas others are more appropriate at the junior high and senior high levels. The Competency Rating Scale (CRS) should assist educators in determining what competencies and subcompetencies have been acquired so appropriate educational programming can be done for each student. It is suggested that the Competency Rating Scale be introduced sometime during the upper elementary grades (5–6). Each section of the competency unit is discussed below:

1. *Objectives*
   Each competency unit contains suggestions for the sequencing of performance objectives for a specific subcompetency. An attempt has been made to arrange the objectives in a logical order although they can be arranged according to the instructor's evaluation of the student needs, to fit a class, or to correspond to the availability of resources. Objectives may be expanded and/or developed into smaller components to meet the specific learning abilities of the students. Additional performance objectives can be added to meet the individual needs of the learner.

2. *Activities/Strategies*
   Activities are the vehicle by which teachers, counselors, parents, administrators and community representatives shape the competencies. The suggested activities and strategies have NOT been arranged in a rigid hierarchy although some consideration has been given to difficulty levels. More appropriate activities may be inserted, depending on the characteristics of the students and available resources. The suggested activities/strategies make use of a wide assortment of resources and plans for instructions to prompt the teacher to approach the teaching task with variety. Utilization of community personnel to provide instructional activities and support is highly encouraged.

3. *Adult/Peer Roles*
   School personnel must continually attempt to bring their students into contact with community representatives—particularly role models for the demonstration of the competencies. In addition to owners of business and industries, it is

recommended that the individuals who have jobs similar to those which handicapped students might later obtain should speak to the class about their work.

The adult/peer section includes adult models, sources of information from a career perspective, former students who are closer in experience, parents and peers (e.g., siblings, fellow students from regular classes and fellow students from the same class). Follow-up studies can identify those individuals to be used in this role. In some cases, parents have been identified as the most appropriate agent. In other cases, parents and peers could participate with the student. The instructor should select the most appropriate agency, based on agent availability, student's level or ability, and the sequence of activities. Numerous activities require the same community source or person.

Infusion

To achieve the goals of the Life-Centered Career Education Curriculum, educators must examine new ways to realistically provide career relevant experiences and content within a career education context. The career educational construct (or vehicle) brings new life role meanings to the existing curriculum. Therefore, a change process referred to as infusion is suggested.

Infusion refers to the process of integrating career development goals based on student career development competency needs with current subject matter, goals, and content. This curriculum development concept is used to assure the delivery of an integrated career education program.

Two important tasks must be considered in both the development and the use of the competency units. Relationships among the units must be established and the points at which they are infused most effectively into the total curriculum must be determined. The relationship of some units to a single discipline or subject will be obvious while others will not be as easily identifiable. The progression of skill development, concept difficulty, and application of knowledge may also need refinement as the units are used in a given sequence.

Guidelines for Effective Use of Competency Units

Effective Instructional use of these units is contingent on certain conditions or factors. As in any instructional program, teachers and counselors are obligated to make decisions and adjustments regarding the use of each unit activity in the light of (a) the needs and motivations of their students, (b) varying teaching/learning styles, (c) factors of the physical and psychological environment, and (d) standards of excellence and the instructional policies of the school administration. Thus, most specific questions which teachers and counselors may ask about the use of these units should be answered with reference to (a) what is more facilitative and growth producing for individual student(s); (b) the given or appropriate mode of interaction among faculty and students, considering, for example, their individual teaching/learning styles; and (c) the requirements or expectations of our school district.

Faculty members may pose questions and express concern regarding issues such as scope and sequencing, grade level specification, modification of learning activities, use of alternate activities and resource time restrictions, team teaching arrangements, etc. to exercise their personal and professional judgment. The best choices a teacher or counselor can make are those which are most advantageous to the individual student in the quest to achieve career development growth. Thus, the welfare of the student, given all of the implications of the teaching/learning environment (community, school, and classroom) should guide the users of this curriculum.

The Life Centered Career Educational Curriculum advances the belief that curriculum development should take place in the local school system. A curriculum framework for teaching competencies is suggested; however, this framework has been designed to be easily modified to meet special needs in local settings.

The competency units recommended here are intended to serve as a guide for teaching the 22 life centered competencies.

E. PROGRAM IMPLEMENTATION

The Life Centered Career Education Curriculum utilizes a competency based approach to career education. To integrate these competencies into the curriculum for handicapped students at the senior high school level, the following items have been developed:

1. RECOMMENDED FOUR YEAR PROGRAM
2. CRITERIA FOR STUDENT ELIGIBILITY
3. ROLE/RESPONSIBILITIES OF EEN TEACHER

1. Recommended Four Year Program*

  A. Required Credits

    3 credits—English
    3 credits—Social Studies
    1 credit—Mathematics
    1 credit—Science
    1/4 credit—Health
    1/4 credit—Driver Education
    1/4 credit—Pool
    1/4 credit—Gym
    1/4 credit—Physical Education
    10 1/2 credits—Total

  B. Electives

    1 credit—Vocational Ed I/Vocational Ed II (Course Title, Career Orientation)
    1 credit—Work Sample I/II
    3 credits—Work Experiences
    1 credit—Refresher/Consumer Math**
    5 credits—Electives**
    11 credits—Total

2. *Criteria for Student Eligibility*

The criteria for a student is as follows:

A. Be enrolled in an EEN program in the district.
B. Maintain a satisfactory attendance record. Because attendance is paramount for a good work record, we feel it is important to develop this behavior while still in school.
C. Attend, accompanied by parent, a yearly group conference with program personnel.
D. Pass all scheduled non-elective classes required before placement in any career/vocational education classes.

3. *Role/Responsibilities of the EEN Teacher*

The role and responsibilities of the EEN teacher include the following:

A. Act as a liaison between employer and student.
B. Arrange for extensive vocational testing which would include a variety of hands-on tasks.
C. Observe students at their work sites.
D. Provide additional remediation in academic subjects.
E. Teach any entry level skills needed to succeed in career, vocational or elective classes.

F. INSTRUCTIONAL MATERIALS

Before selecting new instructional materials, it is suggested that the teacher review all material available locally through either regular or exceptional education. In addition, individual subject area supervisors should be consulted for their input into the selection of new instructional materials.

The Life Centered Career Education Manual, pages 100–128, lists instructional materials for each competency. A wide range of prices, maturity levels, and achievement requirements are presented. It should be possible to select material that fits both the budget and the individual needs of the learners.

G. EVALUATION

To utilize this curriculum successfully, a uniform method of evaluating student performance and progress in career education is needed. This must be both specific and comprehensive to be of value.

The Competency Rating Scale (CRS) evaluates changes in individual performance over a period of time. The user completes the Scale by judging a student's mastery of the subcompetencies.

H. RESOURCES/REFERENCES

1. *Community Resources*

Local Business and Industry
    Field trips to observe on the job activities
    On the job experiences/tryouts

399

Governmental Agencies
Vocational Rehabilitation
Bureau of Indian Affairs
Immigration
Social Security Administration
Veterans Administration
Employment Services
Job Corps
VISTA
Comprehensive Employment
Training Act (CETA) Program
Community Action Program
Law Enforcement Agencies
Legal and Judicial Agencies
County Commissioner
County Extension Agent
Taxation Agencies

Parks Department
Welfare offices
Motor Vehicle Bureau
Agricultural Extension Agent
Public Health Nurse
Fish and Game Commission
Adult Basic Education Program
Parent-Teacher Association (PTA)
Migrant Programs
Military Service Representatives
Correctional Institutions
Mental Health Agencies
Sheltered Workshops
Governor's Commission for
Employment of the Handicapped
Planned Parenthood

Community Service Organizations
YMCA
YWCA
Red Cross
League of Woman Voters
Urban League

American Legion
Veterans of Foreign Wars
Salvation Army
Heart Association

Civic Clubs
Chamber of Commerce
JAYCEES
Rotary Club
Kiwanis
Civitan

Elks
Lions
Business and professional workers
Knights of Columbus

Special Resources, Private, Nonprofit and Volunteer Organizations
Airports
Weather stations
Colleges
Universities
Monasteries
Association for Retarded
Citizens
4–H Clubs
Boy Scouts
Indian Guides
Churches

Hospitals
Nursing Homes
Libraries
Museums
Goodwill Industries and other
rehabilitation facilities
Private mental health associations
Girl Scouts
Campfire Inc.
Big Brothers/Big Sisters

The above list suggests resources that can be used. However, you may have ideas for additional resources. The following references will furnish you with more specific information on available resources.

I. RECOMMENDATIONS

1. Provide inservice training for school personnel, community resource individuals and parents for purposes of assimilating EEN students more effectively into the total community life. This should include:

   A. presentation of this Career Education Plan
   B. agencies to explain career opportunities available for EEN students
   C. informing teachers and counselors of the legal rights of EEN students
   D. sharing of information with regular education staff of prerequisite skills required in vocational/elective courses
   E. informing parents of the difference between career education and vocational education

2. A joint effort between the vocational/elective teachers and EEN teachers is needed to create mini-courses to develop prerequisites required to enter the various vocational/elective courses.

3. Provide release time for EEN and regular education teachers to:

   A. work cooperatively with other teachers in providing for EEN students
   B. observe EEN students on the job
   C. observe EEN students in other academic settings
   D. observe already existing vocational/education programs in other school districts
   E. observe extensive testing programs available in the area

4. Continue summer curriculum writing, and include staff from the entire educational environment as required for the specific project.

5. Encourage input from teachers and administrators for effective implementation of the program ideas and activities stated in this document.

6. Provide extensive vocational appraisal with a follow through to create appropriate opportunities for work sampling to help determine the area of work experience in the last two years of senior high school.

7. Update and add relevant materials/equipment needed to:

   A. present the inservice programs mentioned above
   B. develop self-awareness, career and vocational awareness
   C. transport students for evaluation and visitation purposes

8. Develop Life Simulation Center in the junior/senior high school, similar to the proposed program at Irving School of West Allis-West Milwaukee School District.

9. In order to determine the effectiveness of the LCCE program, a periodic follow-up study of all EEN students no longer enrolled in the school setting will be conducted.

10. Develop procedures for parental input in the construct of vocational and career education programs.

401

11. Investigate the possibility of developing projects that can be marketed. These projects can lend to a total career/vocational experience; i.e., sales, building, site erection, concrete work, painting, possible landscape work to finish project.

12. Investigate with MATC and WCTI the possibility of some of the EEN population taking vocational classes in conjunction with their academic classes in West Allis-West Milwaukee Schools.

Brigance Essential Skills and Career Education Competencies

403

404

406

407

Title	Test	Page	LCCE Competency
Y. Food and Clothing			
Food Vocabulary	Y–1	327	5.2, 5.4
Food Preparation Vocabulary	Y–2	328	5.4, 5.5
Basic Recipe Directions	Y–3	329	5.4
Food Labels	Y–4	330	5.3, 5.4
Conversion of Recipes to Different Servings	Y–5	331	5.4
Foods for a Daily Balanced Diet	Y–6	332	5.2
Computes Cost of Purchasing Different Quantities	Y–7	333	1.2, 5.3
Food Quantity at Best Price	Y–8	334	5.3
Personal Sizes of Clothing	Y–9	335	6.4
Clothing Labels	Y–10	336	6.1, 6.2, 6.4
Z. Oral Communication and Telephone Skills			
Speaking Skills	Z–1	339, 340	16.1, 16.4, 13.1
Speaking Skills Rating Scale	Z–2	341	16.4
Listening Skills	Z–3	344–353	13.1
Listening Skills Rating Scale	Z–4	354	13.1
Telephone	Z–5	357, 358	8.4, 16.1
Telephone Book	Z–6	359	22.1, 16.1, 22.3
Telephone Yellow Pages	Z–7	360	8.4

Source: Information provided by Sherrie Chrysler, Central Washington University, Ellensburg, Washington 98926.

Some Commonly Used Vocational Aptitude Measures D

Name of Test	Publisher	Type Handicap	Description
Appraisal of Occupational Aptitudes	Houghton-Mifflin Co.	All but VI	Measures clerical ability such as checking letters and numbers, filing names and numbers, math, and reasoning.
Bennett Hand Tool Dexterity Test	Psychological Corporation	All but VI	Measures proficiency with ordinary mechanics' tools. Testee assembles and disassembles different-size nuts and bolts. Timed.
Bennett Mechanical Comprehension Test (BMCT)	Psychological Corporation	All but VI (some mild MR)	Group-administered, paperpencil test. Six illustrations demonstrate the relationship of physical forces and mechanical elements in practical situations.

Code: LD—learning disability HI—hearing impaired MR—mentally retarded OH—orthopedically
      CP—cerebral palsy ED—emotionally VI—visually impaired handicapped
                                   disturbed

Name of Test	Publisher	Type Handicap	Description
Crawford Small Parts Dexterity Test	Psychological Corporation	LD, ED, MR, HI (some CP, OH)	Assess fine eye-hand coordination, using small tools. Testee inserts small parts into work surface—small pins into holes and collar on top, using tweezers. Uses screwdriver to insert screws into plate.
Differential Aptitude Test (DAT)	Psychological Corporation	All but VI	Group administered, pencil-paper. Eight sections: verbal reasoning, numerical ability, abstract reasoning, clerical speed and accuracy, mechanical reasoning, space relations, spelling, language usage. Two hour limit. Requires 6th-grade reading.
General Aptitude Test Battery (GATB)	U.S. Department of Labor	All handicaps but VI, but considerations for CP, MR, OH, HI	Measures nine aptitudes with 12 subtests. Requires 6th-grade reading. Aptitudes measured: general learning, verbal, numerical, spatial, clerical, form perception, motor coordination, finger dexterity, and manual dexterity.
General Clerical Test	Psychological Corporation	CP, ED, OH, HI	Group administered, paper-pencil test. Requires 6th-grade reading. Nine skill areas: checking, alphabetizing, arithmetic computation, error location, arithmetic reasoning, spelling, reading comprehension, vocabulary, grammar.
MacQuarie Test for Mechanical Ability	California Test Bureau	All but VI	Measures eye-hand coordination and finger dexterity required for office and factory tasks. A nonverbal, paper-and-pencil test with seven subtests: tracing, tapping, dotting, copying, location, blocks, and pursuit.

412

Name of Test	Publisher	Type Handicap	Description
The Minnesota Rate of Manipulation Test	American Guidance Service	LD, ED, MR, HI (limited with CP, OH)	Group or individually administered. Board with 60 blocks; testee performs five different manipulation tasks. Measures hand and finger dexterity.
Minnesota Spatial Relations Test	American Guidance Service	All handicaps	Measures speed and accuracy in discriminating among odd sizes and shapes. Consists of four form boards containing 58 cutouts each.
Nonreading Aptitude Test Battery (NATB)	U.S. Department of Labor	All but OH and VI	The nonreading counterpart of the GATB—especially for persons who are retarded.
O'Connor Finger and Tweezer Dexterity Tests	C. H. Stoelting Co.	All but VI	Measures motor coordination and manual dexterity. Finger test to insert pins into 100 small holes. Tweezer task to pick up the pins and put them into holes.
Pennsylvania Bi-Manual Test	American Guidance Service	All handicaps	Measures five-finger dexterity, gross arm movements, and eye-hand coordination. Task to assemble 105 nuts and bolts on a board and then disassemble them.
Purdue Pegboard	Science Research Associates, Inc.	All handicaps, but special provisions needed for OH, VI, HI	Measures dexterity for two types of activity: gross movements of hands, fingers, and arms, and fingertip dexterity. Timed.
Revised Minnesota Paper Form Board Test	Psychological Corporation	All handicaps but VI	Group administered, paper-pencil test. Measures mechanical aptitude and spatial perception. There are 64 two-dimensional diagrams, five figures per diagram. Testee must select correct shape of original diagram. Twenty-minute limit.

413

Name of Measure	Publisher	Type Handicap	Description
Stromberg Dexterity Test	Psychological Corporation	All but VI	Measures speed and accuracy. Consists of 54 red, blue, and yellow discs along with a board containing 54 holes on one side.
Typing Test for Business	Psychological Corporation	All but VI (some MR, CP, OH)	Group or individually administered. Five units: straight copy, revised manuscript, letters, numbers, and tables. One-hour limit. Requires 6th-grade reading.

Source: Brolin, D. E. *Vocational preparation of persons with handicaps* (2nd ed.). Columbus, OH: Charles E. Merrill, 1982, 106–108.

Some Commonly Used Interest Measures

Name of Measure	Publisher	Type Handicap	Description
Career Assessment Inventory	National Computer Systems, Inc.	All but VI (requires 6th-grade reading)	Measures vocational interests related to John Holland's occupational-types theory. Testee indicates preferences for various activities, school subjects, and occupations. Group or individually administered.
Geist Picture Interest Inventory	Western Psychological Corporation	All but VI (some reading)	Measures interests in 11 areas. Has 44 items, three pictures per item. Also looks at the motivating force behind the choice.
Gordon Occupational Checklist	Harcourt, Brace, and World, Inc.	All handicaps (if verbally presented)	Checklist of 240 activities grouped into five interest clusters that relate to many different jobs. Person chooses activities of interest.
Minnesota Importance Questionnaire (MIQ)	Vocational Psychology Research at Univ. of Minn.	All handicaps (If read) 5th-grade reading	Measures 20 vocational needs—ability utilization, achievement, activity, advancement, authority, etc. Testee chooses the one of two statements that would be the more important in an ideal job.

415

Name of Measure	Publisher	Type Handicap	Description
Minnesota Vocational Interest Inventory (MVII)	Psychological Corporation	All but MR and VI (9th-grade reading)	Self-administered, has 474 items grouped in 158 trades, describing different activities performed by skilled tradesmen.
Occupational Interest Inventory (OII)	California Test Bureau	All but MR and VI	Measures: Fields of interest: personal-social, natural, mechanical, business, the arts, and the sciences; Types of Interests: verbal, manipulative, and computational; and Levels of Interests. Paper-and-pencil administered in groups or individually. Related to D.O.T.
Picture Inventory Interest (PII)	California Test Bureau	All but VI	Nonreading measure that identifies fields and patterns of occupational interests. Testees rate sketches of situations having vocational significance.
Reading-Free Vocational Interest Inventory	American Association in Mental Deficiency	MR	Pictorial measure—three choices to determine interest areas. Male: automotive, building trades, clerical, animal care, food service, patient care, horticultural, janitorial, personal service, laundry, and materials handling. Female: laundry, light industrial, clerical, personal service, food service, patient care, horticultural, and housekeeping.

Name of Measure	Publisher	Type Handicap	Description
Wide-Range In-terest and Opinion Test (WRIOT)	Jastak Associ-ates, Inc.	All handicaps	Pictorial measure, 150 sets of three pictures. Has 18 clusters of occupational in-terests (art, literature, mu-sic, drama, sales, etc.). Eight clusters refer to one's attitudes, particularly toward work conditions. Given individually or in groups.
Code: LD—learning disability CP—cerebral palsy	HI—hearing imparied ED—emotionally disburbed	MR—mentally retarded VI—visually impaired	OH—orthopedically handicapped

Source: Brolin, D. E. *Vocational preparation of persons with handicaps* (2nd ed.). Columbus, OH: Charles E. Mer-rill, 1982, 108–109.

Journals with an Emphasis on Career Development

CAREER DEVELOPMENT FOR EXCEPTIONAL INDIVIDUALS
Division on Career Development
The Council for Exceptional Children
1920 Association Drive
Reston, VA 22091
(two times yearly)

CAREER EDUCATION NEWS
Bobit Publishing Co.
2500 Artesia Blvd.
Redondo Beach, CA 90278
(twice monthly September through June, monthly during July & August)

CAREER EDUCATION WORKSHOP
Parker Publishing Co., Inc.
Rt. 59A at Brookhill Drive
West Nyack, NY 10994
(monthly, September through June)

CAREER PLANNING AND ADULT DEVELOPMENT JOURNAL
Career Planning and Adult Development Network
1190 S. Bascom Ave.
San Jose, CA 95128
(quarterly)

JOURNAL OF CAREER DEVELOPMENT
College of Education
University of Missouri-Columbia
Columbia, MO 65211
(quarterly)

JOURNAL FOR VOCATIONAL SPECIAL NEEDS EDUCATION
Division of Occupational and Vocational Studies
110 Rackley Building
Penn State University
University Park, PA 16802
(three times a year, January, May, and October)

Journals with Information Related to Career Development G

Accent on Living
P.O. Box 700
Bloomington, IL 61701
Quarterly

American Rehabilitation
United States Rehabilitation Services Administration
Ordered through Superintendent of Documents
Washington, D.C. 20402
Bi-monthly

CANHC-GRAM
Association for Neurologically Handicapped Children
Box 61067
Sacramento, CA 95860
Monthly

Disabled USA
The President's Committee on Employment of the Handicapped
Washington, D.C. 20210
Bi-monthly

Education and Training of the Mentally Retarded
Division on Mental Retardation
The Council for Exceptional Children
1920 Association Drive
Reston, VA 22691
Four times yearly in February, April, October, and December

Education of the Handicapped
Capitol Publications
1300 N. 17th St.
Arlington, VA 22209
Bi-weekly

Exceptional Children
The Council for Exceptional Children
1920 Association Drive
Reston, VA 22091
Eight times a year, September through May, excluding December

The Exceptional Parent
Psy-Ed Corp.
296 Boylston St.
Boston, MA 02116
Bi-monthly

Journal of Rehabilitation
National Rehabilitation Association
633 S. Washington St.
Alexandria, VA 22314
Quarterly

Journal of Rehabilitation of the Deaf
American Deafness and Rehabilitation Association
814 Thayer Ave.
Silver Springs, MD 20910
Quarterly

Journal of Visual Impairment and Blindness
15 West 16th St.
New York, NY 10011
Monthly, September through June

Mental Retardation
American Association on Mental Deficiency
5101 Wisconsin Ave.
Washington, D.C. 20016
Bi-monthly

Paraplegia News
Veterans of America, Inc.
5201 N. 19th Ave.
Phoenix, AZ 85015
Monthly

Personnel and Guidance Journal
American Association for Counseling and Development
Two Skyline Pl.
5203 Leesburg Pike
Falls Church, VA 22041
Monthly, September through June

The Pointer
Heldref Publications
4000 Albemarle St., N.W.
Suite 510
Washington, D.C. 20016
Three times yearly

Programs for the Handicapped
Office of Information and Resources for the Handicapped
Room 3119 - Switzer Bldg.
Washington, D.C. 20202
Six times yearly

Rehabilitation Gazette
4512 Maryland Ave.
St. Louis, MO 63108
Annual

Rehabilitation Literature
National Easter Seal Society for Crippled Children and Adults
2023 W. Ogden Ave.
Chicago, IL 60612
Bi-monthly

Rehabilitation/World
Rehabilitation International USA
20 W. 40th St.
New York, NY 10018
Quarterly

School Counselor
American Personnel and Guidance Association
Two Skyline Pl.
5203 Leesburg Pike
Falls Church, VA 22041
Five times a year

Teaching Exceptional Children
The Council for Exceptional Children
1920 Association Drive
Reston, VA 22091
Quarterly

Vocational Evaluation and Work Adjustment Association Bulletin
1522 K Street, N.W.
Washington, D.C. 20005
Quarterly

Vocational Guidance Quarterly
National Vocational Guidance Association
Two Skyline Pl.
5203 Leesburg Pike
Falls Church, VA 22041
Quarterly

VocEd
American Vocational Association, Inc.
2020 N. 14th St.
Arlington, VA 22201
Monthly, September through May

Volta Review
Alexander Graham Bell Association for the Deaf, Inc.
3417 Volta Place, N.W.
Washington, D.C. 20007
Seven times a year

REFERENCES

ACCD Action, February 16, 1982, 1–4.

Aiello, B. (1976). Especially for special educators: A sense of our own history. *Exceptional Children, 42,* 244–252.

Akey, D. (Ed.). (1982). *Encyclopedia of associations* (17th ed.). Detroit, MI: Gale Research.

Alper, S. (1981). Utilizing community ideas for developing vocational curriculum for severely handicapped youth. *Education and Training of the Mentally Retarded, 16,* 217–221.

A matter of inconvenience [film]. Santa Monica, CA: The Stanfield House, 1974.

American Coalition of Citizens with Disabilities. (1982, February 16). *ACCD Action,* 1–4.

American Legion. (1980). *The American Legion and career education.* Indianapolis, IN: The American Legion.

American Legion. (1983). *Post auxiliary community together in education.* Indianapolis, IN: The American Legion.

Anderson, L. E. (1976a). CANHC Vocational Committee Report, 1972–76. *CANHC Gram, 10*(6), 5.

Anderson, L. E. (Ed.). (1976b). *Vocational kit: Steps in vocational readiness for adolescents and adults with the hidden handicap.* Los Angeles: California Association for Neurologically Handicapped Children.

Apple Computer Inc. (n.d.). *Personal computers for the physically disabled: A resource guide.* Cupertino, CA: Apple Computer.

Arni, T. J., Magnuson, C. S., Sparks, W. C., & Starr, M. (1977). *Missouri career education delivery system.* Jefferson City: Missouri Department of Elementary and Secondary Education.

Asner, E., Hartman, T. S., & Schallert, W. (1982, December 26). TV and the disabled (letter to the editor). *Los Angeles Times.*

Association for Retarded Citizens. (1980). *Making job opportunities for mentally retarded people a reality.* Arlington, TX: Association for Retarded Citizens.

Association for Retarded Citizens. (n.d.). *Working together with mentally retarded employees.* Arlington, TX: Association for Retarded Citizens.

Bailey, L. J. (1976). *Career & vocational education in the 1980's: Toward a process approach.* Carbondale: Southern Illinois University.

Bartel, N. R., & Guskin, S. L. (1971). A handicap as a social phenomenon. In W. M. Cruickshank (Ed.), *Psychology of exceptional children and youth* (3rd ed.). Englewood Cliffs, NJ: Prentice-Hall.

Baskin, B. H., & Harris, K. H. (1977). *Notes from a different drummer: A guide to juvenile fiction portraying the handicapped.* New York: R. R. Bowker.

Bateman, B. D. (1967). Visually handicapped children. In N. G. Haring and R. L. Schiefelbusch (Eds.), *Methods in special education.* New York: McGraw-Hill.

Baum, D. D. (Ed.). (1982). *The human side of exceptionality.* Baltimore, MD: University Park Press.

Becker, R. L. (1976). Job training placement for retarded youth: A survey. *Mental Retardation, 14*(3), 7–11.

Bellamy, G. T., Horner, R. H., & Inman, D. P. (1979). *Vocational habilitation of severely retarded adults.* Baltimore, MD: University Park Press.

Berkeley Planning Associates. (1982). *A study of accommodations provided to handicapped employees by federal contractors: Executive summary.* Berkeley, CA: Berkeley Planning Associates.

Bernstein, A., & Karan, O. (1979). Obstacles to vocational normalization for the developmentally disabled. *Rehabilitation Literature, 40*(3), 66–71.

Bethell, T. (1979, November). *What's happening.* Department of Rehabilitation, State of California.

Biklen, D., & Bogdan, R. (1978, October 28). Handicappism in America. *Win.*

Bocke, J., & Price, D. (1976). Experiential approach for the exceptional adolescent. *Thresholds in Secondary Education, 2*(3), 12–13.

Bowe, F. (1978). *Handicapping America: Barriers to disabled people.* New York: Harper and Row.

Bower, E. M. (Ed.) (1980). *The handicapped in literature.* Denver, CO: Love Publishing Co.

Boyer, E. L. (1983). *High school: A report on secondary education in America.* New York: Harper and Row.

Brantman, M. (1978). What happens to insurance rates when handicapped people come to work? *Disabled USA, 1*(8), 16–18.

Brock, R. J. (1977). *Preparing vocational and special education personnel to work with special needs students: State of the art, 1977.* Menomonie, WI: University of Wisconsin-Stout.

426

Brolin, D. E. (1973). Career education needs of secondary educable students. *Exceptional Children, 39*, 619–624.

Brolin, D. E. (1974, September). *Preparing the retarded in career education* (Project PRICE, Working Paper 1). University of Missouri-Columbia. (Ed 096 777)

Brolin, D. E. (1976). *Vocational preparation of retarded citizens.* Columbus, OH: Charles E. Merrill.

Brolin, D. E. (1982). *Vocational preparation of persons with handicaps* (2nd ed.). Columbus, OH: Charles E. Merrill.

Brolin, D. E. (1978 & 1983). *Life centered career education: A competency based approach.* Reston, VA: The Council for Exceptional Children.

Brolin, D. E. (1983). Career education: Where do we go from here? *Career Development for Exceptional Individuals, 6*, 3–14.

Brolin, D. E., & D'Alonzo, B. J. (1979). Critical issues in career education for handicapped students. *Exceptional Children.*

Brolin, D. E., & Elliott, T. (1983). Meeting the lifelong career development needs of students with handicaps: A community college model. *Career Development for Exceptional Individuals, 7*, 12–21.

Brolin, D. E., & Kolstoe, O. P. (1978). *The career and vocational development of handicapped learners.* Columbus, OH: ERIC Clearinghouse on Adult, Career, and Vocational Education.

Brolin, D. E., Malever, M., & Matyas, G. (1976, June). *PRICE needs assessment study* (Project PRICE, Working Paper 7). Columbia, MO: University of Missouri-Columbia.

Brolin, D. E., McKay, D. J., & West, L. L. (1977a). Personnel preparation for career education of handicapped students, *Journal of Career Education, 3*(3), 52–74.

Brolin, D. E., McKay, D. L., & West, L. L. (1977b). Inservice training of educators for special needs children. The PRICE Model. *Career Education Quarterly, 2*(1), 6–17.

Brolin, D. E., McKay, D. J., & West, L. W. (1978). *Trainers guide for life centered career education.* Reston, VA: The Council for Exceptional Children.

Brolin, D. E., & Thomas, B. (Eds.) (1971). *Preparing teachers of secondary level educable mentally retarded: A new model.* Project Report No. 1. Menomonie, WI: University of Wisconsin-Stout.

Brolin, D. E., & Thomas, B. (1972). *Preparing teachers of secondary level educable mentally retarded: Proposal for a new model. Final report.* Menomonie, WI: University of Wisconsin-Stout.

Brown v. *Board of Education,* 347 U.S. 483 (1954).

Browning, P. L. (Ed.). (1974). *Mental retardation: Rehabilitation and counseling.* Springfield, IL: Charles C. Thomas.

Brownson, C. B. (Ed.). (1982). *Congressional staff directory.* Mount Vernon, VA: Congressional Staff Directory, Ltd.

Buchan, L. G. (1972). *Roleplaying and the educable mentally retarded.* Belmont, CA: Fearon.

Buscaglia, L. (1975). *The disabled and their parents: A counseling challenge.* Thorofare, NJ: Charles B. Slack.

REFERENCES

Cain, L. F. (1976). Parent groups: Their role in a better life for the handicapped. *Exceptional Children, 42,* 432–437.

Campbell, L. W., Todd, M., & O'Rourke, E. (1971). *Work-study handbook for educable mentally retarded minors enrolled in high school programs in California public schools.* Sacramento: California State Department of Education.

Capitol Observer. (1983). Section 504 to be limited by cost. *2*(5), 1.

Career Education Workshop. (1977, February). Career clips. 14–15.

Chamber of Commerce of the United States. (1975). *Career education. What it is and why we need it from leaders of industry, education, labor and the professions.* Washington, D.C.: Author.

Charles, C. M. (1976). *Individualizing Instruction.* St. Louis, MO: C. V. Mosby.

Clark, G. M. (1979). *Career education for the handicapped child in the elementary classroom.* Denver, CO: Love Publishing Co.

Clark, G. M., & White, W. J. (1980). *Career education for the handicapped: Current perspectives for teachers.* Boothwyn, PA: Education Resources Center.

Clarkson, M. C. (1982). *Mainstreaming the exceptional child: A bibliography.* San Antonio, TX: Trinity University Press.

Clearinghouse on the Handicapped. (1980, March/April). Library of Congress convenes conference on application of technology to handicapped individuals. *Programs for the Handicapped,* 8–10.

Clearinghouse on the Handicapped. (1983a, January/February). SSA publishes major work disability survey. *Programs for the Handicapped,* 7–8.

Clearinghouse on the Handicapped. (1983b, January/February). Meeting the needs of handicapped delinquent youth. *Programs for the Handicapped,* 4–5.

Clearinghouse on the Handicapped. (1983c, May/June). Administration decides against revisions to 504 guidelines. *Programs for the Handicapped,* 1.

Clearinghouse on the Handicapped. (1983d, May/June). Projects with industry: A partnership with promise. *Programs for the Handicapped,* 8–9, 20.

Cobb, R. B. (1983). *External and internal access for handicapped students in vocational education in Illinois.* Unpublished doctoral dissertation, University of Illinois.

Cohen, S. (1977). *Special people.* Englewood Cliffs, NJ: Prentice-Hall.

Conn, G. A. (1982). New concepts and directions in rehabilitation. *American Rehabilitation,* 7 (4), 18–20.

Costa, E. L., & Welch, F. (1981). Simulated traffic scene. *Teaching Exceptional Children, 14*(2), 85–86.

Council for Exceptional Children. (1976). Official actions of the delegate assembly at the 54th annual international convention. *Exceptional Children, 43*(1), 41–45.

Council for Exceptional Children. (1978). *Position paper on career education.* Reston, VA: CEC.

Cruickshank, W. M., & Paul, J. L. (1980). The psychological characteristics of children with learning disabilities. In W. M. Cruickshank (Ed.), *Psychology of exceptional children and youth,* (4th ed.). Englewood Cliffs, NJ: Prentice-Hall.

Cunerd, E. H. (1980). Interview. *Disabled USA, 3*(4), 11.

Cuvo, A. J., Jacobi, L., & Sipko, R. (1981). Teaching laundry skills to mentally retarded students. *Education and Training of the Mentally Retarded, 16*, 54-64.

Dahl, P. (1981). Counteracting stereotypes through career education. *Career Development for Exceptional Individuals, 4*, 13-24.

Darley, J. M., & Latane, B. (1968). When will people help in a crisis? *Psychology Today, 2*(7), 54-57; 70-71.

DeJong, G. (1981). *Environmental accessibility and independent living outcomes: Directions for disability policy and research.* East Lansing: Michigan State University, Center for International Rehabilitation.

Deno, E. (1970). Special education as developmental capital. *Exceptional Children, 37*(3), 229-237.

Diana v. *State Board of Education of California,* C-70 37 RFP, District Court of Northern California (1970).

Dunn, L. M. (Ed.). (1973). *Exceptional children in the schools: Special education in transition* (2nd ed.). New York: Holt, Rinehart & Winston.

E. I. du Pont de Nemours and Co. (1982). *Equal to the task.* Wilmington, DE.

Edgerton, R. B. (1967). *The cloak of competence.* Berkeley: University of California Press.

Egelston-Dodd, J., & DeCaro, J. (1982). National project on career education: Description and impact report. *Career Development for Exceptional Individuals, 5,* 87-97.

Ellner, J. R., & Bender, H. E. (1980). *Hiring the handicapped.* New York: AMACOM, American Management Associations.

Elmfeldt, G., Wise, C., Bergsten, H., & Olsson, A. (1983). *Adapting work sites for people with disabilities: Ideas from Sweden* (English translation). New York: World Rehabilitation Fund.

Employment Development Department, State of California. (1981). Advertisement. *Mainstream, 6*(12), 9.

Epilepsy Foundation of America. (1977a). Employer education seminars designed to build job opportunities in Maryland. *National Spokesman, 10*(3), 3.

Epilepsy Foundation of America. (1977b). News item. *National Spokesman, 10*(6), 1.

Epilepsy Foundation of America. (1983). News item. *National Spokesman, 16*(3), 6.

Epilepsy Foundation of America. (1982). People with epilepsy at work. *National Spokesman, 15*(3), 4.

Epilepsy Foundation of America. (1983). Section 504 to be limited by cost. *Capitol Observer, 2*(5), 1.

Federal Organization Service. (1981). Washington, D.C.: Carroll Publishing Co.

Fenderson, D. A. (1983, March/April). Fenderson gives congress overview of NIHR activities. *Programs for the Handicapped,* 5 & 7. (ISSN No. 0565-2804)

Foote, C. (1982). Personal correspondence.

Foss, A., & Peterson, S. (1981). Social-interpersonal skills relevant to job tenure for MR adults. *Mental Retardation, 19*(3), 103-106.

429

Foster, J. C., Szoke, C. O., Kapisovsky, P. M., & Kriger, L. S. (1977). *Guidance, counseling and support services for high school students with physical disabilities.* Cambridge, MA: Technical Education Research Centers.

Frieden, L., Richards, L., Cole, J., & Bailey, D. (1979). *ILRU source book.* Houston, TX: Institute for Rehabilitation and Research.

Fuhrman, L. (1982). Personal correspondence.

Galloway, C. (1982). *Employers as partners: A guide to negotiating jobs for people with disabilities.* Sonoma, CA: California Institute on Human Services, Sonoma State University.

Gearheart, B. R. (1980). *Special education for the '80s.* St. Louis, MO: C. V. Mosby Co.

Gilhool, T. K. (1973). Education: an inalienable right. *Exceptional Children, (1980). 39,* 597–609.

Gillet, P. (1980). Career education in special elementary education program. *Teaching Exceptional Children, 13*(1), 17–21.

Glasser, W. (1969). *Schools without failure.* New York: Harper and Row.

Gliedman, J., & Roth, W. (1980). *The unexpected minority: Handicapped children in America.* New York: Harcourt Brace Jovanovich.

Goffman, E. (1963). *Stigma: Notes on the management of spoiled identity.* Englewood Cliffs, NJ: Prentice-Hall.

Gold, M. (1976). Task analysis of a complex assembly task by the retarded blind. *Exceptional Children, 43*(2), 78–84.

Gowan, J., Demos, G. D., & Kokaska, C. J. (Eds.). (1972). *The guidance of exceptional children* (2nd ed.). New York: David McKay.

Graves, C. (1970). Levels of existence: An open system theory of values. *Journal of Humanistic Psychology, 10*(2), 131–155.

Gray, P. (1982, April 1). Personal interview. *Los Angeles Times.*

Gysbers, N. C. (1973). *The three faces of needs assessment: Periodicals, programs and staff.* Paper presented at a joint ERIC-CAPS American Research & Guidance Association Conference, Ann Arbor, MI.

Haines, R. R. (1982). *Project useful hands.* Renton, WA: Renton School District No. 403, Department of Special Education.

Hallenbeck, C. E. (1973). Curriculum standards in the United States for training blind persons in computer occupations. *New Outlook for the Blind, 67,* 266–271.

Halloran, W. E. (1978). Handicapped persons: Who are they? *American Vocational Journal, 53*(1), 30–31.

Halpern, A. S., Lehmann, J. P., Irvin, L. K., & Heiry, T. J. (1982). *Contemporary assessment for mentally retarded adolescents and adults.* Baltimore, MD: University Park Press.

Haraguchi, R. (1981). Developing programs meeting the special needs of physically disabled adolescents. *Rehabilitation Literature, 42*(3–4), 75–78.

Haring, D. (1978, January 1–3). *Learn and earn with Project WORK.* Paper presented at the meeting of the Career Education Workshop.

430

Hartley, N. (1980). Needs assessment in post-secondary vocational education for handicapped learners. In Greenan, J. (Ed.) *Post-secondary vocational education for the handicapped.* Champaign, IL: Leadership Training Institute, University of Illinois.

Hartman, T. S. (1983, February/April). Media. *Communique, 7*–10.

Hensley, G. (1977). Enhancing business and industry participation in career education. In *Two studies on the role of business and industry and labor participation in career education.* Washington, D.C.: National Advisory Council for Career Education, U.S. Government Printing Office.

Herr, E. L. (1976). *The emerging history of career education: A summary view.* Washington, D.C.: National Advisory Council on Career Education, U.S. Government Printing Office.

Herr, E. L. (1977). *Research in career education: The state of the art.* Columbus: ERIC Clearinghouse on Career Education, Center for Vocational Education, Ohio State University.

Hewett, F. M. (1968). *The emotionally disturbed child in the classroom.* Boston: Allyn & Bacon.

Hippolitus, P. (1982, September 22–23). *A blueprint for action.* Paper presented at the Pathways to Employment Meeting, Missouri Governor's Committee on Employment of the Handicapped, Kansas City, MO.

Hively, W. (Ed.) (1974). Domain-referenced testing. *Educational Technology.*

Hobson v. *Hansen,* 393 U.S. 801 (1968).

Hofmeister, A., & Preseton, C. (1982). *Curriculum-based assessment and evaluation procedures.* Monograph prepared for Dean's Grants Projects. Minneapolis: University of Minnesota.

Horst, G., Wehman, P., Hill, J. W., & Bailey, C. (1981). Developing age-appropriate leisure skills in severely handicapped adolescents. *Teaching Exceptional Children, 14*(1), 11–15.

Hoyt, K. B. (1975). *An introduction to career education: A policy paper of the U.S. Office of Education.* Washington, D.C.: Office of Education.

Hoyt, K. B. (1976a). Refining the career education concept. *Monographs on career education.* U.S. Department of Health, Education, and Welfare: U.S. Office of Education.

Hoyt, K. B. (1976b). Community resources for career education. *Monographs on career education.* Washington, D.C.: U.S. Office of Education.

Hoyt, K. B. (1977a). A primer on career education. *Monographs on career education.* Washington, D.C.: U.S. Office of Education.

Hoyt, K. B. (1977b). Community resources for career education. *Occupational Outlook Quarterly, 21*(2), 10–21.

Hoyt, K. B. (1977c). Why Johnny and Joann can't work. *Occupational Outlook Quarterly, 21*(2), 1–3.

Hoyt, K. B. (1979). Career education for exceptional individuals: Challenges for the future. In Kokaska, C. J. (Ed.), *Career futures for exceptional children.* Reston, VA: The Council for Exceptional Children.

REFERENCES

Hoyt, K. B. (1980, June 24). *Career education for persons with visual handicaps.* Paper presented at the Helen Keller Centennial Conference, Boston.

Hoyt, K. B. (1982a) Career education: Beginning of the end? Or a new beginning? *Career Development for Exceptional Individuals, 5,* 3–12.

Hoyt, K. B. (1982b).Federal and state participation in career education: Past, present, and future. *Journal of Career Education, 9*(1), 5–15.

Hoyt, K. B. (1983, June). *How to fix the public's schools in eight not-so-easy steps.* Working paper. Council of State Planning Agencies, National Governors Association.

Huff, B. (1983). Personal correspondence.

Hughes, C. (1981). Personal correspondence.

Hughes, C. (1983). *Life centered career skills: A handbook for parents.* Sacramento, CA: California Department of Education.

Ianacone, R. N., Hunter, A. E., Hiltenbrand, D. M., Razeghi, J. A., Stodden, R. A., Sullivan, W. F., & Rothkopf, L. R. (1982). *Vocational education for the handicapped: Perspectives on vocational assessment* (Document 7). Champaign: Office of Career Development for Special Populations, University of Illinois.

International Business Machines Corporation. (1983). *Computer programmer training for the severely physically disabled* (Report). Armonk, NY.

Irvine Unified School District. (1982). *Applied career tasks.* Irvine, CA.

Itard, J. M. G. (1932, 1962). *The wild boy of Aveyron.* (G. Humphrey and M. Humphrey, Eds. and trans.). New York: Appleton-Century-Crofts (Prentice-Hall). (Originally published in Paris by Gouyon, 1801.)

Jamison, S. L. (Ed.). (1976). *Computing careers for deaf people.* New York: Association for Computing Machinery, Inc.

Jamison, S. L. (1977a). IBM work experience program for deaf people. *American Rehabilitation, 2*(5), 3–5.

Jamison, S. L. (1977b, April 22). Professional careers for deaf people in business and industry. Paper presented to the California Governor's Committee for Employment of the Handicapped, San Francisco, CA.

Jesser, D. L. (1984). Career education: Challenges and issues. *Journal of Career Education, 11*(1).

Johnson, J. (1976, March 4–5). School stores: A vital part of your career education program. Paper presented at the meeting of the Career Education Workshop.

Johnson, R. T., & Johnson, D. W. (1982). Effects of cooperative and competitive learning experiences on interpersonal attraction between handicapped and nonhandicapped students. *Journal of Social Psychology, 116,* 211–219.

Johnson, R. T., & Johnson, D. W. (1983). Effects of cooperative, competitive, and individualistic learning experiences on social development. *Exceptional Children, 49,* 323–329.

Johnson, R. T., Johnson, D. W., & Rynders, J. (1981). Effect of cooperative, competitive, and individualistic experiences on self-esteem of handicapped and nonhandicapped students. *Journal of Psychology, 108,* 31–34.

Jordan, T. E. (1976). *The mentally retarded* (4th ed.). Columbus, OH: Charles E. Merrill.

Kanner, L. (1964). *A history of the care and study of the mentally retarded.* Springfield, IL: Charles C Thomas.

Kenney, A. P. (1981). Independent minds: Scholarship and disability. *Scholarly Publishing, 13*(1), 79–91.

Kenney, A. P. (1982). The pursuit of independence: A survey of scholars with disabilities. *Career Development for Exceptional Individuals, 5,* 75–86.

Killilea, M. (1960). *Karen.* New York: Dell.

King, F. (1975). Treatment of the mentally retarded character in modern American fiction. *Bulletin of Bibliography, 32*(3), 106–113; 131.

Knorr, K. H., & Hammond, N. C. (1975). Data processing: A vocation for severely handicapped persons. *Journal of Rehabilitation, 41*(6), 26–29.

Kokaska, C. J. (1968). *The vocational preparation of the educable mentally retarded.* Ypsilanti: Eastern Michigan University Press.

Kokaska, C. J. (1974). Normalization; Implications for teachers of the retarded. *Mental Retardation, 12*(4), 49–51.

Kokaska, C. J. (1976). Recent expansions in careers for the handicapped. *Thresholds in Secondary Education, 2*(3), 14–15; 23–24.

Kokaska, C. J., & Kolstoe, O. P. (1977). Special education's role in career education. *Journal of Career Education, 3*(3), 4–18.

Kokaska, S., & Kokaska, C. J. (1971). Individualized work centers: An approach for the elementary retarded child. *Education and Training of the Mentally Retarded, 6*(1), 25–27.

Kolstoe, O. P. (1976). Developing career awareness: The foundation of a career education program. In G. B. Blackburn (Ed.), *Colloquium series on career education for handicapped adolescents.* West Lafayette, IN: Purdue University.

Kolstoe, O. P., & Frey, R. M. (1965). *A high school work-study program for mentally subnormal students.* Carbondale: Southern Illinois University Press.

Krents, H. (n.d.). Selected comments. In *How to communicate to and about people who happen to be handicapped.* Washington, D.C.: The President's Committee on Employment of the Handicapped.

Lamkin, J. S. (1980). *Getting started: Career education activities for exceptional students (K–9).* Reston, VA: The Council for Exceptional Children.

Landau, E. D., Epstein, S. L., & Stone, A. P. (Eds.). (1978). *The exceptional child through literature.* Englewood Cliffs, NJ: Prentice-Hall.

Larson, C. (1981). *EGCE state of Iowa dissemination model for MD and LD students.* Fort Dodge: Iowa Central Community College.

Larson, C. (1982). A community college service model of lifelong career development for adult persons with handicaps. *Journal of Career Education, 8,* 293–300.

Lawrence, E. A., & Winschel, J. F. (1973). Self-concept and the retarded: Research and issues. *Exceptional Children, 39*(4), 310–319.

433

Levitan, S. A., & Taggart, R. (1977). *Jobs for the disabled.* Baltimore, MD: The John Hopkins University Press.

Lewis, M. J., Rimai, C., DiPalma-Meyer, F., & LeFevre, K. (1981). *Training parents in career education* (Preliminary report). New York: Teachers College, Columbia University.

Lippman, L., & Goldberg, I. (1973). *Right to education: Anatomy of the Pennsylvania case and its implications for exceptional children.* New York: Teachers College Press, Columbia University.

Loomis, R. (1980). *The ARC, 29*(4), 1.

MacArthur, C. A. (1982). Inservice in career/vocational education: Strategies and examples. *The Pointer, 26*(4), 45–47.

Magic Valley Rehabilitation Services, Inc. (1978). *Activities of daily living curriculum for handicapped adults.* Twin Falls, ID: Magic Valley Rehabilitation Services, Inc. (Distributed by Materials Development Center, Stout Vocational Rehabilitation Institute, University of Wisconsin, Stout.)

Magnuson, C. (1974). Creating a facilitative classroom climate. In *Career education methods and processes.* Columbia: University of Missouri-Columbia.

Mainstream, Inc. (1981). *Speaking of employment: A symposium on disabled people in the workplace.* Washington, D.C.: Mainstream, Inc.

Malouf, D. (1982). Is your school helping or hindering the career/vocational development of handicapped students? *The Pointer, 26*(4), 18–20.

Marland, S. P., Jr. (1976, November 8). Career education update. Speech presented at the Commissioner's National Conference on Career Education, Houston, TX.

Masland, R. L., Sarason, S. B., & Gladwin, T. (1958). *Mental subnormality: Biological, psychological, and cultural factors.* New York: Basic Books.

Mattson, H. A. (1976, December). Career information centers for students. *Career Education Workshop,* 11–13.

McClain, P. J. (Ed.). (1982). . . . Parents. *Missouri Lincletter, 3*(4), 4.

McCray, P. M. (1982). *Vocational evaluation and assessment in school settings.* Menomonie: Research and Training Center, Stout Vocational Rehabilitation Institute, University of Wisconsin-Stout.

McMahon, B. T., & Spencer, S. A. (1979). A systems selling approach to job development. *Journal of Rehabilitation, 45*(2), 68–70.

Melstrom, M. (1982). Social ecology of supervised communal facilities for mentally disabled adults: Productivity and turnover rate in sheltered workshops. *American Journal of Mental Deficiency, 87,* 40–47.

Merchant, D., & Coriell, St. (1981). *Educators with disabilities: A resource guide.* Washington, D.C.: American Association of Colleges for Teacher Education.

Mesa (Arizona) Public Schools. (1976). *Talking with your child (teenager) about your career.* Mesa, AZ: Center for Career Development, Mesa Public Schools.

Meyen, E. L., Vergason, G. A., & Whelan, R. J. (1983). *Promising practices for exceptional children: Curriculum implications.* Denver, CO: Lover Publishing Co.

Michaelis, C. T. (1979, February 9). My son, the doctor: Helping parents understand and accept the career education concept. Presentation at the National Topical Conference on Career Education for Exceptional Individuals, St. Louis, MO.

Miller, T. W. (1983, June 14). Technology and the changing labor market. Paper presented at the National Conference on Making Education Grow in America, Louisville, KY.

Mills v. *Board of Education of District of Columbia*, 348F. Supp. 866 (D.D.C., 1972).

Missouri Lincletter. (1982). *3*(4), 4.

Mithaug, D. E., Mar, D. K., & Stewart, J. E. (1978). *Prevocational assessment and curriculum guide*. Seattle, WA: Exceptional Education.

Mohr, P. (1971). *Current research and development efforts in in-service training and curriculum planning*. Washington, D.C.: U.S. Department of Health, Education and Welfare, Office of Education (ERIC Document Reproduction Service No. 083 148).

Moody, M. T. (1971). *Bibliotherapy: Methods and materials*. Chicago: American Library Association.

Moore, E. J., & Gysbers, N. C. (1972). Career development: A new focus. *Educational Leadership, 30*, 1–8.

Murphy, A. T. (1981). *Special children, special parents*. Englewood Cliffs, NJ: Prentice-Hall.

Nacson, J., & Kelly, E. M. (1980). *Vocational education: Meeting the needs of special populations*. Executive summary. Washington, D.C.: A.L. Nellum Associates.

Naisbitt, J. (1982). *Megatrends: Ten new directions transforming our lives*. New York: Warner Communications Co.

Nave, G., Browning, P., & Carter, J. (1983). *Computer technology for the handicapped in special education and rehabilitation: A resource guide*. Eugene, OR: International Council for Computers in Education.

Neil, S. B. (1977). Clearing the air in career education. *American Education, 13*(2), 6–9; 13.

Nevin, A., Johnson, D. W., & Johnson, R. (1982). Effects of groups and individual contingencies on academic performance and social relations of special needs students. *Journal of Social Psychology, 116*, 41–59.

Nichols, D. L. (1977, February). What is advocacy all about? *New Hampshire Association for Retarded Citizens Newsletter*.

Nichols, W. H. (1970). Blind persons in data processing: The attitude of industry. *New Outlook for the Blind, 64*, 293–296.

Noar, G. (1974). *Individualized instruction for the mentally retarded*. Glen Ridge, NJ: Exceptional Press.

Noland, R. L. (Ed.). (1971). *Counseling parents of the ill and the handicapped*. Springfield, IL: Charles C. Thomas.

Occupational Curriculum Laboratory. (1982). *An implementation manual for vocational assessment of students with special needs*. Commerce, TX: Author.

435

REFERENCES

Official actions of the delegate assembly at the 54th Annual International Convention of the Council for Exceptional Children. *Exceptional Children, 1976, 43*(1), 41–45.

Orlansky, M. D., & Heward, W. L. (1981). *Voices: Interviews with handicapped people.* Columbus, OH: Charles E. Merrill.

Owens, J. A., Redden, M. R., & Brown, J. W. (1978). *Resource directory of handicapped scientists.* Washington, D.C.: American Association for the Advancement of Science.

Palmer, J. T. (1980). *Career education for physically disabled students: Development as a lifetime activity.* Albertson, NY: Human Resources Center.

Papke, R. F. (1980, May). Placement of the handicapped—a view from the private sector. *Job placement division professional supplement.*

Pati, G., Adkins, J. I., & Morrison, G. (1981). *Managing and employing the handicapped: The untapped potential.* Lake Forest, IL: Brace-Park.

Patterson, L. L. (1956). Some pointers for professionals. *Children, 3*(1), 13–17.

Payne, J. S. (1977). Job placement: How to approach employers. In R. Carpenter (Ed.). *Colloquium series on career education for handicapped adolescents, 1977.* West Lafayette, ID: Special Education Section, Department of Education, Purdue University.

Payne, J. S., & Chaffin, J. D. (1968). Developing employer relations in a work-study program for the educable mentally retarded. *Education and Training of the Mentally Retarded, 3*(3), 127–133.

Payne, J. S., Mercer, C. D., & Epstein, M. H. (1974). *Education and rehabilitation techniques.* New York: Behavioral Publications.

Pennsylvania Association for Retarded Children v. *Commonwealth of Pennsylvania.* 334, F. Supp. 1257 (E.D.Ua., 1971).

Perske, R. (1972). The dignity of risk and the mentally retarded. *Mental Retardation, 10*(1), 24–27.

Peterson, M. (1980). Development of a model of vocational education assessment. Unpublished doctoral dissertation. Denton: North Texas State University.

Petzy, V. (1979). A model for employer commitments to job development. *Career Development for Exceptional Individuals, 2,* 80–90.

Phelps, L. A. (1976). *Instructional development for special needs learners: An inservice resource guide.* Urbana: Department of Vocational and Technical Education, University of Illinois.

Phillips, G. B. (1975). Specific jobs for deaf workers identified by employers. *Journal of Rehabilitation of the Deaf, 9,* 10–23.

Plato, (1941). *The republic.* (B. Jowett, trans.) New York: Random House.

Pollard, N. E. (1977). Career education in the classroom. In R. Carpenter (Ed.), *Colloquium series on career education for handicapped adolescents, 1977.* West Lafayette, ID: Special Education Section, Department of Education, Purdue University.

Popham, W. J., & Husek, T. R. (1969). Implications of criterion-referenced measurement. *Journal of Educational Measurement, 6*(1), 1–9.

The President's Committee on Employment of the Handicapped. (1975). *Hiring the handicapped: Facts and myths.* Washington, D.C.: U.S. Government Printing Office.

The President's Committee on Employment of the Handicapped. (1977a, September). *Newsletter.* Washington, D.C.: U.S. Government Printing Office.

The President's Committee on Employment of the Handicapped. (1977b). *Bibliography of secondary materials for teaching handicapped students.* Washington, D.C.: U.S. Government Printing Office.

The President's Committee on Employment of the Handicapped. (1977c). *Pathways to employment.* Washington, D.C.: U.S. Government Printing Office.

The President's Committee on Employment of the Handicapped. (1979). *Affirmative action for disabled people: A pocket guide.* Washington, D.C.: Government Printing Office.

The President's Committee on Employment of the Handicapped. (1981). *Special report: Disability and employment.* Washington, D.C.: Author.

The President's Committee on Employment of the Handicapped. (1982). *Newsletter, 22*(3), 1–2.

The President's Panel on Mental Retardation. (1963). *Report to the President: A proposed program for national action to combat mental retardation.* Washington, D.C.: U.S. Government Printing Office.

Puorro, T. (1983). Personal correspondence.

Raths, L. E., Harmin, M., & Simon, S. B. (1966). *Values and teaching.* Columbus, OH: Charles E. Merrill.

Razeghi, J. A. (1983, March 3). Statement before the Subcommittee on Education, Art, and Humanities, Committee on Labor and Human Resources, Senate.

Razeghi, J. A., & Ginyard, E. J. (1980). *Resource guide for parents: Career education and vocational education rights and opportunities for disabled students and youth.* Washington, D.C.: American Coalition of Citizens with Disabilities.

Regan, M. K. (1979). The parents' role in vocational education starts early. *Perceptions, 1*(7), 4.

Reynolds, M. C. (1962). A framework for considering some issues in special education. *Exceptional Children, 28*(7), 367–370.

Reynolds, M. C. (1975). Trends in special education: Implications for measurement. In Hively, W., & Reynolds, M. C. (Eds.), *Domain-reference testing in special education.* Reston, VA: The Council for Exceptional Children.

Reynolds, M. C., & Birch, J. W. (1982). *Teaching exceptional children in all America's schools.* Reston, VA: The Council for Exceptional Children.

Rice, J. (1976). An interstate consortium of directors of special education confront the problems of mainstreaming. In P. H. Mann (Ed.), *Shared responsibility for handicapped students: Advocacy and programming.* Coral Gables, FL: University of Miami Training and Technical Assistance Center.

Riggs, C. (1971). *Bibliotherapy.* Newark, DE: International Reading Association.

Roberts, E. V. (1979). Career development for the disabled: A prophecy. In Kokaska, C. J. (Ed.), *Career futures for exceptional individuals.* Reston, VA: The Council for Exceptional Children.

437

Roberts, E. V. (1982, February 27). Presentation to the First Annual Vocational Education Special Needs Conference, State of California, Los Angeles.

Robinson, J. H., & Morrison, L. (1981). *An estimation of the job titles potentially available to the retarded.* Oberlin, OH: The Northern Ohio Special Education Regional Resource Center.

Rogers, C. R. (1951). *Client-centered therapy: Its current practice, implications, and theory.* Boston: Houghton-Mifflin.

Rohr Industries, Inc. (1981). Advertisement. *Mainstream, 6*(5), 4.

Rosner, J. (1975). Testing for teaching in an adaptive educational environment. In Hively, W., & Reynolds, M. C. (Eds.), *Domain-referenced testing in special education.* Reston, VA: The Council for Exceptional Children.

Ruffner, R. (1981). Just where's the barrier? *Disabled USA, 4*(9–10), 3–6.

Rusch, F., & Menchetti, B. (1981). Increasing compliant work behaviors in a non-sheltered work setting. *Mental Retardation, 19,* 107–111.

Rusch, F., & Mithaug D. (1980). *Vocational training for mentally retarded adults.* Champaign, IL: Research Press.

Sankovsky, R., Arthur, G., & Mann, J. (Eds.). (1971). *Vocational evaluation and work adjustment.* Auburn, AL: Materials and Information Center.

Schalock, R., Harper, R., & Carver, R. (1981). Independent living placement: 5 years later. *American Journal of Mental Deficiency, 86,* 170–177.

Schoepke, J. M. (1979). *Lifelong career development needs assessment study.* Working paper No. 3. Columbia: University of Missouri.

Sears, J. H. (1975). The able disabled. *Journal of Rehabilitation, 41*(2), 19–22.

Sigler, G. R., & Kokaska, C. J. (1971). A job placement procedure for the mentally retarded. *Education and Training of the Mentally Retarded, 6*(4), 161–166.

Siller, J. (1977). Personal interview. In S. Kleinfield, *The hidden minority.* Boston: Little, Brown and Company.

Simpson, E. J. (1973). The home as a career education center. *Exceptional Children, 39,* 626–630.

Sitlington, P. L., & Wimmer, D. (1978). Vocational assessment techniques for the handicapped adolescent. *Career Development for Exceptional Individuals, 1,* 74–87.

Smith, E. I. (1973). The employment and functioning of the homebound disabled in information technology. *American Journal of Occupational Therapy, 27,* 232–238.

Steinmiller, G., & Retish, P. (1980). The employer's role in the transition from school to work. *Career Development for Exceptional Individuals, 3,* 87–91.

Stewart, D. M. (1977). Survey of community employer attitudes toward hiring the handicapped. *Mental Retardation, 15,* 30–31.

Stewart, J. C. (1978). *Counseling parents of exceptional children.* Columbus, OH: Charles E. Merrill.

Stieglitz, M., & Cohen, J. S. (1980). *Career education for physically disabled students: Speakers' bureau.* Albertson, NY: Human Resources Center.

438

Super, D. E. (1976, June). Career education and the meanings of work. *Monographs on Career Education*. U.S. Department of Health, Education and Welfare, U.S. Office of Education.

Taber, F. (1983). *Microcomputers in special education: Selection and decision making process*. Reston, VA: The Council for Exceptional Children.

Taymans, J. M. (1982). Career/vocational education for handicapped students: A joint venture throughout the school years. *The Pointer, 26*(4), 13–17.

Technical Education Research Centers. (1983). *Promoting collaborative planning of career education for disabled students*. Cambridge, MA: Author.

Turnbull, A. P., Strickland, B. B., & Brantley, J. C. (1982). *Developing and implementing individualized education programs* (2nd ed.). Columbus, OH: Charles E. Merrill.

United States Bureau of Education for the Handicapped. (1973). *Selected career education programs for the handicapped*. Washington, D.C.: U.S. Government Printing Office.

United States Department of Health, Education, and Welfare. (1977, October 17). Memorandum: Collaboration between educational and vocational rehabilitation agencies. Washington, D.C.: Department of Health, Education, and Welfare.

United States Department of Labor. (1983, November 15). The economy in 1995. *News*. Washington, D.C.: Bureau of Labor Statistics.

United States Department of Labor, Employment and Training Administration. (n.d.). *Placing handicapped applicants: An employment service handbook*. Washington, D.C.: U.S. Department of Labor (Mimeograph).

United States Office of Education. (1976). *The unfinished revolution: Education for the handicapped*. In *1976 Annual Report*. Washington, D.C.: National Advisory Committee on the Handicapped, U.S. Government Printing Office.

United States Office of Education. (1978). *Helping children make career plans: Tips for parents*. Washington, D.C.: Office of Education.

United States Office for Handicapped Individuals. (1980). *Directory of national information sources on handicapping conditions and related services*. Washington, D.C.: Office for Handicapped Individuals.

Van Riper, C. (1978). *Speech correction: Principles and methods* (6th ed.). Englewood Cliffs, NJ: Prentice-Hall.

Varelas, J. T. (1976, April). The career seminar: Ideas and techniques. *The Career Education Workshop*. 1–4.

Vasa, S. F., Meers, G. D., & Steckelberg, A. (1980). *Mom and dad can help: Parents' role in career education for the handicapped child*. Lincoln: Department of Special Education and Center for Vocational Education, University of Nebraska.

Vasa, S. F., & Steckelberg, A. L. (1980). Parent programs in career education for the handicapped. *Career Development for Exceptional Individuals, 3*, 74–82.

Vasa, S. F., & Steckelberg, A. L. (1980). Parents' roles in the education of special vocational needs youth. In G. D. Meers (Ed.), *Handbook of special vocational needs education*. Rockville, MD: Aspen Systems Corp.

439

Vasa, S. F., Steckelberg, A. L., & Meers, G. D. (1979). *Career education for the handicapped child: A guide to parent education programming.* Columbus: The ERIC Clearinghouse on Adult, Career, and Vocational Education, The Ohio State University.

Vasa, S. F., Steckelberg, A. L., & Meers, G. D. (1979). Mom and dad can help: Parents' role in career education for the handicapped child. In C. J. Kokaska (Ed.). *Career futures for exceptional individuals.* Reston, VA: The Council for Exceptional Children.

Veatch, D. J. (1980). A videotape series for teaching job interviewing skills. *American Annals of the Deaf, 125,* 747–750.

Viscardi, H. (1976, April 29). Speech presented at the President's Committee on Employment of the Handicapped Annual Meeting, Washington, D.C.

Vocational Biographies Inc. (1980). *Don't call me handicapped.* Saul Centre, MN: Vocational Biographies Inc.

Walker, J. E., & Shea, T. M. (1980). *Behavior modification: A practical approach for educators* (2nd ed.). St. Louis, MO: C. V. Mosby.

Ward, M. J. (1982). Handicapped adults as resources in career education. *The Pointer, 26*(4), 30–33.

Wehman, P. (1981). *Competitive employment: New horizons for severely disabled individuals.* Baltimore: Paul H. Brookes.

Wehman, P. (1983). *Selected references in vocational education and habilitation of the severely handicapped* (bibliography). Richmond: Rehabilitation Research and Training Center, Virginia Commonwealth University.

Wehman, P., & Hill, M. (Eds.). (1982). *Vocational training and placement for severely disabled persons: Project employability,* Vol. III. Richmond: Virginia Commonwealth University.

Weisgerber, R. A., Dahl, P. R., & Appleby, J. A. (1981). *Training the handicapped for productive employment.* Rockville, MD: Aspen Systems Corp.

West, L. (1977). Suggested teaching strategies for classroom use. In D. J. McKay (Ed.). *Selected PRICE topical papers for career education* (Project PRICE, Working Paper 8). University of Missouri-Columbia.

West Virginia State Department of Education. (1977). *Expanding options for handicapped persons receiving vocational education: Run into the future run.* Proceedings of the West Virginia Training Institute, West Virginia College of Graduate Studies.

White, W., Alley, G., Deshler, D., Schumaker, J., Warner, M., & Clark, F. (1982). Are there learning disabilities after high school? *Exceptional Children, 49,* 272–274.

Wolfensberger, W., & Tullman, S. (1982). A brief outline of the principle of normalization. *Rehabilitation Psychology, 27,* 131–145.

Wright, A. R., Padilla, C., & Cooperstein, R. A. (1981). *Local implementation of PL 94-142: Third year report of a longitudinal study.* Menlo Park, CA: SRI International Educational and Human Services Center.

Wright, B. A. (1960). *Physical disability—A psychological approach.* New York: Harper & Row.

440

Wright, B. A. (1974). An analysis of attitudes: Dynamics and effects. *New Outlook for the Blind, 68,* 108–118.

Wright, W. H. (1973). *Project success* (EHA Title VI-B, No. 19–73452–1423–2–01, Final Report). Rowland Heights, CA: Rowland Unified School District.

Wyeth, D. (1981). Presentation. In *Speaking of employment: A symposium on disabled people in the workplace.* Washington, D.C.: Mainstream, Inc.

Zadny, J. J., & James, L. F. (1976). *Another view on placement: State of the art 1976. Studies in Placement Monograph No. 1.* Portland, OR: School of Social Work, Portland State University.

Zohn, J., & Bornstein, P. (1980). Self-monitoring of work performance with mentally retarded adults: Effects upon work productivity, work quality, and on-task behavior. *Mental Retardation, 18,* 19–25.

Zuger, R. R. (1971). To place the unplaceable. *Journal of Rehabilitation, 37*(6), 22–23.

Name Index

NAME INDEX

Subject Index

Charles J. Kokaska

Donn E. Brolin

Charles J. Kokaska (Ed. D., Boston University, 1968) has been involved with exceptional individuals since 1959. After graduating from Valparaiso University, he taught in a private school for children with behavioral disorders. He obtained his Master's degree from Northwestern University in 1961 and was hired by the Phoenix (Arizona) High School System to teach students who were mentally retarded. During a workshop conducted by the Phoenix system, he met Burton Blatt, then chairman of the Department of Special Education at Boston University, who encouraged him to pursue advanced training. He entered Boston University's program in 1964 and studied with such professors as Burton Blatt, Frank Garfunkel, Albert Murphy, Seymour Sarason, Lewis Klebanoff, and Louis Orzack.

Dr. Kokaska currently coordinates the special education credential and master's degree programs at California State University, Long Beach and teaches introductory courses and graduate seminars in special education. He has written and co-authored numerous articles,

served as a consulting editor to five journals, and edited such publications as *The Guidance of Exceptional Children* (with John Gowan and George Demos), *Career Futures for Exceptional Individuals*, and *Career Education for Behaviorally Disordered Students* (with Albert Fink). He was the founding editor of the journal *Career Development for Exceptional Individuals* which is published by the Division on Career Development, The Council for Exceptional Children.

Since 1962 Donn E. Brolin (Ph.D., University of Wisconsin, 1969) has worked in the fields of education, rehabilitation, and psychology to serve the career and developmental needs of persons with handicaps. From 1962 to 1963 he was a psychologist in the Pediatrics Department at the University of Wisconsin Hospital, and from 1963 to 1969 he worked as a prevocational coordinator at Central Wisconsin Training School. Since 1969 he has launched training programs in special education, rehabilitation services, and vocational assessment and has initiated several federal and state grant projects on career and vocational education. The most noteworthy program that he proposed is the Project PRICE, which resulted in the Life-Centered Career Education (LCCE) curriculum presented in this book. In 1984 he received two federal special education program grants that will help him to further the development of the LCCE curriculum.

Since 1972 Dr. Brolin has been a professor in the Department of Educational and Counseling Psychology at the University of Missouri-Columbia. He is also active as a lecturer, consultant, and director of inservice workshops on career development and has worked closely with several state and local educational agencies. One of his most satisfying accomplishments has been spearheading an organizational committee to form a new international division within the Council for Exceptional Children (CEC). This effort resulted in the Division on Career Development (DCD), one of the fastest growing and dynamic CEC groups. Dr. Brolin served as its charter president from 1976–1978.

Donn Brolin has also written *Vocational Preparation of Retarded Citizens* (1976), and *Career Education for Handicapped Children and Youth* (1979) with Charles Kokaska, and *Vocational Preparation of Persons with Handicaps* (1982). In addition, he has written many journal articles, chapters, and monographs on the career development of persons with handicaps.